Benjamin Lincoln

AND THE

American Revolution

Benjamin Lincoln
AND THE
American Revolution

DAVID B. MATTERN

UNIVERSITY OF SOUTH CAROLINA PRESS

© 1995 by the University of South Carolina

Published in Columbia, South Carolina, by the
University of South Carolina Press

Manufactured in the United States of America

99 98 97 96 95   5 4 3 2 1

Library of Congress Cataloging-in-Publication Data

Mattern, David B., 1951–
    Benjamin Lincoln and the American Revolution / David B. Mattern.
        p.   cm.
    Includes bibliographical references and index.
    ISBN 1–57003–068–5
    1. Lincoln, Benjamin, 1733–1810. 2. Generals—United States—
    Biography. 3. United States. Continental Army—Biography.
    4. United States—History—Revolution, 1775–1783—Campaigns.
    I. Title
    E207.L7M38 1995
    973.3'092—dc20
    [B]   95–4399

To the memory of my father and mother,
Paul Guyer Mattern Jr.
and Miriam Barnhart Mattern

Contents

Illustrations

Acknowledgments

One of the pleasures of finishing a book is the chance to thank all those who helped speed it along. My thanks go first to Robert McCaughey, who directed this study at Columbia University, and to Eric McKitrick, Herb Sloan, Richard Bushman, and Demetrios Caraley, for their comments and criticisms. I owe a special debt of gratitude to Alden Vaughan, who introduced me to graduate study and the highest standards of scholarship; to Jim Shenton, for his enthusiasm and support; and to Marcia Wright, for opening my eyes to a world of exciting ideas.

Few survive the rigors of graduate study without a cadre of close (and gently critical) friends. For their sharp eyes and unswerving encouragement, I am grateful to Steve Deyle, Randy Bergstrom, Doron Ben-Atar, Bernadette McCauley, and Betty Dessants.

This book was conceived during the year I was a National Historical Publications and Records Commission fellow at *The Papers of Robert Morris* at Queens College. My thanks go to John Catanzariti, for encouraging the project, and, particularly, to Mary Gallagher and Betty Nuxoll, for generously sharing their sources, for the stimulating discussion provoked by their painstaking research, and for their friendship.

Thanks are also due to those who read and commented on the manuscript in whole or in part: W. W. Abbot, Frank Grizzard, Don Higginbotham, John Stagg, Dorothy Twohig, and the reviewers at the University of South Carolina Press. To John Stagg, editor-in-chief of *The Papers of James Madison,* I am additionally grateful for support at a critical time which enabled me to finish the book. And I could not have completed the index without the help of my colleague Sue Perdue.

Many others have been particularly kind. Warren Slesinger was the soul of patience and good humor as he waited for the finished manuscript. Mapmaker Tom Roberts was equally calm in the face of many questions and requested changes. Rebecca Hobart dug into her archives and provided rare photographs from Dennysville, Maine. Elizabeth

Beveridge, owner of the Benjamin Lincoln House in Hingham, Massachusetts, and a descendant of the general's, graciously gave me a tour of the house, while her son, Franklin, generously provided photos of family members and scenes of Hingham. Thanks are also due to Kitty Thuermer, an old friend from Africa days, for her cheery pep talks.

I'd also like to thank the librarians and staffs of the Alderman Library, University of Virginia; the Boston Public Library; the Charleston Library Society; the Columbia University Library; the Connecticut Historical Society; the Duke University Library; the Georgia Historical Society; the University of Georgia Library; the Houghton Library, Harvard University; the Independence National Historical Park; the Library of Congress; the Massachusetts Historical Society; the Morristown National Historical Park; the National Archives; the New-York Historical Society; the New York Public Library; the University of North Carolina Library at Chapel Hill; the South Carolina Historical Society; and the Yale Art Gallery. A special thank-you goes to the staff of the Middletown Public Library in Middletown, Connecticut.

I've saved my greatest debts for last. For my son, Ben, whose arrival provided the final impetus to get the manuscript out the door, a hug and a host of free Saturdays. And to my wife, Charlotte Crystal, whose sharp blue pencil proved equal to the most tangled phrases and muddy thinking and whose own writing is an inspiration to me, I can only say: *ne b'i fé fo ka dama témé.*

Abbreviations

BL	Benjamin Lincoln
CHi	Connecticut Historical Society
DLC	Library of Congress
DNA	National Archives
GHi	Georgia Historical Society
MB	Boston Public Library
MH	Houghton Library, Harvard University
MHi	Massachusetts Historical Society
NHi	New-York Historical Society
NjMoHP	Morristown National Historical Park
NN	New York Public Library
NNC	Columbia University Libraries
NNU	New York University Libraries
PMHB	*Pennsylvania Magazine of History and Biography*
WMQ	*William and Mary Quarterly*

Benjamin Lincoln

AND THE

American Revolution

Introduction

On the eve of the American Revolution Benjamin Lincoln was forty-two years old, a prosperous farmer, a deacon of his church, and town clerk of the small village of Hingham, Massachusetts. As a member of the New England gentry, he could look forward to being, as his father had been, a well-known and respected member of Massachusetts provincial society. But, by the time of his death thirty-five years later, Lincoln had helped guide the Massachusetts Bay Colony to independent statehood, commanded armies against British invaders, coordinated the military affairs of a confederation of new states, and become a known and respected figure in the new American nation. The distance Lincoln traveled between his life as a comfortable middle-aged farmer in rural Massachusetts in 1775 and that of a Revolutionary War hero and pillar of the dynamic republic in 1810—the challenges he faced, the sacrifices he made, and the triumphs he enjoyed—are the subject of this book.

Historians have not been kind to Lincoln. In contrast to the judgments of his contemporaries, whose appreciation of his military abilities and political contributions was widespread, modern characterizations of the general are for the most part skewed, misleading, or wrong. Variously described as a "fat, gouty and lethargic" failure or as a corrupt aristocrat, Lincoln appears in most histories of the American Revolution as a slow, ineffectual soldier clearly out of his depth. Yet, as a major general in the Continental army, Lincoln was one of George Washington's trusted commanders, displaying courage, energy, and leadership on battlefields as diverse as Saratoga and Savannah, Charleston and Yorktown. Congress recognized Lincoln's organizational abilities and administrative savvy when it made him secretary at war during 1781–83, the crucial final years of the war. Massachusetts entrusted him with the politically difficult job of suppressing Shays's Rebellion in 1786–87, a task he accomplished with a minimum of bloodshed. And Lincoln's reputation as an honest and judicious man gave luster to the infant national government when President

Washington appointed him to a number of federal posts. Lincoln's role in these pathbreaking events is detailed in his voluminous correspondence, which provides the foundation for this study. There, in the collected papers of his military campaigns, his sharp observations on contemporary affairs, and his lively exchanges with Washington, Henry Knox, John Adams, and other revolutionaries, is the dramatic record of a complex and interesting man. And, more important, Lincoln's life so mirrored his times that it provides the opportunity to tell the oft-told tale of the American Revolution in a fresh and compelling way.[1]

Benjamin Lincoln's life reflected many of the broad themes of the Revolutionary era which historians are still working to understand. Why would a man leave a prosperous farm and thriving family to endure without complaint seven years of hardship? Why was a man like Lincoln chosen for positions of greater and greater responsibility despite his defeats and setbacks? How did a man who so loved his native town and state become a confirmed supporter of the new nation? While the answers to these questions lie in the story of one man, on another level they provide clues to the Revolutionary era's larger themes: the motivation of American soldiers, the nature of republican leadership in wartime, the development of nationalism, and the creation of the new republic.

Lincoln was in many ways much like his New England neighbors. He was a farmer, whose wealth and status were bound to the land. Being a deeply religious man, he was strongly tied to his church. Like most of his countrymen, he had not attended college but had received a good common school education. He was born, and would die, in the clapboard house in Hingham which his forebears had built four generations earlier. In all this Lincoln resembled his fellow New Englanders. What set him apart was his remarkable rise to positions of high public trust.

How did a man like Lincoln rise from relative obscurity to posts of great responsibility in the new republican world? Lincoln's contemporary, the historian David Ramsay, pointed out that "the Revolution called forth many virtues and gave occasion for the display of abilities which, but for that event, would have been lost to the world." That was certainly Lincoln's case. Lincoln proved to be a talented organizer, manager, and leader of men. But, more important, it was Lincoln's character that led his fellow revolutionaries to entrust him with power. These were men who distrusted power, who jealously eyed those who wielded it, and who delegated it with great care. They realized, however, that Lincoln would be scrupulous in the exercise of power, that he could hold an independent military command or put down an insurrection without threat to civil government. They knew that Lincoln believed passionately in the ideal of republican virtue.²

Revolutionary Americans were obsessed with the moral character of their society. The political experiment they launched with such enthusiasm and optimism in 1776 rested upon the assumption that a republic was extraordinarily fragile and needed the public virtue of its citizenry to succeed. To most revolutionaries public virtue was defined simply as the sacrifice of private interest for the good of the public. This was, of course, difficult for a citizen to do for any length of time, but it did not stop revolutionaries from recognizing, applauding, and rewarding public virtue when they saw it.³

As a man of public virtue put his country's needs before his own, so Lincoln shouldered his public duty through seven years of war. The source of Lincoln's extraordinary exertions on behalf of his fellow revolutionaries lay in his New England upbringing: his family, his community, and his faith. His understanding of the world and his place in it were shaped by the provincial world of Hingham, perched on the periphery of the town of Boston and the Atlantic world of the mid-eighteenth century. His ideas were rooted in a colonial world of deference and rough equality, patronage and duty, faith and reason. His political experience in town offices provided him with a practical education, one that recognized the value of consensus, compromise, and persuasion. It was a world in which a man's worth and independence were tied to his land and his ability—by frugality, industry, and self-denial—to wrest a living from the stony New England soil.

Lincoln was a deeply religious man who espoused moderation, reason, balance, and order. He believed that God had created a magnificent world of order and harmony and that, if man used his reason to control his passions, he could bring himself into harmony with nature. He was a man for whom religious enthusiasm was suspect yet for whom daily prayer was the key to a calm and reasoned life. He worked hard all his life to master his emotions—his anger, frustration, fears, and pain—and to discipline his mind. Despite this, he found himself leading armies in an intensely emotional revolutionary struggle.

These were the ideals that lay at the heart of Lincoln's republicanism. This was not the classical republicanism of the Latin writers studied by James Madison at Princeton or John Adams at Harvard. Nor were they the ideas of the English "country" writers, whose criticism of the British government had such a profound effect on many Americans in the years before the Revolution. Lincoln's republicanism was derived from

Hingham's Puritan past—from the strictures of his father and the elements of his faith. They were propounded from the pulpit during Sunday services and weekday prayer meetings and reinforced within the family circle: hard work, economy, and duty to family, town, and country. A Hingham villager would have explained that Lincoln answered God's call to leadership, much as another was called to be a carpenter or a minister. And this calling required, like all others, that one labor for the benefit of society. Lincoln explained it differently but used a word similarly fraught with meaning: he had "covenanted" with his countrymen to fight until independence from Great Britain was achieved. It was a contract that no amount of hardship could break.[4]

In the process of fighting the war, Lincoln expanded the definition of his country from the confines of Hingham and Massachusetts to encompass the new nation. He developed a continental vision. Like his fellow Bay Staters, Lincoln felt all the ambiguities inherent in conflicting loyalties to state and nation. He never lost his regional prejudices entirely, yet the compelling idea of a union of states melded with his war experience to forge a fierce loyalty to the United States. If at times Lincoln was discouraged by the vast differences that characterized the individual states and despaired of the union's survival—he even advocated creating regional confederations at one time—it was with the idea that the breakup of the union would be a catastrophe. With the adoption of the Constitution Lincoln became one of its staunchest supporters, a federal diplomat and holder of federal office.

With the end of the war and his retirement from active service Lincoln faced a dilemma. His wartime experiences had advanced him to the first rank of citizens of the new nation. He was acquainted with nearly all the Americans who had played a prominent role in the Revolution. The war had thrust him into public life on a national stage, and it had changed the circumstances of his life. He could not return to his life as a farmer and still maintain his ties to the first men of the nation. Thus, he had to strike out in new directions to acquire the financial means to bolster the status he had won in the war. He launched a commercial venture, tried his hand at manufacturing, and built a community in the Maine wilderness. None of these endeavors sustained him financially. It took a federal appointment by President Washington to guarantee his future. It was a situation faced by many revolutionaries, to a greater or lesser degree, in the postwar era.

After the devastating American defeat at Charleston in the summer of 1780, for which he bore responsibility, Lincoln received a letter from an

4

acquaintance in South Carolina. "You are very sensible," the man wrote, "that want of Success is with most of mankind, deemed a sufficient proof of want of Abilities, Industry, or Honesty, & that we are obliged to make our last appeal for Justice to posterity. And where I know a man deserving of the highest Applauses & public Thanks of his Country, it distresses me to think it is possible his Merit may not be clearly discerned." In one sense, his friend need not have worried. To his contemporaries Lincoln was a patriot, whose later years were full of honors and the plaudits of his countrymen. It is posterity that has treated Lincoln harshly. Lincoln would have agreed with Benjamin Rush when he wrote that "the proper and the dearest compensation for the labors, sacrifices, and achievements of public spirit is *justice to character*. Everything short of this is nothing but Shakespeare's purse—'all trash.'" This book seeks to tell Lincoln's story more completely than ever before and, in the process, recapture what it was that his contemporaries so admired in him.[5]

CHAPTER ONE

The Wellsprings of Ambition

When I was young, the *summum Bonum* in Massachusetts was to be worth ten thousand pounds sterling, ride in a chariot, be colonel of a Regiment of Militia and hold a seat in his Majesty's Council. No Mans Imagination aspired to any thing higher beneath the Skies.

John Adams

Of the many influences that shaped the life and character of Benjamin Lincoln, none proved so profound as the trinity of town, church, and family. Each, in different but mutually supportive ways, helped mold his idea of the world and his place in it. As he once pointed out, "See the care taken of man by the benevolent creator of the world, in the order and system so conspicuous in all creation around us. We must feel our safety on knowing that there cannot be any clashing of parts but that each will move on in its own orb." Order and system were indeed conspicuous in the New England of his day. Men and women were tied by bonds of obligation, or kinship, or by covenant with one another. All knew their place in the hierarchical order, and most found satisfaction in moving about within this frictionless world. So solid and secure was Lincoln in his various guises as townsman, church member, kin, and neighbor that he could write with satisfaction in old age that "there never was a moment of my life when I was not made happy on the reflection that I was born in the town of Hingham." In one sense the story of Lincoln's early life is the story of Hingham's own.[1]

When Benjamin Lincoln was born, in 1733, the town of Hingham, Massachusetts, had been settled for more than one hundred years. In that time four generations of the Lincoln family had helped clear the forest and sent shiploads of timber, planks, and barrel staves to Boston and as far south as the West Indian island of Barbados. The Lincolns and their neighbors carved hardscrabble farms from the rocky landscape, planted

6

orchards and fields of barley, wheat, and corn, and grazed herds of cattle and swine. With patience, hard work, thrift, and discipline, they created a thriving community in this sheltered cove just fourteen miles southeast of Boston.[2]

Those who settled Hingham in the 1630s, including Benjamin Lincoln's great-great-grandfather, Thomas Lincoln, a cooper, were Puritans from Hingham, in Norfolk, England. They came as part of the great Puritan migration to New England to create a New Jerusalem. In Hingham, as in most New England towns, the church served as the focus of individual lives and of the community. The goal of Hingham's founders was to establish a godly community, an "assembly of saints." One hundred years later, though the candle of religious fervor had guttered occasionally, it still burned with a strong, steady flame.[3]

The story of Benjamin Lincoln's family in New England began with the arrival in Massachusetts Bay of Thomas Lincoln and his wife, Annis Lane, in August 1638. They and their neighbors in the new Hingham attempted to build a world strikingly similar to the one they had left behind by recreating the same social and economic relationships that existed in old Hingham. This meant that, despite the vast acreage available, land was distributed according to a man's stature among his neighbors, his value to the community, and the needs of his family. Each "Town Man" received on the average a little over twenty acres of land, scattered about in enclosed, irregularly shaped parcels. Consequently, no great changes of status occurred in the move to the New World, nor were there great extremes of wealth within the town limits.[4]

In the years from its settlement to the 1680s Hingham remained astonishingly homogeneous—88 percent of its townspeople could be traced to forty-seven families that had settled there before 1641. And, in 1790, 81 percent of the heads of families represented in the census had a male ancestor in the town before 1660. Those who bore the surname of Lincoln made up one quarter of the population. Another feature of Hingham life was the extent to which a tightly knit circle of men controlled positions of leadership within the town. Until the 1680s a coterie of Hobarts, Beals, and Cushings held well over one-half of all town offices. Old Hingham had been characterized by an oligarchy; in New Hingham the same pattern was reproduced.[5]

In its early years Hingham was "susteined chiefly by Grasinge, by Deyries, and by rearing of Cattell," pursuits familiar to those from the mixed-farming region of Norfolk. But townspeople also specialized in the commercial use of wood, and it was not long before woodsmen and coo-

7

pers, such as Thomas Lincoln, began "transporting Timber; plank and mast for shipping to the Town of Boston, as also Ceder and Pine-Board to supply the wants of other Townes." Access to the sea linked Hingham closely to the burgeoning Atlantic economy. While, socially, Hingham resembled most New England towns, economically, it provided opportunities that were unavailable to inland communities.[6]

Life in Hingham was good to Thomas Lincoln. He built a house on North Street and, with his wife, began a family. To support the five children, who came in quick succession, Thomas, in addition to coopering, built a malt house in which he malted barley to brew beer. While he held no town offices before he died in 1691, the community recognized his status as an elder and one of the town patriarchs by assigning him a "seate under the pulpit" in the Old Ship Meetinghouse.[7]

To his youngest son Benjamin (1643–1700), the first of four Benjamins in succeeding generations, Thomas bequeathed a triangular lot at the corner of North and Lincoln streets and the malt house. Benjamin proved a successful malster—enough so to accumulate some property, build a house, and support a family of seven children. His prosperity extended to investing twenty-five pounds in Harvard College stock and serving one year as a selectman of the town.[8]

Of Benjamin's four sons the eldest followed his grandfather's trade, becoming a cooper, while two left Hingham to settle in Harwich on Cape Cod. It was the second son, his father's namesake, who achieved a solid position within the town oligarchy. This Benjamin (1672–1727) inherited the Lincoln homestead and the malt house and quickly rose to prominence in the little town. As selectman for four years and deacon of the church, he began a fifty-year family monopoly of the town clerkship with his appointment to office in 1721. Above all, despite his sudden death at the age of fifty-seven, he managed to transfer to his only child, Benjamin (1699–1771), the rank, wealth, and social status that his family had slowly acquired over several generations in the New World.[9]

This third-generation Benjamin—or Colonel Lincoln, as he came to be called—was a successful man, not only in Hingham but also in the province of Massachusetts Bay. The Colonel "served his generation with uncommon Diligence and exemplary Fidelity," holding nearly every office of responsibility in his town. His neighbors elected him to sixteen terms as selectman, thirty terms as town clerk, and twice as representative to the General Court, the colonial Massachusetts legislature (1746–48). He held the king's commission as justice of the peace and colonel of the Suffolk militia. And he served the province for sixteen years as a member of the Governor's Council. By the end of his long and busy life Colonel Lincoln had certainly achieved all that was within the grasp of a New England gentleman; he had attained the *"summum Bonum"* that John Adams remembered from his youth.[10]

Colonel Lincoln's life was not without its cares. His first marriage to a Hingham neighbor, Mary Loring, ended with her death five months after the nuptials. But his second wife, Elizabeth Thaxter Lincoln, though a widow some years the Colonel's senior, delivered five girls within eight years after their marriage in 1723. Their sixth child was born on 24 January 1733. They named this first-born son Benjamin, after his father, continuing a line that stretched back to the son of the first settler, Thomas Lincoln. The continuity of names expressed more than a concern with the viability of the family. As Ben grew older, his name was a constant reminder of family expectations that he be worthy to walk in his father's footsteps.[11]

It also reinforced the boy's awareness of the dense network of kinship and community relationships that had been built over a century of small-town life. Being Benjamin Lincoln of Hingham meant that the boy had a secure and prominent place in village life from the outset. As a grown man, this sense of security would manifest itself in a calm sense of self-possession in the face of crisis. Life in a small town also taught the growing child the reciprocal obligations due from one neighbor to another. As Lincoln would write later to his own son, "We are constituted in a manner that our happiness is united with and is inseparable from the happiness of others." But the family legacy created a burden as well. Ben was expected to follow his family's tradition of leadership and service. Yet to excel he must somehow surpass his father's achievements, an unlikely outcome given the narrow range of provincial possibilities and Colonel Lincoln's success.[12]

A contemporary of Benjamin Lincoln's noted that he "was accustomed to mention the opinions and remarks of his father in a manner which showed their authority over his mind and conduct." And, if Lincoln's subsequent behavior is any indication, he was raised by affectionate parents who inculcated in him a strong sense of duty. They taught him his obligations to those above and below him in the hierarchical chain of social standing as well as respect for and obedience to the law. He was taught to rein in his passions so as to present a calm and rational face to the world. Here he learned to check his personal ambition, sublimating it by recasting it as concern for the public good. If unlimited ambition was evil, a dutiful regard for one's community and country was to be applauded.

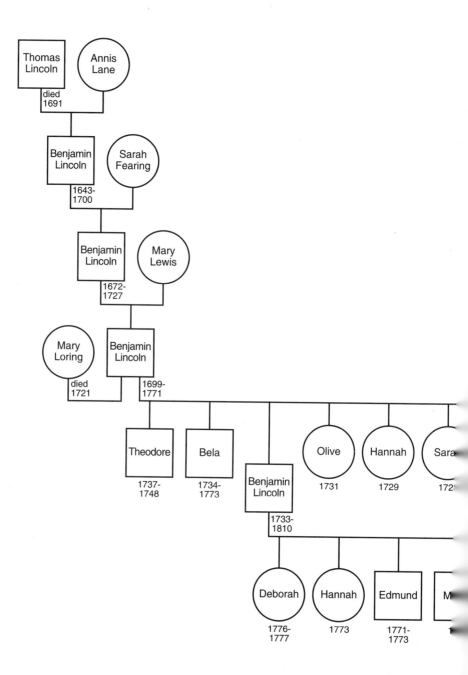

George Lincoln, *History of the Town of Hingham* (3 vols; Hingham, Mass.) 3:3-10

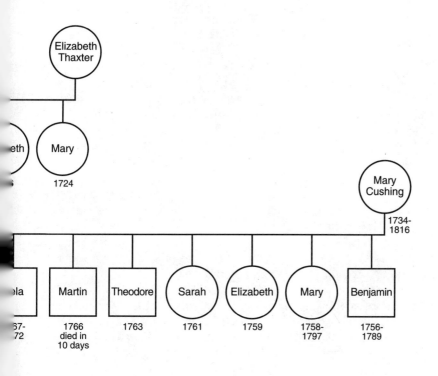

In private life pleasures were to be enjoyed in moderation. A gentleman was temperate in his tastes, simple in his dress, and frugal in his surroundings. Lincoln imbibed these precepts at home, along with his cornmeal mush and molasses, and used them as a guide throughout his life.[13]

While the Colonel's authority over Ben's mind and conduct was marked, there were other influences at work on the young man. The celebrated Ebenezer Gay, pastor of the first church in Hingham, was one of Massachusetts's greatest spokesmen for congregational liberalism. Gay, called by some the "Arminian panjandrum," believed that man was a rational being, in whom "God implanted an inner moral sense," and that, "if properly guided, man's reason would naturally choose good over evil." Gay also believed that God's grace could be gained through action: daily prayer, attendance at church, and participation in the spiritual life of the community. These ideas deeply impressed Ben Lincoln, who practiced them throughout a long life in which his experiences in war and politics must have often argued the contrary. He may have become discouraged at times, but he never lost his faith. "You are just stepping out into the world, a world of wickedness folly and temptation," he wrote his son Theodore during the Revolutionary War, yet "God has made us capable of happiness and that we might be pointed to the path in which it is to be found he has been pleased to reveal his will." In the rough and impious world of military camp life, Lincoln was not afraid of being known as a pious man. He found great solace in public worship and often visited churches of different faiths on his travels, finding there "suitable reflections to warm his zeal, love and gratitude." And he recommended prayer to his sons, especially in the morning "before the World crowds in upon our Minds." His faith wove the Arminian and pietistic strands of Puritanism into a comfortable garment he would wear all his life.[14]

For the present Ben worked his father's farm, doing the thousand and one things necessary to make it successful. The boy's chores were dictated by the weather and the time of year: spring plowing gave way to digging stones, planting corn to haying, hoeing corn to harvesting, building and mending stone fences, then gathering wood for the long winter's break. Field work was interrupted only by Sunday meetings and Thursday evening services and by occasional visits to markets in surrounding towns.[15]

As the eldest son, Ben could expect a double share of his family's wealth as his patrimony. The ancestral home, the malt house, and the farm land so laboriously accumulated over generations would eventually fall to him, as his five older sisters were given dowries and married and his brother, Bela, received a college education as his legacy. For his part Ben was responsible for managing and enriching the family properties under his father's supervision, and it was expected that he would follow his father in the councils of the town should he prove worthy of office. For this role only a common school education seemed necessary, and so Ben studied the three Rs in Hingham. He later felt the lack of a classical education, particularly its emphasis on public speaking and writing, as he took on positions of increasing responsibility. He worked hard to overcome this impediment and his early unpolished efforts at writing gave way in his later years to letters and essays written in a bold and fluent style. Even so, throughout his life he had someone read aloud what he wrote, claiming that in his ignorance of the rules of grammar he could only judge the correctness of the language by its sound. And Lincoln, like other ambitious men who were poorly educated, emphasized the value of education for his children.[16]

Perhaps Colonel Lincoln judged that Ben was not cut out for the life of a lawyer or minister. Blue-eyed and of light complexion, he was of average height, standing about five feet nine inches tall, but "of so uncommonly broad person, as to seem to be of less stature than he was." Though he had grown into a robust young man, he was afflicted with a speech impediment. Evidence suggests that he spoke "with apparent difficulty, as though he were too full." On top of that Lincoln suffered throughout his life with narcolepsy, a condition in which a person lapses into brief periods of deep sleep. A contemporary wrote that, "in the midst of conversation, at table, and when driving himself in a chaise, he would fall into a sound sleep." Lincoln would fall asleep while dictating dispatches, wake, and carry on as if nothing had happened. While disconcerting to others, this condition did not seem to slow him down. It provided the substance for more than one jest and many occasions in which Lincoln was warmly defended by those who knew him well. Once a gentleman disparaged Lincoln in the presence of Major William Jackson by saying that the general was always falling asleep. Jackson, who had served as Lincoln's aide during the war, retorted, "Sir, General Lincoln was never asleep when it was necessary for him to be awake." Lincoln himself "considered this as an infirmity, and his friends never ventured to speak to him of it."[17]

In contrast to Ben, the Colonel had other hopes for Bela, his younger son by one year. Colonel Lincoln "had very flattering expectations that he would destinguish himself as a scholar; although some of his friends entertained a different opinion of him, and thot there was no hope of his holding a mediocrity with his class." Bela surprised them all, graduating from Harvard College in 1754 and afterward settling down to practice medicine in Sherbourne, Massachusetts. Bela married Hannah Quincy, the daughter of Colonel Josiah Quincy, "the Squire of Braintree," in May of 1760, an event that brought great satisfaction to Colonel Lincoln. Bela studied medicine in London and received a degree from King's College, Aberdeen, in 1765. Already having represented Sherbourne in the General Court in 1764, Bela returned to settle in Hingham to practice medicine and resume a promising political career.[18]

As Ben took over more of the family farm's day-to-day responsibilities, Colonel Lincoln was freed for other pursuits. When Ben was sixteen, the Colonel served a term as representative of Hingham to the General Court, service that required prolonged visits to Boston. As one of the wealthiest men in Hingham, the Colonel also began to invest what ready money he had in trade. Four years later, in 1753, he was elected a member-at-large of the Governor's Council, and his concerns grew to embrace those of Massachusetts Bay.[19]

As Bela was finishing his last year at Harvard, in 1754, Ben was showing an aptitude for leadership and paying his political dues by becoming town constable. The job required a man of honesty, tact, and abilities, for a constable kept order in the town, watched over peoples' behavior, and collected taxes. The post was often refused because it was so unpleasant. At the age of twenty-one Ben accepted it and carried out his duties as he had been taught to do. One year later Ben received another practical lesson in leadership when he was appointed adjutant in his father's militia regiment, the Third Suffolk.[20]

In January 1756, when most of his peers were working to accumulate enough assets to marry, Benjamin Lincoln took Mary Cushing of nearby Pembroke, Massachusetts, for his bride. Benjamin was twenty-four; his wife was twenty-two. Only his father's wealth and social standing enabled the two to marry at such a young age. They set up housekeeping in Hingham, and their first child, Benjamin Jr., was born the same year. They would have eleven children in all, four of whom would die before reaching the age of five.[21]

We know little about Mary Cushing Lincoln beyond what can be inferred from several surviving letters from Benjamin to her and bits of evidence in other family letters. That the marriage was a happy one seems a fair guess. Lincoln described quiet evenings at home before the war when the two sat comfortably before the fire in conversation. Given the long and detailed description of American affairs Lincoln wrote her on the occasion of the British surrender at Yorktown, it is clear that he valued her opinion on political matters. And, given Lincoln's long absences from home, Mary Lincoln must have been a strong character, who managed her household with firmness. There is some evidence that she was considered by outsiders to be a domestic tyrant, but by Lincoln's own testimony her actions must have been thoroughly leavened with good humor. Judged by the respectful tone used when her husband and sons referred to her, the Lincoln family was knit together by bonds of affection.[22]

After Lincoln had established his family and demonstrated a certain amount of economic independence, the town elected him to succeed his father as town clerk in 1757. It was an office that he would fill for twenty years, and it positioned him as a leader in town affairs at the age of twenty-five. That a young man would be given such responsibility was extraordinary. Most New England towns required a long apprenticeship before electing men to such offices. But in certain towns in which the top offices were tightly controlled by a small number of families, young men like Benjamin Lincoln were elected to office through family influence despite their lack of experience.[23]

As Benjamin settled into farming in earnest, British North America faced the threat of French and Indian attacks, as hostilities began in the Seven Years' War. As adjutant of the Third Suffolk, Benjamin carried out duties related to recruitment, training, and supply, but he saw no combat. Unlike most young men his age, who lacked the resources to farm on their own, Lincoln was a young father, established on the land, and with town responsibilities. Most of those from Hingham who volunteered to campaign in the colonial wars were young men who hoped to earn enough to buy a farm or to marry. Few men like Benjamin participated in those expeditions. Lincoln helped organize and administer Suffolk County's war effort. Apparently, his activity gained the approval of his superiors, for by the end of the war, in 1763, they promoted him to major.[24]

In 1764 Colonel Lincoln, increasingly busy with provincial business, deeded to his son Benjamin for the nominal fee of £5 "all my dwelling house which he now lives in all the malt house and one half the barn with one half the land adjoyning to the said building, also one half my orchard at broad cove, one half my land adjoyning to both the places last mentioned." That same year his wife's father, Elijah Cushing, died and bequeathed to his daughter £133. The two inheritances provided the Lincolns and their five children a comfortable living and a degree of independence. The town recognized this when it elected Lincoln, now thirty-two and a solid townsman, a selectman in 1765, retaining him in that office for the next six years.[25]

The news of the passage of the Stamp Act that same year shattered old loyalties and friendships and created a new political landscape. The old "court" and "country" animosities that had driven provincial politics since the turn of the century quickly became irrelevant, as the focus of conflict shifted from squabbles within the colony over the royal preroga- tive to the relationship between England and the American colonies. Colo- nel Lincoln was a man of "country" sentiments who had served as a member of the Governor's Council for more than a decade. His tenure there had taught him moderation; the new radical politics of bitter pro- test, street demonstrations, and property destruction filled him with dis- may. John Adams noted with disdain that the Sunday evening "Clubb" where Colonel Lincoln gathered with other Hingham notables such as Ebenezer Gay and Colonel Thaxter was "wholly inclined to Passive Obe- dience—as the best way to procure Redress. A very Absurd Sentiment indeed." And after Lt. Gov. Thomas Hutchinson's house was destroyed by the Boston mob in August 1765, Colonel Lincoln wrote to a friend, "My very soul has been moved with compassion to the Lt. Govr. but for yr consolation as well as mine the last attempt made upon him has en- gaged perhaps Ten friends to one even among what was their own Club." He ended by noting sadly, "I cant but envy yr retirement."[26]

And no wonder. A moderate man of independent judgment found himself walking a tightrope between what he perceived as two principled courses of action. The speaker of the House of Representatives, Thomas Cushing, referring to a member of the General Court in a letter to his brother, wrote: "You ask how your representative conducts. Why truly it is a difficult time with him, he does not well know how to conduct. The Gov. on one side and the People on the other press him pretty severely— I pity him, poor man." After 1766 the House of Representatives elected progressively more radical members to the Governor's Council, many of whom Governor Bernard rejected as too extreme. The Colonel managed to navigate between the government and the people, but his efforts be- came increasingly ineffectual. His resignation from the council in 1769 was probably the result of ill health, but there is no doubt that the politi- cal world had changed so as to render the old rules inoperable.[27]

One sign of the times was the increasing radicalization of Hingham— and the Colonel's son, Benjamin. Passage of the Stamp Act spurred many people to take an active part in politics; fifty Massachusetts towns in- structed their representatives to oppose it. When news of its repeal reached New England in May 1766, Hingham's reaction, according to John Adams, was conspicuously joyful, as "bells [were] rung, Cannons fired, Drums beaten and Land Lady Cushing on the Plain, illuminated her House." The towns had taken the initiative in opposing the act. The town meetings and the petitions they generated lay at the heart of the resistance. Towns like Hingham carefully instructed their representatives on how to conduct themselves as new controversies continued to arise. As town clerk, Benjamin was instrumental in setting the limits within which Hingham's representative could act. The town's instructions to Joshua Hearsey in 1768, for example, which Lincoln drafted with the aid of two fellow townsmen, were primarily aimed at preserving "peace and good order in the province and loyalty to the king," hardly a radical notion. But the town was also concerned that Hearsey "take every legal and constitutional method for the preservation of our rights and liberties" and, especially, "encourage the inhabitants to keep up military duty, whereby they may be in a capacity to defend themselves against foreign enemies." The enemies, for the moment, remained nameless.[28]

Another indication of the change in Hingham and elsewhere in Massachusetts was the reaction of Ebenezer Gay's parishioners to a sermon he delivered in December 1765. Using the occasion of a Day of Thanksgiving proclaimed to celebrate the repeal of the Stamp Act—not the most politic occasion—Gay asserted that "the ancient Weapons of the Church, were Prayers and Tears, not Clubbs," and, according to one report, he "inculcated Submission to Authority, in pretty strong Expressions." That kind of talk did not go down well with the Hinghamites, who accused the parson of being a tax distributor. But a week later they welcomed a sermon preached by William Smith, a good Whig, who recommended "Honour, Reward and Obedience to Good Rulers; and a Spirited Opposition to bad ones, interspersed with a good deal of animated Declamation upon Liberty and the Times." In a town that had consistently voted with the "country" party, that sounded like good religious doctrine.[29]

Evidence suggests that Benjamin Lincoln was a leading Hingham Whig; his later statements are framed in classical revolutionary language. One contemporary described Lincoln as a "sincere and determined, though temperate whig," a profile that fits well with what we know of Hingham's politics. As late as November 1772, an anonymous letter datelined Hingham appeared in a Boston newspaper, taking Boston radicals to task for the violence of their political writing and describing the people of Hingham as "moderate Whigs, real Friends to Liberty." That characterization did not sit well with men like James Warren, who wrote privately that the letter was "a low dirty Business founded upon the Pillars and chief Corner Stones of the Tory Cause." Yet Hingham was in step with the revolutionary movement. During the town meeting in March 1770 Lincoln drafted Hingham's letter to the Boston Committee of Merchants supporting a nonimportation agreement. While the emphasis was still on a "constitutional way to procure a redress of those grievances," occasioned by the Townshend Acts and the "measures gone into to enforce obedience to them," the decision to boycott British goods was a radical act.[30]

Lincoln's temperament explains to some extent his political moderation. For someone who valued self-control the nearly hysterical tone of much of the revolutionary literature would have been as distasteful to him as the Boston radicals' use of mobs and mob action. But there was another aspect to Lincoln's moderation. Given the respect he had for his father's opinions and high public office, it is probable that he did not give full rein—at least in public—to his feeling that, as he put it later, "the British Administration are still pursueing their plan for enslaving America with a zeal and impetuosity proportionate to the injustice and madness of their designs formed against us." Thus, it must have been with a feeling of relief that Lincoln greeted his father's resignation from the council in 1769.[31]

The death of Colonel Lincoln two years later dissolved the last tie that held Benjamin Lincoln to the old order and freed him to take command of the town's Whigs. A newpaper notice of the Colonel's long and honorable career read simply: "A good man and a good magistrate. He feared God, honoured the King, and loved his Country." This was a legacy to live up to, as much a part of Benjamin Lincoln's inheritance as the malt house, orchards, and rich meadowlands in Hingham. For the Colonel's generation, as the newspaper noted, "more needeth not, and more cannot be said, to preserve his memory ever precious." For Benjamin Lincoln and his generation it would not be as simple. Something more than the fulfillment of duty would be required. As Lincoln dropped the *Junior* from his name, he must have realized that his long apprenticeship for leadership was over.[32]

Benjamin Lincoln's uncontested status as an influential spokesman for Hingham and the Lincoln family was reinforced by the long illness and subsequent death of his brother, Bela. The younger brother had long since consigned his affairs to Benjamin and retired from any participation in politics. When he died, in July 1774, a friend wrote that "for knowledge of Physic, strength of Judgement, clearness of apprehension, and a facility in Communication few if any exceeded him, of which, had his life been spared, the world would have had, I am confident, the most incontestable proofs." Bela, armed with a Harvard degree, connected through his wife with a wealthy and influential family, articulate and worldly, had been poised to rise to eminence. While Benjamin grieved the loss of his brother, with whom he had been close, Bela's death removed a potential rival. And it gave Benjamin, a man of fewer natural gifts perhaps, an additional spur to his ambition.[33]

The late 1760s and early 1770s were a busy time for Lincoln. He began to consolidate property that he had acquired in the past decade as he settled his father's and brother's estates. Besides operating the malt house, he and a neighbor manufactured potash for fertilizer, a business they sold for a hefty profit in 1767. Lincoln immediately invested in a similar venture closer to home. His energetic management of these enterprises and the patient accumulation of land made him a wealthy man by Hingham standards.[34]

At the same time that Lincoln was consolidating his personal affairs, Hingham elected him to serve as their representative to the General Court in May 1772. That same year Lincoln was appointed lieutenant colonel of the Second Suffolk Regiment. This press of public and private responsibilities induced him to buy from Robert Robins for eighty pounds "my nigro man named Cato aged about twenty years, his time labor and service." Cato was the first of several slaves Lincoln owned throughout his life. His own sentiments about slavery, once he had seen it practiced in South Carolina and Georgia in later life, were unequivocally against "this unjustifiable and wicked practice." But, at the time, Lincoln might have felt only a slight uneasiness about slavery or possibly, like most of his neighbors, no qualms at all. Cato probably worked side by side with Lincoln at the malt house or the potash factory or in the field. Most likely, he ate with the family and lived under the same roof, integrated into the family on terms of relative intimacy. Slavery in New England had a distinctive pattern that was unlike plantation systems elsewhere.[35]

And Lincoln needed a laborer. He had ambitions for his son, Benjamin Jr., who was preparing for Harvard by studying the classics. The young man had little time to help manage his father's various enterprises. Lincoln's other sons were too young to be much help—Theodore was nine and Martin three.[36]

After two years in the General Court Lincoln was elected chairman of the Hingham committee of correspondence, in January 1774. He framed the answer to a letter from the Boston committee in which the town made clear that "a virtuous and steady opposition to the ministerial plan of governing America is necessary, to preserve even a shadow of liberty; and it is a duty which every freeman in America owes to his country, to himself, and to his posterity." In August the townspeople of Hingham went one step further toward an open break with Great Britain by forming a covenant among themselves "not to import, purchase, or consume" any articles coming from the metropole, nor allow anyone in the town to do so.[37]

In September 1774 the town again elected Lincoln to sit in the General Court that the new governor, Gen. Thomas Gage, had ordered to convene in Salem. Though Gage soon dissolved the meeting, the elected representatives declared themselves a Provincial Congress and, in that capacity, met three times between September 1774 and July 1775. The task of the congress was to carry out the day-to-day governance of the colony, prepare for possible hostilities, and at the same time refrain from provoking the British authorities. The congress chose Lincoln as its secretary, and he served on the permanent standing committee as well as committees charged with reorganizing and supplying the militia. Lincoln focused on creating minute companies within militia units which could respond faster than larger bodies of troops. And his committee was responsible for procuring cannon, small arms, and ammunition and depositing them in secure places.[38]

It was the British attempts to find and confiscate these supply caches that led to the fighting at Lexington and Concord and which altered the nature of the political conflict between Great Britain and its North American colonies. After the shocking bloodletting of 19 April 1775 there was little chance of a negotiated settlement of differences. Angry militiamen, like those of the Second Suffolk Regiment, hurriedly marched to Boston, while refugees from the fighting crowded the roads. The politicians hastily tried to gain control of the situation. The Provincial Congress reconvened three days after the battle, and Lincoln went straight to Watertown. There he was quickly chosen muster master of militia and appointed to the newly created Committee of Safety as well as being assigned a seat on the committees of supply and governmental organization. His final duty as secretary of the congress was to serve as acting president during its final days, in June 1775, in the absence of its elected president, James Warren.[39]

In July 1775 a newly elected House of Representatives constituted itself the legal government of Massachusetts. A week later the House elected a council of twenty-eight members to assume the executive functions of the government. Lincoln was appointed a councillor on 28 July. With that appointment he ceased to be a representative from Hingham. During the past several years Lincoln had begun to see issues and events in a larger context. His seat on the council was a formal acknowledgment of his ability to help formulate policy for Massachusetts Bay, just as his neighbors had recognized his talent for leadership twenty-odd years before. When Lincoln wrote to the selectmen of Hingham to inform them of his new office, he thanked the town for its trust—"for I consider that it is partly owing to their favorable notice of me that I have been brought into public view. I recollect with gratitude that they have conferred upon me most if not all the places of honor that were in their power to bestow."[40]

Benjamin Lincoln had undergone a long apprenticeship to assume the position held years earlier, under different circumstances, by his father. His family's status in Hingham and his father's influence in provincial politics had provided him with opportunities to display his energy, talents, and ambition. Of these he took full advantage. At forty-two he had achieved all his father achieved, with this difference: he stood ready to risk it all on a desperate experiment. What moved Lincoln, and tens of thousands like him, to step so confidently out of the imperial fold and defy an empire?

During the war Lincoln tried to explain his personal decision to break with Great Britain to his sons. "I might perhaps have waded through life with as little difficulty as I experience in the present cause," he wrote, "but the growing encroachments of Britain would I think have fallen with too much weight on the necks of my children and would have deprived them of those natural rights, which are the sweetness of life, and which to preserve are among the duties enjoined on us by our creator." The next seven years would be full of honors, cruel disappointments, and personal sacrifice, but Lincoln's "particular eye to posterity" would sustain him to the end.[41]

CHAPTER TWO

From Boardroom to Field Command

I hear General Lincoln is appointed in the room of [Artemas] Ward. Has
he Spirit enough, has he activity, has he ambition enough for the place?
Abigail Adams

The siege of Boston began immediately after the skirmishes at Lexington and Concord, when thousands of militiamen from Massachusetts
and its neighboring colonies mustered on the city's outskirts, angrily awaiting an opportunity to drive the British army into the sea. Throughout the
spring and summer of 1775 the Provincial Congress struggled to bring
order to this spontaneous army of twenty thousand men, which, although
necessary, was viewed with alarm. "We tremble at having an army (although consisting of our own countrymen) established here," the Massachusetts Congress wrote the Continental Congress, "without a civil power
to provide for and control them." To place the army on a legal footing the
Massachusetts authorities asked the Continental Congress to adopt it and
take over its direction. This the Continental Congress did in June of 1775,
appointing the Virginian George Washington as commander.[1]

By the late summer of 1775 about fourteen thousand troops were
entrenched in the newly created fortifications surrounding Boston, from
the Mystic River in the north to Dorchester in the south. As a councillor
in the upper chamber of the new Massachusetts state government, Benjamin Lincoln was mostly occupied with providing the vast quantities of
supplies demanded by the new army. He procured scarce gunpowder and
lead as well as £8,000 worth of blankets. Lincoln also served on a committee that fit out ten vessels as privateers, ships that would capture British ships laden with badly needed supplies in the months to come. On
another committee he took "into consideration the state and circumstances
of the Sea-Coast," to determine which harbors in Massachusetts Bay would
be defended by the state and which by the Continental army. Above all,

22

his previous experience as a militia officer, a committeeman on crucial provincial committees, and muster master was invaluable in helping the state government grapple with the questions of militia organization and recruitment for the Continental army.[2]

From the start Lincoln proved to be a tireless and willing leader in the cabinet. The council handled provincial issues, such as finding accommodations for prisoners, dealing with petitions seeking compensation for wounds and property damage suffered in the service of the province, creating a loyalist policy, and taking measures to avoid a smallpox outbreak. In addition, as Washington struggled to create an army out of a mob of militiamen, he frequently turned to the council for aid in such matters as reconciling the payment of soldiers on the lunar and calendar months and finding reinforcements for the Continental army. Besides this array of duties Lincoln tried to solve one of the nagging problems of the Continental army—how to secure a dependable supply of gunpowder. During the fall recess of the General Court, Lincoln and fellow councilman Azor Orne "made tryalls" in the manufacture of saltpeter, an ingredient in gunpowder. They demonstrated "the process to be simple and easy, and that great quantities may be made." After being shown samples, James Warren pronounced it "undoubtedly good." The council was not satisfied, however, and in February 1776 authorized a committee, with Lincoln a member, to experiment further.[3]

By January 1776 the new organization of the Massachusetts militia was complete. Lincoln's energetic service on the council and his military bent were recognized on 30 January, when the General Court appointed him brigadier general for Suffolk County. John Hancock, James Warren, and Azor Orne were named major generals. When Warren declined the appointment, due to illness, Lincoln was appointed major general in his stead. In February, citing his new appointment as "incompatible with my holding any office in this town," he resigned as town clerk of Hingham.[4]

Lincoln had barely settled into his new responsiblities when the British evacuated Boston on 17 March 1776. For nearly a year the British and Americans had eyed each other warily from strong defensive positions. The stalemate finally was broken by the fortification of Dorchester Heights and the placement there of heavy artillery brought from Fort Ticonderoga in New York by Henry Knox. The Heights, now bristling with heavy guns, enabled the Americans to shell British positions in the city and their ships in the harbor. British general William Howe had no choice but to take the Heights or evacuate the city. He chose the latter and sailed off to

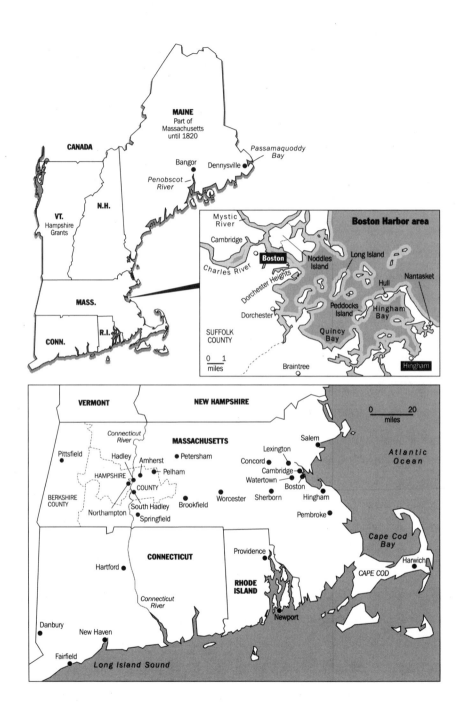

CANADA

MAINE
Part of
Massachusetts
until 1820

Bangor

Penobscot
River

Dennysville

Passamaquoddy
Bay

VT.
Hampshire
Grants

N.H.

MASS.

CONN.

R.I.

Boston Harbor area

Mystic
River

Cambridge

Boston

Charles River

Dorchester Heights

Dorchester

Noddles
Island

Long Island

Hull

Nantasket

Peddocks
Island

Hingham
Bay

SUFFOLK
COUNTY

Quincy
Bay

0   1
miles

Braintree

Hingham

VERMONT

NEW HAMPSHIRE

0   20
miles

Connecticut
River

Pittsfield

Hadley

Amherst

Petersham

MASSACHUSETTS

Salem

Lexington

Concord

Atlantic
Ocean

HAMPSHIRE
COUNTY

Pelham

Cambridge

Watertown

Boston

BERKSHIRE
COUNTY

South Hadley

Northampton

Springfield

Brookfield

Worcester

Sherborn

Hingham

Pembroke

CONNECTICUT

Providence

Cape Cod
Bay

Hartford

RHODE
ISLAND

Harwich

CAPE COD

Connecticut
River

Danbury

New Haven

Newport

Fairfield

Long Island Sound

Halifax, Nova Scotia, to regroup and plan his next move. Washington, convinced that Howe would try to take New York City and use it as his primary base, drew off the Continental army and marched for New York. The defense of Boston and the long Massachusetts coastline was left to the state militia and a small detachment of Continentals under the command of Gen. Artemas Ward.[5]

Despite the evacuation of Howe's troops, British warships still lurked in Boston's outer harbor, harassing rebel shipping and threatening coastal villages. Justifiably concerned for his hometown, Lincoln wrote the Hingham selectmen to keep the town's guards "very vigilant" and sent a militia officer to appraise the village's defenses. But Boston's safety was his first priority; it had to be fortified in case of another attack. Anxious Bostonians complained about the sluggish effort being made to defend the city. Lincoln worked with General Ward to erect small forts at Dorchester Point and Noddles Island in April, but the lack of energy in fortifying the harbor shocked him.[6]

The fear of a British attack on the coast prompted the state legislature to advise Lincoln to order the brigades under his command "to hold themselves in readiness to march at a moments warning," orders that he passed on to the brigadiers commanding those units in a circular letter. Believing that the "British Administration" still "retain their disposition to make this colony the first victim of their folly and malice and that a large army may soon be expected here," Lincoln admonished the brigadiers to see that "nothing will be wanting on your part to put the Militia of your brigade" into a state of readiness.[7]

In May Lincoln took time from his military duties to help draft the instructions of the Hingham town meeting to its representatives to the legislature. The town agreed that, if the question of separation from Great Britain should arise in the coming session of the Massachusetts legislature, the three Hingham representatives should vote for independence. This action, while a logical extension of the past year's events, was still a momentous step and one not taken lightly. But, given Lincoln's conviction that a British conspiracy existed to deprive Americans of their rights as Englishmen, independence seemed the only course.[8]

By early June the fortification of the harbor was sufficiently advanced that an attempt could be made to drive the British warships from its outer reaches. Lincoln planned the expedition, and the Massachusetts council authorized him to call out the militia to execute it. On the night of 13 June 1776 a combined force of Continentals and militiamen erected batteries on Long and Peddocks islands and Nantasket Head. The next morning their artillery fire drove the remaining British warships from the harbor, an event that the Reverend Samuel Cooper gleefully reported to John Adams. "We have now not a British Ship of War in any Harbor," the clergyman exulted, "not a British Soldier uncaptivated in all N. England." Despite Lincoln's disappointment in failing to lure a fleet of British troop transports into the harbor a few days later, he could bask in the congratulations of friends over the "late expedition and the success attending it."[9]

As if war were not enough, an outbreak of smallpox ravaged the Boston area in the summer of 1776 with such devastating effects that thousands decided to "take" the disease. "Such a spirit of innoculation never before took place," wrote Abigail Adams from Boston. "The Town and every House in it, are as full as they can hold." Lincoln, no doubt convinced that if he remained in the army he would be inevitably exposed to the disease, left his command post at Hull and repaired to a friend's house in Boston, where he was innoculated with a mild form of the disease. Though quarantined for weeks, he emerged in as good health as ever.[10]

Despite the interruption of Lincoln's military services, his stature had grown to the point that it was rumored he would replace the chronically ill Artemas Ward as commander of the Continental troops in Massachusetts, a move that John Lowell described as "universally agreeable." Although Ward agreed to continue despite his illness, it was clear that Lincoln was angling for a command in the Continental service. In August and September 1776 Lincoln dined with influential politicians, such as Elbridge Gerry, a delegate to the Continental Congress, and was present at large political gatherings. Joseph Ward was aware that Lincoln "would like to engage in Service" and recommended him to John Adams as "a good man for a Brigadier General; he has never been a Continental officer nor had much experience, but he is a man of abilities and appears to me to have a good mind." Adams was not so sure, despite having recommended Lincoln to replace him in the Continental Congress, and shared his wife's doubts about Lincoln's military abilities.[11]

In September the Massachusetts legislature decided to draft every fifth man from its alarm and train band list, about five thousand men, to serve as "temporary forces" in the New York area under Washington's command. The Continental army, which they were to join, had been badly mauled on Long Island in August and was evacuating New York City in the face of the frightening weight of the British expeditionary force. To lead the Massachusetts forces the legislature appointed James Warren, giving him the rank of major general. Once again Warren declined the position, explaining to John Adams that he "could not at this time support the fatigue." The House of Representatives then selected Lincoln "to command the whole." This was Lincoln's first major command; he must have felt a rare excitement as he mobilized his troops for the march. By dint of hard and successful service in the past year and willingness to take on jobs others had shirked, his opportunity had come. Others were watching his comportment with a critical eye. John Adams, complaining of cowardly officers, "men not worthy of the Commissions they hold," expressed the hope that Lincoln would do better.[12]

By 28 September Lincoln was in Danbury, Connecticut, where the militia were mustering. Washington had ordered Lincoln to bring the Massachusetts troops as fast as possible to reinforce the army, most of which was concentrated on northern Manhattan. On 30 September, however, Washington's plans changed, and he wrote Lincoln to return to Fairfield, Connecticut, and meet with Gen. George Clinton in order to plan an attack on Long Island, a raid to "aid the inhabitants in removing or destroying the stock, grain, etc. which must otherwise fall into the hands of the enemy." The excursion would serve the secondary purpose of drawing off some of the pressure the British were exerting on the Continental army.[13]

For three days Lincoln and Clinton discussed the expedition over glasses of wine at Isaac Beer's New Haven tavern. Governor Jonathan Trumbull of Connecticut was unable to join them but promised everything in his power to promote the success of the operation. As a precautionary measure, Lincoln collected all the boats on the Connecticut shore to prevent the Tories from communicating with the enemy on Long Island and to control Loyalists in his immediate area. Provisions and shipping were being readied for the cross-sound raid, when Washington, on 16 October, ordered two regiments from the force to the main army north of New York. Despite strong support and enthusiasm for Lincoln's raid, the expedition was aborted. Washington's need for reinforcements now was critical. Lincoln marched his militiamen to the support of the main army, where they were designated as one of its seven divisions.[14]

The Continental army was in full retreat, straggling from Kingsbridge across the Harlem River from Manhattan Island to White Plains, fifteen miles to the north. Howe intended to outflank the retreating Americans by landing at Pell's Point in Pelham Bay on 12 October, but the slow, deliberate British advance and the determined opposition of John Glover's brigade allowed Washington to gather his forces and dig in around the village of White Plains. Lincoln's troops secured the rear of Washington's marching army by occupying Valentine's Hill, some miles to the south of White Plains. From that defensive position a harried Lincoln wrote a note of apology to "Brother" John Browne: "Such has been our uncertain state and that of the army as to deny me an opportunity of writing. I have been scarcely two days at the same place." As the British approached, Lincoln pulled his men out of their entrenchments and joined the main American line in anticipation of a pitched battle with the enemy.[15]

The British struck on 28 October, attacking Chatterton's Hill on the extreme right flank of the entrenched American line. Despite a determined defense, the Americans were forced to abandon the hill; that night they retreated to strong positions just north of their former lines. For four days the Americans busily erected earthworks while watching every British move. The American defenses stimulated a change of heart in the British command. During the night of 4 November Howe pulled his forces out of their positions and marched southwest toward Manhattan Island and the American garrison at Fort Washington. Two days later Lincoln attended a council of war which agreed to garrison the Hudson Highlands with three thousand Continentals and move a strong body of troops into New Jersey.[16]

Lincoln would not participate in the advance into New Jersey. His division, drafted for three months' service, was scheduled to be discharged on 17 November, despite nearly a month's delay in arriving in camp. On 21 October Lincoln had written privately to a high government official in Massachusetts about the problem Congress faced keeping an army in the field. Congress had authorized a new army of eighty-eight regiments enlisted for the duration, but in the meantime the terms of "the greatest part of the army engaged to serve [would] expire." The consequences of the dissolution of the old army were clear. As Lincoln explained, there was "no great reason to suppose that a sufficient number of men will be raised upon the new plan, by the time it will be necessary for them to be in the field." Nor did he think it possible to hold his men "beyond the time for which they engaged to serve," for that would have "a tendency to give them a distrust of the service." In Lincoln's opinion the best thing would be "to see what number of men here can be prevailed upon to continue a longer time in the service." Washington agreed but was not optimistic about the outcome. On 6 November he wrote to the Massachusetts legislature, urging them to recruit four thousand men to replace those whose time was about to expire. Washington's fears were justified. Despite Lincoln's pleadings, the men of his division turned homeward when their time was up. There was nothing for him to do but follow.[17]

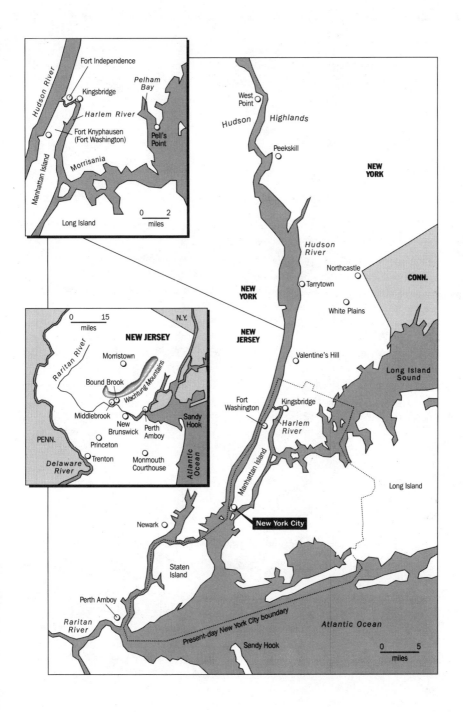

Inset 1 (top left):

Hudson River

Fort Independence

Kingsbridge

Pelham Bay

Harlem River

Fort Knyphausen
(Fort Washington)

Pell's Point

Manhattan Island

Morrisania

Long Island

0   2
miles

Inset 2 (middle left):

0   15
miles

N.Y.

NEW JERSEY

Raritan River

Morristown

Bound Brook

Wachtung Mountains

Middlebrook

New Brunswick

Perth Amboy

Sandy Hook

PENN.

Princeton

Trenton

Delaware River

Monmouth Courthouse

Atlantic Ocean

Main map:

West Point

Hudson   Highlands

Peekskill

NEW YORK

Hudson River

Northcastle

Tarrytown

CONN.

NEW YORK

White Plains

NEW JERSEY

Valentine's Hill

Long Island Sound

Fort Washington

Kingsbridge

Harlem River

Long Island

Manhattan Island

Newark

New York City

Staten Island

Perth Amboy

Raritan River

Present-day New York City boundary

Atlantic Ocean

Sandy Hook

0   5
miles

The problem of keeping soldiers in the field was not new, nor would it be solved during the course of the war. The military experience of colonial Americans had been extensive but limited. The colonial militias were particularly adapted to defensive fighting close to home; they were not trained or equipped for offensive campaigns in far-off places. Moreover, the New England militia system was based less upon a military ethos of loyalty, subordination, and discipline than on the traditional idea of the covenant. The "contract" that a militiaman made when he signed on for an expedition included an understanding that he would be commanded by the officer who had enlisted him, that he would serve for a certain time in order to do a certain job in a certain place. Any violation of those terms, or those of pay or provisions, would mean the dissolution of the contract.[18]

Lincoln knew the New England militia system intimately through his twenty-odd years of experience as a militia officer. To be successful in it, a leader had to develop a fine sense of balance between the competing interests of his men and the requirements of any given military situation. Lincoln would have learned this lesson from circumstances like those his father had handled during the Seven Years' War. During the 1759–60 Quebec expedition a number of Suffolk County men had become "uneasy" and complained "of their treatment of their Country" for having to spend the winter on campaign. Colonel Lincoln wrote to encourage their commanding officer, noting how difficult it was to lead such independent men. "An exact discipline must be kept up, and Orders most strictly Observed," he wrote, "which to undisciplined men, men of your Own Town, your Schoolmates, & perhaps Some of your Intimate Acquaintance must seem grevous." He went on to assure the man that, though the colony had ordered that "not one man be dismis'd," that winter he had no doubt that the General Court would "do something hansom for both Officers and men in Consideration of their being exposed this winter to an Extraordinary expence" and that there was "not a Single Instance" of which he had heard in "the whole Town of a wife, or family, but what has been provided for." And he promised, "Nothing on my part shall be wanting in order to yours being treated with the utmost Care and Tenderness by the Government." The lengths to which Colonel Lincoln went to assuage those militiamen's concerns was characteristic of a system based on a covenant of exacting terms.[19]

In the public mind, however, the militia consisted of citizen-soldiers, men of property who voluntarily enlisted to serve their country from sheer virtue. After all, volunteerism lay at the very heart of the struggle for independence. In 1776 most Americans felt that only a virtuous people moved to take up arms could hope to defeat professional British soldiers. Thus, it was hard to understand the militia's insistence on service performed according to strictly legal forms rather than a calculus based on its country's need. Particularly infuriating to army commanders was the militia's insistence on returning home when their time of service was concluded, even if that time occurred on the eve of a battle. Continental army officers, from Washington on down, quickly came to see the militia as being worse than useless; its members were poorly trained, ill disciplined, unreliable, and wasteful of scarce supplies. These officers based their hopes upon the creation of a professional army, one in which a soldier's self-interest—in the form of land and money—was linked to the national interest rather than the disinterested virtue of the citizen volunteer.[20]

Lincoln was a militia officer whose sole experience had been in commanding his fellow townsmen, neighbors and friends. He knew the advantages of the militia, for he had seen its work in New England. The militia was the right arm of the civilian authorities, enabling them to maintain control over the political and law inforcement institutions of a state. The battles of Lexington and Concord had shown that the militia could keep the British on the defensive outside of areas in their immediate control. And during the war the militia would tip the balance in more than one critical battle, if used intelligently by its commanders. Yet the White Plains campaign forced Lincoln to begin thinking continentally, and, in doing so, he began to see the disadvantages of the militia. The prospect of a long war waged along an immense seacoast was vastly different from confining the British in Boston. Given his own unswerving commitment to the cause, Lincoln was troubled by the evidence that the militia lacked virtue, that their management was difficult and would remain so until, as he put it later, "all of them are really influenced by those principles of patriotism, that love of their country, and concern for their freedom and independence, which induced America, in the first instance, to oppose the tyranny of Britain." Lincoln, like many of his brother officers who served in the Continental army, had begun to think of the Revolution as a national effort, rather than a strictly local defense of hearth and home.[21]

Lincoln had barely returned home when he was appointed to command the new recruits levied to reinforce the Continental army. Nevertheless, his short stay in Hingham enabled him to settle some personal affairs. Unable to say when, or whether, he would return home, he made arrangements with friends to watch over his family and provided the means for their support in his absence. He also resigned his position as deacon in the First Congregational Church. Despite their political differences, Pastor Gay wrote Lincoln to thank him for his service to the church and recommended him "to the divine protection, guidance, and blessing in the important and difficult offices" that he was "called to undertake." In mid-December, with his family comfortable and his affairs settled as best they could be, Lincoln turned his attention to his new troops.[22]

Something of Lincoln's style of command can be seen in his orders to General Warner as the new levies prepared to march. Lincoln ordered Warner to rendezvous his brigade at Danbury, while he spent a few days in Rhode Island inspecting the defenses of that state. "It is impossible for me to give you particular orders with regard to matters in general," he wrote. "I need not do it. I can safely confide in your wisdom and fortitude if any thing very material should take place of importance for me to know you will send an express off without loss of time." Lincoln preferred the light rein of command, couching his orders in tactful reminders, which allowed his subordinates as much responsibility as each could handle without interference.[23]

As Lincoln battled a fierce snowstorm on his way south to Rhode Island, Washington considered how best to use the six thousand men promised him by the Massachusetts government. The appearance of British men-of-war off the coast of New England suggested to Washington that most of the men would be employed there; few, if any, would ever make it to the main army. If they did, he wrote Gen. William Heath, some should be sent to the Hudson Highlands and the others to New Jersey, where they could "cover the upper parts of that province and afford . . . support and assistance to the well affected." Washington's analysis proved correct, for Massachusetts split up its force, sending nine hundred men to Ticonderoga and three thousand to Providence to counter the British attack and occupation of Newport, Rhode Island.[24]

While the diversion of force disappointed Washington, he was pleased that the state had appointed Lincoln to command. "This appointment," he wrote Lincoln after he received the news, "gives me the highest satisfaction, as the proofs you exhibited of your zeal for the service, in the preceding part of this campaign, convinces me, that the command could not have devolved upon a more deserving officer." Washington then ordered Lincoln to join Heath at Peekskill, New York. Washington reiterated the compliment when he ordered Heath to "consult and cooperate with Genl. Lincoln, of whose Judgement and Abilities I entertain a very high opinion."[25]

What Lincoln had done to deserve this judgment, beyond a competent display of his leadership during the White Plains campaign, is unknown. Perhaps Washington remembered Lincoln's decisiveness and willingness to work as a Massachusetts councilman in 1775, when they first met. Or perhaps the two men of nearly the same age, of similar temperaments and commitment to the revolutionary cause, felt a kinship that went beyond that of commander and subordinate. In any case, this was the beginning of a long and warm association that proved critical to Lincoln and his subsequent career.

Washington also made his opinion of Lincoln known outside the confines of headquarters. The New York campaign had run roughshod over the reputations of some general officers, highlighting the shortcomings of many of the early commanders. Washington was reluctant to lose the services of any deserving officer. In a letter to John Hancock, the president of Congress, he recommended Lincoln as "a gentleman well worthy of notice in the Military Line. He commanded the Militia from Massachusetts last summer, or Fall rather, and much to my satisfaction, having prov'd himself on all occasions an active, spirited, sensible Man. I do not know whether it is his wish to remain in the Military Line," he continued, "or whether, if he should, anything under the rank he now holds in the State he comes from, would satisfy him." Washington was well aware that the question of rank and promotion was a quagmire in which even the best intentioned could lose their way. The appointment or promotion of any capable officer had to be considered carefully to avert the jealousy of other commanders. "How far an appointment of this kind might offend the Continental Brigadiers I cannot undertake to say," he went on, "many there are, over whom he ought not to be placed, but I know of no way to discriminate."[26]

Although the British laughed at the way farmers and booksellers were made American officers (the New York *Royal Gazette* said of John Sullivan's appointment, "Make him a Gen'ral, Gen'ral strait he grows"), Washington had reasons to recommend men such as Lincoln as Continental generals. Lincoln, after all, was eager and willing to serve without qualification or restriction. There were many qualified men who refused to serve outside their states—James Warren is a good example. Despite the pleadings of his friends to take a larger role in public affairs, he declined time and again. The one Continental office he did fill, that of paymaster general of the army, he held for less than a year and resigned when the army left Massachusetts in the spring of 1776, because "the situation of his affairs and engagements in the business of the Colony, are such, as to prevent him from personally attending the Army." Continental service required civic virtue, a willingness to sacrifice personal profit for the public good.[27]

Washington also looked for men who had at least a modicum of military experience. Personal bravery was necessary but was not a sufficient qualification for command. A general officer also had to be able to maneuver large numbers of men and provide for their discipline and well-being. Few American generals had experienced the chaos of battle, and none had ever operated at the level of responsibility which their new positions required. Clearly, something other than military experience figured into the command equation.

In a revolutionary struggle, in which men fought less because they were disciplined and commanded to do so than because they believed in their cause, Continental generals were expected to inspire their men by force of character. Thus, a virtuous leader animated his men through the example of his bravery and selflessness. Charles Lee, one of the few American generals with extensive military experience, thought that the success of the army depended upon the appointment of men of "the first distinction and property" as officers. Men of the first "character" had to demonstrate their readiness to share the risk to lives and fortunes that their countrymen were being asked to undergo. Richard Montgomery, whose death at Quebec in 1775 deprived the army of one of its most promising leaders, thought that confidence in a general was based on his "spirit and activity." The personality of a leader, therefore, was of the highest importance because his ability to command rested largely on the example he set for his men. Lincoln's bravery, energy, and republican style all recommended him for a posting in the Continental army.[28]

Lincoln arrived in Providence on 18 December and remained there for several days. Some thought he had come to supervise the defense of Rhode Island, but, after examining the situation and sending on a report to Washington, he hurried to Danbury to meet his men. Leaving that place with two regiments and orders for the others to follow, he arrived in Peekskill on 4 January 1777. Washington, fresh from successful attacks on Trenton and Princeton and wishing to annoy the British on two fronts, ordered Heath to attack down the Hudson valley and menace New York City. Washington was optimistic and wrote to Lincoln: "The greatest part of your troops are to move down towards New York, to draw the attention of the enemy to that Quarter, and if they do not throw a considerable body back again, you may in all probability carry the City, or at least blockade them in it." Even a blockade would be useful, he argued, for, having occupied New Jersey, the British had seen no need to stockpile supplies—thus, "if we oblige them to evacuate Jersey, we will cut off their main source of supply."[29]

The first obstacle to an attack on New York City was a British outpost near Kingsbridge on the north bank of the Harlem River which guarded the bridge to Manhattan Island. A British officer described it as a "stockade, along which there are many strong forts; the hills very high and vastly strong ground." Even so, Lincoln was eager to attack. "The Massachusetts troops are fast collecting here," he wrote from North Castle in Westchester County on 12 January to the other division commanders. "I expect we may soon proceed to Kingsbridge." And to George Clinton he wrote to assure him that the Massachusetts militia "are Lovers of Freedom, and are determined to fight in support of it."[30]

On 14 January Lincoln moved his troops to Tarrytown and three days later began his march down the Albany road to Kingsbridge. On 18 January Lincoln's and Heath's two other divisions converged on the outskirts of the enemy camp, which they called Fort Independence. After surprising a guard outpost, the advance was halted by the outworks of the fort. Heath sent the British a summons to surrender. The move proved unwise, for the Americans had no heavy artillery to breech the British defenses, and it was the unanimous opinion of Heath's subordinates, including Lincoln, that storming the entrenchments with militia would fail. This left them little choice but to lay siege to the position, making every attempt, "by feint or otherwise, to draw the enemy out of the fort."[31]

Lincoln's troops, while equipped for rapid movement, were unprepared for a long siege. Colonel Timothy Pickering, who shared a hut made of rails, straw, and leaves with Lincoln and the general's son, Benjamin Jr., noted in his diary that they spent nearly a week in the bitterest weather. On the night of 23 January, he wrote, it began to snow, and by morning it lay three or four inches deep. "This morning it rained hard, by which the soldiers were generally wet, in their huts, through to their skins." Lincoln, who could see no advantage in remaining in these miserable conditions, especially as the men's powder was wet, ordered Pickering's regiment back to Tarrytown. In the face of another snowstorm on 28 January all the American forces retreated to their previous quarters.[32]

Thus ended the campaign against Fort Independence. It had been, as Pickering said, "a very idle not to say disgraceful expedition." Heath's lack of energy and judgment made him the object of ridicule within the army. Even Washington lost some of his famous composure when he wrote

Heath: "Your conduct is censured (and by men of sense and judgement who were with you on the expedition to Fort Independence) as being fraught with too much caution by which the Army has been disappointed, and in some degree disgraced. Your summons, as you did not attempt to fulfill your threats, was not only idle but farcical, and will not fail of turning the laugh exceedingly upon us." For the hard-pressed Washington, determined to achieve respect for a ragtag army of citizen-soldiers, the British derision proved the most humiliating aspect of the affair. Heath never recovered his reputation in Washington's eyes, and he served the remainder of the war in commands far from any active theater.[33]

In the critical early days of the war Congress and the army command were absorbed by the need to find leaders of energy, decision, and judgment. It was not an easy process. As John Adams explained: "Many persons are extremely dissatisfied with numbers of the genral officers of the highest rank. I don't mean the commander in chief, his character is justly very high, but Schuyler, Putnam, Spencer, Heath, are thought by very few to be capable of the great commands they hold." William Tudor, one of Adams's correspondents in the army, thought that some of the mud that spattered Heath would cling to Lincoln, though without his deserving it. Fortunately for Lincoln, others did not share Tudor's opinion. Washington once again recommended Lincoln to Congress as "an excellent officer and worthy of your notice in the Continental Line."[34]

Soon after Lincoln and his division arrived at Washington's headquarters at Morristown, New Jersey, on 14 February 1777, Congress acted on that recommendation and appointed him a major general in the Continental line. Although he felt himself unequal to the task, Lincoln accepted the position—"happy in the confidence you place in my attachment to the liberties of America and my ardor to support her cause." John Adams was more interested in winning battles than in the patriotic fervor of Congress's generals. Having voted for Lincoln, he wanted reassurance that he had chosen the right man. Adams asked William Tudor how Lincoln's appointment was regarded at headquarters and "how he [Lincoln] behaves." Adams confided appologetically, "I wish We had better Materials than we have, but We must use the best We can." Tudor did not share Adams's gloom and replied that the "appointment of General Lincoln is approv'd of here. He was considered at Headquarters last Fall as an industrious vigilant and brave Man."[35]

By the end of February the new major general commanded more than a thousand soldiers at his post in Bound Brook, New Jersey, an advanced position on the army's right flank, guarding a pass through the Wachtung Mountains. Bound Brook was a small village about eight miles from

British-occupied New Brunswick, with the Raritan River to its south and the mountains behind it to the north. The British had posted their advanced guards only three miles away. Despite continuing cold weather and heavy snows, there were frequent skirmishes between small detachments of both armies throughout February and March. Details of army administration, the apprehension of Tories, and foraging for food and supplies took up most of Lincoln's time. It was an active life—one that challenged even the fittest of men. Between inspection tours along the defensive line, on 3 March Lincoln rode forty miles roundtrip to Morristown to meet with General Washington about the pay and discharge of the Massachusetts militia, whose tour of duty was to expire on 15 March.[36]

As spring came to New Jersey, activity in the opposing camps heated up. Desertion stripped American ranks as hundreds of farmer-soldiers headed back home for spring planting. The Massachusetts militia left camp on 22 March, leaving Lincoln painfully aware of his exposed position. After inspecting the lines of defense, he wrote a despondent letter to Washington. Given current troop dispositions, Lincoln warned, many units could not "render the least assistance to this post in case it is attacked by the enemy." Responding to Washington's desire that wagons be kept ready in case "a sudden movement" proved necessary, Lincoln replied that "the weakness of our troops hath induced us at all times to take this precaution," however "painful the idea" of a retreat might be.[37]

Lincoln soon found out exactly how painful it could be. Early on Sunday morning, 13 April, just a day after his letter to Washington, a British force of four thousand men, led by Lord Cornwallis, launched a raid on the post at Bound Brook. The American pickets guarding the approaches to the encampment fled without sounding the alarm, and "the enemy were at the general's quarters before he had any knowledge of their approach." Lincoln's small force of five hundred men was in danger of being trapped by Cornwallis's converging columns. Lincoln "had a choice of difficulties, and but a few moments to determine and act in, of which he made the best improvement," rallying his men and guiding them to escape through the "warm fire" of British musketry. American losses amounted to sixty casualties and prisoners. The British also captured three artillery pieces and most of Lincoln's personal papers—"a great misfortune as it will inform the Enemy of many disagreeable circumstances." But Lincoln, by his coolness and decisiveness, had averted disaster.[38]

The British left Bound Brook soon after breakfast, and the Americans reoccupied the town in time for Lincoln to dine there. Washington shrugged off the loss as "trifling." Nathanael Greene wrote to an agitated John

Adams that Lincoln "is deservedly acquitted from any blame." Greene censured, instead, the "negligence of the militia" and the "intrigues of the Tories." Lincoln's peers, such as Massachusetts general Joseph Ward, judged that his "generalship was good" and insisted that "he took every precaution which wisdom and vigilence would dictate in his situation." Yet Lincoln found his narrow escape hard to forget. Ordered a month later by Washington to "be guarded in the best manner possible to elude and baffle" British designs, Lincoln felt an implicit reproach and replied that "the unhappy affair of Sunday April 13th is too recent in my mind to admit my neglecting the former, while a duty indispensible (to say nothing of a desire to retaliate) call me to every exertion in a fullest manner to effect the latter."[39]

Through May and most of June time hung heavy on Lincoln's hands as the Americans watched the British camp warily, trying to guess where the British would move next. In this war for information the soldiers were Tory informers, ardent Whigs, and deserters from both sides. Lincoln kept a finger on the pulse of New Brunswick with the aid of discontented Hessian deserters, whose treatment by the British was "so very different from what they had expected." From the reports he received Lincoln thought it likely that New Brunswick would be evacuated soon, and, unless reinforced, the British would postpone any plans to attack Philadelphia.[40]

A semipermanent posting had at least one consolation: mail from home came at regular intervals. And Lincoln's eldest son, Ben, was a lively and faithful correspondent, filling his father in on all the local news. For a man absent from his farm during spring planting for the first time in his life, it was bittersweet to hear that "there never was since my remembrance a fairer prospect for large crops of the fruits of the earth than the present." Ben Jr. wrote that the cool weather had produced English hay and "rainy apples" in plentiful supply. The family was "tolerably stocked for wool," and even flax promised a good harvest.[41]

Ben Jr.'s letters revealed a constant concern for little economies in the management of the farm and "the almost immeasurable expences of the family for the necessaries of life." Lincoln's pay had gone to buy cattle and a considerable amount of supplies, which Mary Lincoln stockpiled in case the family was "obliged to retire" from their home under attack from the British. Besides these ordinary outlays the family strained to supply Lincoln "with the very great variety of articles" he had asked for, such as "Russia duck" for breeches, Irish sheeting for shirts, and a favorite of Lincoln's, good aged cheese. Unlike most of Lincoln's needs, which could be supplied from the family farm, these scarce items had to be purchased with cash.[42]

Word from home could be painful. It was not uncommon for a new soldier, away from home for the first time, to experience shock and depression and to manifest physical symptoms such as loss of appetite, restlessness, and melancholy. Lincoln's promotion to the Continental line meant that his army service no longer consisted of three-month cycles. By accepting his commission, he had signed on for the duration of the war. And, as the summer campaign was just beginning, there was no chance that he could get away from camp to visit Hingham. That news hit the family hard. "My mother was very disagreably disappointed when she was informed that you was not to return this summer," Ben wrote. "She wishes you would let her know when you are to return. The period is desirable by us all and her in particular."[43]

For Lincoln, in camp at Bound Brook, most of June passed quietly. Unable to fathom why the British had remained inactive so long, the Americans braced themselves for an attack. On 12 June Howe, with eighteen thousand men, left New Brunswick and advanced slowly into central New Jersey, hoping to draw Washington from his secure position on the heights at Middlebrook. Ten days later, having failed to lure the American army into a general engagement, Howe retired to Staten Island. New Jersey was free of British troops.[44]

"The retreat of the enemy from the Jerseys," wrote Ben Jr. from home, "exhilerated to a very great degree the spirits of the people in this part of the continent." As well it should have. But the army command anxiously watched throughout July as Howe's army, like a great snake coiling to strike, regrouped in New York. Would Howe join Burgoyne, now marching south to Albany from Canada? Or would he try to smash the political center of the rebellion in Philadelphia? Even Charleston, in distant South Carolina, seemed a plausible target in the summer of 1777.[45]

Howe's huge fleet of 260 ships finally sailed from Sandy Hook on 23 July. Washington guessed that Philadelphia was the enemy's destination and the next day ordered his army south. For Lincoln, however, the commander had other plans. Gen. John Burgoyne's invasion of New York from Canada threatened to divide the United States and isolate New England. Gen. Philip Schuyler, whom Congress had appointed to command in the Northern Department, had done little but retreat in the face of Burgoyne's advance. Fort Ticonderoga, for decades a major strongpoint in the defense of British North America, had been evacuated without a fight—an action that shocked and angered New England. As Washington explained to Lincoln, "I have this day received two letters from General Schuyler in such a stile, as convinces me that it is absolutely necessary to send a determined officer to his assistance." He urged Lincoln to move with all possible speed to the northern army and there take command of the New England militia, over which, he said, "I am informed you have influence and who place confidence in you." Despite a slow fever, which troubled him until early August, Lincoln bid his division good-bye and rode north to join General Schuyler.[46]

In September of 1776 Lincoln had left Boston as a militia officer, virtually untried, whose only real experience consisted of maneuvers on the town green. He had a reputation as a good administrator and a good committeeman, but some, such as Abigail Adams, wondered if he had the "spirit, activity and ambition" for higher responsibilities. By August 1777 Lincoln had laid those doubts to rest. Acting under the command of Washington, he had proven himself to be cool under fire and capable of directing large bodies of troops. Equally important, Lincoln commanded the loyalty of his men; he lent "dignity and lustre" to his office. Even so sour a New Englander as Timothy Pickering wrote that, while Lincoln was with the main army, he "gained the love and respect of all men. The officers of his division admire him and much regretted his departure." Washington realized this quality would be critical to the outcome of the northern campaign. If the militia turned out, Burgoyne could be stopped in his tracks. As Washington wrote to Connecticut's Governor Trumbull, he feared that "distrust, jealousy, and suspicion of the conduct of the officers [already present] might arise in the Militia, and that degree of confidence in them wanted, which would be necessary to success." He was sending Lincoln and Benedict Arnold because, he explained, "their presence, I trust, will remove every Ground of diffidence and backwardness in the Militia, and . . . they will go on when and where their Services are demanded, with a Spirit and Resolution, becoming Freemen and the Sacred Cause in which they are engaged." As Lincoln covered the dusty miles to Albany, he had every reason to believe that they would.[47]

CHAPTER THREE

Saratoga

I have directed General Lincoln to repair to you. . . . This gentleman has
always supported the character of a judicious, brave, active Officer.
George Washington

What Lincoln found in the American camp on his arrival in Albany
on 30 July 1777 was discouragement and disorganization. Gen. Philip
Schuyler, commander in the Northern Department, had retreated in the
face of Gen. John Burgoyne's steady advance south from Canada. He had
given up the stronghold of Fort Ticonderoga and fallen back in stages,
from Skenesborough to Saratoga and then to Stillwater. By 12 August the
Continental army was ordered to Van Schaick's Island, at the confluence
of the Mohawk and Hudson rivers, just a few miles north of Burgoyne's
goal, Albany.

Schuyler's delaying tactics were militarily effective but politically disastrous. Constant retreat punctured army morale. The fall of Ticonderoga
caused such an uproar in New England, where complaints of Schuyler's
incompetence gave way to muttered accusations of treason, that the New
England militia refused to serve under him. "The Indignation and Distrust that prevails here are Extreem," James Warren wrote from Boston to
John Adams in Philadelphia. "The want of Confidence in your Commanders [are] that way such, that if it be not removed by Lincolns being sent
there to Command the Militia will very much impede our Reinforcements."[1]

By sending Lincoln north, Washington was betting that the New
Englander's reputation in Massachusetts would stem the widespread desertion of militia already in camp, while encouraging men at home to
march. The move also was designed to bolster the spirits of state leaders
in New York and Connecticut, who were on the verge of panic. Consoling
the New York Council of Safety on the loss of Fort Ticonderoga, Wash-

ington tried to hearten them with news of the arrival of two "very valuable officers," Lincoln and Benedict Arnold—"particularly the former, than whom there is, perhaps, no man from the State of Massachusetts who enjoys more universal esteem and popularity."[2]

Schuyler had proposed the idea of stationing a body of militia in "the Grants" (present-day Vermont) on Burgoyne's left flank which could harass the British and profit from any missteps Burgoyne made. Washington concurred, writing that such a move "would certainly make Gen. Burgoyne very circumspect in his advances, if it did not totally prevent them. It would keep him in continual anxiety for his rear and oblige him to leave the posts behind him, much stronger than he would otherwise do." The mere threat of an attack on Burgoyne's lifeline to Canada might induce him to weaken the main body of his troops, and that might be critical in a pitched battle before Albany. After a discussion with Schuyler near Fort Miller on 30 July, Lincoln was ordered to "repair to Manchester" (Vermont) and take command of the small unit of Continental troops and militia stationed there. More men were expected soon, including John Stark's New Hampshire militia, and with these troops Lincoln was to move toward Skenesborough if he could do so "without risking too much." Schuyler concluded by urging Lincoln to "exercise your own judgement as contingencies arise."[3]

Lincoln lost no time in joining his command, arriving in Manchester on 2 August. He found about five hundred troops there, with an estimated two thousand more on the way. Waiting for his little army to grow, Lincoln set about organizing his camp and fixing his operational plan. Writing to Schuyler on 4 August, he was full of optimism. In a few days he expected to march twenty miles north to the fork of the roads heading to Skenesborough and Ticonderoga. From there Lincoln's army would be close to the enemy and could watch their movements and attack them "more suddenly" if the opportunity arose. The movement would "cover a much larger part of the country" and thus protect farmers who had abandoned their harvest in the face of the enemy. It also might divert Burgoyne into dividing his force, Lincoln continued, a move that would be advantageous for the Americans. Lastly, he suggested that frequent skirmishing with the enemy would "give spirit to our men" and make them more "vigilant and active," a reference to the dispiriting effect the recent months of retreat had had on the morale of the northern army. Lincoln also wrote to Artemas Ward to forward the newly requisitioned Massachusetts militia, taking care that those chosen were familiar with "partisan duty" and were commanded by men "able, active and experienced." Given the grim

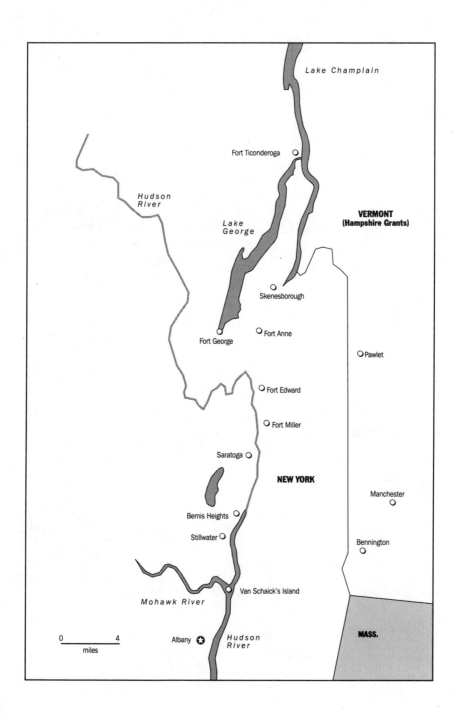

Lake Champlain

Fort Ticonderoga ○

Hudson River

VERMONT
(Hampshire Grants)

Lake George

○ Skenesborough

○ Fort Anne

Fort George ○

○ Pawlet

○ Fort Edward

○ Fort Miller

Saratoga ○

NEW YORK

Manchester
○

Bemis Heights ○

Stillwater ○

Bennington
○

○ Van Schaick's Island

Mohawk River

0   4
miles

Albany ✪   *Hudson River*

MASS.

scenes of battle he already had witnessed, Lincoln insisted that a number of good surgeons be sent, with amputating tools and a large supply of medicine. "The great sufferings and distresses brought on the Troops the last campaign from the Want of these things," he wrote, "were enough to fill a man of a very moderate share of humanity with the most sensible grief." Lastly, because of the lack of roads and the difficulty of movement in the wilderness, Lincoln recommended that personal belongings be kept to an absolute minimum.[4]

That was good advice. Though Lincoln was unaware of it at the time, Burgoyne's army was hampered by a horde of camp followers and baggage carts laden with such essential items as dress uniforms and champagne. The British army crawled south at a snail's pace through the boggy wilderness between Skenesborough and Fort Edward on the Hudson. It arrived at Fort Edward on 29 July, where Burgoyne paused to collect stores and prepare for the push down the Hudson to Albany. But Schuyler, aware only that Burgoyne was within striking distance of Albany, expected him to take advantage of American weakness by quickly crossing the Hudson and launching an immediate advance on the city. Convinced that the critical moment had arrived, Schuyler countermanded his orders of 31 July and ordered Lincoln to join him at Stillwater. Lincoln replied on 6 August that he could hardly reinforce Schuyler with troops he did not have, assuring him that he would come as soon as he had gathered the Massachusetts militia. On 9 August Schuyler, shrugging off Lincoln's reasoning, reiterated his order, adding, "You cannot make too much Expedition to join us with whatever force You can possibly bring."[5]

Lincoln was in a bind. He had been reinforced by Gen. John Stark and the New Hampshire militia on 7 August, but Stark soon made it clear that he wanted nothing to do with the Continental army or its generals. As Lincoln wrote Schuyler: "He seems to be exceedingly soured, and thinks he hath been neglected, and hath not had justice done him, by Congress. He is determined not to join the Continental army until the Congress give him his rank therein. His claim is to command all the Officers he commanded last year; as also all who joined the army after him." Lincoln was unsure whether Stark would march to Stillwater, but he was sure that, if Stark did go, he would "act there only as a separate Corps and take no orders from any officer in the N. Dept." As it was, Stark refused to leave the Grants, despite Schuyler's pleas that he cooperate.[6]

While the tiff over command annoyed Lincoln, he and Stark were in basic agreement on the course they should take. Both saw the vast benefits to be reaped from harassing, as Lincoln put it, Burgoyne's "naked and uncovered rear." After smoothing Stark's ruffled feathers, which doubtless required a great deal of self-control, and drawing up a plan of operations, Lincoln rode to Stillwater to persuade Schuyler to stick with the original idea. Lincoln was successful and wrote Stark on 14 August: "Our plan is adopted. You will please to meet us, as proposed, on the morning of the 18th." By the time Stark got that message, however, his New Hampshiremen were in the midst of destroying a large force of the enemy sent on a foraging expedition to Bennington. It was a victory so complete and so crippling to Burgoyne that it vindicated Stark's insubordination and Lincoln's tactics of irregular warfare.[7]

The victory at Bennington infused new spirit into the officers and men of the northern army, but it came too late to save Schuyler's command. Congress, in early August, had already decided to replace him with Gen. Horatio Gates, a former British officer, whose yearlong feud with Schuyler had left a trail of bitterness throughout the Northern Department and in Congress. Gates had the confidence of the New England delegates in Congress; his appointment, in addition to that of New Englanders Lincoln and Arnold, promised, in the words of John Adams, to "restore our Affairs in that Department."[8]

Word of Gates's appointment reached Schuyler on 10 August, although Gates did not arrive until 18 August. In the meantime Lincoln prepared for his flanking expedition and readied his men to join Stark at Bennington. Yet, for the second time, he was uncertain whether his plans would be approved. Schuyler wrote Lincoln on 15 August that he should inform Gates of "the Business you are going upon" but that "the orders he may have may make it necessary either to alter your rout or perhaps intirely desist from the Enterprize." Thus, from his command post at Bennington on 20 August, Lincoln once again repeated his arguments for a flanking movement against Burgoyne's line of communication, this time to the newly arrived Gates. Lincoln gave two reasons why his plan would be more effective than a concentration before the enemy. First, adding great numbers of ill-disciplined militia to the main army would do little to strengthen it in the case of a general action; instead, it would make the whole unwieldy. Lincoln knew from experience that militia in a pitched battle were little more than an armed mob. But, he added, "should we be in force here, and advance towards the enemy and fall in their rear, it will reduce Burgoyne to the necessity of reinforcing the several posts he now possesses, where he hath left small garrisons, on the holding of which, the salvation of his army may depend." This move would greatly weaken his main force, "or he will detach a force superior to us with a design to attack us. In either case it will divide him and may give you an opportunity to attack him with success." Implicit in Lincoln's plan was the idea that the militia was tailor-made for small operations that depended on surprise, sniping, and hit-and-run attacks.[9]

Gates was persuaded and asked Lincoln to come to headquarters, where on 23 August they met with New York governor George Clinton to coordinate their strategy. Once agreed upon, there was little for Lincoln to do but organize and supply the militia forces that trickled into camp at Bennington. Despite his urgent pleas to the various state governments and his encouraging letters to Gates, it was not until the middle of September that Lincoln had enough manpower to execute his plan of attack. By that time Arnold had eliminated the threat to Gates's left wing by forcing Lt. Col. Barry St. Leger to suspend his attack on Fort Schuyler, a key position in the Mohawk Valley. And Burgoyne had crossed the Hudson, beginning his march southward along the west bank of the river. Unknown to the Americans, Burgoyne had cut his line of supply and thrown all his strength into the effort to reach Albany before winter set in.[10]

By 12 September Lincoln had two thousand militia troops at Pawlet, New York, and felt strong enough to launch attacks on the string of British posts that guarded Burgoyne's line of communication with Canada. He wrote Gates on 14 September and disclosed his operations:

> On being apprized of the weak state of Ft. Ticonderoga and the considerable number of prisoners there and the vessels at Lake George landing under very weak guard—plus a magazine of stores—and thinking that a movement that way is what [I] was sent here fore, (to divide and distract the enemy), [I] sent Col. Brown with 500 men to the Lake George landing to release the prisoners and destroy the stores—500 under Col. Johnson to Mt. Independence to divert the enemy, 500 under Col. Woodbridge to Skeensboro thence to Ft. Anne and then on to Ft. Edward. Hope these moves meet your approval.

On 17 September Lincoln wrote that he and the remainder of his men—about six hundred—were on their way to reinforce Col. Woodbridge on his drive south.[11]

On 14 September the Americans were relieved of the uncertainty of British intentions by Burgoyne's crossing the Hudson River. Two days later Gates, still in the dark about Lincoln's troop dispositions, wrote Lincoln to seize the "opportunity to gall that part of the enemy's forces yet upon the east side of the river." Ending with a typical flourish, he assured Lincoln that "yr scouts and spies, must, joined to your own wisdom and experience direct you in the glorious task." Lincoln, however, was already committed to his plan of dispersed attacks. News of Col. John Brown's successful assault on the British post at Lake George reached Lincoln on 20 September, and he hesitated to withdraw his troops before they had attempted to overwhelm Ticonderoga. Gates, however, was peremptory. On 19 September, and again three days later, he ordered Lincoln to march his army to Stillwater ("You may be sure New York and not Ticonderoga is Burgoyne's destination") and directed him to post five hundred men on the heights on the east side of the Hudson to anchor the American line. Lincoln left Brown and Johnson to test the defenses of Fort Ticonderoga with orders to follow him if it proved too strong to take. Recalling Woodbridge from Skenesborough, Lincoln then marched to join the main army near Stillwater.[12]

Lincoln arrived at Gates's headquarters at Bemis Heights near Saratoga in the evening of 22 September. The news of Brown's success at Lake George "produced universal joy in the camp," as well it might. Brown had captured nearly four hundred soldiers, had freed about one hundred American prisoners, and had taken a "vast Quantity of Plunder." As Lincoln wrote to Gen. John Warner the next day, "All our movements to the north have met with Gen. Gate's approbation." In Burgoyne's camp the effect was more subdued. While Fort Ticonderoga was still held by the British, it was clear that the Americans could operate at will in the wilderness surrounding Burgoyne's army. Retreat, if ever an option, had grown more and more unlikely. As supplies grew tight, any chance of resupply by heavily laden wagons disappeared. A half-pound of bread and an equal portion of meat were cut from soldiers' daily rations.[13]

Lincoln's arrival in camp on 22 September came in the midst of a vicious quarrel between Gates and his second-in-command, Benedict Arnold. Bitter words were exchanged over petty incidents, while the real grounds for their antagonism rested on their appraisals of the military situation. Gates, given the large proportion of militia forces in his army, was content to entrench and block Burgoyne's advance, fielding in strong position whatever attacks the British might make. Arnold preferred to take on the enemy in a pitched battle and did not hesitate to say so. Gates made it plain that Arnold was not indispensable, by replacing him with Lincoln as commander of the right wing and taking the left wing for himself. This was particularly galling to Arnold, since Lincoln had been promoted over his head six months before, and the Connecticut general had been working ever since to have his seniority reinstated. Arnold, in a fit of pique, asked for a pass to Washington's headquarters and threatened to leave but was prevailed upon to remain, when a petition begging him to stay was signed by most of the general officers. Lincoln, significantly, did not sign it.[14]

Arnold's resentment was all the greater because, three days before, he felt the Americans had lost an opportunity to crush the British through Gates's lack of initiative. Burgoyne had attempted on 19 September to outflank Gates's entrenchments on Bemis Heights, but the British had run into forward elements of the American left wing commanded by Arnold. In the general action that followed Arnold's troops, made up of Daniel Morgan's riflemen and units of the Massachusetts line, stopped the British advance, but Gates's refusal to reinforce Arnold for a major assault left the British in possession of the field. Arnold blamed Gates for the inconclusive nature of the battle of Freeman's Farm. In retrospect, however, Gates's decision was probably wise. Few of the American units were a match for British and German regulars in the open field. And, if Burgoyne's army could be contained, its lack of supplies would slowly starve it, forcing either a surrender or a last-ditch assault against the strong American defenses. The Americans had only to watch and wait.[15]

For the next two weeks the American forces harassed the British encampment, attacking foraging parties and advanced pickets and using snipers to good advantage. While the infusion of militia units strengthened the American lines, the British could not stanch the hemorrhage of desertion. Finally the deteriorating situation forced Burgoyne to act. A British council of war agreed to send out a "reconnoisance in force" to test the American left flank. Their objective was a hill that, if taken and fortified, would command the American defenses at Bemis Heights. On the morning of 7 October the British advanced with about fifteen hundred regulars into the no-man's-land between the two armies. The British force was neither quick enough nor in great enough force to withstand the attack ordered by Gates and launched by Morgan and Arnold. By the end of the day the British had not only been forced back to their original lines, but the battle of Bemis Heights had so weakened the British lines that Burgoyne thought it prudent to withdraw to a strong position closer to the river.[16]

That evening Gates ordered Lincoln, commanding the troops on the American right, to reconnoiter the British camp during the night. As Lincoln later recalled it, "On my return a little before day on the Eighth I reported that the enemy appeared in a state of inquietude lying upon their arms and that appearances indicated a retreat if not a flight." Gates then ordered Lincoln to move forward "to feel of the enemy." As the right wing advanced, the British "immediately abandoned their works and retired unto a rising ground covered with a thick wood." Lincoln's troops, hard on the heels of the retreating British, occupied the former British lines.[17]

Lincoln reported the British retreat to Gates and suggested that Burgoyne's next move might be to recross the river and attempt a full-scale retreat to Fort Ticonderoga. In that case, Lincoln said, the Americans should take possession of the ford at Fort Edward. Gates agreed and ordered Lincoln to accomplish the task. As Lincoln later wrote:

> In attempting to execute this order I fell in with a body of the enemys troops in a thick wood detached as a cover to their right, while I was absent at head quarters. I entered an open cart path which led thro the wood and rode in it some distance and did not discover any troops untill I turned an angle in the road: when a body of men opened to my view. At first I could not distinquish them by their dress from our troops, two of them having on scarlet cloths others being in blue the Hessian uniform and some being clad as our militia. A few of our men two or three in a company had British Uniforms, taken in a prize, and the other continental troops were in blue. . . . In this state of uncertainty I continued my route until I was within a few yards of that body so near as perfectly to discover my error—as soon as the enemy perceived this and that I was checking and spurring my Horse I saw the two in british uniforms present & fire. The ball from one of their pieces intered my right leg. On that the party opened a scattering fire upon me and kept it up untill I returned the angle before mentioned.[18]

The British musket ball had shattered Lincoln's right ankle. He was evacuated to Albany, where doctors fought to save his leg. "The appearance of the wound was at first so bad as left not the least probability of saving the leg," but by 19 October Lincoln could write General Washington, "My surgeons encourage me to hope not only for the salvation of my limb but that I shall by the spring have the use of it again." Gates felt the loss of Lincoln keenly, noting in his report to Congress of the victory at the battle of Bemis Heights that Lincoln's wound "has deprived me of the assistance of one of the best officers as well as Men." New York governor George Clinton agreed. Somewhat later he wrote to Lincoln that "exclusive of the most sincere personal friendship I owe you, believe me, Sir, I regard'd your Presence in the field in the Critical Hour in which you was constrained to retire as a matter in which the Public was deeply interested." When news reached Washington's army near Philadelphia the commander was solicitous. Timothy Pickering also "lamented the misfortune of that good man," adding, "I hope he will not lose his leg; his life and health will at a future as well as in the present period be important to our State."[19]

Meanwhile, Burgoyne's army thrashed about like a rabbit in a snare under the gathering fire of the Americans. Retreating under pressure from front and flanks, Burgoyne was finally surrounded on 13 October. On that day he convened a council of war, which decided that negotiations for an "honorable capitulation" were in order. On the morning of 17 October 1777 the British laid down their arms, and the Saratoga campaign came to a stunning and victorious close. The importance of the battle could not be overestimated. For a body of amateur soldiers to induce an army of proud veterans to surrender was an astounding achievement. The victory not only boosted the confidence of the American army but also won the political recognition and military support of France, in the form of a treaty of alliance signed in February 1778.[20]

From his Albany hospital bed Lincoln surveyed the result with satisfaction. A congressional resolution of 4 November honored him, along with Gates and Arnold, for his part in the victory over Burgoyne. Friends such as Gen. Henry Knox wrote to congratulate him, revealing a twinge of jealousy at Lincoln's good fortune: "We at the Southward are quite put out of countenance by the brilliancy of your success." And Dr. James Browne assured him that he was "in a fair way of recovery." Browne attributed Lincoln's progress to his character, which "united the patient philosopher and pious Christian." Though the process of healing was painful and slow, Lincoln bore it with good cheer. One of his aides, Nathan Rice, commented that "during the most painful operation by the surgeon, while bystanders were frequently obliged to leave the room, [Lincoln would] entertain us with some pleasant anecdote, or story, and draw forth a smile from his friends." By 1 December Lincoln was writing to friends at home that the wound was healing fast, free of inflammation, that the "fractured pieces of bone are all extracted," and that he should be home about the middle of January. But that account was too sanguine. The wound would continue to "throw off" bits of bone for years, leaving it open to infection and making it difficult for the leg to acquire strength. Lincoln's son Ben made the trip to Albany to nurse his father and accompany him back home. But it was not until 23 February that the twosome, traveling in a sleigh over the snow-choked Massachusetts roads, arrived in Boston.[21]

However patient Lincoln appeared on the surface, his long convalescence in Albany proved frustrating. In late August his son Ben had written him of the extreme illness of his youngest daughter, Debby. She died on 11 September, but news of her death did not reach Lincoln until after his wounding in October. His son wrote: "My mother is as well as can be expected under the present situation of the family. She sends her love to you and hopes much to see you the next winter if you tarry at home but for a day." Letters like these could only serve as a painful reminder of the family responsibilities Lincoln neglected in fulfilling what he considered a higher duty. For his family it would prove equally difficult. The first word that reached them of Lincoln's wounding was a public letter from Gen. John Glover published in the Boston *Independent Chronicle and Universal Advertiser,* which declared that Lincoln's leg would have to be amputated. It was not until early December, when Glover "luckily met" Mary Lincoln in Boston, that the family received a number of Lincoln's letters and "the true state" of the wound. When Glover reported back to Lincoln he betrayed the anxiety of Lincoln's family and friends in a shaky joke: "I tell all your Friends (who are very anxious for you) that you'll bring it [the leg] home again; Pray dont make me a liar."[22]

In addition to his slow and painful recovery Lincoln also received a blow to his pride. Washington wrote to inform him that Benedict Arnold had been restored by Congress to a seniority higher than Lincoln's. Arnold, who clearly merited promotion, had been passed over when Lincoln and four others had been made major generals. The resolution of Congress of 29 November 1777 placed Arnold ahead of Lincoln in order of senority on the army list, an act that Lincoln believed left him subordinate to any Continental officer, despite his rank. Washington, who realized how touchy an issue this was, wrote, "I am too sensible, My Dear Sir, of your disposition to justice and generosity, of your wishes to see every Man in the possession of his rightful Claim, not to be convinced that you will cheerfully acquiesce in a measure calculated for that end." Word of Lincoln's disgruntlement over the arrangement reached Congress very quickly. James Lovell, one of the Massachusetts delegates, hastily wrote to Lincoln that he was not "altogether suprised" that Arnold's advancement had made Lincoln "uneasy." But he hastened to explain the rationale that had led Congress to make the decision, while assuring him that "your Name and Character is as highly esteemed in Congress as at both Camps, than which I cannot find a more honorable Comparison."[23]

Lincoln's reply to Lovell is characteristic of the jealousy and pique with which Continental officers defended their honor. Lincoln, who was by no means as choleric as Arnold or as proud as John Stark, believed that Arnold's promotion meant, in his words, that "either I was found unequal to the command, or that I was inattentive to my duty," and that, the moment it was known that Arnold had "a right to command me," his own usefulness would be terminated. He ended the letter with an indirect threat to resign: "Will the Congress after holding me up to the Public eye, disgrace and compel me to leave the Service. I trust they will not."[24]

Lincoln's plea fell on deaf ears. Nor did he carry out his threat to resign. The claims of duty proved stronger than the personal pride Lincoln was forced to swallow. Yet it is remarkable that neither a crippling wound nor a blow to his self-esteem, either of which could and did deter other men, forced him from the service of his country. It is difficult to explain such extraordinary dedication. One clue to Lincoln's behavior, however, can be found in a discussion that took place in 1779 in the midst of his efforts to fill the Continental battalions by drafting South Carolina militiamen. These men objected to the draft as an infringement on their rights as citizens. Lincoln felt otherwise: "Did not the inhabitants of this state prior to, and at the commencement of the present war covenant, each with the other, that they would support the contest with Great Britain at the hazard of every thing dear to them in life, and would resign that rather than enjoy it under her galling yoke?" These "covenanters," he went on, "accepted the invitation" to join the army not from a conviction that they would fight alone but that, should it become necessary, others "also would take the field." Should, he wrote, "those, who have survived thus far the fatigues and dangers of the war . . . after having sacrificed their ease, spent their fortunes, ruined their families, and become, by their exertions, peculiarly obnoxious to the enemy," be left to the mercy of this enemy? Lincoln thought not.[25]

The concept of the covenant was central to puritan theology and the social structure of New England life, and it resonates with the power of the deepest obligations to God and men. For Lincoln his decision to serve during the Revolution was a sacred trust, absolutely binding until independence had been achieved. And he believed that all who had decided in favor of independence were similarly bound to support the war effort by any means necessary. Lincoln's devotion to duty, instilled at a young age by church and family, was reinforced by the intellectual and emotional power of this covenant. To resign his post would be to betray this trust.[26]

In addition, much of the sting of the personal affront was drawn by Washington's gift of "Epaulets and sword knott," a gift, he wrote to Lincoln, which bore "testimony of my sincere regard and approbation of your conduct." Lincoln accepted them as "among the first honors which have been confered upon me in life" and, in the blizzard of sentiment that followed, expressed his gratitude to Washington for the opportunity to serve under him. Just below the surface of these comments rode the guilt that Lincoln must have felt for having considered, however briefly, deserting the cause.[27]

Lincoln's leg continued to bother him. In March, from his home in Hingham, he reported to Gates that, though the leg was stronger, "unfortunate for me it is about two inches shorter than the other, which defect ariseth from a greater loss of the Tibula than was at first expected. I hope in some measure to remedy the inconveniences by a corked shoe and a high heel." Yet, as spring became summer, he hobbled about the farm on his oak crutch despairing "of joining the army til the hot season shall be over." To Gates he wrote again at the end of June, "The openings are yet considerable and the limb weak." The corked shoe was "unwieldy," and Lincoln's hopes that the "meliorating hand of time will make it more agreeable" proved too optimistic. He would limp badly for the rest of his life.[28]

Lincoln's return to the army was further delayed by the grave illness of his wife, Mary. The two had taken a trip in late May to Worchester to visit their son Ben, who was studying law. Mary came down with smallpox "in the natural way," which was far more dangerous than through innoculation. It took her a long time to recover, especially her eyes, which remained "weak and tender" and prevented her from writing until September.[29]

To fill the time while he waited for his wound to heal Lincoln studied the strategic situation of the American states in the war with Great Britain. The fruits of this study, a long letter to George Washington, bear examining in some detail, for they demonstrate how far Lincoln had traveled in his thinking from provincial New Englander to officer of the Continental army.

From the beginning of the war, he wrote, America has been on the defensive, suffering "the enemy to take their own measures" while "their movements have directed hers." Lincoln wanted to go on the offensive and thought he saw a way to do it. Since British strategy revolved around the capture and possession of the American "capitals," he suggested to

Washington that a major effort be undertaken to recapture New York City. Even if the attempt were only partially successful, Lincoln felt that there were a number of benefits to be gained. First, "collecting a respectable body of men" in the vicinity of New York would "put them [the British] on the defensive and oblige them to govern their movements by ours." Second, Lincoln realized the strategic importance of the Hudson corridor. Operations in that area would secure communications between New England and the rest of the states. Third, by massing around New York, "we should have our rear open to a strong and plentiful country, filled with men friendly to the common cause." Supplies would be plentiful and the climate healthier for New England men. And, finally, "we should draw the enemy from an open campaign country to one strong by nature less favourable to their designs and more friendly to ours." In short, what Lincoln was suggesting was a chance to repeat the success of the Saratoga campaign, in which Americans profited from their natural advantages and avoided the kind of pitched battles at which the English excelled.

Lincoln also had grown aware of the political realities presented by the war. "I hope these suggestions do not convey the most distant idea of a measure injurious to the southern states," he wrote. "Nothing can be further removed from my mind than the thought that the cause can be supported but by our united, vigourous and confidential assertions. We are all embarked on the same bottom and shall be saved or lost together." It was a statement that would have done credit to a member of the Continental Congress and demonstrated how quickly command in the Continental line produced an appreciation of continent-wide problems.[30]

Lincoln finally felt well enough to resume his divisional command in the Continental line. He arrived at Washington's headquarters in White Plains, New York, on 6 August 1778, nearly a year after his injury. The main army was at full strength, warily watching the British in New York and trying to anticipate their next move. The past summer had seen Continentals slug it out with British regulars at Monmouth Court House in an attempt to prevent Gen. William Howe's retreat from Philadelphia to the safety of New York. And a joint Franco-American operation against Newport, Rhode Island, was the first cooperative venture of the new alliance. It proved tantalizing but unsucessful.[31]

The entry of the French into the war against Britain had shifted the locus of the conflict to the West Indies. Unbeknownst to the Americans, the British had decided to forgo northern campaigns in favor of a southern strategy. The lull in the fighting thus afforded Washington the chance to conduct business that was long overdue: the courts-martial of generals Arthur St. Clair and Philip Schuyler. Lincoln was named president of the court and presided over both trials. The charges were serious. St. Clair was accused of neglect of duty, cowardice, and treachery in abandoning Fort Ticonderoga in 1777; Schuyler was arraigned on charges of neglect of duty. The trials dragged on until October, when both men were acquitted, ending more than fourteen months of agonizing suspense. Despite their acquittal, the damage to their reputations was irreparable. Lincoln's close association with these trials, and the havoc created by politically motivated accusations, left an indelible impression on his mind. Schuyler and St. Clair had made decisions from military necessity which were politically imprudent and had suffered grievously for them. Though he never explicitly referred to their trials, Lincoln could not help being reminded of their plight when he was forced to decide whether to defend or evacuate Charleston later in the war.[32]

When not occupied with the trials, Lincoln settled into the old, and by now comfortable, army routine. Once again he commanded a division of the main army under Washington. The army found itself in much the same position as it had been two years before, with the British holding small but solid beachheads in New York and Newport. The great British effort to subdue the rebellion had foundered in the northern wilderness and been squandered in a senseless campaign to occupy Philadelphia. Now, ironically, at a time when the main American army had reached its greatest strength and was ready for a trial by combat, the British shifted their attention southward. No one as yet suspected that the British had suspended operations in the north. Lincoln expected an attack on either the Hudson Highlands or Boston, but, given the American advantages in those two locales, this was probably wishful thinking. His advice to Washington was taken in part, however, when the army was stationed by divisions in a wide arc from Danbury, Connecticut, in the east to West Point on the Hudson. There it remained on a quiet front throughout the winter and spring of 1779.[33]

For Lincoln, however, there was to be no comforting routine, no rude fellowship of winter quarters, no long furlough in Hingham. As the British cast their eyes to the south, so did the Continental Congress. The Southern Department was in chaos, its defenses in tatters, its commander, Gen. Robert Howe, in conflict with civil and military authorities. Congress sought a strong and confident hand to reorganize the department and lend the luster of victory to the South. And for that task it chose Benjamin Lincoln.

CHAPTER FOUR

Independent Command

A general of an American Army must be everything; and that is being
more than one man can long sustain.

Horatio Gates

At first glance Benjamin Lincoln was a strange choice to command
the Southern Department. Lincoln was a New Englander unfamiliar with
the geography, climate, and people of the South. Unlike some of his New
England colleagues, he had never served in the Continental Congress, where
friendships were made between men of different parts of the continent.
He had never held an independent command, let alone shouldered responsibility for organizing the defense of several states. Furthermore, as
his foray into Continental strategy attests, he believed the war should be
fought in the North, where topography, population density, and ardor for
the common cause favored the American interest.

Yet there were several excellent reasons why Lincoln was a good choice
for the post. First and foremost was the stature he brought to the position
as a hero of Saratoga. The battle, still fresh in the minds of congressional
delegates, made Lincoln a celebrated and successful figure who could unite
a divided South and lead it to victory. Second, given the uproar that Gen.
Robert Howe, a North Carolinian, had caused during his tenure as southern commander, the choice of the tactful, diplomatic, and discreet Lincoln
also made sense. Lincoln may have been the only general officer who
managed to serve for the entire war without alienating any of his peers.
Certainly, he is the only one who served under Washington, Gates, and
Schuyler and managed to keep the respect of all three—at the same time.
Third, there were few generals of Lincoln's rank who had exercised independent command, and, of those who had, none was available for the
appointment at the time. Philip Schuyler, John Sullivan, and Charles Lee

were viewed with disfavor by Congress at the moment, and Washington would no doubt have blocked the appointment of Horatio Gates.[1]

The choice of a New Englander was shrewd as well. Unfamiliar with the internal squabbles of southern factions and animated by his devotion to the revolutionary movement, Lincoln had no axes to grind. He could be expected to make decisions that were best for the "common cause" rather than in the interests of the southern tidewater or the piedmont. Furthermore, the choice of Lincoln tied northern interests more tightly to the South in much the same way that Washington's appointment as commander-in-chief had tied Virginia to an overwhelmingly New England army.[2]

Finally, the South Carolina delegates to Congress who requested Lincoln's appointment were aware of the chaotic nature of the military situation in the South. They also must have considered Lincoln's reputation for military organization and administration as well as his reputation for leading militia. Though Congress promised Lincoln a Continental army of seven thousand men and encouraged him to plan an offensive campaign to wrest control of Florida, its southern members must have known how empty those promises were. Those aims could only be accomplished if the southern commander had the energy and strength of will to build an army from scratch. That was the challenge that awaited Lincoln in South Carolina.[3]

"In the evening Oct. 3d 1778 at Quaker Hill in the state of New York I received a resolve of Congress sending me to South Carolina immediately to take command in the Southern Department." In this laconic style Lincoln began the journal of what were to be the most significant years of his life. Leaving camp on 8 October, Lincoln passed by easy stages to Philadelphia, where he stayed for nearly a week, dining with members of Congress and acquainting himself with the military situation in the South. To Washington, whom he had missed in his stop at headquarters, he revealed some of his misgivings about the appointment: "I wish the Congress had fixed their minds on some other officer for the Southern department as well from a consciousness that many others would render there more important services to the public as from an apprehension that I may suffer in the journey from my wound which is not yet healed but," he added, "I have not objected because to make excuses is painful."[4]

The danger of injury or illness was real. An exasperated Dr. Browne, Lincoln's Albany surgeon and friend, wrote: "I am sensible you are aquainted with the difficulties of the command and the dangers to which you expose your health in the climate to which you are going; but with

Genl. Lincoln all obstacles vanish when the interest of his Country demand his services. Do not take this as a compliment." Browne went on to give Lincoln some medical advice. As "the seat of action is a low marshy country, abounding with ponds of stagnant water from which exhales a fetid, putrid vapour," you should never "expose your person to the night; nor without the greatest necessity ride out in the morning before the sun has dispelled these noxious vapours." While those strictures proved impossible to follow in the exigencies of a campaign, Lincoln probably found Browne's prescription against scurvy more congenial. Every day Lincoln was to take "quontam sufficient of the following mixture . . . Jamaica spirits, spring water, lemon or lime juice and good leaf sugar." As Lincoln would note later, rum was considered essential to the health of those in hot climates.[5]

An optimistic Lincoln left Philadelphia on 24 October armed with his commission and letters of introduction to prominent southerners. The trip was uneventful, apart from a carriage accident in Virginia in which Lincoln hurt his knee, forcing a two-day layover. He spent an agreeable week in Williamsburg at Col. Carter Braxton's, dining out with Virginia society and conversing with Gov. Patrick Henry. Once south of the James River the pace of his journey quickened, often reaching thirty to forty miles a day. His journal observations were those of a farmer and naturalist, commenting on the soil, trees, appearance of crops, and the natural features of the terrain. Many of the notes he took on this trip provided grist for the essays he wrote in later life.[6]

Lincoln arrived in Charleston on 4 December to a warm welcome by prominent South Carolinians. Edward Rutledge wrote to thank Washington "for introducing to my acquaintance a gentleman of his character and merit," assuring the commander-in-chief that Lincoln was "much caressed" by Charleston society. Upon assuming his military responsibilities, however, Lincoln had little time for socializing. As he began to assess the situation of the department, Lincoln was ill prepared for what he found. There were few supplies in the quartermaster departments in Georgia or South Carolina, little in the way of ordnance stores, and the six Continental fieldpieces were unfit for use. Matters in Georgia were so confused that, two weeks after his request, Lincoln had still not received a proper report on men and supplies. As for soldiers, the three thousand militia promised by Virginia were being withheld until "more authentic evidence of the enemies designs against South Carolina should be obtained." More than one thousand North Carolina militia were expected to arrive any day, but their time would be up four months later, and no more troops were expected from that state.[7]

Nor was that news the worst. Gen. Robert Howe, acknowledging the transfer of authority to Lincoln, wrote from Georgia to explain why the latter would find the Continental troops ill clothed, ill paid, and hungry. "Destitute as we have been of a military chest the army has been in a state of abject dependence upon the civil authority for every shilling they received," he confessed. As Lincoln explained when he relayed this news to Washington, however urgent the need, Howe could not even march his troops without the consent of the president of South Carolina, given the army's dependence on state authorities for supplies. "I hope things will be better settled," wrote Lincoln, "and that I never shall be driven to the hard necessity of altercating with the civil power, than which nothing [could] be more disagreeable." That hope died quickly. Lincoln was not in South Carolina three weeks before he came into direct conflict with Pres. Rawlins Lowndes over the question of army supply.[8]

From the time of his December arrival in Charleston, Lincoln faced British aggression in Georgia. A small force led by Gen. Augustine Prevost from the garrison at St. Augustine had threatened the American outpost at Sunbury, a port town south of Savannah, returning to East Florida after "spreading waste and distruction" and "carrying with them a number of negroes, cattle and other valuable articles." More threatening still were reports from deserters that a British fleet and invasion force were en route from New York—their destination either Savannah or Charleston.[9]

Unknown to American leaders, the British had made a major strategic shift in their approach to the rebellion. Unsuccessful in their bid to control large areas of the North and faced with the entry of France into the war, the British had seized on a southern strategy to carry the conflict to a sucessful conclusion. For any number of reasons, taking the war southward promised to solve the central dilemma of the conflict: how to turn military victory into political stability. The British had demonstrated in three years of fighting how easy it was to win nearly all the battles—and still lose the war. In the South the British hoped to neutralize American advantages by exploiting what they assumed were great numbers of Loyalists eager for a fight and several elements of "strategic and social geography." These included a thinly scattered population, the proximity of British West Indian naval bases, the southern fear of a slave revolt, and the support of powerful and pro-British Indian nations on the borders of white settlement. Their initial gambit was the invasion of Georgia.[10]

Lincoln's orders, by resolution of Congress on 25 September, required him to defend Georgia and South Carolina against a British invasion. If the British did not attack those states, the new commander was to take the offensive by invading East Florida and eliminating the British garrison at St. Augustine. Thus, in addition to assessing the overall military situation, Lincoln spent his initial weeks in Charleston contemplating an expedition against St. Augustine. By the end of December Lincoln had concluded that "it would be embarrassing and unsafe to attempt an expedition on either of the plans" forwarded to him by Congress. One of these plans, conceived by the Marquis de Bretigney, proposed that an army invest St. Augustine by land while a fleet blockaded the port by sea. Another proposed a sea expedition and a storming of the fort. Lincoln's criticism of these plans shows a practical understanding of the difficulties posed by eighteenth-century military campaigning, especially the problem of supply. His own plan, "in case another attempt should be made for the reduction of that fort," was a combined operation that required superiority on the seas, water transportation of all baggage and artillery, and a land force to "be marched as light as possible" and met at the river crossings by the naval forces with portable boats, provisions, and forage. Lincoln also insisted on fortifying the river passes to secure any retreat.[11]

General Prevost's incursion into southern Georgia from St. Augustine preempted any invasion of Florida and provided an excellent excuse for an immediate offensive by the Continental troops in Georgia under Gen. Robert Howe and the North Carolina militia slowly filtering into Charleston. As Lincoln explained to President Lowndes, Prevost's defeat in Georgia would be the best defense that Charleston could imagine—a defense in depth. Thus, it was a shock to Lincoln when his request to Lowndes for "arms, accoutrements, and camp utensils" to equip the North Carolina militia was turned down. Despite Congress's promise that the southern states would cooperate with the new commander, Lowndes insisted that he could not "think of delivering these stores while this State [South Carolina] is in so precarious a situation with respect to the Enemy." As the arms had been purchased for the defense of South Carolina, "it would never do to leave themselves defenceless—no: he would not deliver them, should he receive an order of Congress for it." Such a narrow definition of state interest and lack of comprehension of the military situation was appalling. Lincoln, though privately incensed by Lowndes's decision, remained publicly calm. On one hand, he put pressure on the president to release the supplies by making it clear he was keeping a written record of Lowndes's failure to cooperate. On the other hand, he offered Lowndes a graceful way of backing down from his intemperate outburst by implying that his verbal message had been misunderstood and giving him "an opportunity to set it right." Lowndes took advantage of Lincoln's tact, writing on 24 December that he promised every support for the military effort to defend South Carolina and, "if compatible with our own safety, towards the defense of Georgia." Without giving up the principle, Lowndes released the arms and supplies to Lincoln the next day.[12]

Lincoln was reacting in part to the pleas of Gov. John Houstoun of Georgia, who earlier in the week had implored Lincoln to turn his attention to his state. "I can assure you," he wrote, "with the greatest Truth, that the situation of this State is truly perilous, & unless some vigorous Impression is made, in the Course of the Winter, on our Southern Neighbours, I do not know whether the Existence of Georgia as a free & independent State is not endanger'd." Already panicked by Prevost's earlier invasion, Georgians were ill prepared to deal with the greater threat of a full-blown attack on Savannah. As Lincoln was mustering the North Carolina militia and two Continental regiments to march to Howe's aid in southern Georgia, Houstoun notified him of the arrival of "twenty seven sail of transports and other vessels belonging to the enemy" off the bar at Tybee, the entrance to Savannah harbor. Houstoun wrote, "We shall make every exertion against them and depend on what succour you can afford us."[13]

Unfortunately, what "succour" Lincoln could provide was too little and too late. British forces led by Lt. Col. Archibald Campbell landed unopposed and immediately attacked the American lines drawn up across the main road leading to Savannah. With over three thousand troops the British outnumbered the Americans by three to one. In addition, the defense of the town was handled poorly. Even a delay of several days would have enabled Lincoln to arrive with reinforcements. Howe's force of Continentals and militia had its flanks protected by swamps, but the commander neglected to post guards at the little-known passes through them. The British, guided by a local black man, sent a strong column through one of those passes and attacked the Americans from behind, causing panic and confusion. The British victory was complete, and they took possession of Savannah.[14]

In a matter of hours the strategic situation facing Lincoln had changed dramatically. Instead of contemplating an attack on East Florida, Lincoln was reduced to plotting the retaking of Savannah. Yet he remained optimistic. On his way to join the remnant of Howe's scattered force, Lincoln paused at Pocotaligo, just twenty-eight miles from the Savannah River (the border between South Carolina and Georgia) to write to Henry Laurens, the South Carolinian president of Congress. After reporting Howe's defeat, Lincoln promised that "as early as a sufficient force can be collected we shall recross the river, and our wishes are to dispossess the enemy; if we should not be able to do that, at present, from the want of men, artillery & supply, our next object will be to cover the country, & convince them that, notwithstanding they are in possession of a town, they have not conquered a State."[15]

The British, however, were in the process of doing just that. Campbell issued a proclamation inviting all Georgians to take the oath of allegiance to King George and to receive royal protection of their persons and property. Prevost, retracing his steps into southern Georgia from Florida, captured the Sunbury garrison on 10 January 1779 and soon joined Campbell in Savannah. The combined British forces then advanced north along the Savannah River, taking Augusta easily by the end of the month. Although organized resistance to British forces in Georgia collapsed, small bands of Whig partisans began to form to protect their families from newly formed Tory militia units and in anticipation of an eventual American push across the river.[16]

While the British secured control over Georgia, Lincoln scoured the countryside for troops. Encamped at Purysburg, South Carolina, on the banks of the Savannah River, about thirty miles from its mouth, Lincoln had managed to rally about fourteen hundred men of various description: militia units from the southern states and a handful of Continental soldiers. It was not an encouraging sight. Asking Lowndes for more militia was like trying to draw blood from a stone. "There was no law," Lowndes told Lincoln, "which obliged the militia to leave the State, and if there were a law made for that purpose, he was not without his doubts whether there was efficacy enough in the Government to execute it." That judgment posed a conundrum: Lincoln needed more troops for offensive operations in Georgia, but the only troops he could get would not serve there. The sole solution, as Lincoln wrote to Henry Laurens, was money. "The lack of a military chest impedes progress and renders the military commander impotent." With cash the ranks of the Continental battalions could be filled and supplies purchased.[17]

To Washington, Lincoln unburdened himself further: "I have met with almost every disappointment since I came into this department." Nothing was as Congress had promised, yet Lincoln was still responsible for stemming the tide of British regulars washing over the state of Georgia. "I have daily the unhappiness to see families of affluence fleeing before the

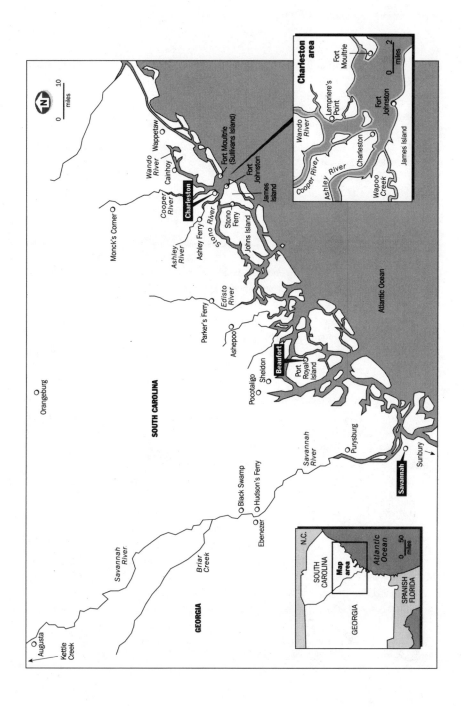

enemy, reduced in a few hours to a state of want." Lincoln's frustration was apparent, but he could do little until he brought his little army to fighting strength. To add to his woes, his days and nights were filled with pain. "My wound," he wrote Washington, "which was nearly closed when I left camp, is opening again, and in a worse condition than it was seven months ago." The new year had not opened auspiciously either for Lincoln or for the American cause.[18]

Throughout January Lincoln posted what militia joined him at the fords along the Savannah River to "prevent excursions into this state, and to cover our flanks." He spent a great deal of time reorganizing the supply system, finally replacing one recalcitrant contractor who resisted the new regulations. Much of his time was spent inspiring political leaders and army officers. As the shock of the December invasion receded and Lincoln's strong hand took hold, energy and purpose replaced despair. Lincoln began to look forward to the day when he might cross over into Georgia. In reply to an offer of a large Indian reinforcement, Lincoln declined, noting that "we soon expect a large body of men here," when "our affairs will shortly put on a good face." Lincoln meant Gen. John Ashe, who·was due in camp any day with a considerable number of North Carolina militia.[19]

In addition to preparing an advance into Georgia, Lincoln encouraged the militia units forming in the backcountry of that state and South Carolina. "You will have every aid in our power to give," he wrote one militia leader. "To hold the upper part of your state is of importance as thereby you will curb the disaffected, restrain the savages, give countenance to our friends and support the common cause." That kind of support had good effect, as bands of militia crossed and recrossed the Savannah River, harassing British troops and skirmishing with Loyalists bent on subduing the countryside. On 14 February a sharp encounter took place at Kettle Creek, Georgia, in which Whig militia under colonels Andrew Pickens of South Carolina and John Dooly and Elijah Clarke of Georgia surprised about seven hundred Tories, defeating and scattering the lot. Some of the prisoners were dragged back to South Carolina, where they were tried for murder; five were hanged.[20]

Such behavior was symptomatic of war in the South. It was a civil war in all respects. The inability of Continental army forces to control disputed areas placed enormous importance on militia units. Many of these, in turn, changed their loyalties as quickly as their coats, depending on who had the upper hand at the time. The penalty for being caught with a coat wrong side out could be severe. After 19 February, for example, any South Carolinians who withdrew from the defense of the state or attempted to go over to the enemy were sentenced to death as traitors and would be stripped of their estates—all this on the oath of two "creditable" witnesses. Lincoln sought to control the more savage aspects of the Whig-Tory conflict by issuing orders against plundering and insisting that warrants be issued for specific people and places, rather than giving blanket permission "to secure the persons and property of the unfriendly." But the frequency of his letters on this subject suggests he could do little to moderate the ferocity of the conflict.[21]

To add insult to injury, Lincoln found that the South Carolina militia—paid, supplied, and fed by Congress—refused to put itself under the command of Continental officers or submit to discipline under the Continental articles of war, the army's legal code. This conflict arose when a militiaman assaulted a Continental officer. When the man was brought to trial before a panel of judges made up of officers of the man's militia unit, the officers refused to hear the case, insisting that it could only be tried under the state's civil law. If the civil government upheld this decision, it would have meant the end of any effective control Lincoln might have exerted within the Southern Department. Besides protesting to President Lowndes, Lincoln sent all the Continental officers he could muster, including Gen. William Moultrie and Col. Charles Cotesworth Pinckney, to Charleston for the opening session of the legislature. There, though the matter was hotly debated, an ordinance was passed giving Lincoln the authority he needed. The law proved unenforceable, however, and Lincoln continued to have problems commanding the officers and men of the South Carolina militia.[22]

The arrival of Ashe and his eleven hundred North Carolina militia in Charleston on 30 January bolstered the confidence of the American forces even as the British occupied Augusta and forced the last remaining Continental troops from Georgia. A young Continental officer reflected the new, aggressive attitude and optimism when he wrote that "Lincoln is anxious and uneasy at being obliged from the enemy's superiority, or at least equality of numbers, to remain so long inactive, and will assuredly take the first opportunity of paying them [the British] a visit." Lincoln sent Ashe to the fords opposite Augusta, where he joined General Williamson and Colonel Elbert "to digest a plan of defense for the country and future offensive operations." Their combined force of about sixteen hundred nearly matched the estimated seventeen hundred men of the enemy. Lincoln held Moultrie's Continentals in reserve, hoping to push them across the Savannah River below Augusta and form a pincers that would trap Campbell and force him to fight his way back to Savannah. Instead, Moultrie's force was engaged by a party of British soldiers, who moved onto Port Royal Island. Their defeat and expulsion took some time. Nonetheless, the American concentration across the river from Augusta led Campbell to rethink his exposed position.[23]

Lincoln soon abandoned his two-pronged strategy in favor of concentrating his forces before Augusta "to check the progress of the enemy and protect the friends of America." Ashe spoke for Lincoln and his generals when he wrote that "the motion of the British troops at Augusta ought to be attended to and opposed in force. I consider them as a snowball, that should they move any distance into the frontiers of this state, will collect all the lukewarm and disaffected in each of the Carolinas, and should they reach Camden will become so large, that no force can be raised in these parts . . . would be sufficient to oppose their march to Charlestown." Before Lincoln could march his force to Augusta, however, the British hurriedly evacuated the town in the early morning hours of 14 February, retreating down the Savannah River to Hudson's Ferry. Lincoln, hearing the news on 16 February, wrote Ashe that he hoped the latter "crossed the first opportunity you had and that you will follow them with all the force you can muster and as quickly as you can." It was important to keep pressure on Campbell, Lincoln wrote; otherwise, he might attempt to cross the river in force at a lightly guarded ford further downstream from Augusta in order to flank the American left. For his part Williamson felt little of the urgency of the situation, suggesting that some of his militia units be furloughed for a few days, now that "the War, in all Probability, will be transferr'd into the lower Parts of the Country." He was so relieved at the disappearance of the British that he suggested that this was a good time to meet with the Creeks and Cherokees.[24]

That left Ashe and his North Carolinians to pursue Campbell. On 18 February Lincoln ordered him to cross the river and move "with all the dispatch possible consistent with the precaution necessary to be observed in marching in an enemies country." On 22 February Lincoln ordered Ashe to remain at Briar Creek, some miles upriver from Hudson's Ferry, where Campbell's troops lay. That, Lincoln wrote, will be "a good stand for you until some plan of cooperating be digested." And he ordered Ashe to meet him at the Two-Sisters, a ford on the South Carolina side of the river, for a council of war.[25]

The tone of the meeting, which included generals Lincoln, Ashe, Moultrie, and Rutherford, must have been ebullient. Campbell's retreat, as Lincoln wrote to John Jay, the new president of Congress, "gives great spirit to the upper country" and "blasts the hopes of the disaffected." Most important, it would convince "the timid and deluded" that they cannot expect protection from the British. As long as Ashe's troops protected Augusta, plans could be made for the inhabitants to return home and reestablish the legislature and reorganize civil authority. The council of war agreed that Briar Creek was a strong defensive point and that Ashe should be reinforced there.[26]

Yet all hopes of immediate offensive operations in Georgia were stifled by the surprise and defeat of Ashe at Briar Creek on 3 March. Lincoln reported the "very disagreeable news" of the debacle to newly elected governor of South Carolina, John Rutledge, in tones of disbelief. "I thought him very secure," Lincoln wrote. But when he was attacked "his men were not even embodied." As Ashe described it, the surprise was such that "the troops in my division did not stand fire for five minutes. Many fled without discharging their pieces." Most deaths were caused by drowning as soldiers attempted to escape by swimming the river. The defeat was so complete that, of Ashe's 1,500 men, no more than 450 ever served with American forces again. Although Ashe was found not guilty of personal cowardice at a court-martial held a week later, he was found to have failed to secure his camp and to get good intelligence of the enemy's movements.[27]

The defeat was another setback for Lincoln's offensive plans. At a council of war held at Purysburg on 4 and 5 March, Lincoln asked the Continental officers gathered there for advice on the next course of action. The American forces numbered perhaps eighteen hundred rank and file, the British about thirty-five hundred. Given those odds and the likelihood of Campbell's pursuing his victory by crossing into South Carolina, the officers agreed that the American forces should be concentrated at Purysburg and that no posts should be set out of support range from the main body of the army. That meant another period of enforced waiting for Lincoln until he could again rebuild his army to a respectable level by replacing the men lost at Briar Creek.[28]

A departmental commander dealt with a host of problems in the normal course of a month. Tactical questions took up a great deal of time. The placement of troops required a keen sense of terrain. Other decisions had to be made: Which posts should be defended at all costs and which given up for stronger positions in a unit's rear? Where should batteries be placed? Where should cavalry patrols be sent out? Supply issues were equally vexing. One unit was nearly naked; another had no rum; others had had no bread for weeks. Problems of supply were aggravated by the jealousies of each state in providing for its own soldiers—whether militia or Continentals. As time went on, Lincoln tried to assume the responsibility of supplying all the troops in the Continental pay as a means of controlling them and quashing their complaints.

No problem, however, matched that of recruiting and maintaining adequate forces in the field. Lincoln's early run-in with President Lowndes foreshadowed further troubles in raising sufficient numbers of militiamen and placing them under effective Continental command. Lincoln spent a staggering amount of time corresponding with the governors of Virginia and North Carolina, diplomatically pleading for yet another three-month levy of troops or for a draft to fill depleted Continental rosters. He also noticed a change in the attitude of the rank and file recruited for the conflict. "The object that first induced us to take arms," he wrote, "is now winked out of sight. Too many there are who content themselves with having done what they call their turn . . . and pay little attendance either to the good of the service, justice to the public, or to a line of conduct which will promote a speedy termination of the present war." This, he added, was not peculiar to the South; unfortunately, Lincoln had seen it everywhere. For Lincoln and his Continentals there was no going home until the war was won. That made it all the more frustrating to see the militiamen march home when their short stints were over, forcing the suspension of offensive operations. During his term in the South Lincoln did less fighting than preparing to fight.[29]

Little wonder, then, that he felt discouraged. Sick with fever, his wound festering and aching, beset by the thorny problems of high command, Lincoln had authorized an aide to suggest to Congress that his recall from the southern command would be welcome. In a long letter to James Lovell of 12 April summarizing the state of affairs, Lincoln made his request explicit: "I have been too long accustomed to a Northern climate to think of risquing a seasoning at this time of life to a Southern one. I hope my friends will not suffer me to be kept here long." It was not only the danger to his health that Lincoln feared but also the risk to his pride and hard-won military reputation from a situation in which the southern states lacked the will to carry on the war. "I hardly know how to reconcile myself to the Fabian principles," he wrote Lovell, when Georgia is held "by the enemy with a force so inconsiderable compared to what might have been sent into the field by this and the neighboring states." He was convinced that Congress was unaware of the situation when it refused to provide badly needed reinforcements. Southerners could not manage alone, he argued, for "there is not that union of Sentiment among the inhabitants of this

State I expected to find." In other words, South Carolina was not Massachusetts.[30]

While Lincoln waited for Congress to act on his resignation request, the military situation slowly began to improve. In early April Williamson and his militia gave a large war band of Creeks and "disaffected" Cherokees a severe "drubbing," preventing all but a few of the Indians from joining the British forces. This was especially satisfying to Lincoln, who felt that the British design in recruiting Indians was "to terrify and keep at home the militia." The British use of Indians in the Saratoga campaign had backfired, resulting in a concentration of angry militiamen from all over a ravaged countryside. In Georgia the danger lay in dispersed attacks by Indians on a wide and isolated front, with the result that militia units would desert in order to defend their farms and families. Williamson's victory eliminated that danger for a time.[31]

Recruitment also took a turn for the better. For once the Americans began to show superiority in numbers. The British received no reinforcements in the spring of 1779, but the energetic efforts of governors Richard Caswell (North Carolina) and John Rutledge (South Carolina) provided replacements and more for the men whose time of service had expired. Rutledge took personal charge of recruitment efforts, concentrating his state's militia forces at a central location, Orangeburg. From his headquarters at Black Swamp, Lincoln encouraged Rutledge to think about offensive operations. With our numbers, he wrote, "I think we might act offensively with every rational hope of success. . . . Now seems to be the time for our greatest exertions—the weather is good, the season healthy & the enemy not reinforced."[32]

Consequently, Lincoln marched toward Augusta on the northern bank of the Savannah, leaving Black Swamp on 23 April. He took with him all the troops he could muster, except for two regiments of South Carolina Continentals left under Moultrie's command at Black Swamp and a handful of troops guarding the Savannah River fords. Moultrie's task was to form a counterweight to British forces concentrated at Ebenezer, Georgia. Should the British attempt to cross the river, Moultrie was to oppose their crossing and stop their advance by holding the strong passes behind him. Lincoln intended to cross the river and descend along the southern bank. In that way he could protect Augusta, where a new Georgia legislature was called to meet on 1 May, and force the British back to Savannah. In short, Lincoln sought to "give a new existence to the State of Georgia."[33]

Unfortunately for the Americans, the British did not wait for Lincoln's plan to develop, for on 30 April they crossed the river into South Carolina at Purysburg. Moultrie fell back on a strong defensive position at Tulafinny. Lincoln believed that the British had no intention of marching toward Charleston. It was a feint "thrown out to distract and divert us from our present intention." But, just to be sure, he ordered a reinforcement of three hundred picked Continental troops to join Moultrie and asked Rutledge to send the South Carolinian the militia intended for Lincoln's army as well as any other troops the governor could spare. That, Lincoln was confident, would give Moultrie a force superior to the enemy.[34]

That confidence was misplaced. Moultrie wrote on 2 May that the enemy numbered about three thousand men, far too many for the Americans to oppose. By 5 May Moultrie was in full flight. Only a forced march allowed him to stay ahead of the British, reaching Ashepoo, where he hoped to meet up with Rutledge and make a stand. By now Moultrie estimated the British at four thousand men, who definitely intended to take Charleston. In contrast, Moultrie's "little army" of twelve hundred was melting away, as each militiaman went "running to look after his wife, children and property. The enemy carried everything before them with fire and sword." Lincoln, on 6 May, was moving toward Savannah on the Georgia side of the river, still in the belief that his movements would divert Prevost back to his Georgia base. To his credit Lincoln also realized that his movement downriver brought him closer to Charleston's relief, if that should prove necessary.[35]

Prevost, however, was encouraged by the weak American defense offered by Moultrie's fleeing troops and, abandoning Georgia, pushed on to grasp the far greater prize of Charleston. Lincoln's grave mistake was to confuse his real goal, which was to eliminate the British presence in Georgia, with the less important one of taking Savannah. By eradicating Prevost's army, Lincoln would have accomplished both goals. But, by letting Prevost slip through his fingers, he risked the loss of Charleston for the empty victory of securing Georgia. Up to 6 May Lincoln was still unconvinced that the British intended to attack Charleston. By hesitating, he wasted valuable time that would have allowed him and Moultrie to trap Prevost between them, a possibility that Moultrie clearly had in mind when he pleaded with Lincoln to "pray follow them and let us Burgoine him."[36]

On 6 May Lincoln held a council of war and decided to march to Moultrie's assistance. He was still unaware of the collapse of the American front. Indeed, Moultrie had barely managed to escape into the relative safety of Charleston's unfinished defensive lines. On 8 May Moultrie wrote that he had just arrived in Charleston only to find "a strange consternation in Town, people frightened out of their wits." Another of

Lincoln's correspondents wrote that "all the timorous ones here are packing their beds, Bedding Crockery ware etc and sending them off as fast as they can." Charleston had panicked. Once Moultrie was thoroughly apprised of the situation he wrote Lincoln, the evening of the same day, that it was "absolutely necessary you should march immediately here—and hurry."[37]

Lincoln did not receive Moultrie's letter of 8 May—and an equally importunate one from Rutledge of the same date—until 10 May. Finally convinced of the seriousness of Charleston's plight, Lincoln's army, "full of spirits," was proceeding by forced marches to Moultrie's relief. "We are making every exertion," he wrote Rutledge. "The inability of the men only will put a period to our daily marching." The chance to catch Prevost between two fires, a chance for which the Americans had waited months, was within reach. Only Moultrie's tone of desperation bothered Lincoln, who added a further note, "*Do not give up, or suffer the people to despair.*"[38]

Lincoln had good reason to worry. The British army reached Ashley Ferry on 10 May and crossed over onto Charleston neck the next morning. By that evening Prevost and his men stood before the gates of Charleston prepared to take the town by storm. On the morning of 11 May an American horseman under a flag of truce carried a message from Moultrie into the British camp. The message demanded to know under what conditions Prevost would accept the capitulation of Charleston. Rutledge and a majority of the council believed that the town was outnumbered and its defenses so weak as to make a defense against a storm impossible. Moultrie disagreed but was induced by the civil authorities to send the message.[39]

Prevost replied that those who wished to take an oath of allegiance to the king would be restored to the king's peace and protection; all others would be treated as prisoners of war. On the receipt of this, the council met to determine an answer. Estimates were made of the relative strength of each army, and a report was made on the state of the defensive lines. The council then voted five to three to propose to Prevost that the state be neutral during the rest of the war and its status a matter of negotiation at its conclusion.[40]

The message was sent on 12 May. Prevost, for some unexplained reason, rejected the offer and demanded the surrender of the garrison, governor, and council. This Moultrie refused to do, saying, "We will fight it out." It was a courageous decision that also proved to be wise. The day before, the British had intercepted Lincoln's letter of 10 May to Rutledge, indicating that Lincoln was moving fast to close the trap on Prevost. Thus, during the night of 12 May the British slipped the noose, quietly left their lines, and retreated over Ashley Ferry. Charleston was saved, but Lincoln's first chance to end the British threat to the South was lost.[41]

With few light horsemen for reconnaissance Lincoln could not find the enemy for several days. On 17 May Lincoln, at Parker's Ferry, picked up intelligence of the enemy's whereabouts from prisoners taken by forward units. The British were retreating down the south bank of the Ashley River toward James Island, pillaging and destroying plantations as they went. By 19 May the British were stretched in a long line along the Stono River from Wapoo Cut to Stono Ferry. Rutledge, whose plantation had been plundered, was particularly incensed and urged Lincoln to crush those "Thieves, Robbers & Plunderers" once and for all. Lincoln, however, advanced cautiously, not willing to give too much credence to the reports of prisoners. On 24 May he was at last at Ashley Ferry and two days later had solid intelligence of the British deployment through a reconnaissance in force by the Polish nobleman Kazimierz Pulaski.[42]

Lincoln conferred with Moultrie to settle on a plan of attack, one that would put the American superiority of force to work and make good use of militia. They agreed on a frontal assault by Lincoln's troops on a series of entrenchments the British had thrown up on the west side of Wapoo Cut. While that attack pinned the British down, Moultrie would attack the British rear on James Island, preventing British reinforcements from reaching the front. But, as Lincoln moved his force to within striking distance of Stono, intending to attack on 1 June, the British shifted their main army to James Island and dug strong entrenchments to cover Stono Ferry. When Pulaski brought back news that the British were "too strongly posted and in too great force for us to attack," the plan was postponed.[43]

For the next three weeks Lincoln's army waited watchfully six miles from enemy lines for a chance to attack the British. It was during this time, on 8 June, that Lincoln received word from Congress that his recall from the southern command had been approved. Lincoln's aide, Everard Meade, had been sent to Philadelphia in April with dispatches and firsthand accounts of the southern situation. Lincoln had asked Meade to lobby privately for his removal, which the latter did, testifying before a committee of Congress that he was certain that Lincoln's wound would prove fatal if he remained in South Carolina during the hot season. Congress, after long debate, voted to give Lincoln permission to resign and appointed Moultrie in his place.[44]

Lincoln informed Rutledge and Moultrie of his permission to resign on 9 June. Moultrie had already received a letter from the president of

Congress promoting him to major general and investing him with the command of the department on Lincoln's departure. Moultrie immediately wrote to Lincoln begging him not to relinquish the command "in this critical hour, but stay to see us extricated from our difficulties." "I would not for the universe have the command fall upon me at this time," he continued. "I am so unequal to the task, it would be placing me in such a point of view as might ruin my reputation for ever." Lincoln remained unconvinced, especially since word had reached him of discontent with his leadership in Charleston. Some of the frustration and bitterness of the past six months of effort escaped in his reply to Moultrie: "The same motives, which led me here, would retain me so long as my health should permit me to act, if there was now the same prospect of rendering service to my country as when I took command, in this department." But, Lincoln went on, "as it appears, from the unkind declarations daily thrown out in your Capital, that I have lost that confidence of this people . . . I ought to retire. . . . A man should sacrifice his own feelings to his country's good."[45]

It was Rutledge's letter of 13 June which persuaded Lincoln to retain his command. Lincoln could brush off Moultrie's sentiments as a fit of nervousness or a momentary lack of confidence. But Rutledge made it clear that he and the South Carolina council wanted Lincoln to stay, that his "character, and knowledge and Experience in the Art of War are such, and the publick has so much Confidence in you, that your remaining here will ensure great good to this, and the Neighboring state." That vote of confidence and the critical situation of affairs, with the British still within striking distance of Charleston, persuaded Lincoln to remain a while longer. He would stay on for another year.[46]

On 20 June, dusting off his old plan of a combined assault with Moultrie, Lincoln attacked the British entrenchments at Stono River. Given to believe that the British works were "inconsiderable" and the enemy's force about five hundred men, Lincoln brought up "the principal part of our force," about fifteen hundred men, and formed them in a wood three hundred to four hundred yards from the British lines. The attack began about eight in the morning and lasted an hour. The Americans drove the British back to their lines but found that the entrenchments were much stronger than they had believed. Moultrie was unable to make the attack on James Island as planned, and the British soon received reinforcements. The exchange of fire continued until Lincoln, realizing that his hopes of carrying the works were dashed, ordered a withdrawal. This was carried out in good order: "We halted and formed several times in leaving the ground." Casualties on both sides were heavy, yet Lincoln put a bold construction on the battle. "Though we had not the wished-for success; yet I think good will arise from the attempt," he wrote Governor Rutledge. "Our men now see that little is to be feared either from musquetry or field pieces; they are full of spirit, & are sure they can beat the enemy on equal grounds at any time." With Moultrie on James Island, Lincoln still hoped to strike a decisive blow before the British slipped back to Savannah. But the British kept a strong force near Beaufort on Port Royal Island and ferried their main army to Georgia.[47]

By the end of July 1779 both armies held approximately the same positions that they had six months before. Apart from the mountains of plunder the royal army had seized from the plantations of southern Whigs, the British had scarcely gained a thing. Prevost and his army held a beach-head at Savannah, with the Georgia backcountry for the most part controlled by roving bands of Whig militia. The British had added a small foothold on Port Royal Island in South Carolina. But their vaunted southern strategy, the reestablishment of the king's peace, had failed. Despite the invasion of backcountry Georgia and tidewater South Carolina, their gambler's foray had weakened, rather than strengthened, their ties to southern loyalists. Tories had learned they could not rely on protection from the British army.[48]

For Lincoln and his ragtag army of Continentals and militia the past six months had been a dizzying struggle, one in which alarm alternated with high hopes, only to give way to anxiety and frustration. Discouraged at first by Congress's failure to carry out its promises, Lincoln soon found that to keep an army in the field was a triumph, to maneuver it and lead it into battle a major victory. No wonder that when his little army withdrew under fire at Stono without panic Lincoln noted with pride that "they behaved well." A good retreat under fire was a far cry from Lincoln's expectations when he took command in the fall of 1778, nor did it match the expectations of Congress and the public. But Lincoln could take comfort in the advice of his friend Henry Knox: "My friend has lived so long and seen such a variety of events, that he well knows there are times which demand a tenfold exercise of patience. I take yours to be the case." Lincoln would need all the patience he could muster to survive the year ahead.[49]

The past six months had also revealed the strengths and weaknesses in Lincoln's generalship. To his credit Lincoln had shown a strong and steady hand in organizing disparate elements into a disciplined force and in supplying his men against great odds. He had reinvigorated the war effort in the South, providing a steadying influence despite a number of reverses. Lincoln maintained the respect of the civil authorities and cooperated well with them. But he had been unsuccessful in the field. Lincoln had made at least two mistakes. He had been too aggressive in his Georgia campaign, confusing the recapture of Savannah with his true goal—the destruction or neutralization of the British army. And he had overestimated the role militia could play in the war. Militia forces had defeated the Indians and controlled the Tories in most of upper Georgia. But giving them too large a role against British regulars proved unwise. Lincoln realized this from his own experience but felt he had no choice, given the small number of Continental soldiers at his disposal. The situation would not improve.

It took great strength of character to continue as southern commander under the hardships Lincoln had faced in the past and would find in the future. The best measure of the New Englander's devotion to the cause was his willingness to risk health and reputation in the treacherous swamps of the South. While mistakes had been made, Lincoln was a fighter—and the fighting had just begun.

CHAPTER FIVE

Storm over Savannah

Our Militia are daily increasing. Gen. Lincoln is very well and tho'
undergoing great fatigue [is] in fine Spirits.

Joseph Clay

As the heat of a Carolina summer baked the opposing camps, the
American forces melted away—first the South Carolina then the North
Carolina militias left for home. Only the two South Carolina Continental
battalions and Count Pulaski's legion (a total of about eight hundred men)
under the command of General Moultrie remained encamped at Sheldon,
South Carolina, facing about a thousand British regulars led by Lt. Col.
James Maitland on Port Royal Island. The rest of the British army sum-
mered in Savannah.[1]

From his vantage point at Charleston Lincoln looked carefully at the
events of the past six months to prepare for the coming campaign. The
key to his problems, he believed, lay with Congress. Despite the best efforts of energetic and forceful men such as John Rutledge, support for the
war in South Carolina and Georgia had been lukewarm at best. Some
militia units, like the Charleston Artillery, fought well. But most were
prone to insubordination and desertion at critical moments. Even the loyalty of Charleston, after the recent British foray, was suspect. To hold the
South Lincoln needed a renewed commitment from Congress in the form
of money and reinforcements of regular soldiers.

It also galled him that Congress failed to provide guidance, much less
show interest, in the affairs of the Southern Department. Lincoln's letters
to Congress went unanswered throughout the spring of 1779, and his
sense of isolation increased. Even turning to Washington provided no relief. The commander-in-chief politely declined to offer any advice, holding strictly to his policy of noninterference in other departments. Lincoln

found some solace in opening a back channel to James Lovell, a Massachusetts delegate in Congress, whom he pressed to influence Congress to support a greater effort in the South. "Matters are not going on right here," he wrote Lovell in June, "and if this department is not immediately attended to by Congress and an army sent more respectable than the one already here, this State must be lost." While Lincoln did not expect the British to move offensively during the hot season, he knew that by October, at the latest, reinforcements of Continental troops would be needed as well as the replenishment of funds in the military chest.[2]

There was little Lincoln could do but put on a good face and prepare for the coming campaign, pestering whomever he could for men, money, and supplies. To Washington he noted, "My particular attention now is to the supplies for the next campaign; many are wanted, and without them we cannot keep the field." To John Jay, the president of Congress, he wrote that the British retreat to Georgia offered an opportunity "of putting this country in a State of defence, and providing the necessary supplies." Finding Congress unresponsive, Lincoln organized the export of fifteen hundred barrels of rice to Martinique for the purchase of military stores unavailable on the continent. He apologized to Jay if this was not the "regular mode" of proceeding: "Nothing but the sincerest desire to render service to my country, betrays me into the error." Just the provision of food for the coming campaign was a staggering challenge. Lincoln estimated that three hundred tons of wheat flour, fourteen hundred tons of beef and pork, two thousand bushels of salt, three hundred hogsheads of whiskey, and one hundred hogsheads of vinegar were necessary for the health and vigor of his little army.[3]

The oppressive heat did not slow the pace of preparation. Lincoln ordered "all the publick boats be immediately numbered and registered," along with the number of men each could carry, and their oars replaced with paddles, so that "the confusion too frequent in embarkations" could be avoided. "Method in all transactions is essential to dispatch," he wrote, thinking obviously of the missed opportunities of the past campaign. The defenses of Charleston and Fort Moultrie were in scandalous condition, with people stealing the wooden stakes of the abatis—lines of sharpened timber buried in the ground and slanting outward—for firewood and cattle grazing on the unfinished walls. "This place . . . under its present situation," Lincoln wrote John Rutledge, "would fall an easy prey to a few hundred brave, determined men." He urged the governor to make finishing the fortifications a priority, using either the militia remaining on duty or battalions of slaves.[4]

Still, not all the news was grim. Gen. Lachlan McIntosh, a spirited Georgian, had by his own request been assigned to the Southern Department. Lincoln immediately ordered him to take command of the tattered American forces in Georgia, which still kept a tenuous grip on the upper reaches of that state. Lincoln could promise McIntosh little but his cooperation. In return the New Englander demanded a great deal. McIntosh was to collect the "scattered Inhabitants" and form them into "regular Corps" and to keep the "Indians in awe, restrain the disaffected & prevent their supplying our Enemy." Above all, McIntosh should encourage the establishment of civil government for Georgians. "I have observed great divisions among them," Lincoln wrote, "to heal which is among the first objects of our duty." It was a tall order, but whatever McIntosh could accomplish would lighten Lincoln's burden of command.[5]

The arrival in July of the first regiment of light dragoons under Maj. John Jameson and a detachment of four hundred infantrymen of the Virginia line under Col. Richard Parker was a heartening sight. This was to be only the first of several delayed reinforcements of Virginia troops ordered by Congress. Lincoln posted the Virginians forty miles from Augusta on a ridge in terrain as healthy as he could find. There they could assist McIntosh should he need them. Also encouraging for Lincoln was the pleasure both Parker and Jameson expressed at serving under him. Both were eager to begin readying their men for the coming campaign. They had, however, been "sent off totally unprepared," as Parker put it, lacking ammunition, shoes, supplies, and money. But Parker at least was aware of Lincoln's difficulties and wished not "to add to [his] perplexity." That kind of delicacy provoked a candid, even grateful, response from Lincoln: "You are right about my embarrassments, but apply to me for all necessary articles. What I can do, I will do readily."[6]

Thus, by the beginning of August Lincoln had about fifteen hundred troops to defend the Georgia backcountry and the state of South Carolina. Most of these were Continentals, except the garrison at Charleston, which was two-thirds militia, "a number quite unequal on which to risque the defence of this town." While Lincoln requested more militia as a stopgap measure, he realized that an effective defense depended upon the skills of professional soldiers such as Parker, Jameson, and Moultrie and troops recruited for the duration of the war, trained to obedience and disciplined to stand against the king's regulars. Filling the ranks of the six South Carolina regiments was an absolute necessity, a measure that alone would provide nearly five thousand men. To Lincoln's disappointment—but not to his surprise—the South Carolina Assembly rejected a draft to fill the Continental line, relying instead on voluntary enlistment and increased bounties: for twenty-one months of service a recruit would receive a slave and one hundred acres of land.[7]

In arguing for a militia draft, Lincoln cut to the heart of his conception of the Revolution. The principal objection to a draft to fill the Continental regiments, he wrote, "is that it would too materially infringe the right of the citizen." Yet, when a man contracts with another and fails to fulfill his obligation, his property becomes forfeit, and he is imprisoned until he makes good his debt. All this against his consent. "But no one pretends because it is distressing it is therefore not to be binding. The only enquiry is whether the covenant was made, and whether it has not been broken." By joining in the political separation from Great Britain and the creation of new states, Lincoln insisted, all Americans had contracted with one another to see the war through to a successful conclusion. The contract, he said, was now due, and, distressing or not, a citizen's obligation was to serve. And, he added earlier, in a statement on the importance of Continental unity, "Besides this contract, which seems to be of a more private nature, the covenant the people entered into as one of the United States, is not only indissoluble except by mutual consent, but their obligations to support the Union indispensable." Though in Lincoln's mind a draft was an act born of necessity, it had also a rough measure of justice. If the people were not virtuous enough to volunteer, they must be compelled to fulfill their obligation.[8]

Citizens disliked the idea of Continental army service because of the long period of enlistment. At this point in the war men were recruited for the duration. But equally alarming to most men was the fear of being subjected to the articles of war, a much more rigorous code of laws than those that regulated the state militia. Lincoln, believing the articles of war necessary to the proper discipline and control of soldiers, made no distinction between militia and Continentals in this regard. When Rawlins Lowndes told him that he hesitated to inform South Carolina militia units that they were to be governed by the articles, Lincoln burst out, "Do the militia think that the Continental officers have lost all ideas of the citizen? have a separate interest, and therefore ought to be avoided?" Later Lincoln would take up this refrain and answer his rhetorical question. The citizens, he argued, by an act of their Congress, provided articles of war for the government of all who were called to the battlefield, not just "for any particular set of men." Since the citizens had already "engaged to take the field when necessary," they were, in essence, "making the laws for their own government." In short, Lincoln saw all the citizens of the

79

United States as potential soldiers, "a large army in the field," as he put it. This was a true portrait of a nation in arms, in which the distinctions between militia and Continental were superfluous and even dangerous. All American soldiers were fighting in the common cause and should be treated alike, governed by the same laws, fed the same rations, and given the same pay. "I know of no service but the continental," Lincoln wrote. "Let us throw by all distinctions of states, such have been kept up too long already." That few shared his vision was a constant source of irritation and frustration to Lincoln.[9]

For a short time in the early fall of 1779, however, new developments eclipsed the ordinary struggles involved in fielding a unified army. A French fleet dropped anchor off the coast of Georgia. Count d'Estaing, fresh from victory in the West Indies, had decided once again to cooperate with American forces in an assault on a British-held seaport. One year earlier d'Estaing had withdrawn midway through a joint operation with the Americans against Newport, Rhode Island, leaving Gen. John Sullivan and his troops stranded and vulnerable to defeat. The encounter had left bitter feelings on both sides. Thus, informed by Rutledge and Plombard, the French consul at Charleston, that only a short visit would be necessary for the reduction of Savannah, d'Estaing decided to risk an expedition during the hurricane season.[10]

The surprise was complete. The French fleet of more than forty sail swooped down on Tybee Island on 1 September and captured four British ships carrying supplies and army pay. D'Estaing sent General François, Vicomte de Fontanges, to Charleston to coordinate a plan of attack with the Americans, who, already aware of his arrival, were busily preparing an expedition to Georgia. Word of d'Estaing's arrival reached Lincoln the evening of 3 September; the next day he ordered all officers to rejoin their regiments. Lincoln also sent an express to McIntosh to gather all the troops he could find within twenty-four hours and march for Ebenezer, where Lincoln would meet him with the army on 11 September.[11]

D'Estaing made it clear from the start that he wished to spend no more than ten days on the coast. Any longer would greatly increase his fleet's vulnerability to the destructive autumn storms. Lincoln thought a fortnight ample time to take Savannah, given its small garrison and the "insufficiency of its works." Consequently, the allies drew up a plan of operations that stressed speed. Lincoln was to collect at least one thousand soldiers and march them into Georgia by 11 September, where they would proceed along the south bank of the Savannah River to the town. The French were to land three thousand men at Beaulieu, south of Savannah, and confine the British within the town. The French would also prevent the British detachment on Port Royal Island from reinforcing the Savannah garrison while cutting off any possible British retreat south to St. Augustine. Both elements of the French role were critical to the success of the operation.[12]

Lincoln prepared his army to march, made troop dispositions for the defenses of Charleston, and reached headquarters at Sheldon on 9 September. Without a pause the thousand-man army composed of the Continental troops and the best units of South Carolina militia—the Grenadiers, Light Infantry, Fusiliers, Volunteers, and True Blues—began its march toward the Savannah River, stopping only to repair bridges across the rivers along its path. By 11 September the Americans stood on the north bank of the Savannah River at Zubley's Ferry, anxious to cross. An earlier reconnaissance mission to secure boats to ferry the troops across had found one canoe, which could carry only three men. McIntosh had been ordered to bring boats down from Augusta but had not yet arrived, nor were there boats to be had, he claimed, when he did arrive.[13]

Some of Lincoln's men knocked together a raft, and on the morning of 12 September the army began to cross the river. The Savannah was "tho narrow yet one of the most difficult to pass on the Continent," wrote Lincoln. "The land adjoining is mostly swamp and often overflowed from 2–4 feet deep, the breadth of them is generally 2 miles on both sides." Passage across the river was long and arduous, taking most of the day. By noon two larger canoes had been found so that by nightfall most of the troops were encamped on the south side of the ford. The next two days were spent bringing over the artillery and supply wagons and repairing the bridges along the road to Savannah. Lincoln, who had had no word from d'Estaing since leaving Charleston, was further delayed by his ignorance of the French army's situation. Eager as he was to come to grips with the enemy, Lincoln realized the American forces were not sufficient to move against Savannah alone. Lincoln sent messages by several routes and anxiously awaited a reply.[14]

While the Americans crossed the Savannah River to Georgia, the French landed unopposed at Beaulieu, about thirteen miles south of Savannah. By 16 September the French forces, some twenty-four hundred men (ultimately, to number about four thousand) were within a mile of the town. D'Estaing, confident of victory, sent in a summons for the British garrison to surrender "to the arms of the King of France." In a vainglorious display d'Estaing threatened Prevost with sole responsibility should the town be pillaged as the result of an assault. No mention was made of the Americans, an omission that Lincoln would resent and which was symptomatic of the friction between the allies.[15]

At this point Prevost had about twelve hundred men in Savannah, and, though he had had two weeks to improve the fortifications, the town's defenses were still in a very poor state. Time was vital to the weak garrison, for it would allow the British to build new redoubts, batteries, and abatis. A few more days would enable them to strip the cannons from their ships and mount them on the walls of the town. Another few precious hours might allow Lt. Col. James Maitland's eight hundred regulars to slip into the town and reinforce the garrison. And all this could delay the joint French and American attack, discouraging the French, whose shipping lay exposed to the season's storms, and forcing the Americans to give up the attempt as well. Prevost, therefore, demanded to know the terms the French offered for his surrender. When this delaying tactic was played out, he asked for, and received, a twenty-four-hour truce.[16]

D'Estaing was so little concerned with Prevost's frantic efforts to build entrenchments that, even in upbraiding him for the lapse of military etiquette in continuing the works, during a parley the French admiral wrote, "It is a matter of very little importance to me." It proved, however, to be the key to the allied failure before Savannah. Lincoln, who finally had made contact with the French, marched to Cherokee Hill, eight miles from Savannah, on 15 September. He met d'Estaing around noon on the fateful day of 16 September. After "remonstrating to the Count against his summoning them [the British] to surrender to the arms of France only" and settling the matter to his satisfaction, Lincoln was preoccupied the rest of the day with the disposition of his arriving troops. D'Estaing granted the truce that evening without consulting Lincoln. "It did not seem to me to be worth disturbing you about after the fatigue of a long march," he explained. Lincoln's immediate reaction went unrecorded, but some of his officers were incensed. That the Americans were junior partners in the alliance was probably the only thing that kept Lincoln from quarreling a second time in as many days with d'Estaing.[17]

The Americans had much to be angry about. On 16 September, as they marched into camp and d'Estaing wasted the day exchanging letters with Prevost, Maitland reinforced the embattled Savannah garrison with the first half of his eight hundred men. The next day, as Lincoln and d'Estaing watched from Brewton Hill, where they had gone to survey the lines, the other half slipped into the town. The British were jubilant—"all in high spirits, and the most pleasing confidence expressed on every face. The sailors not to be prevented from giving three cheers." The French and

Americans indulged in an orgy of recrimination, but neither had counted on Maitland's resourcefulness or determination. Nor had either ally tried very hard to keep him bottled up at Beaufort. As a consequence, what had promised to be a quick and easy conquest now looked doubtful.[18]

Relations between the allies, which had been strained, now proved rancorous. D'Estaing reported that the Americans provoked "altercations" and threw "reproaches and false accusations" at the French. Junior American officers, such as Francis Marion and John Laurens, proved just as touchy about their honor as the haughty French. Lincoln was forced to order the French camp off-limits to American soldiers to minimize friction. Knowing that American hopes still rested with the French, Lincoln remained conciliatory, even inviting d'Estaing to dine at his quarters. Uppermost in his mind was the successful completion of the operation, and he turned all his persuasive powers on the French admiral. During a reconnaissance trip along the lines on 18 September Lincoln noted that d'Estaing "appeared exceedingly anxious about his Fleet," and, if the admiral's private notes can be trusted, he repeatedly told Lincoln of "the dim outlook I had as to our operation" now that Maitland had reinforced the British garrison. Over "a massive cake of rice and corn cooked under the ashes on an iron platter," washed down with a "*mélange* of sugar, water and fermented molasses," Lincoln persuaded D'Estaing to stay. The American, D'Estaing noted, "never stopped begging, even demanding, our perserverance." This, and the shame d'Estaing would face should he back out of a second allied operation, were decisive. Despite the admiral's misgivings, a siege was ordered.[19]

The Americans had never experienced a formal siege and remained optimistic that the great weight of artillery the allies could bring to bear upon the town would ensure a quick capitulation. Even after torrential rains, which began on 16 September, made a quagmire of the roads from the French anchorage, doubling the difficulty of transporting cannons already lacking wheeled carriages, Lincoln's resolution remained fixed. As d'Estaing acidly noted about Lincoln later, "My tranquil colleague, happy in his indomitable placidity, entertained no doubts." What d'Estaing conveniently overlooked was that Lincoln's "placidity" veiled an energy that enabled the French to transport their artillery, dig their trenches, and feed their army.[20]

What Lincoln thought of his French allies, and of d'Estaing in particular, he nowhere indicated for posterity. If he yielded to the urge to complain or criticize the French, it is likely that he destroyed the evidence later. In his journal of the siege and in both his private and his public letters, no hint of anger or reproach can be found. D'Estaing and other French officers were not so discreet. Their contempt for the "*insurgents*," as they called the Americans, and for their commanding officer must have been apparent, even through the thin mask of politesse. Characteristic of French opinion was this mixed estimate of Lincoln provided to d'Estaing by Colonel de Bretigny, a French officer who held rank in the Continental army and was posted to Charleston: "General Lincoln is an honest man, easily impressionable, prickly [*pointilleux*], who has few ideas of his own, but who is ready to adopt those of anyone he comes across; while valuing what is good, he does not have the strength to accomplish it. . . . [S]o far as military affairs are concerned, the General is another man entirely." In this estimate d'Estaing agreed, complaining that Lincoln had "no opinions of his own," while conceding the general's bravery: "He is not afraid of cannon fire."[21]

The French confused indecision with the American penchant for councils of war, in which decisions were reached by consensus. In an army in which military experience was lacking, this kind of decision making guarded against rash judgments. Lincoln expressed his opinions with force but also with tact. D'Estaing was unable to look beyond the ragged men in the American camp nor to see Lincoln as anything more than a farmer with a game leg. Thus, as one American officer would later recall, "Lincoln's wisdom, Lincoln's patience, Lincoln's counsel would be very limited in effect."[22]

When the rain stopped at midday on 22 September the allies prepared to begin their entrenchments. D'Estaing did not plan a regular siege, in which the enemy's lines are approached and finally breached by a system of trenches. Instead, allied hopes rested on a massive bombardment of Savannah which would induce the British to surrender. For this, ground was broken during the night of 22 September. By morning the French had dug themselves in less than three hundred yards from the British lines. In the week that followed the allies edged closer to the town and established a series of batteries, including cannons and mortars, just to the left of the British center. Two British sorties were repelled with losses on both sides, but the work was not delayed.[23]

On 3 October the allied batteries, thirty-three cannons and nine mortars, began the bombardment of Savannah. The firing continued for five days, in which more than a thousand shells rained down on the inhabitants. Initially, the townspeople panicked, but many were evacuated to an island across from the town. Others took refuge in cellars and the front lines. About forty civilians died in the bombardment, women and chil-

dren among them. Only one soldier was killed. Nor were the fortifications of the town much damaged. Lincoln refused a British request to
remove the women and children, much as the British had earlier refused a
request by McIntosh to allow his wife to leave Savannah. Lincoln had
argued previously that civilians by "their entreaties might sway the commanding officer to surrender" and thus save lives and avoid a protracted
siege.[24]

Nonetheless, the bombardment did not achieve, as Lincoln put it,
"the desired purpose, that of compelling a surrender." Nor was d'Estaing
agreeable to changing tack and beginning a regular siege. Anxious for the
safety of his fleet and warned by his engineers that regular approaches to
the town would "be a work of considerable time," the French admiral
agreed to what he had avoided all along, a frontal assault on the fortress.
On 8 October a plan of attack for the next day was quickly agreed upon
over heated opposition from most of the French officers. Lincoln also was
unhappy with the idea of a storm but had no choice but to acquiesce. It
was either the assault or lifting the siege.[25]

The attack focused on the British right at a point where a swamp
joined the town's fortified line. A total of four columns, two French and
two American, would attack points along the Spring Hill redoubt, which
the allies believed was manned by Loyalist militia. Pulaski's cavalry would
sweep to the left of all the allied attackers in an attempt to flank the
entrenchments. The plan, for all the opposition to it, was carefully worked
out. But, to be successful, it required coordination and timing, two elements difficult enough to attain with professional troops. Add the difficulty of commanding an allied army whose members spoke different
languages and the usual confusion of a night movement, and it is easy to
see why the attack had little chance of success. In addition, according to
d'Estaing, the element of suprise was critical. That proved unfortunate
because a deserter revealed the plan to the British in time for them to shift
their best troops to the threatened sector. The ninth of October would be
a grim day for the allies.[26]

The attack, scheduled for 4 A.M., began late, proceeded in confusion,
and was repulsed with heavy losses. The allies never were able to bring
the force of their combined weight to bear on a single point. D'Estaing
and Lincoln led one column, courting "danger to give effect to the assault," but to no avail. Though the column pierced the British lines, lack
of support at the critical moment allowed the attackers to be thrown back.
Caught in a crossfire between the abatis and the redoubt, the French and
Americans were cut to pieces. D'Estaing was wounded twice, and Pulaski

was killed in a fruitless cavalry charge. The allies lost 250 killed and nearly 600 wounded, about one-fifth of those engaged. The British suffered only 100 casualties in all.[27]

Over Lincoln's vigorous protests d'Estaing hurriedly prepared for departure. To his mind an honorable attempt had been made to aid the allies of France, and no more could be asked. For Lincoln, however honorable the attempt, failure at Savannah could only mean the renewal of war, more than likely in South Carolina. As he wrote dejectedly to Rutledge the day after the attack, "It cannot be doubted that if Great Britain is reinforced they will attack the place [Charleston]." And he asked the governor to see that the town's fortifications were completed and everything put in readiness for a siege. With this in mind Lincoln persisted in his arguments with the admiral, pointing out all "the evils which would attend the measure." But d'Estaing could not be dissuaded. During the next three days, while flags of truce were exchanged with the British to bury the dead, Lincoln and D'Estaing discussed the best means of lifting the siege and conducting the retreat. On 13 October an agreement was signed between the allies regulating the retreat. The artillery and the sick and wounded were evacuated first. Then on the evening of 18 October the Americans left their camp, reached Zubley's Ferry by morning, crossed the river, and bivouacked in South Carolina that night. The French, after covering the American retreat, returned to their ships on 19 October. A month after it had begun the siege of Savannah was over.[28]

"Our disappointment is great," wrote Lincoln to Samuel Huntington, the president of Congress. Writing to a friend after reaching Charleston in November, Lincoln remained convinced that, had d'Estaing stayed, "nothing could have prevented our success." Yet, realizing the importance of the French alliance, he was careful to stifle any feelings of resentment which might escape him. Even in his journal he noted that "the causes of failure were such as attend the uncertain events of War and are rather to be lamented than at present investigated." Publicly, he had only praise for d'Estaing and his troops. The count, he reported to Congress, "has undoubtedly the interest of America much at heart. This he has evidenced by coming to our assistance, by his constant attention during the siege, his undertaking to reduce the enemy by assault . . . and by bravely putting himself at the head of his troops and leading them to the attack." Furthermore, before the French had brought the prospect of victory, Americans had to remind themselves, their situation had been bleak. Dashed expectations should not lead them to seek a scapegoat. Lincoln ended his letter with words that he would no doubt recall in six months' time. He hoped that d'Estaing "would be consoled, by an assurance . . . that his want of success will not lessen our ideas of his merit."[29]

"The disagreeable news from Genl. Lincoln, that our army have not succeeded against Savannah," reached Philadelphia on 10 November. It was doubly disagreeable because the "most sanguine expectations of success" had been held by Congress and the public. Some blamed the French. One congressman invoked the Lord, writing that "Providence by another Striking Instance has . . . tumbled our Towring Expectations to the ground." A Philadelphia Quaker noted gleefully in his diary that he found the defeat "remarkably providential in preventing the French from Getting footing on this continent." And one young man noted with more than a grain of truth that "this continent is certainly hostile to the Monsieurs."[30]

For General Washington the news came as a "mortification." He consoled Lincoln on his misfortune by praising the behavior of his troops and thanking him for the "delicacy and propriety" of his conduct. "Instead of the mutual reproaches which too often follow the failure of enterprises, depending upon the cooperation of troops of different nations," Washington wrote, this campaign resulted in increased "confidence in and esteem for each other." That, the commander-in-chief was sure, was in great part thanks to Lincoln.[31]

But, as Lincoln surveyed the wreckage of the past year's campaign, Washington's rueful thanks must have come as small consolation. On the anniversary of his arrival in the Southern Department he was—despite the energy, resources, and sacrifice expended—in much the same position as when he had started. Two chances to defeat the enemy had failed. The British presence in Georgia, once reduced to a toehold, was now in danger of becoming permanent. The citizens of South Carolina, who so recently had marched eagerly to Savannah, now despaired of mounting their own defense and talked openly of neutrality. In addition, reliable news reached Lincoln of a large enemy expedition from New York bent on invading the southern states. It would require renewed confidence, energy, stamina, and a measure of luck to counter the defeatism souring the Carolina air. Swallowing his disappointment in the past campaign, Lincoln accepted his biggest challenge yet and prepared for the defense of South Carolina.

CHAPTER SIX

The Siege of Charleston

You must work with the tools in your possession. If you succeed
applause will follow you. If you do not, disappointed ambition and
every species of rascality will be in an uproar against you.

Henry Knox

In 1780 Charleston, South Carolina, was the fourth largest city in the
United States. It was a small town for all that. About twelve thousand
people, half of them black, clustered on a low sandy spit of land at the
confluence of the Ashley and Cooper rivers. Its harbor was magnificent.
From Charleston's wharves rich cargoes of rice, indigo, and naval stores
made their way to Europe and the West Indies. Small as it was, Charleston dwarfed other southern ports in the amount of its commercial traffic.
It was the economic jewel of the lower South.[1]

It was also the political heart of the rebellion in the deep South. Whig
leadership was rooted in the city and in the wealthy, low-country plantations of the surrounding districts. It was generally believed that the loss of
Charleston to the British would cause the collapse of revolutionary resistance in the lower South. As David Ramsay, a South Carolina Whig and
historian of the Revolution put it, Charleston is "the *viniculum* that binds
three States to the authority of Congress. If the enemy possess themselves
of this town, there will be no living for honest whigs to the southward of
the Santee."[2]

Lincoln realized the importance of Charleston and only once questioned the necessity of defending it to the last extremity. Immediately after
his return from the failed assault on Savannah, Lincoln wrote to Washington that in Charleston "we remain unsupported by troops, unsupplied
with many essential articles, and uncovered with works; and, what adds
to the unhappiness, is the little prospect that our affairs will speedily be in
a better channel." This was hardly news. Lincoln had peppered the gover-

nor of South Carolina, Congress, and Washington with agonized appraisals of the weak state of the Southern Department since arriving in December 1778. Little had changed since then. Yet Lincoln persisted in thinking
that "this town might be defended against a very formidable attack, if all
was done for its security which ought to be done."[3]

Lincoln regarded "a respectable body of disciplined troops"—Continentals sent from the main army in the north—as essential. Thoroughly
disgusted with the part played by the militia at Savannah, Lincoln placed
little faith in them. Not only were they unreliable, they were expensive, too.
The hidden costs of militia included time wasted in raising the men and
marching them to and from the field, the loss of the men's civilian productiv-
ity, and the many deaths of those unaccustomed to military service. Nor did
Lincoln have much hope that Continentals could be recruited in South Carolina. Large reinforcements of militia had been promised from North Carolina, but the prospect of taking the field with short-term soldiers was
unsettling. Lincoln could muster only a thousand Continentals in the entire department, while the British garrison in Savannah contained three
times as many regulars. With those odds the Americans might hold on to
Charleston, but they could never hope to retake Georgia.[4]

In his plea to Congress for reinforcements Lincoln pointed out the
advantages the British would acquire should they take the city: a rich
trade, a valuable harbor, and provisions for the West Indies. The acquisition of a large territory and great numbers of disaffected citizens would
boost the British war effort. The Indians would be "inspirited" and easily
supplied. As far as the United States was concerned, if the South were lost,
the southern states' proportion of the common debt would have to be
shouldered by the remaining ten states, a burden to be borne along with
providing for thousands of refugees. Finally, if Great Britain conquered
America's "extremities," the United States would be "encircled by land
and cooped by sea." It was a persuasive argument, ably delivered.[5]

Congress was not immune to such arguments. The failure to liberate
Savannah had shaken its complacency, especially since they had expected
the town to fall easily. Now came worse news: a major British expedition
was forming at New York whose destination was rumored to be Charleston. Thus, dispositions were underway to reinforce Lincoln even before
his letter of 27 October arrived in Philadelphia. The additional resources
to be sent south included three Continental frigates for "the defence of
the Harbour" and the remainder of the Virginia and North Carolina lines,
amounting to about three thousand men, half of whom were recruited for
the duration of the war. These reinforcements were approved "after much

altercation." Many in Congress, and especially in Virginia and North Carolina, resented South Carolina's lack of energy and support for the Revolutionary cause. John Matthews, a member of Congress from South Carolina, tried to quash "hints," like the following, thrown out in Congress: "How can South Carolina expect we will send our men to their support, when they will do nothing for themselves." And James Lovell, a Bay Stater, after reading Lincoln's plea for aid, caustically wrote: "The State of Sth. Cara. have *thought* we neglected them, we *know* they neglected themselves. They will not *draught* to fill up their Battalions, they will not raise *black Regiments,* they will not put their militia when in Camp under continental Rules." "However," he sneered, "we must exert ourselves for them in every Way."[6]

Meanwhile, in Charleston Lincoln and his Continentals prepared for the inevitable siege. Nothing was to interfere with the effort to defend the town. When Col. John Laurens spoke optimistically of peace negotiations with Britain, Lincoln replied that the news, while wonderful, should not put a halt to the ongoing work. "My wish is that the people here may be *roused* and put this Town & State in some better posture of defence than it is at present." The next few months brought a flurry of activity. Lincoln presented a shopping list to Governor Rutledge: twenty thousand pounds of powder and thirty thousand pounds of lead, cartridge paper, felling axes, gun flints, and cordage—all necessary for the coming fight. Long days in the saddle and nights at his desk made Lincoln less patient and more forceful. Responding to a group of planters who were attempting to drive up the price of corn, he threatened to move "the army to some place where it can be supported with less expense." Work continued on the fortifications, but progress was slow. An outbreak of smallpox emptied the town of laborers, as plantation owners kept a tight hold on their slaves. It was a frustrating time for Lincoln.[7]

As work continued on 10 January, the Americans received news of a British fleet sailing off Charleston bar with troops bound for Georgia. The size of the fleet and its intentions were not confirmed until two weeks later, when a brig flying the Union Jack was lured into Charleston harbor. The ship was part of 163 sail that had left New York City on 27 December with a British army of eight thousand on board. By the time news arrived of the fleet's departure Lincoln was already aware that a major invasion of the Southern Department was afoot. Instead of the anticipated attack from a reinforced Savannah garrison, Lincoln faced the flower of the British army in North America, led by its commander-in-chief, Sir

Henry Clinton. Its destination was Charleston, and its mission was to bring South Carolina under the British heel.[8]

Clinton, stymied in his attempts to force Washington into a decisive battle, had launched his southern expedition according to instructions given in March 1778 by the British ministry and plans he had drawn up in the spring of 1779. At the heart of Britain's southern strategy lay the belief that the majority of southerners were nominally loyal to the Crown and waiting only for an opportunity to show it. Taking the war to the South, the ministry believed, would mobilize the Loyalist population, cut off vital supplies of raw materials to the rebellion, and demonstrate the efficacy of the king's peace—all with a minimal expenditure of troops and treasure. One by one the states would fall to victorious British and Loyalist troops, to be controlled and governed by the Tory majority. The possession of South Carolina would ensure the pacification of Georgia; that of North Carolina, its namesake to the south. The first step to ending the war was the "liberation" of Charleston.[9]

To oppose the eight thousand British troops, Lincoln could muster only about fourteen hundred Continentals and another thousand North Carolina militia. He had been promised reinforcements from the North— Continentals from the main army and two thousand more North Carolina militia. This, he wrote to Congress, "is our whole force, and more we may not soon expect." Lincoln pleaded for troops from the governors of Virginia and North Carolina. And he wrote to Rutledge, asking him once again to consider "arming some Blacks, agreeable to the repeated recommendations of Congress."[10]

A year earlier, in the spring of 1779, Congress had passed a resolution calling on South Carolina and Georgia to raise three thousand black troops to be divided into battalions officered by whites and integrated into the state Continental lines. Ironically, the idea was that of John Laurens, son of Henry Laurens, a former president of Congress, a prominent South Carolinian, and a former slave trader. The elder Laurens introduced the measure in Congress, where it was strongly supported by Carolinians William Henry Drayton and Isaac Huger. Under the plan Congress would reimburse slave owners up to one thousand dollars for each recruit. Blacks received no bounties or pay but would receive their freedom if they survived the end of the war. Some in Congress, including William Whipple of New Hampshire, believed the plan would "be the means of dispensing the Blessings of freedom to all the Human Race in America." Others, more pragmatically, sought to ensure the needed manpower for the southern army. In any case the resolution was overwhelmingly rejected by the South Carolina legislature in its summer session of 1779.[11]

Lincoln was an enthusiastic supporter of the measure, arguing its expediency in the face of recruitment shortfalls in the Continental line. Disappointed by the legislature's rejection of the plan, Lincoln continued to seek ways to exploit this relatively untapped resource. He suggested to Rutledge that a pioneer battalion made up of slaves be formed and permanently attached to the army. When that proved unacceptable and British intentions became clear in January of 1780, Lincoln instead asked for fifteen hundred blacks to build Charleston's fortifications. Then he again asked for black soldiers. "I know it has already been rejected once by the Assembly," Lincoln wrote, "but circumstances were different then. It was a providential measure, now it is an absolutely necessary one."[12]

Lincoln sought to make the issue of black soldiers a test of South Carolina's commitment to its own defense. As it became clear that few militia would be raised, Lincoln candidly described his situation to Rutledge:

I find myself in a peculiar and very critical situation from the novelty of having continental troops shut up in a besieged Town. To this no general officer, has during the war, submitted, but, under similar circumstances with ours, an attempt has been made to cover the country and leave the City to its fate. No consideration could induce me to adopt a new mode of conduct or would justify my doing it, but the hope I have of being supported by the people of the country, and of this I ought to have the fullest assurance.

Part of this assurance, Lincoln went on, was provision for two thousand militia. If that number of citizens could not be raised, he insisted, an equal number of blacks should be armed to defend the city. Thus, from the beginning Lincoln was aware of the dangers of a siege. But he expected the South Carolinians to recognize their desperate situation and make extraordinary exertions for the cause. In this he would be disappointed.[13]

When Rutledge failed to answer Lincoln's request, the New Englander resorted to threats. He reiterated his arguments, even assuring the governor that he never would have urged a measure "so opposite to the general sentiments of the people" if not for sheer necessity. Yet, if this measure were rejected and the army forced to withdraw, Lincoln wrote, "you must say I have tried all in my power to defend the Town." Two weeks later he still had received no answer. Lincoln then requested a formal answer for the record, one that would "determine whether I stay in Town or not." Rutledge was uncowed. True to its colors, the state's Privy Council "fully canvased" Lincoln's request and found the matter "totally impracticable." As young Col. Alexander Hamilton, a friend of John Laurens, had dourly predicted, "Prejudice and private interest will be antagonists too powerful for public spirit and public good." But Rutledge not only rejected the plan; he held Lincoln's feet to the fire. "I flatter myself," he wrote in the same letter, "that as our holding the Town and Harbour is evidently of great importance to the United States, nothing but an invincible and extreme necessity will induce a determination to withdraw the continental Troops from its defence and that such necessity will never exist." Lincoln had his answer: South Carolina expected Lincoln to defend Charleston while denying him the tools he needed to do so. The extraordinary sacrifices for the "Glorious Cause" which Lincoln expected from Americans as a matter of course, sacrifices that he himself had made, would not be forthcoming.[14]

Under these circumstances why did Lincoln stay to defend Charleston, rather than withdraw his troops, as his better judgment indicated? Because he believed that Congress agreed with Rutledge and, without expressly ordering him to do so, expected him to defend the town. The acts of Congress investing him with the command of the Southern Department implied as much. A year earlier Congress had sent Lt. Col. Louis-Antoine-Jean-Baptiste, chevalier de Cambray-Digny, a military engineer, to design and construct the city's defenses. More recently, it had sent three frigates to bolster the defense of the harbor. At no time, Lincoln wrote afterward, did Congress "intimate to me that my ideas of attempting the defense of it were improper." Defending Lincoln's decision years later, John Sullivan agreed with Lincoln's assessment, attributing the misfortune at Charleston to "the positive orders of Congress to keep possession" of it.[15]

Lincoln also believed that Charleston was a very defensible site. "Its natural strength," Lincoln wrote, "promised a larger delay than any other part of that country." The narrowness of the peninsula above the city presented a manageable front for a small garrison. The marshy ground on the American flanks complicated the enemy approaches. The harbor was strong, the Americans believed, protected by forts Moultrie and Sullivan and by a long sandbar that blocked large warships from entering the inner harbor.[16]

There was also extreme pressure on Lincoln from South Carolinians such as Rutledge to remain in the city. One Scottish merchant, Alex

Macshorter, wrote afterward that "the ignorant, self-important gentry of Charlestown as it were compelled Gen. Lincoln to shut himself up in that place. Southern judgements are feeble and southern imaginations and fancies are strong . . . to these Lincoln fell a sacrifice." But Lincoln's own instinct led him to bow to civil authority. As a New Englander, he shared the strong tradition of civil precedence over the military. He always sought cooperation with government leaders when possible and went out of his way to avoid conflict. In a revolutionary war Lincoln could hardly make decisions on a purely pragmatic basis without the support of those he had been sent to defend.[17]

Finally, Lincoln disliked the Fabian strategy he had been forced to adopt. In 1778 Congress had promised him an army and sent him south to invade East Florida. Since then he had spent most of his service biding his time, hoarding his strength, and preparing, marching, and countermarching in anticipation of a decisive battle. Here, at Charleston, was the chance to stake all on one throw. In the final analysis Lincoln could not bring himself to abandon the city. In the back of his mind rested the image of Arthur St. Clair, the general who had given up Fort Ticonderoga without a fight. St. Clair had spent a year and a half as the butt of American scorn for the sound military decision he had made in the summer of 1777. Lincoln had presided over his court-martial. While Americans praised their generals' policy of cautious maneuver, retreat, and limited engagement, "nothing aroused them so much as the loss of fixed posts and cities." To abandon Charleston without a fight would expose Lincoln to accusations of cowardice and dereliction of duty as well as cries of betrayal from the American public.[18]

In the midst of the dispute over black soldiers came another jolt. The defenses of the harbor were not strong enough to stop a determined fleet from entering the inner harbor and blockading the city. Lincoln learned this from Commo. Abraham Whipple, whose arrival on 23 December 1779 with the three Continental frigates had seemed to ensure the harbor's security. Lincoln had been assured that Whipple's force, which included a number of smaller ships of the South Carolina navy, could block the entrance to the harbor by lying broadside outside of the bar. In early February, however, Whipple informed him that the tide made it impossible for the ships to be moored broadside to the bar, a situation that would allow the enemy under full sail to pass easily into the inner harbor. The matter was critical because British control of the harbor would pin the American army within the city. An anchorage in the channel within the bar was proposed, but that proved impracticable. Finally, Lincoln ordered the commodore to act in conjunction with Fort Moultrie, and so matters stood until early April.[19]

If the naval situation was worrisome, the future movements of the British army were a mystery to the Americans. Lincoln, as he wrote to Washington, found himself "greatly embarrassed to know what ground to occupy" in order to oppose Clinton's advance. If, for example, Lincoln concentrated his army in Charleston and Clinton should march overland from Savannah, the Americans would "lose the advantages of opposing them at the several strong passes between this town and the Savannah." If, on the other hand, Lincoln posted his army on the Savannah River, the British could land between him and Charleston, thus shutting him off from its defense. And if he were to try to do both, by dividing his "few troops," Lincoln added, "there is danger that we shall be beaten in detachment." British command of the seas made any defensive strategy problematic.[20]

Nor did Lincoln have confidence any longer in his own judgment. He wrote to Washington that he needed "the advantage of [his] advice and direction," because Lincoln said, "I feel my own insufficiency and want of experience." That might have been true, but Lincoln was now one of the most experienced commanders in the Continental army and the one with the greatest knowledge of the Southern Department. Yet the past year had taken a devastating toll on Lincoln's self-confidence. The string of defeats, the quarrels and wrangling with civil leaders, and the heat, sickness, and fatigue had sapped his strength. "I can promise you nothing," he wrote Washington, "but a disposition to serve my country." And once again he promised to defend Charleston "as long as opposition can be of any avail."[21]

Clinton did not leave the Americans long in the dark. In a move that would have outflanked an American concentration on the banks of the Savannah River, the British commander used his seapower to approach close to Charleston. On 11 February elements of the British army landed on Johns Island. By the end of the month the enemy occupied James Island, concentrated at Fort Johnston across the Ashley River from Charleston. Throughout March, Clinton cautiously edged north along the southern shore of Ashley River, crossed over Stono River and the scene of the past year's bloody fighting, and moved on to Wapoo Neck. From Drayton's Ferry the army crossed over to Charleston Neck on 29 March. Two days later the British had marched to within several miles of Charleston. There they extended their lines across the neck from the Ashley River to the Cooper River and prepared to lay siege to the town.[22]

In the eighteenth century a formal siege was a highly stylized affair. It formed a kind of minuet, in which besieged and besieger danced intricate and familiar steps, each of which carried a clear and precise message. A complete investiture had to be made and the town invited to surrender. Then ground was broken on the first parallel, a long trench just out of the enemy's cannon shot. Once completed the first parallel formed the "jumping off point" for the attack. Trenches perpendicular to it were advanced toward the town's defenses, and a second parallel was dug about four hundred feet away, and so on. Batteries were built to protect those working on the trenches and to batter the enemy's defenses and create a breach in the walls which would permit an assault. A well-conducted siege ended by negotiation and capitulation, for few fortresses could withstand this "scientific approach." Nor would most garrisons submit to an assault, an act that inevitably meant the sack of the town. Once a breach was made surrender was only a matter of time.[23]

The besieged hoped to delay the enemy long enough for a relieving army to arrive and raise the siege. The garrison did this by strengthening and repairing the defensive works and by making sorties against the enemy to impede its progress. With sufficient supplies and well-engineered defenses a garrison could hold out for a long time. Its ultimate fate, however, hinged on the arrival of reinforcements or events that would force the enemy to retreat.[24]

The defenses of Charleston were extensive. By 8 March the French engineer Col. Jean-Baptiste-Joseph, chevalier de Laumoy, had prepared a design that strengthened the existing works by raising the height of the parapet walls, creating a wet ditch, or canal, and adding a series of *chevaux-de-frises,* or abatis. Laumoy estimated that the job required the work of sixteen hundred men. Lincoln made due with some six hundred requisitioned slaves, who worked alongside "fatiguemen" drafted from the Continental troops. Needless to say, many southerners were reluctant to soil their hands with manual labor, tasks they thought suitable only for slaves. To persuade them to pitch in, Lincoln worked side by side with blacks and whites, slinging pick and shovel to build the works. "And this was not only the exertion of one hour to excite emulation, but his [Lincoln's] constant practice, going out with the foremost in the morning, and returning with the last in the Evening." It was as if the old farmer sought relief from the frustrations of past years in the hard sweat of familiar toil.[25]

The Americans "worked with untiring effort on the fortification," wrote one enemy observer. Trenches, batteries, "like mushrooms . . . sprang from the soil." When the Americans paused to take stock in April, the British faced a chain of redoubts, lines, and batteries, with more than eighty cannons and mortars, stretching across the peninsula from the Ashley to the Cooper rivers. These lines were flanked on either side by swamps connected by a canal. In the center, regarded as the weakest point, a "hornwork of masonry," or citadel, guarded the road into the city. On the harbor side more heavy guns were emplaced in batteries made of palmetto trees and earth. These menaced any British vessel that approached within cannon shot.[26]

Also on 8 March Lincoln ordered Colonel Malmédy, another French engineer, to take two hundred soldiers and three hundred blacks to Cainhoy on Wando Creek to build fortifications to protect that important ford. The Americans controlled the Cooper River crossings, which provided a line of communications for supplies and reinforcements to reach the city. Should that route be closed, Charleston would be surrounded and evacuation of the garrison impossible. Within a few days Lincoln ordered a series of points fortified along the line beginning with Lemprieres Point, just across the Cooper River to the northwest of Charleston, and extending into the country to better secure this critical link to the north.[27]

Earlier, in February, Lincoln had sent Moultrie with a mixed force of infantry and cavalry to Bacon's Bridge, some twenty miles west of Charleston, to rally the militia and "hang on the enemies flanks and oppose them at every advantageous pass. Remove everything which might aid the enemy." When no militia materialized, Moultrie's small force kept a watchful eye on British movements but could do little else. Moultrie himself fell ill in early March and had to be evacuated to Charleston. Gen. Isaac Huger took Moultrie's place. By 15 March Lincoln had ordered Huger to send the infantry to Charleston while keeping the cavalry outside to harass the enemy and guard the American lines of communication to the north. Huger eventually concentrated his horsemen at Monck's Corner, north of the city.[28]

In the evening of 3 March Gen. James Hogan, with a brigade of North Carolina Continentals, marched into Charleston. As Lincoln put it, the arrival of reinforcements "gives great happiness and spirit to the garrison; for we were before, and are now, much too weak." Hogan's men, all of six hundred rank and file, might have buoyed Charleston's spirits, but a host they were not. Lincoln still counted on the promises of reinforcements made by the governors of Virginia and North and South Carolina. Those militiamen, when added to the Continental line marching toward Charleston, would have amounted to reinforcements of ninety-nine hundred men. Given his past experience, Lincoln had little reason to believe the promises would be kept. Yet he did. But only a thousand North Carolina militia were in camp, out of the three thousand soldiers promised him by Governor Caswell, and these troops left Charleston for home on 24 March when their time of service expired. At least North Carolina responded; the South Carolina militia, of which two thousand were pledged, refused to enter the city. In this situation Hogan's arrival was a godsend. Above all, Lincoln anxiously awaited the Virginia Continentals, whom he hoped would stiffen the city's resistance.[29]

On 20 March a crucial, but not unexpected, blow was given to the Charleston defense when the British admiral Marriot Arbuthnot sailed his ships over the bar into the harbor. Despite Lincoln's proddings and misgivings, it had already been decided that the American navy, under Commodore Whipple, could not prevent the British from crossing the bar. In spite of Lincoln's positive orders to attack the British ships as soon as they crossed (the British ships had to remove some of their guns in order to get over the bar), all of them entered the harbor unscathed. This effectively closed the harbor and made an American evacuation of the city extremely dangerous. Washington, when he heard the news, thought it amounted "to the loss of the town and garrison." While he had "the greatest confidence in General Lincolns prudence," Washington thought that the attempt to defend Charleston should have ended at this point. Unfortunately, when Lincoln earlier had begged him for advice, Washington had punctiliously refused. Now it was too late.[30]

The American garrison still had hopes that the guns of Fort Moultrie could turn back the British fleet, just as they had in 1776. But on 8 April seven British warships ran the narrow channel under tremendous fire and emerged with one ship slightly damaged. "It was," wrote a Hessian officer, "the most majestic and beautiful spectacle that one can imagine. The fort was veiled in fire and smoke, and the roar of forty-three heavy guns resembled a terrible thunderstorm. Despite all dangers threatening the fleet, it sailed quite slowly past the fort with colors flying proudly, one ship behind the other, without firing a shot. As soon as it had passed the enemy fort, each ship made a sudden turn, fired a broadside, and sailed to its designated anchoring place." There had been no firing from the American ships. Most of Whipple's squadron had been scuttled to block the entrance to the Cooper River. The ships' guns had been taken off to bolster the city's defenses and the sailors recruited to man them. The navy, upon which Lincoln had counted so much, had proved to be just another empty promise.[31]

The successful British fleet action left Lincoln with only one narrow escape hatch across the Cooper River along the fortified points from Lemprieres Point to Cainhoy and on to North Carolina. It was along this road that Gen. William Woodford and his 750 Virginia Continentals double-timed, arriving in Charleston on 7 April. The men were in "good health and spirits," despite having marched 505 miles in thirty days. They were received with "great joy" and immediately thrust into the line of defense. The enemy had watched the Virginians sail down the Cooper River to town, unable to prevent their noisy arrival. "The besieged shouted for joy three times from their works," wrote one enemy officer, "which mingled with an hourly pealing of bells and a continuous cannon and mortar fire at our parallels and redoubts." In spite of the rejoicing for these hearty veterans, Lincoln could tote up the odds. Added to his other Continentals, the Virginians boosted Lincoln's forces to about 2,500 men. To these he could add another 2,500 assorted militia and volunteers. Lincoln estimated that there were 3 miles of entrenchments to be manned by this force, against a British army that had swelled to nearly 10,000 regulars. The newly arrived Woodford wrote that "the garrison appears in high spirits, and our arrival seemed to give them fresh confidence." But Lincoln kept his own counsel, aware of the desperate situation he faced.[32]

Clinton professed to be happy about the reinforcement of the garrison. "They will now defend the town," he noted in his diary, "and when we take it, we shall take all in it." The British on Charleston Neck had broken ground some days earlier, in the early morning hours of 2 April, building three redoubts some eight hundred yards from the American lines and beginning their first parallel. The sandy ground proved easy digging, and the work progressed quickly. Once the Americans were aware of the British activity they began to pound the area heavily with cannon fire. The British sustained some losses but not enough to stop the work. On 4 April the two American frigates in the Cooper River set sail upriver and, having flanked the work parties, opened fire on the British lines. The ships were only driven away by stubborn cannon fire from a makeshift battery. The next day British guns began to "play upon the city" for the first time. "A terrible clamor arose among the inhabitants of the city," wrote Captain Johann Ewald, a Hessian officer. "[I] approached quite close to the city to discover the effect of those batteries, and in the short intervals between shooting I could often hear the loud wailing of female voices."[33]

With several batteries completed and Arbuthnot's fleet occupying the inner harbor, Clinton summoned the Americans to surrender on 10 April.

Lincoln replied without hesitation: "Sixty days have been past, since it has been known that your intentions against this town were hostile, in which time has been afforded to abandon it; but duty and inclination point to the propriety of supporting it to the last extremity." Clinton thought the answer "very proper, very modest," and noted that "if he [Lincoln] is a firm man he will hold out to extremity."[34]

From 10 April until the surrender of the town there was hardly a peaceful moment, as batteries on both sides pounded each other's defensive lines. The expenditure of powder, shot, and shell was the most extravagant yet seen in North America. By the end of the siege more than six hundred guns had been active. The British bombarded Charleston from their entrenchments on the neck, from Fort Johnson on James Island and from batteries across the Ashley River. Their warships in the harbor threw an occasional broadside into the town. Charlestonians heaped earth around the foundations of their houses and dug caves in their basements. Some houses were destroyed by fire; others were damaged by cannonballs. Civilians and soldiers alike were killed in this indiscriminate fire. Solid shot, up to twelve pounds of iron, ricocheted against buildings and caused havoc among the population. Roundshot battered enemy fortifications. Caracasses were incendiary shells that started numerous fires. Howitzers and mortars threw screaming explosive shells at high trajectories. The Americans returned fire enthusiastically but, as time wore on, less and less effectively.[35]

Given the extreme peril in which the garrison found itself, Lincoln now tried to persuade Governor Rutledge to leave the city to provide for the continuation of South Carolina's civil government in case Charleston should fall. On 12 April Lincoln gathered his general officers in council and asked them to sign a plea to the governor, which they did. As a consequence, Rutledge and three councilmen crossed the Cooper River on their way to the backcountry about noon the next day. They left behind the newly appointed Lt. Gov. Christopher Gadsden and the rest of the Privy Council. From areas outside British control Rutledge attempted to muster enough men to force Clinton to give up the siege. It was a faint hope and, despite Rutledge's energetic efforts, came to nought.[36]

On 16 April Lincoln held another council of war to seek advice on a possible attack on a British force of 750 at Wappetaw, a few miles north of Cainhoy. The generals unanimously opposed it. Although Lincoln made no mention of this in his official minutes of the meeting, McIntosh wrote that Lincoln, after giving the council a "State of the Garrison, the Men, provisions, Stores Artillery, etc.," asked the council to "Consider of the

Propriety of evacuating the Garrison." For his part McIntosh insisted that "we should not lose an hour longer in attempting to get the Continental Troops at Least out, while we had one side open yet over Cooper River." And he thought that his impassioned speech had convinced the rest of the officers. But Lincoln vacillated, unwilling to give up the city. He replied, according to McIntosh, that "he only desired now that we should consider maturely of the expediency & practicability of such a Measure by the time he would send for us again." Unknown to him, it was already too late.[37]

On 14 April Loyalist cavalry commanded by Banastre Tarleton swooped down on Isaac Huger's cavalry, guarding the American line of communication at Monck's Corner, north of the city, crushing their resistance and capturing nearly all their horses. When word reached Lincoln several days later he could see that the British had tightened their grip on the city and narrowed the remaining escape route to a corridor along several small fortified points at the river crossings of the Cooper and Wando. Since the British were too thinly scattered over the countryside to stop all traffic into and out of the city, some Charlestonians left, dodging enemy patrols, and made their way to safety. But the way was not open for long. On 18 April a "considerable reinforcement" of twenty-six hundred British regulars arrived from New York and was immediately formed into a corps under Lord Cornwallis to complete the encirclement of the city, a move they accomplished within a fortnight.[38]

With his escape hatch slowly being sealed and the British advancing from their second parallel, penetrating to within seventy yards of the American lines, Lincoln once again gathered his general officers in a council of war to discuss what should be done. Generals Moultrie, McIntosh, Woodford, Scott, and Hogan, along with colonels Laumoy, Beekman, and Simons, met with Lincoln on 20 and 21 April in marathon sessions to hammer out a response to their critical situation. Lincoln began by reporting "the strength of the Garrison, the state of the provisions [and] the situation of the enemy." Some of the officers, including McIntosh, still believed an evacuation possible and proposed that the Continental troops be sent out of the city while the militia manned the walls. Most, however, agreed with Laumoy that Lincoln should parley with the British and attempt to get the most honorable terms of capitulation he could. At this point Lieutenant Governor Gadsden "happened to come in whether by Accident or design," and Lincoln proposed that he be allowed to sit in on the council, most likely to ensure that any decision the military took would be agreeable to the government. Gadsden, in fact, "appeared surprised and displeased that we had entertained a thought of a Capitulation or evacuating the Garrison," and he insisted on discussing the matter with the Privy Council. The meeting adjourned until that evening.[39]

When night fell the general officers met again. Laumoy persuaded them to offer terms of capitulation, testifying to "the insufficiency of our Fortifications (if they were worthy of being called so) the improbability of holding out many days Longer, & the impracticability of making our Retreat good as the Enemy are now situated." The matter thus seemed settled when Gadsden and the four council members arrived. Gadsden "used the Council very Rudely" and protested the decision, arguing that "the Militia were willing to Live upon Rice alone rather than give up the Town upon any Terms." Lincoln, after two years of struggling to bring the militia to do their duty, could hardly believe his ears. But he found councilman Ferguson's threat more credible. As McIntosh recorded in his journal, Ferguson said that he had observed for some time the boats collected to ferry the Continental troops over the Cooper River to safety. "If it was ever attempted he would be among the first who would open the Gates for the Enemy and assist them in attacking us before we got aboard." It was clear that Lincoln was no longer master of the situation. Another man might have clapped the governor and council into jail and proclaimed martial law. But Lincoln's respect for civilian authority left him ill equipped to counter this kind of sabotage.[40]

As if this were not enough for one night, after Gadsden and his party had gone Charles Cotesworth Pinckney, the commander of Fort Moultrie, burst into the meeting and "forgetting his usual Politeness, addressed Genl. Lincoln in great warmth & much the same Strain as the Lt. Governor had done." Pinckney lashed out at the assembled brass and declared that "those who were for business required no Councils." Lincoln was silent. McIntosh at this point had had enough. "I was myself so much hurt by the repeated Insults given to the Commanding Officer in so public a Manner," he wrote, that "I could not help declaring . . . I was for holding the Garrison to the last extremity." Despite protestations from Laumoy, all agreed to continue the siege, and they parted for an uneasy night.[41]

The next morning Lincoln convened the group again. To carry on the siege under the circumstances seemed futile. The council reversed its decision of the night before and agreed unanimously that "offers of Capitulation, before our Affairs become more critical, should be made to General Clinton." Care was taken to explore the reasons why an evacuation was problematic. The obvious objection was that "the civil authority were utterly averse to it." But the opinion of the council was that a retreat in the face of a much superior enemy, across a river three miles wide, would be perilous and have little chance to succeed. Even if the river crossing could be made safely, the Americans would face heavy British resistance at the various river crossings on their way north and would have infinite trouble crossing the Santee River to safety. By this time, whether Lincoln or any of his officers had the necessary energy and stamina for this difficult maneuver is doubtful. It was just too late. Lincoln had relied too long on the promises of Congress and the states, had clung too long to the chimera of rescue. There was no longer any chance of escape.[42]

At noon on 21 April Lincoln sent out a flag of truce to request a six-hour cessation of hostilities for the Americans to propose terms of surrender. This was granted, and articles of capitulation written the night before by Lincoln and Ternant were sent off to the British. Lincoln proposed that the town, forts, and fortifications be exchanged for permission for the garrison to retreat for ten days unmolested, with its arms, artillery, baggage, and stores. The articles included free passage for the American ships out of Charleston harbor. And all citizens were to be protected in their persons and property. Those who wished to do so were to be given a year in which to liquidate their assets and move out of the city. This "free evacuation" with the honors of war was the most lenient surrender a besieger might allow an enemy in a formal siege. Clinton refused to consider these terms and issued an ultimatum, which he said was "exactly what we sent before." This was refused, in turn, by Lincoln and his assembled officers, with the message that the British "might begin firing again when they pleased—which they did immediately abot. Nine at night with greater Virilence & fury than ever."[43]

The artillery duel continued as the British finished their third parallel and edged ever closer to the American lines. The *jagers*, German marksmen serving with the British, occupied the front lines, pouring deadly fire into the cannon embrasures in an attempt to slow the fire of the American artillerymen. Parker, who had marched his Virginians south one year earlier, was killed "by a Rifle ball looking over the Parapet of the half Moon battery." American fire took its toll on the enemy but had to be rationed to economize on dwindling stocks of shot and shell. Even so, it found its mark from time to time. A hundred cannonballs might bury themselves harmlessly in the sand, but just one strike could wreak havoc. One morning, as the guard was changing, "a cannon ball struck among seven *jagers* this side of [redoubt] No. 3. One of them lost a leg, a second received a wound in the thigh (from the same shot), and the other five were injured by splinters of a felled tree against which the ball struck." The Americans, one Hessian officer noted, "threw their shells in a masterly manner." The cannonade continued day and night; the Americans "let few nights pass in which they fired fewer than three hundred shots." Besides this danger were the nearly unbearable conditions experienced by men on both sides in the front lines. The Hessian Captain Ewald wrote:

> The dangers and difficult work were the least of the annoyance: the intolerable heat, the lack of good water, and the billions of sandflies and mosquitoes made up the worst nuisance. Moreover, since all our approaches were built in white, sandy soil, one could hardly open his eyes during the south wind because of the thick dust, and could not put a bite of bread into his mouth which was not covered with sand.[44]

On the morning of 24 April, just before daybreak, a group of Hessians were digging in the advanced works just in front of the American lines when a shout rang out: "Damn me the Rebels are here." A party of two hundred Continentals slashed through the Hessian work party and "compleatly Surprized them, in their trenches abot. fifteen of them were killed with the Bayonet in their ditches, & twelve Prisoners brought off." The British attempted to counterattack but were discouraged by cannon fire—"so excessive a shower of canisters which were loaded with old burst shells, broken shovels, pickaxes, hatchets, flatirons, pistol barrels, broken locks, etc." The Americans made good their retreat but were unable to destroy any fortifications. In addition, Moultrie's brother Thomas was killed in the attack. Spirits within the city were raised by the raid, but no more sorties were made, in order to conserve the garrison in case it was stormed.[45]

A day after the sortie Gen. Louis Duportail arrived from Philadelphia. He brought grim news that they could expect no reinforcements from the main army. Duportail, a French engineer, had clearly impressed Washington with his extensive military knowledge and judgment. The commander-in-chief had recommended the Frenchman to Lincoln as a "valuable acquisition." Unfortunately, Duportail arrived too late to make much difference. The French engineer was appalled by the "desperate State" of the city and declared almost immediately that "the fall of the Town was unavoidable unless an Army came to her assistance." Duportail's judgments, while true, were harsh and rang with European contempt for Lincoln and his army. The British, he declared, "had surmounted difficulties which were generally looked upon as insuperable without experiencing scarce any resistance." He pressed Lincoln to order an immediate evacuation of the garrison.[46]

Once again, on 26 April, Lincoln called together his general officers in a council. The only question he asked them was whether or not an evacuation was an "expedient & practicable measure." Duportail argued strongly for the evacuation, a measure he thought "only appeared difficult and hazardous and such as we ought to risk in our present situation." The council agreed unanimously, however, not to retreat. At that point, as Duportail noted, given rejection of the plan, "the only object was to protract the term of our Capitulation."[47]

From 26 April to 8 May the siege progressed. Duportail worked incessantly to strengthen the crumbling fortifications. The engineer "changed and remedied as much as he could in this short time." Most of the fatigue duty fell on the hard-pressed enlisted men, "the few Negroes remaining in Town are obliged to be pressed daily, & kept under guard, as the masters as well as the Slaves, were unwilling they should work." Even so, Ewald noted after the surrender that, had Duportail "arrived in Charlestown sooner, I believe we would not have obtained such a cheap bargain." Lincoln was determined to hold out, even if it meant a British assault on the lines. Privately, he informed the general officers, on 29 April, that "he intended the Horn Work [central citadel] as a place of retreat for the whole Army in Case they were drove from the Lines." It was a little late to think about the preservation of the Continental troops, but it shows to what length Lincoln was prepared to go to defend his men.[48]

Despite "very heavy fire of grapeshot," occasional rains, and "a violent wind," the British continued work on the third parallel, which was nearly finished. By 29 April they had advanced so far as to pierce the canal and begin to drain it. The next day Arbuthnot landed two hundred sailors on Lemprieres Point on the north side of the Cooper River and occupied the entrenchments deserted by the Americans. The encirclement was now complete. What little communication the city had maintained with the surrounding countryside was now cut off. Fresh beef and other food supplies could no longer be ferried across the Cooper River. The garrison would have to get by on its meager stockpiles. It was not long before the general cry was: "Hungry guts in the garrison."[49]

If the British had slammed the cage door shut, they had yet to subdue the dangerous army within it. The Hessian sharpshooters in the most advanced trenches of the British works during the early days of May commented on the ferocity of the American fire. On 5 May Ewald wrote that "in the evening at ten o'clock the cannon and musketry fire of the besieged was so violent and directed with such good effect that the workers could do little." And again: "There were at least one hundred sharpshooters in the hole, whose fire was so superior to mine that the jagers no longer dared to fire a shot." The Americans dug counterapproaches and built new batteries to flank the British parallels. Tar barrels were placed in front of the American lines and lighted to burn all night to prevent a surprise attack. The American defense thus was active, but, while it could delay the British, it could not stop them from extending their works.[50]

Nor could it prevent the final steps of the siege from being played out. On 7 May came the shocking news that Fort Moultrie had surrendered without firing a shot. As one American officer put it, "This fort by many people was reckoned impregnable." The bastion of palmetto and earth which had turned back Sir Henry Clinton's fleet in 1776 surrendered its two hundred men as prisoners of war and added its forty guns to the British booty bag. Undermanned and unsupported, it had been in no position to defend itself.[51]

At seven o'clock on the morning of 8 May, with the third parallel bristling with cannon less than a hundred yards away from the American lines, Clinton once again sent Lincoln a summons to surrender. He offered the same terms as before and added that, if the Americans persisted, "whatever vindictive severity an exasperated soldiery may inflict" on the city would be Lincoln's responsibility. The American officers, both general and field officers, huddled all day in council. The assembly quickly decided by a great majority to ask for terms. The discussion grew heated over what the terms should be. Eventually, twelve articles of capitulation were written, proposing among other things that the town be surrendered, the sailors and Continentals be prisoners of war, the militiamen return to their homes, and the officers keep their sidearms, horses, and baggage. Sent to Clinton, the general revised the document article by article, defining the town, for instance, to include all artillery, shipping, and public stores. He also required that the militia and all civil officers be considered as prisoners on parole. These changes were then revised by Lincoln and sent back to the British. Clinton considered them "inadmissable," and on the afternoon of 9 May he sent that message to Lincoln.[52]

For an hour after the reception of Clinton's letter the silence of the day's truce was maintained. "At length," wrote General Moultrie,

we fired the first gun and immediately followed a tremendous cannonade, and the mortars from both sides threw out an immense number of shells. It was a glorious sight to see them like meteors crossing each other and bursting in the air; it appeared as if the stars were tumbling down. The fire was incessant almost the whole night; cannon-balls whizzing and shells hissing continually amongst us; ammunition chests and temporary magazines blowing up; great guns bursting, and wounded men groaning along the lines. It was a dreadful night! It was our last great effort, but it availed us nothing.[53]

American fire slackened as spirits fell, but the British guns boomed throughout the next day and night. Red-hot shot set fire to several sections of the city, in one quarter destroying at least twenty houses. Troop details were sent to fight fires, "to seize every steer and cow in the town for the use of the garrison," and to search private homes for hoarded caches of rice and other provisions. On 10 May, one soldier noted, "the militia abandoned the lines and [could] not be prevail'd upon to Join." The next day Lincoln received four petitions signed by a combination of 753 militiamen, begging him to "send out a Flag in the name of the People intimating their acquiesence in the Terms proposed" by the British. That same day Gadsden and the Privy Council told Lincoln that "no time should be lost in renewing negotiations." In consequence, Lincoln sent out two flags of truce, the latter of which was accepted. In his letter to Clinton, Lincoln declared his willingness to accept the conditions set down in Clinton's letter of 8 May, and these were, accordingly, granted by the British. The guns fell silent for good.[54]

Late in the morning of 12 May, as one British officer noted, "Lincoln limp'd out at the Head of the most ragged Rabble I ever beheld." Clinton had denied the garrison the honors of war, so the fifteen hundred Continental soldiers marched out of the Horn work along the main road to the drumbeat of a Turkish march, with their flags and banners cased, and piled their muskets in front of their own lines. When the men were ordered back to town, Gen. Alexander Leslie, appointed by Clinton to be military governor of Charleston, said to Lincoln, "I take this, Sir, to be your first division." The New Englander replied, "This body, Sir, contains my first and my last division; they are all the troops I have." Moultrie noted that the British were "astonished and said we had made a gallant defense." As for the militiamen, only five hundred of them could be rounded up on 12 May to make a surrender of their arms. The next day, however, the threat of having British grenadiers search private homes for arms brought out, in Moultrie's words, "the aged, the timid, the disaffected and the infirm, many of them who had never appeared during the whole siege." Their surrender to the British brought the number of prisoners taken by the British, in Moultrie's estimate, to "three times the number of men we ever had upon duty."[55]

The loss of the Charleston garrison was a severe blow, the heaviest the Americans would suffer in the entire Revolutionary War. More than 5,000 Continental soldiers, militia, and private citizens officially surrendered to the British. How many of these men actually were involved in the defense of the city is questionable. In his official returns Lincoln counted about 2,200 Continentals, of whom more than 500 were sick or wounded. Added to this were only about 500 reliable militia troops. These men were held as prisoners of war and were lost to the Continental army for the rest of the war. Given the appalling treatment of prisoners by the British, many would die in captivity. A wealth of military ordnance was also captured: 391 artillery pieces, nearly 6,000 muskets, 33,000 rounds of ammunition, and 3 frigates. Despite the tremendous volume of cannon shot exchanged and the long duration of the siege, casualties were relatively light. The Americans lost 89 killed and 138 wounded, the British 76 killed and 189 wounded.[56]

It was a military disaster—much greater than the loss of the town alone would have been. Lincoln, a general known for his "prudence," had jeopardized the entire Southern Department by his unwise decision to defend Charleston to the bitter end. However understandable his reasoning, however unrelenting the pressures placed upon him, the fact remained that Lincoln had sacrificed his better judgment to the threats and entreaties of South Carolina's civil authorities. Unable to imagine a military effort without the support of the civil authorities, Lincoln bowed at critical moments to the desires of civilian leaders. Imbued with the idea of military subordination to civil authority, he allowed himself to be trapped in a siege he had neither the experience, the resources, nor the ruthlessness to win.

It was some comfort that in the eyes of the world, as Duportail would write, "the honor of American Arms is secure and the Enemy have not great subject to triumph. To remain forty two days in open trenches before a Town of an immense extent fortified by sandy intrenchments raised in two months . . . defended by a Garrison which was not sufficient by half of what was necessary . . . is nothing very glorious." But, if the British reaped little honor and glory from the siege, they still held the prize—Charleston. Who knew what effect that victory would have on the rest of South Carolina and the surrounding states? Lincoln might have speculated about the course the southern war would take as he waited for a ship to take him to Philadelphia. More likely, he was wondering what his reception by Congress would be like. Quite possibly, he recalled Washington's last letter to him, in which the commander-in-chief had written: "Whatever may be the event [of the siege], of this we are assured, that no exertion, prudence or perserverance on your part, will be wanting to defeat the attempts of the enemy." That, at least, Lincoln knew to be true.[57]

CHAPTER SEVEN

The Long Road to Yorktown

But do you feel pain, my dear sir, because it is probable one more has misconstrued or misrepresented your conduct? I think you know the operations of the human heart too well to suppose that any person who has acted in the high station which you have done can escape the malevolence of disappointment or the reproaches of the ignorant and interested. . . . To be envied is a tax which a Man pays for being eminent. I am sure you are too good a member of the community to wish not to pay your proportion.

Henry Knox

Though Charleston surrendered on 12 May, it was not until the first week in June that Sir Henry Clinton allowed Benjamin Lincoln and his military "family" to sail for Philadelphia. The delay was inexplicable, for Lincoln quickly made the necessary arrangements for the administration of his prisoner army during his absence. The delay rankled him, despite the fact that, once readied to sail, Clinton showed Lincoln only the greatest politeness and respect, giving orders that "every comfort which can be given him be put on board" ship for the voyage. As a prisoner of war, Lincoln was allowed to report to Congress, but the terms of his parole restricted his movements to New England thereafter. After his short visit to Philadelphia Lincoln would head to Hingham and a long-anticipated reunion with his family.[1]

Throughout May Congress and the American public remained in a state of suspense over the fate of Charleston. Within the army most of the general officers had long expressed anxiety over Lincoln's decision to defend the city against a siege. Both generals Steuben and Greene, for example, thought that Lincoln was risking the loss of a valuable and irreplaceable army for a victory that, like the occupation of Philadelphia, would prove of little strategic value to the British. Civilian leaders, in Congress and elsewhere, alternated between moods of optimism and pessimism and were buoyed by every rumor that made its way from the South. One congressman wrote that "Charlestown holds out to Admiration," while another noted that he was certain the city had fallen. Some hoped, along with the president of Congress, Samuel Huntington, that the large French force, whose arrival was expected, would force the British to raise the siege. But most observers ultimately relied on Lincoln's "good sense and cool firmness" to snatch victory from the jaws of defeat. If he did not have the means to hold the city, one congressman wrote, "an officer of Gen. Lincoln's prudence would not have suffered himself to be so compleatly invested, when by a timely and safe retreat he could have prevented it."[2]

A report of Charleston's fall reached Philadelphia on 2 June in a special printing of James Rivington's New York *Royal Gazette*. But, given Rivingston's "notorious character for lying" and contradictory reports from the South, hope persisted until Lt. Col. Jean Ternant arrived in Philadelphia on 14 June with Lincoln's dispatches. Despite the long period of uncertainty, the news still came as a shock. As James Lovell wrote: "False reports kept up a hope that makes it all the more cutting now." Ternant was eagerly sought after to fill in the story hidden between the lines of Lincoln's official letters. Nor was he loathe to put his spin on the news. One Philadelphian who had tea with him wrote that Ternant said the army was traded to the British for the safety of the townspeople and their property. By this account Lincoln surrendered the town against his better judgment. The scramble to lay the blame for the disaster had begun.[3]

Lincoln arrived in Philadelphia on 22 June and immediately sent a letter to Congress requesting a formal inquiry into the causes of the loss of Charleston. (Congress had passed a resolution on 28 November 1778 which required a court of inquiry on the loss of any post or battle.) He was, Lincoln wrote, "stimulated by the double motive of regard to the honor of Congress and his own reputation." Congress resolved to initiate the inquiry on 23 June, and Samuel Holten, for one, "had reason to believe it will be to his honor." In the meantime Lincoln made the rounds of Philadelphia society, squired no doubt by Holten and James Lovell, members of the Massachusetts delegation to Congress. There was a good deal of curiosity about the man whose actions the country had followed in newspaper accounts for the past two years. It is likely that Lincoln disappointed them a bit. Here was no choleric Benedict Arnold or fierce Anthony Wayne but, instead, as one man described him, "a plain, familiar man . . . very solid and polite." To the world he presented a calm and imperturbable face, whatever humiliation he felt.[4]

He needed all the self-command he could muster. There was a great deal of resentment over the loss of Charleston, and it was not always privately expressed. At one and the same time Lincoln was criticized for making insufficient efforts to defend the city and for going to extremes in its defense. Some lambasted him for shutting himself up in the city and sacrificing the Continental units he commanded. Another critic wrote that the city was "ingloriously and unnecessarily surrendered." One newly elected member of Congress, who openly censured Lincoln, was dressed down by Matthew Clarkson, one of Lincoln's aides-de-camp, to the delight of his listeners.[5]

To be sure, Lincoln had his defenders, not the least of whom was Philip Schuyler, a man well acquainted with public invective. Another military man who came to Lincoln's defense was Horatio Gates, who replaced him as commander of the Southern Department. Gates sympathized with Lincoln, who he believed had been "doomed to the command of the Southern Dept." He made a point of asking Lincoln's advice about the coming campaign, advice that he would especially value since it came from "a good head and a sincere heart." Most surprising of all those who stuck with Lincoln were a number of prominent South Carolinians. In the immediate aftermath of the siege, members of the South Carolina delegation to Congress expressed their gratitude to Lincoln in friendly correspondence. A year later Dr. David Ramsay, one of the South Carolina Privy Council, who had spent the year after the surrender in a St. Augustine prison, wrote Lincoln: "Much does Carolina owe to you. In your time, and with your materials, it was greatly meritorious to keep things together so long as they were. *It is not in mortals to command success; but you have done more, you deferred it.*"[6]

Still, there were those, such as William Clajon, who respected Lincoln's "good sense and integrity" but failed to see "how the General's reputation [would] be preserved." It was for this very reason that Lincoln had requested the formal congressional inquiry into his command to clear his name of any dishonorable taint. Thus, it came as a particular blow to Lincoln when Washington decided that "the circumstances of the campaign" would not immediately allow the kind of investigation the New Englander wanted. Washington gave other reasons for the decision, first among them being the lack of any documentation from the Southern Department. There was also the absence of a number of key figures in the affair as well as Lincoln's own status as a prisoner of war. But, quite possibly, Washington also wished to avoid a proceeding that would have pointed out the shortcomings of Congress, the military command, and the southern states as well as Lincoln's command decisions. Pointing fingers at this critical juncture would only be counterproductive. The inquiry was postponed, never to be held.[7]

If the public's reaction to Lincoln's role in the Charleston disaster was mixed, so too was its response to the disaster itself. Initially, many felt as William C. Houston did that "no greater Stroke has befallen us since the Commencement of the War." That general sentiment was echoed by another: "God knows what will become of us." Yet days later the shock began to wear off, and Houston would write: "[The] catastrophe is indeed disastrous, but it is only a Fall in the Race. The Business is to be up and forward, not to sit still and lament." Some had hopes that the defeat would stir the country from the lethargy that had gripped the war effort since Saratoga. In fact, reports from Philadelphia indicated that the news had done precisely that. "Far from producing Despondency," wrote James Duane, the defeat "has pointed out the Necessity of Vigour in Government, and Exertion in the Citizens, in such strong Colours that the Flame of patriotism once more illuminates and revives our slumbering spirits." Alexander Hamilton might grouse that, if the loss of Charleston were a blessing, it was "a blessing in a very strange disguise." But, from Boston, Abigail Adams reflected a more generous spirit. Writing to her husband, John, in France, she noted that the loss of the city "excites not the Rage" that other defeats had. Charleston, she wrote, "after a Gallant Defence yealded to superior force, and is considerd as a misfortune, and each one is reanimated with spirit to remedy the Evil." By recognizing the importance of a "Gallant Defence" to the war effort, Lincoln might have been right when he chose to defend the city instead of giving it up without a fight.[8]

Once through the ordeal in Philadelphia, Lincoln returned to Hingham and a joyful family reunion. His two-year absence had been deeply felt. His children were growing up without a father's guidance; his wife, Mary, had shouldered the burden of running the farm with whatever help she could find. During the spring of 1780, while Lincoln was shoring up the defenses of Charleston, Ben Jr.'s letters from home demanded attention he could not give. Lincoln's second son, Theodore, was having difficulties preparing for Harvard. Martin, his third son, was sensitive and a good athlete but an indifferent scholar. As usual, money was a problem as "the expenses of the family are necessarily exceedingly great." Ben Jr. tried his best to oversee his brothers' and sisters' education by arranging for tutors and writing long letters to them on manners and comportment. But it was a heavy responsibility. "The older I grow," he wrote his father, "the more I lament your absence."[9]

Ben Jr. also was at a turning point in his career and needed his father's advice. After graduating from Harvard, he had studied law with Levi Lincoln, a prominent local lawyer and distant relation in Worchester, Massachusetts. Ben reasoned that he could gain more experience at less expense there than in Boston. Now, however, Ben wanted to finish his studies in Boston, to widen his circle of connections and "acquire some further acquaintance with the etiquette of the polite world necessary to unite the Gentleman with the schollar." He was an ambitious young man, whose father supported his ambitions. Lincoln's exposure to southern manners and society and his army service throughout the continent had opened his eyes to the grand opportunities open to ambitious, bright young men like his son. Ben had already outgrown Hingham; soon Massachusetts would no longer hold him. To take advantage of these new opportunities, however, a man needed a continental vision and the ability to move in society wherever he went. Lincoln felt so strongly about this that he proposed to Ben that they make "a tour of America" to expose him to each state's "constitution, lands, customs, genius and political economy." He also advised Ben to spend time "in the best and most polite company" and even to attend a dancing school. A new world was being created, a new "constellation," whose bounds were only limited by a man's imagination. And Lincoln wanted Ben to be ready to exploit it to the full.[10]

Life would have been sweet that summer had it not been for the "mortification" of being a prisoner of war and knowing that some 1,500 soldiers lay ill treated and confined in far-off South Carolina. Lincoln pushed for a general exchange of prisoners but was rebuffed by Washington for reasons of policy. An exchange of general officers and their "families" would be admissible, wrote Washington, but to release the thousands of private soldiers held prisoner by the Americans would provide critical reinforcements to an enemy for the first time stretched thin between north and south. Despite Lincoln's repeated arguments, policy won out over "justice and humanity." On 19 September 1780 Lincoln met with William Phillips, a British general taken prisoner at Saratoga and then free on parole, for a personal exchange in Elizabethtown, New Jersey. While this conference proved unsuccessful, an exchange was agreed to in early November which freed 140 officers, including Lincoln and his aides, William Jackson and Hodijah Baylies, and 476 privates. None of the private soldiers of the southern army were exchanged.[11]

Lincoln's exchange was welcome news. So was Washington's request that Lincoln supervise the recruitment of Massachusetts' quota of Continental troops, a job that would permit Lincoln to remain near home until spring. It also would give him time to renew old friendships and political ties and allow him to become acquainted with a Massachusetts undergoing some unsettling changes. The Charleston debacle apparently had not damaged Lincoln's stature in his home state. Immediately after his return from Philadelphia, in the summer of 1780, Lincoln was awarded an honorary master's degree from Harvard College. And in the fall rumors circulated that Lincoln would make a good state governor. But in Hingham, as a town meeting in early December revealed, the townspeople were so discouraged "by the Insupportable Burthens" laid on them for the war that they "declared it was high time to know the state of our Finances, and what Genl. Lincoln's pay & rations were." The assertiveness that once rocked the British Empire was now aimed at Hingham's first citizen. For Lincoln's part, learning that his neighbors thought he was profiting from their sacrifices no doubt stung him to the quick. Nonetheless, it was upon these very neighbors that the war effort rested. It was imperative that Lincoln face their questions and regain their confidence. At a town meeting later in the month Lincoln mended his political fences, for nothing more was heard about the incident.[12]

The winter passed swiftly as Lincoln turned his attention to recruiting and clothing the new recruits. In February, in the midst of his official duties, he was called on by John Laurens to enlist some troops to make up the crew of the frigate *Alliance,* headed to France on an official mission. Laurens, who served under Lincoln in the South, signified his appreciation by writing to Washington that the New Englander's "zeal in the service of his country is indefatigable." When the Massachusetts Council requested Lincoln's advice on the best means of securing the defenses of Maine, a region of the Commonwealth, the general presented them with an exhaustive series of questions that covered all aspects of a possible British invasion. He then wrote a letter to the Massachusetts delegation in Congress urging them to strengthen the Falmouth works and provide for the defense of Maine.[13]

Lincoln's recruiting duties were interrupted on 1 March by orders from the Massachusetts Council to take command of the state's militia forces and march to Newport, Rhode Island. The French general Jean Baptiste Donatier, comte de Rochambeau, and some four thousand troops were garrisoned there, awaiting the start of offensive operations against the British, but the sudden appearance of a British fleet threatened the peace of the encampment. Lincoln's militiamen reinforced the garrison until the French and English fleets weighed anchor and the danger of an invasion passed. It is also likely that Lincoln participated in the planning talks that followed Washington's arrival in Newport on 6 March. It was here that the Franco-American allies agreed on an assault on New York City later in the year. Afterward, with Rochambeau's accord, Lincoln dismissed the Massachusetts militia with thanks and returned home.[14]

A few months later Lincoln rejoined the main army under Washington at New Windsor, New York, on 15 June 1781. The army, joined now by the French, under Rochambeau, moved cautiously toward New York City, planning to attack the British stronghold there. The allied force, altogether less than 8,000 men, faced Clinton's 14,500 regulars, strongly entrenched on Manhattan Island. Although the French were unhappy with the idea of attacking the city, Washington insisted on testing British defenses. His opening move was to order Lincoln to attack Fort Knyphausen on Manhattan Island or, if that was not possible, to cooperate with the Duc de Lauzun in trapping a Tory cavalry corps at Morrisania. The amphibious movement took place on the night of 2 July, as Lincoln and 800 men rowed down the Hudson River and landed near Spuyten Duyvil on the northern end of Manhattan. Early the next morning the Americans were discovered near Harlem, and a battle ensued. Lauzan's troops came up in support of Lincoln, and both units were able to disengage and retreat. While unsuccessful, the action permitted Washington and Rochambeau a closer look at British defenses, which confirmed for the Frenchman his opposition to an assault on New York City.[15]

While operations were suspended around New York and the allied high command wrestled with alternative plans, Washington sent Lincoln north to the western counties of Massachusetts to hasten the mustering of militia for the defense of Albany and the western frontier. This he accomplished in little more than a week, returning to camp about the middle of August. He was just in time to participate in readying the main army for its march south to Virginia.[16]

Rochambeau's reluctance to beard the British lion in its den by attacking New York forced Washington to look elsewhere for a chance to strike a decisive blow. He focused on his native Virginia, where Lord Cornwallis had begun to fortify Yorktown, a port on Chesapeake Bay. If the French navy could gain control of the lower bay, a concentration of the allied army around Yorktown could bottle up Cornwallis's army on the York peninsula and force his surrender. Rochambeau had already requested the aid of Adm. François de Grasse, whose ships were cruising in the West Indies. De Grasse could guarantee local naval superiority, and the army reinforcements he could bring would tip the balance in favor of the allies. While allied forces continued to probe the New York defenses with repeated attacks that summer, French and American generals discussed a southern expedition over convivial dinners. The high command waited anxiously for word from de Grasse.[17]

When word came that de Grasse had agreed with the allied plans and was sailing for the Chesapeake, the combined armies shifted into high gear. Washington knew that speed was essential if the plan was to work. De Grasse had promised to continue the blockade until 15 October and no longer. Of the American commanders none knew better than Lincoln that such a deadline could spell the expedition's failure. A swift march was necessary to prevent Cornwallis from breaking out of the York peninsula and escaping southward. At the moment only Lafayette and a thin cordon of Continentals stood between him and safety. Only rapid reinforcement could trap Cornwallis's army.[18]

Among the command decisions made in those critical days that followed was the choice of Benjamin Lincoln to lead the American army southward. Washington explained his decision as simply one of seniority. Heath was in command of the Hudson Highlands, Greene was making his reputation in the South, and Lord Stirling was too ill to make the trip. As a courtesy to the commander of the troops designated for the march to Virginia, Washington reached out of the line of seniority to offer the job to Alexander McDougall. When the New Yorker refused, however, Washington did not press him, and Lincoln was given the job. It was Lincoln's responsibility to shepherd the twenty-five hundred Continental soldiers along the four hundred–mile journey from New York to Virginia, guarding against desertion and the pillaging of citizens along the route and organizing supplies and campgrounds. It was up to him also to move these men along at a desperate pace. As Washington insisted in orders to Lincoln, "The success of our enterprize depends upon the celerity of our Movements; delay therefore, may be ruinous to it."[19]

The allied armies slipped away from New York without provoking a British movement against their vulnerable left flank and rear. Washington kept the army's Virginia destination secret from all but the high command. Using part of his army to feint toward New York, he ordered the rest of the troops to march south. By the time the troops reached Trenton, New Jersey, speculation was at an end. Their destination was known and their escape from New York made good. The road lay before them, open all the way to Yorktown.[20]

The march could have been a logistical nightmare, but Washington's attention to detail, the long experience of the veteran Continentals, and Lincoln's competent hand ensured a smooth trip. By 6 September the

Americans had arrived at Head of Elk, Maryland, at the northernmost tip of Chesapeake Bay. They had marched two hundred miles in fifteen days.[21]

Lincoln encountered his only serious problem when the army marched through Philadelphia. On 2 September the American army, with Lincoln and the other generals at its head, snaked through the dusty streets of the capital city. For Lincoln, as he reviewed the troops, it was a proud but anxious moment. Just over a year earlier he had left Philadelphia under a cloud of defeat. This time, if all the elements came together, he would return a victor. The line of march extended two miles, and the soldiers "raised a dust like a smothering snow storm," blinding themselves and onlookers.[22]

The army's reception by the populace was as warm as the weather. But these rawboned men, lean and toughened by exposure and meager rations, were struck by the contrast between themselves and the well-fed and prosperous Philadelphians. Soldiers who had not seen a penny of pay for years grumbled in anger and frustration. Men thought of mutiny, and word got out that the army would not move without some pay. Since the success of the campaign hung on the rapid movement of the army to Virginia, pay for the troops was essential. When Lincoln told Washington of this new development, the commander-in-chief turned to the superintendent of finances, Robert Morris, for relief. Morris had been appointed by Congress in March 1781 to bring order out of the country's chaotic finances. This crisis was among the first that Morris handled, and he swiftly found a solution. Pledging his own credit, he borrowed twenty thousand dollars in coin from the French. This was not quite enough to give Lincoln's column one month's pay. It was enough, however, to raise the men's spirits, quiet their anger, and get them on their way.[23]

The lack of sufficient shipping to transport the troops and their baggage down Chesapeake Bay forced the allies to split up. Lincoln, repeatedly urged by Washington to hurry, took ship at Head of Elk with two divisions and the artillery, leaving port on 12 September. He sent Gen. James Clinton and his New York regiments to Baltimore to embark; the French found boats at Annapolis, which they left on 17 September. What should have been a rapid trip down the bay was delayed by bad weather and Washington's order to halt. De Grasse had sailed out of the bay to face the British navy off the Virginia Capes. It was only on de Grasse's victorious return that Washington sent word to Lincoln to "hurry on . . . with your Troops upon the wind of Speed." The allied transports completed their journey, arriving in the James River near Williamsburg between 22 and 24 September. Washington himself arrived in the old Virginia capital on 23 September to find Lincoln's troops and stores "in much better condition and with much less loss than could be expected." All was gotten ready for a general advance of the combined army to the British lines before Yorktown some twelve miles away. Those orders Washington gave on 28 September.[24]

Cornwallis, in the meantime, encouraged by Sir Henry Clinton's promises of relief, was digging in and preparing for a short siege. With Clinton certain to relieve him, Cornwallis had decided it was too risky to fight his way through Lafayette's small force. But the presence of the French navy had not only shut the sea door against help from New York; it also had provided reinforcements for Lafayette's thin band. Now the arrival of the allied army increased Cornwallis's predicament by completing the encirclement of his position. His sole hope was that the British navy could fight its way through to him. For the first time in the long war Washington had concentrated an army superior to the enemy in men, artillery, and supplies. Unless something went dreadfully wrong, the British would be forced to surrender.[25]

Washington took care that nothing would go wrong. Assisted by French engineers, Henry Knox's artillery, and the experience of Lincoln and Steuben, Washington prepared for a formal siege along the lines of the siege the British had conducted at Charleston. With the Americans holding the right wing, with Lincoln commanding the post of honor, and the French on the left, siege operations were begun on 7 October. On that night of "extreme darkness" Lincoln led a large detachment forward to open the first parallel. The business was conducted with "great silence and secrecy" and nearly finished by morning. On 9 October Washington began the cannonade with great ceremony. Two days later the second parallel was begun, and it soon became evident that the weight of allied artillery was overwhelming. Lincoln predicted on 12 October that the British would not last another twelve days. In fact, it would be five.[26]

On 17 October Cornwallis sent the allies a cease-fire proposal. The next day two commissioners, one of whom was John Laurens, who had been with Lincoln at Charleston, met with the British to decide the terms of surrender. Laurens insisted on humiliating the British by offering them the same terms that Lincoln had been forced to accept at Charleston. So it was that on the afternoon of 19 October the British army, "Cased Colours" and playing an English tune, paraded out of Yorktown between the French and American armies, standing to attention on either side of the road. In the absence of Cornwallis, who was "indisposed," Gen. Charles O'Hara carried out the formalities of surrender. Lincoln, as second-in-command, took the British surrender and directed the movement of the enemy troops to an open field, where they grounded arms and gave up their battle flags.[27]

It was a sweet moment for the Americans, and especially for Benjamin Lincoln. All the bitterness, fatigue, and frustration of hundreds of campaign days could, for a moment, be forgotten; the gall and humiliation of Charleston was purged by that glorious October sight. John Pierce, who knew Lincoln well, wrote later to Henry Knox that, while the surrender ceremonies at Yorktown would have been particularly pleasing to the defeated commander of Charleston, "his Philosophy 'tis probable to me did not suffer his countenance to betray the feelings of his heart in one Case nor the other." Even in that glorious moment Lincoln did not lose his self-control. As he solemnly directed the British army to the field of surrender, Lincoln could bask in the glory that long had eluded him. Soon other duties, other burdens, would weigh upon him. First would come the long march northward and then new responsibilities. But for this one moment, in a shining field of honor, time must have stood still.[28]

Old Ship Meetinghouse, Hingham. (Courtesy of Franklin Beveridge.)

Burial monument of Benjamin Lincoln in the graveyard of the Old Ship Meetinghouse, Hingham. (Courtesy of Franklin Beveridge.)

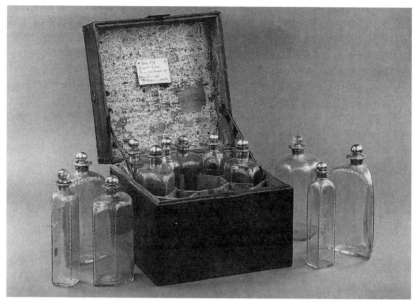

Benjamin Lincoln's traveling liquor case. (Courtesy of Franklin Beveridge.)

Benjamin Lincoln House, Hingham. (Courtesy of Franklin Beveridge.)

Portrait of Benjamin Lincoln, by J. R. Smith, 1809. (Courtesy of Franklin Beveridge.)

Portrait of Mary Cushing Lincoln, by J. R. Smith, 1809. (Courtesy of Franklin Beveridge.)

The Surrender of Lord Cornwallis at Yorktown, 19 October 1781, by John Trumbull. (Trumbull Collection, Yale University Art Gallery.)

Theodore Lincoln House, Dennysville, Maine, ca. 1909. (Courtesy of Rebecca Hobart.)

Portrait of Benjamin Lincoln, by Henry Sargent, 1805. (Courtesy of the Massachusetts Historical Society.)

Benjamin Lincoln's watch. (Courtesy of the Massachusetts Historical Society.)

Portrait of Benjamin Lincoln, by Charles Willson Peale, 1781–82.
(Courtesy of Independence National Historical Park.)

CHAPTER EIGHT

Secretary at War

Congress have at length completed the organization of their executive
departments by the choice of General Lincoln for their Secretary at War.
It is expected that order and system will arise out of this mode of doing
business and the strictest economy.

Robert R. Livingston

A year before the siege of Yorktown a decisive American victory had
seemed unlikely. The catastrophe at Charleston, Benedict Arnold's treason, and a bankrupt and dispirited Congress together marked the low
point in the struggle for independence from Great Britain. The states'
ratification of the Articles of Confederation in early 1781, however, infused new life into a moribund Congress. Expressing a renewed sense of
determination and initiative, Congress departed radically from the past
and created a number of executive departments to replace the congressional committees that previously had directed the war. They placed one
man at the head of each department to carry out the policies of Congress
in the areas of finance, foreign relations, war, and marine affairs.[1]

Despite some difficulties, Congress quickly appointed Robert Morris
as superintendent of finance and Robert R. Livingston as secretary of
foreign affairs in the spring of 1781. When Alexander McDougall declined the ministry of marine, that post was added to Morris's already
onerous duties. That left the appointment of a secretary at war.[2]

As early as February 1781, it was clear that choosing an executive for
the war office would be difficult. Some members of Congress balked at
the very idea, afraid that any new appointee would be worse than the
existing personnel on the Board of War. But the greatest problem was
finding someone with the necessary stature who also was politically acceptable. Gouverneur Morris, soon to become Robert Morris's deputy in
the Office of Finance, briefly sketched his idea of the requirements of such

a man. "Our Minister of War," he wrote, "should have a mind penetrating, clear, methodical, comprehensive, joined with a firm and indefatigable spirit." He should have military experience and a knowledge of American geography and natural resources. Most of all, however, "he should be attached to the civil head of the empire," be "disagreeable to no considerable body or denomination of men, and by all means [be] agreeable to the commander in chief." In the tangled world of congressional intrigue and ambition, that was a tall order.[3]

When he sketched out his idea, Morris clearly had Nathanael Greene in mind. Others in Congress had their favorites, and the factions quickly lined up behind them. Washington privately expressed his pleasure to Philip Schuyler that the New Yorker was "generally spoken of" for the position, and he urged Schuyler to accept the post if the choice should fall on him. Horatio Gates had his proponents, as did John Sullivan, now a congressman from New Hampshire. But each of these candidates proved unacceptable to one or another congressional faction. A New Englander, Sullivan was known for his bad temper and blunt manner, nor did he have the appropriate weight of command. Both Gates and Schuyler had the stature for the position, but either appointment would have reopened the wounds left by their bitter struggle over the Northern Department in 1777, further polarizing a divided Congress. Besides, Schuyler would have taken the position only if he were reinstated to his former rank as major general, a move that would have seriously disconcerted many general officers. And Gates still faced an inquiry into his questionable conduct at the Battle of Camden. Faced with deadlock, Congress postponed further consideration of the appointment until 1 October 1781.[4]

Washington, who thought that a war department with a single executive was the first step toward "system, order and oeconomy" in military affairs, was incensed at the postponement. "I have heard no reason assigned for it," he wrote Schuyler, "and am uncharitable enough to believe that no *good one* can be given." Reasons there were aplenty, but, as Washington suspected, they were purely political. Gates's adherents wanted a postponement of the decision until after the Camden inquiry had absolved their champion of the charge of misconduct. Samuel Adams and other New England delegates wanted a postponement to keep John Sullivan from the appointment because, according to Sullivan, he had "apostasized from the true New England Faith by sometimes voting with the Southern states." Adams, who thought the previous executive appointments were weighted heavily in New York's favor, wanted a New Englander who could be relied on to represent the interests of that region. Finally, New England antipathy for Schuyler was enough to block his selection.[5]

While Congress squabbled, the Board of War muddled along, shifting for itself as best it could. Though hints were dropped to Washington that Congress would be happy to appoint whomever the commander-in-chief wanted for the post, the general was preoccupied with preparations for the allied attack on New York City and, later, the Yorktown campaign. Nor did Washington want to become involved in a political battle over the appointment. In the meantime an energetic Robert Morris took up the slack by providing pay and supplies to the Continental troops marching to Yorktown in September. With all eyes focused on the military campaign there was little pressure on Congress for an immediate decision.[6]

On 2 October Congress again made a vain attempt to elect a secretary at war. The members did agree, however, on two things: the office should be "the reward of continued and active field service," and the candidate should be a New Englander. After a long and inconclusive debate three generals were nominated: Nathanael Greene, Henry Knox, and Benjamin Lincoln. There were objections to each man. Greene, as commander of the Southern Department, was considered indispensable where he was. Knox also, as chief of artillery, and thus head of a special branch of the service, would be difficult to replace in the field. That left Lincoln, who, while he met all the criteria for office, was objectionable to some members of Congress as "too easy in his temper, not sufficiently a man of business, nor sturdy enough to reject importunity." The Charleston defeat still cast a long shadow over his reputation. The post of secretary at war in a period of tight finances would be a difficult one; the man who held it would have to execute unpopular policies. It was not a post for a weak man.[7]

Thus, the election of Lincoln as secretary at war on 30 October 1781, "after Long struggles," came as a surprise. Never having spent much time in Philadelphia, Lincoln was an unknown quantity to many. Robert R. Livingston was probably not alone in his reaction. Lincoln, he wrote, "with all his virtues as a man and an officer . . . will want sufficient activity of Genious for so embarassing a Department." Gouverneur Morris, who was to work closely with Lincoln in the next two years, was more sanguine. Although disappointed that Greene had not won the post, he thought Lincoln had the makings of a "good Minister, if not a great one," because he was honest, sensible, and industrious and would quickly restore "order and regularity" to the chaotic affairs of military administration. The appointment proved popular with the army, if the testimony of the congressional delegates from Rhode Island is any indication: "The confidence that the Commander-in-Chief and the army in general has in the Secretary at War is such, that when we add to his knowledge and experience as an officer, his integrity and attention to business, we cannot but flatter ourselves that the public will receive essential benefits from his appointment." Lincoln accepted the post readily with the usual protestations about the "arduous duties" it entailed and his own "inabilities fully to discharge them." He made sure that he kept his rank in the army (though not his salary) and explained to his son that duty required his acceptance, however much "it greatly interferes with my domestic views." He yearned to go home and repair his tattered fortunes, yet, as he explained, "My country demands of me another kind of service." It made little difference if the post was in the field or in the cabinet—"a public servant must obey."[8]

In retrospect the reasons for Lincoln's appointment are clear. He was a New Englander, available for service and fresh from the triumph at Yorktown. Lincoln was respected within the army and carried the weight of long military experience, including an independent command. Despite the loss at Charleston, he was acceptable to all the factions in Congress. He had a reputation for scrupulously observing the fine line between military and civil power and thus posed no threat to the authority of Congress. He had a comfortable relationship with Washington and worked well with him. And, finally, Lincoln had a reputation as a frugal man, who could be expected to bring a sense of economy into army affairs. All in all it would prove to be an excellent, if not an inspired, choice for the new post.[9]

Lincoln arrived in Philadelphia on 24 November and by 1 December had plunged into the work that had been piling up since spring. The scope of his new duties was staggering, and the disorganization that he found in the records and procedures of the old Board of War was dizzying. In the first few days of his tenure Lincoln received letters requesting action on matters of supply, promotion, prisoners of war, army contracts, and the forced retirement of officers. The office had to be reorganized and a number of subordinates appointed. Authorized by Congress to appoint an assistant secretary and clerks, Lincoln chose William Jackson, one of his former aides-de-camp, as assistant secretary. Jackson proved a diligent and trustworthy man for the job.[10]

In establishing the office of secretary at war, Congress ordered the secretary to keep "the returns and present state of the troops, ordnance, arms, ammunition, cloathing and supplies" of the Continental army, including all the stores and equipment in the country's magazines. In addition, the secretary was to form estimates of the military supplies needed for future campaigns and prepare cost estimates for recruiting and paying the troops. Also, he was to draw up and keep a register of all military commissions and "execute all the resolutions of Congress respecting military preparations." For this the secretary would receive five thousand dollars a year (later reduced to four thousand dollars per year). While seemingly a princely sum, the salary was barely enough even for the economical Lincoln to cover expenses in costly Philadelphia.[11]

As originally envisioned by Congress, the secretary at war was to be little more than a glorified clerk. Yet from the beginning Congress, the commander-in-chief, and the army expected Lincoln to exert a great deal of control over the management of all military affairs except those involving actual field command. Washington wrote a subordinate early in January that "Genl. Lincoln has accepted his appointment of Secretary at War; proper plans of oeconomy are adopting in every department; and I do not despair of seeing, ere long our Affairs under much better management than they have been." Congress officially acknowledged this state of affairs in a resolution of 10 April 1782 expanding Lincoln's powers. His additional duties included the direction of the clothier general and distribution of clothing to the army, the supervision of the commissary general of prisoners and the "care and direction of the prisoners of war," the construction and management of "laboratories, arsenals, foundries, magazines, barracks and other public buildings," and the power to hold general courts-martial in the absence of the commander-in-chief. Also, Lincoln was directed to "give his opinion on all such subjects as shall be referred to him by Congress." Lincoln was to be Congress's military adviser on policy matters as well as its executive in military affairs.[12]

Lincoln's priority as secretary at war was to maintain a strong Continental army in the field. All other goals were secondary. Only by preparing to carry out the war, he believed, could a peace beneficial to the United States be achieved. And the only means to continue the war was to support the army as a striking force. In this Washington agreed. "You know it is an old and true Maxim that to make a good peace," wrote Washington, "you ought to be well prepared to carry on the war." This idea, he continued, was well understood and emphasized "by the Gentlemen at the heads of our three great departments." Once the war office was organized the next big job facing Lincoln was to lay the groundwork for the army's summer plans. "Two things appear to me to be essentially necessary as the Basis and foundation of all the Arrangements of the ensuing Campaign," Washington wrote to Lincoln in January: "effectual measures for filling up the Army, and certain prospects of being able to support it." In the same letter Washington posed a host of policy questions to the new executive of the war office which focused on supply, money, transport, shelter, and clothing—the sine qua non of any military campaign.[13]

Those questions forced Lincoln to turn to Robert Morris, the super-intendent of finance, a blunt, forceful, and immensely competent Phila-delphia merchant. Because of the impoverished state of the Treasury, Morris had been given extraordinary powers to direct the finances of the Confed-eration. Since Morris held the purse strings, it was important that Lincoln reach an understanding with the Financier, as Morris came to be called, about the demands that would be placed upon him by the army. At the beginning of their working relationship it seemed as if that understanding had been reached. Morris was anxious that the heads of the various de-partments, Congress, and the commander-in-chief join in a common ef-fort to conduct the war. It was Morris who suggested that the three department heads—Livingston of foreign affairs, Lincoln of the war of-fice, and himself—meet every Monday evening with the secretary of Con-gress, Charles Thomson, Morris's assistant, Gouverneur Morris, and (whenever possible) George Washington, "for the purpose of Communi-cating to each other whatever may be necessary and for Consulting and Concerting Measures to promote the Service and Public Good." These "cabinet meetings" proved to be a great success and provided a degree of coordination among the departments which had been rare before. It was in these weekly meetings in December and January that the basic require-ments and general arrangements for the coming campaign were hammered out. When Morris promised, early in the winter of 1782, to "make every exertion I am capable of to support the Generals measures so as to enable him to operate Vigorously," it seemed as if the leaders of the Confedera-tion indeed spoke with one voice.[14]

But it was Robert Morris's voice that spoke loudest and set the tone for the "administration." Given the near bankrupt state of Continental finances before his appointment and the shaky ground upon which his own measures were founded, Morris was not alone in feeling that economy must be given priority. The army, Morris believed, while important, was not the pillar upon which the Revolution rested—or, as Henry Knox put it, "the hoop to the barrel, or Cement to the Union." Public credit was. Morris believed that to strengthen the Confederation and bring the war to an end the government had to restore its public credit, which had been destroyed through printing vast amounts of paper money, the paper's sub-sequent depreciation, and the loss of faith in the government which the collapse of the financial system had caused. Restore public credit, Morris believed, and you would restore public support for the war. To accom-plish this, Morris insisted that Congress have a stable source of revenue independent of the states, achieved through the levying of some kind of federal tax. The revenue thus raised must then be spent frugally and honestly. Morris counted on the success of his plan to support the army's continued presence in the field. If necessary, the army could be sacrificed; public credit could not.[15]

Lincoln was not alarmed by Morris's insistence on economy in the administration of military affairs, for it fitted nicely with his own predilections. Frugality was a byword in his personal life and a virtue of his New England upbringing, figuring often in the letters he wrote his sons during the war. "Economy is the parent of greatness," he wrote to his son Theodore. "Nothing should be lost, wasted or wantonly used [and] everything improved so as to yield the greatest good." But Lincoln also made the distinction between economy, "which makes men exceedingly happy," and parsimony, which, he wrote, denies us "the enjoyment of the pleasures of life." Lincoln's experience as commander of the Southern Department had taught him that money was the engine of war: little could be accomplished without adequate funds. No matter how frugal a commander, no matter how lean a budget, wars cost money.[16]

From the beginning, then, the seeds of misunderstanding were sown. Lincoln and Washington valued economy, but not at the cost of the war effort. Morris, on the other hand, believed everything was secondary to reestablishing public credit. When Lincoln agreed with Morris that "the utmost frugality must be practised and every call for Money or Expenditures that can be withstood must be so until the States pay in their Taxes," he did not imagine that Morris would consider bringing the war machinery to a clanking halt. For Lincoln some expenditures were unavoidable. If officers and men could not be paid their salaries or subsistence money, they should at least be well fed. The army must march and thus boots must be supplied; it must be able to fire its cannons and muskets, and so powder and shot must be found. Tents and clothing, wagons and oxen, swords and horses for the cavalry, all were needed to put the army in fighting trim. As Washington succinctly put it, "I am exceedingly impressed with the Necessity of Oeconomizing the public Monies; but we must not spin this Thread so fine as to break it." Lincoln planned that winter and spring for an aggressive campaign, seeking estimates from the quartermaster general, the clothier general, and the commander of the Southern Department.[17]

Lincoln's next task was to place army administration and supply upon a rational, efficient, and economical basis. Congress's decision in 1779 to stop printing Continental money had forced it to turn to the states to support the army. Requisitions from the states had proved to be an abysmal failure; money was rarely supplied, and staple goods and clothing arrived fitfully at best. Without the influx of French gold and silver in 1780 and 1781 the army would surely have disintegrated. But by December 1781, while still dependent on the states for revenue, Robert Morris had taken the first giant step toward bringing order out of economic chaos by pioneering a system of supply contracts for the army, backed by his personal credit. Lincoln's responsibility was to work with Morris and Washington to iron out problems between the army and the contractors, fielding the often bitter complaints of army officers and laying down rules for the equitable distribution of rations among the ranks.[18]

Another unpleasant duty Lincoln immediately faced was the need to retire a number of officers on half-pay. The army's inability to recruit soldiers had required a reduction in the number of regiments, making many officers superfluous. "We are paying an host of useless officers," wrote Henry Knox to Lincoln, "who disgust the country at home and deprive the officers in the field of their proper advantages." A resolution of Congress of 21 December 1781 authorized Lincoln to reduce the number of general officers but said nothing about the lesser ranks. Washington's opposition to the reduction of the officer corps was enough to block any immediate plans for a reform of the army. But the idea continued to percolate in Congress and soon would require a response.[19]

On 10 January, with the general arrangements for the coming campaign nearly completed, Lincoln asked Congress's permission to visit his home to take care of personal business. Along with his own affairs Lincoln carried with him a great deal of public business. When he left Philadelphia on 25 January the New Englander carried seventy-five hundred dollars' worth of Morris's notes, which he was to exchange with the governors of the New England states for ready money. He carried as well a promise he had given to Morris "generally to exert himself to assist [Morris's] claims and Calls as well as those of Congress upon the Eastern States for Money, Revennue &c." The duties of his own department included the disposition of a cargo of gunpowder in Boston harbor, checking into the supply of salted provisions in each of the New England states, and supervising the awarding of supply contracts for Springfield, Boston, and points north. Lincoln spent about a month in New England, returning to Philadelphia around the first of March.[20]

On his return Lincoln once again attacked the mountain of work that awaited him—work requiring not only great attention to detail but all the persuasive powers he could muster as well. The New Englander became a determined advocate of the army's primary place in the war effort. He was, in effect, the army's point man with Congress and the superintendent of finance. As such, he tangled with Morris more than once over the expenses of the army. On the whole, however, Morris valued Lincoln as a "man of sound Sense, sterling Integrity and true Patriotism." And the Financier relied on Lincoln's cooperation to ensure that the administration of the war effort ran smoothly. Morris was especially indebted to Lincoln for his on-site handling of the knotty problems that arose from the new contract supply system, problems Lincoln used his influence and persuasive powers to solve. Although the bluff Morris overshadowed all but Washington in the executive "cabinet," Lincoln could be just as stubborn. In some cases he persuaded Morris to accept a proposal against the latter's better judgment. On a question of clothing purchase, for example, Lincoln humorously asked Morris to note in his diary that "by the Month of December next I [Morris] shall be convinced that his Advice on this Point is perfectly right and wise."[21]

But good humor soon gave way to frustration. When it became clear that the states were no more responsive to Morris's pleas for support than they had been under the old system, the Financier clamped down on the Treasury. Strapped for cash to meet his current obligations and pushed to the edge of his personal credit, Morris refused to pay for many items the army felt indispensable. As the Financier told Timothy Pickering, the quartermaster general, "It is better that the Campaign should Stop than that I should Authorize engagements which cannot be afterwards fullfilled." To get Morris's agreement to even the most essential disbursements now became a tremendous struggle for Lincoln. Finally, on 7 May 1782, Morris informed the secretary at war that he was not able to meet *any* of the estimated expenses of the quartermaster's department for the new campaign, a situation that would bring army operations to a grinding halt. Even for the usually cheerful Lincoln this was a shock. Should the British choose this moment to attack, the army would be helpless to oppose them. Morris, however, was implacable. Though it gave him the "greatest distress and anxiety" to know that this action would prolong the war, Morris wrote, he had no other choice. The states had not paid a penny of the two million–dollar congressional requisition. He, in turn, could not take on any further engagements until that money was paid.[22]

Lincoln passed on the news to Congress on 27 May. It made a grave impression. James Madison wrote to Virginia the next day that the news "shocks, rather than surprises, us." Obviously, Congress should have known, but did not, just how bad the Confederation's finances were. Congressional committees mustered their pens, as did Morris and George Washington, to send a barrage of letters to state leaders, pleading with them to fulfill their pledges of support. Congress even sent envoys to each state to plead its case.[23]

In the meantime relations between Lincoln and Morris soured. Morris's refusal to pay army expenses, however justified by the state of the country's finances, rankled the secretary at war. With the responsibility for the army's welfare on his shoulders Lincoln was humiliated by his inability to provide anything other than the most basic supplies and transportation of the troops. To friends such as Henry Knox he admitted that he was powerless to provide the items the army needed. To Knox alone Lincoln felt close enough to give vent to his resentment of Morris. "Consider how painful it is my friend to apply and be denied," Lincoln wrote. "Consider that my duty is, in time, to make the necessary estimates and lay them before the financier that *he* may take *his* measures for procuring the articles. This has been long since done, do not blame me because you do not receive that supply which I have it not in my power to procure." But, despite the obvious frustrations involved in his position, Lincoln refused to quit. He continued to meet with Morris nearly every day in order to divert a trickle of money to the army from the tiny stream of resources at the Financier's disposal.[24]

Despite its aggravations, the life of the secretary at war in Philadelphia was not all hard work. The capital of the United States had grown during the war years in luxury, culture—and expense. One Frenchman described Philadelphia as "the Paris and the Hague of America, where the brilliancy of our *beau monde* and the Sumptuosity and Elegance of their entertainments rivals those of the old world." It made a decided change from years spent on campaign, living on rum and rice and sleeping in a tent. Lincoln, as one of the first men of the country, was invited to dinners and balls given by the high society of America's greatest city. Some of these affairs were reminiscent of the rough and comradely tables he had shared while on campaign. New Year's Day in 1782 was one of those occasions, when he was among a number of generals at a dinner given by the Friendly Sons of Saint Patrick, in honor of George Washington. But in many cases Lincoln's stature as head of the war office required a degree of social grace which Lincoln found lacking. Dancing, for instance, even without his corked shoe and game leg, proved impossible for the old farmer. Writing to his son Theodore at Harvard, Lincoln insisted that the boy continue his French and dancing lessons. "I suffer exceedingly from the want of this kind of knowledge," he wrote ruefully. "I do not know how to introduce myself, or retire from a room, or even how to give a man my hand." As the symbolic head of the military, Lincoln was required to attend all the great ceremonial occasions, such as the public audiences for the French and Dutch ministers and the magnificent entertainment that the Chevalier de La Luzerne gave to celebrate the birth of the dauphin. Lincoln's portrait was painted by Charles Willson Peale and again by the Frenchman Pierre Eugène Du Simitière. That kind of attention was enough to turn even the most Republican of heads.[25]

There also were simpler pleasures. Lincoln delighted in long dinner conversations with his Massachusetts friends at their common boarding-house or philosophical rambles over a glass or two of wine at the Sign of the Buck tavern. Occasional rides into the countryside around Philadelphia provided relief from the congestion and fetid smells of the crowded city. And Lincoln indulged both his religious nature and his curiosity by visiting various churches in the city, including the Lutheran church, where services were held in German. His days in the office that summer also were broken by two short trips. On a visit to army headquarters at Newburgh, New York, Lincoln ironed out problems in the contract supply system. He also traveled through southern Pennsylvania for a week, visiting the prisoner-of-war camps at Lancaster, York, and Carlisle. In letters to friends Lincoln described the geography, soils, agricultural practices, and people he met. On one trip later that fall he encountered Joel Barlow, a promising poet fresh from Yale College. They rode the length of New Jersey, Barlow related, "without any remarkable occurence except friendship, merriment, and philosophy, which the General [Lincoln] dealt out in large rations . . . we got into several very learned disputes, which are yet unsettled, but which we are to adjudge before I return." Barlow added almost as an afterthought: "He is really one of our first characters, and he is as amiable as he is great."[26]

But there were many nights when neither public business nor social distractions were enough to occupy Lincoln's mind. The extraordinary flood of letters that Lincoln wrote to family and friends during his stay in Philadelphia is testimony to his feelings of homesickness and the inner turmoil and stress created by his position as secretary at war. These letters—which in their length and subject matter have more the character of essays than letters—also bear testimony to Lincoln's great curiosity about the natural and human world as well as his eagerness to engage in intellectual exchange. "Write to me by every post," he pleaded with his son Theodore, then in his first year at Harvard. "It will be good for you and will afford me pleasure." In return Lincoln wrote Theodore letters of advice on the conduct of a gentleman, including homilies on the nature of God and the comfort of prayer, frugality, and the avoidance of gambling, the importance of learning, and the governance of his passions by reason. To various gentlemen associated with the new American Academy of Arts and Sciences, of which he was a founding member, Lincoln wrote essays on plant diseases, surgery cases, trade, commerce, and the usefulness of philosophy to a soldier. To his friend Dr. Barker he wrote pieces on the nature of happiness and on grief and death. But to his son Ben, a young lawyer, whose own letters reveal considerable intellectual accomplishment, Lincoln poured out a remarkable series of letters, reflecting on current events, such as the massacre of the Moravian Indians at Gnadenhutten and the celebrated suicide of Major Galvan; descriptions of natural phenomena, such as the stratum of the James River in Virginia, which led Lincoln to reflect on the origin of the earth; and long descriptive letters about the southern states—their people, resources, and physical features. These letters reveal a restless and active spirit, a mind hungry for good conversation and the exchange of ideas on a wide range of subjects.[27]

But the social gatherings and letters home afforded little relief from the anxiety of administering the war office. The financial situation deteriorated over the summer of 1782, as the states continued to ignore congressional requisitions. Lincoln's desperate pleas for money met with little success, and the flow of funds from Morris's coffers slowed to a trickle. Meanwhile, the Financier was leaving no stone unturned in his search for money. His long-term plans were based on the levy of an import duty, which would provide Congress with a source of revenue independent of the states, a plan he described in a long "Report on Public Credit" sent to Congress on 29 July. But, for the short term, he borrowed large sums from the newly created Bank of North America and from wealthy merchants in Philadelphia on his personal credit. He also sold bills of exchange in anticipation of the proceeds from French and Dutch loans that were either already oversubscribed or still being negotiated. And Morris pleaded with "Gentlemen of influence" to write to prominent men in their respective states to urge the state governments to comply with the requisitions of Congress.[28]

Lincoln responded to Morris's request by writing to his acquaintances in Massachusetts, but the tenor of his letters to John Lowell, a former member of Congress, and to Artemas Ward, the former Continental army officer, would have displeased the Financier. For Morris reliance on the states was only a short-term solution. Nothing would cure the financial ills of the Confederation but an infusion of money from its own taxes.

Lincoln, who was as strong a believer in the union of the states as Morris, was, however, a pragmatist. And Lincoln believed that the 5 percent duty on imported goods upon which Morris based his hopes for an independent income did not have a ghost of a chance of being enacted. "I think it does not require, a very penetrating eye," he wrote Lowell, "to discover that a heavy cloud is fast gathering over the united states. Unless the greatest precautions are taken, and those speedily, it will burst and sweep away our feeble confederation, and endanger, if not overturn, the union of these states." The voluntary compliance of the states, Lincoln believed, was the only way to ensure a continuance of the war effort. Morris had recommended and Congress had proposed a 5 percent duty—"the least exceptional of any" tax yet debated—but it would not pass. And to make matters worse, Lincoln went on, he had heard rumors that the states were going to settle the debts of their own citizens against the United States and then charge the amount against their congressional requisitions. The move would further undercut the authority of Congress and make it impossible to carry on the war. In Lincoln's words, it would result in "the loss of the confederation, the annihilation of the Union and the ruin of the states."[29]

Despite the current crisis, however, Lincoln could not agree with Morris that the powers of Congress should be increased. "There is no medium," he wrote, "between the power they [Congress] now have, and a power of coercion." Giving Congress the power to coerce the states, Lincoln believed, would open a Pandora's box of evils, including a standing army in peacetime and the prospect of one state in arms against another. As Lincoln considered the problem, he was drawn again and again to the ideas of public virtue and voluntarism, which had animated his countrymen in the early days of the war. "I cannot see that we have any real foundation on which we may rest," he concluded, "but on the virtue and justice of the several states." However deeply he believed in the union of the states and the need for further sacrifice to see the war to a successful end, Lincoln could not condone a coercive central government. The states, however fickle to the aims of the Confederation, were the guardians of individual rights and liberties. And safeguarding those rights was, to Lincoln, the aim of the Revolution.[30]

Thus matters stood as news reached American shores that peace negotiations had been opened with Great Britain in early August 1782. The prospect of peace inspired in some Americans prayers of thanksgiving; in others, ambitious plans for the future. But few Americans were aware that one of the most dangerous periods of the Revolution was only just beginning.

CHAPTER NINE

Peace at Last

As long after [the Newburgh affair] as in 1798, the venerable Gen.
Lincoln remarked to me, that it was "then he trembled for his country."
Elbridge Gerry

For many Americans the news of peace negotiations with Great Britain was tantamount to a declaration of peace. Lincoln worried that the country was being lulled into a dangerous state of apathy. "We certainly should be on our guard," he wrote Henry Knox. "It is with us a very critical moment. The people tire under the real or supposed weight of the war and will therefore be easily induced to relax or acceed to terms not so honorable as they ought to claim and insist on." The British still occupied New York City and Charleston. The British ministry was liable to change, bringing a renewed commitment to the war. No one could foretell the shape of the peace to come. It was important, therefore, to maintain a unified front and not splinter into thirteen quarreling states.[1]

The prospect of peace also had disturbing effects on the army and, especially, the officer corps. The army had lived for years under the most scandalous conditions, treated little better than a starving dog. In the past year the soldiers had borne the brunt of Morris's economizing measures. While they had been fed in the year since Yorktown, they had not received a hint of pay from Congress. Morris was even finding it difficult to support his contracting system, warning Washington at the end of August that he soon would have to stop payment, unable to find the eight thousand dollars per month necessary for army rations. If private soldiers were content to return to their homes once peace had been secured, the officers bitterly resented their treatment. Having served for the duration of the war, they had, as a whole, sacrificed more than any other group of Americans—faced years of dangerous service, the loss of their private fortunes, and, in some cases, their health. Many were unable to resume professions

134

they had cast aside in order to serve. Bankrupt, with little more than their tattered commissions, they faced a bleak future. Thus, it was no surprise that, as Henry Knox put it, "the cry of peace has awakened the idea of half-pay, or compensation for service in some way."[2]

The idea of half-pay pensions for the officer corps, based on the British model, originated in the dreary winter at Valley Forge in 1777–78, when it was reluctantly proposed by Washington in order to stem the hemorrhage of officers' resignations which threatened to destroy the army. Washington, and most other military leaders, believed that the officer corps was the heart of the army, without which it could not survive. Private soldiers might, and did, come and go. But without seasoned officers engaged for the duration of the war the army could not maintain a continued presence in the field. Officers that winter, because of the lack of pay, supplies, and support, resigned their commissions in droves. Congress's answer, in a reluctant decision made in the spring of 1778, was to grant a half-pay pension for seven years to Continental officers upon their retirement. In October 1780, during a similar low point in the war, Congress extended the half-pay provision from seven years to a pension for life.[3]

Critics of the pension measure, especially in New England, had been vociferous in their opposition. Many objected to the cost, reasoning that, since all Americans had sacrificed for the war effort, it was unfair to create a special class of citizens and saddle the public with their support. Others equated officers' pensions with the corrupting influence of pensioners and placemen in the British administration. This kind of political corruption had skewed the delicate balance of the British constitution; it was not unreasonable to wonder whether, in the future, officers dependent on the government for their livelihood would not become a pressure group inimical to the public interest. But the greatest objection to pensions was that they offended one of the American revolutionary's strongest beliefs—that the war effort was based on public virtue. By declaring that they would not fight without a financial reward, the officers signaled to their countrymen that they were no better than the Hessian mercenaries hired to fight for Great Britain. Thus, the public perceived the officers as greedy men, bereft of virtue, holding American independence hostage for their own selfish purposes.[4]

The prospect of peace, coupled with the ever troubled state of the Treasury and the knowledge that the public did not support the half-pay pension, only seemed to fan the officers' resentment. They realized that the impetus to provide for them would be gone once peace was achieved. Congress seemed interested only in holding the situation together until peace was signed. For the legislators in Philadelphia the army was a two-edged sword: without it Congress was helpless to conclude a peace, and yet the cost of its support left the Confederation teetering on the edge of dissolution. But for others, such as Robert Morris and Alexander Hamilton, the officers' disgruntlement offered a chance to pressure Congress and the states to adopt legislation that would strengthen the Confederation. They sought to unite the officer corps with another group also interested in justice, the public creditors. This group of wealthy men had loaned money to the government and held securities in the form of loan office certificates, the only form of government security which paid interest. As long as the Confederation lacked independent funds to pay the interest and eventually the principal of these loans, the public creditors were unsecured. Morris hoped to consolidate the debt to the public creditors and the army as a national debt to be secured with national funds. It would be a tough, uncompromising fight, which Morris would lose in the end. And Lincoln's opposition would help to defeat it.[5]

By 1782 Lincoln's influence in military affairs had extended throughout the army and into Congress. This was especially so since the bulk of the Main Army, stationed in the Hudson Highlands, was made up of New England troops, most of whom were from Massachusetts. Among these men and their officers Lincoln had many friends and was highly respected. Morris assumed that Lincoln would use his influence to back the Financier's plan. Lincoln's first concern, however, was the army. He, too, wished to see the officers receive their just due, but, as a practical man, he found Morris's scheme illusory. He opposed the half-pay pension, and he seriously doubted that the states would give Congress the power to tax.[6]

From the beginning Lincoln opposed the pension measure, not for ideological reasons but because the officers would never be able to enjoy it. "The idea of half-pay is so opposed to the genius of New England," he wrote to Henry Knox in January 1781, "that the money will be paid with reluctance, the officers made unhappy in the use of it and his [sic] feelings constantly wounded by insinuations that he is a pensioner on public alms." Lincoln preferred the old colonial Massachusetts practice of a direct grant of money from the legislature "to be paid at the close of the war [with the] acknowledgement that the donation was the just tribute for their services." This belief came not from an idea that the officers did not deserve a special reward for their years of service but, rather, from Lincoln's pragmatism and knowledge of human nature: "I am convinced that one years pay at the close of the war or a fair settlement of past wages would be better for the officer and put more money in his pocket than half-pay for life."

Thus, when the idea of a commutation of the half-pay pension into a lump-sum payment gained currency among the officers at West Point, Lincoln supported it wholeheartedly.[7]

Furthermore, Lincoln wanted the officers to rely on the states for payment of what they were owed but to do so in a way that would reinforce the union of the states. He believed it would be possible for the states to pay in a manner that would support, rather than undercut, the authority of the Confederation government. All the debt should be settled as a national debt, he wrote to John Lowell that September. Once the extent of it was known, the debt would be apportioned among the states, and each state would pay its share by procuring the money in the mode most convenient to it. This would eliminate the need for a national tax, to which Lincoln believed the states would never agree. This was the reason that Lincoln disagreed with Henry Knox's plan to petition the Massachusetts legislature directly for half-pay and settlement of its officers' accounts. "No power had been delegated to congress authorizing the several states to settle the half-pay with their officers," he wrote Col. David Cobb, one of the Massachusetts officers. "The promise of half-pay was made by congress and not by particular states"; thus, Congress must first agree to allow the states to settle with their own Continental lines. Lincoln advised Cobb to encourage the officers of the whole army to apply directly to Congress and ask that each state be empowered to deal with its own troops. The Massachusetts officers ignored this advice and went ahead with their plans, only to meet a dead end when the Massachusetts legislature refused to act on the officers' petition. The effort had ended, as Lincoln predicted it would, in "disappointment and chagrin."[8]

Discontent in the army, which had simmered during the summer, threatened to boil over that autumn. Even Washington was at wit's end. In a despairing letter of 2 October 1782 addressed to Lincoln, with copies to other influential men in Philadelphia, Washington described the officers' discontent: "The Complaint of Evils which they suppose almost remediless are, the total want of Money, or the means of existing from One day to another, the heavy debts they have already incurred, the loss of Credit, the distress of their Families (ie such as are Maried) at home, and the prospect of Poverty and Misery before them." This was certainly an old refrain, but there was a new urgency in Washington's tone. "The patience and long sufferance of this Army are almost exhausted . . . there never was so great a spirit of Discontent as at this instant." Lincoln was sympathetic but held out little hope of an accommodation. "The picture your Excellency gives of the distresses of the Army is horrible," he replied two weeks later. "Their sufferings require the immediate attention of Congress." But, repeating arguments he had made already to Knox and others, Lincoln explained to Washington that the only way the officers would see a penny of compensation was to petition Congress to allow the states to settle with their respective lines. In essence, Lincoln said, forget the half-pay and rely on the states to provide something "handsome" instead.[9]

Ironically, during this autumn and winter of its discontent the army was at its peak of military efficiency and prowess. Several grand reviews were held in September, including a maneuver under arms held on 14 September in honor of the Comte de Rochambeau. Lincoln's pride was palpable as he reported this affair to John Adams, the American minister in Holland: "We now have a better Army in the field than ever before. The Troops are exceedingly well cloathed and their discipline nearly perfect." At the parade for Rochambeau, he continued, the Frenchman "was pleased to say to His Excellency General Washington that he had passed through a Prussian Army." That was high praise, indeed. Throughout the long and arduous years of war the United States had managed to create a "respectable army." Yet this army, modeled on its European counterparts, embodied all the features that made it anathema to orthodox Whigs—professionalism, pride, and esprit de corps and a sense of separation from and superiority to the civil authorities. These qualities, along with the army's belief that it was being driven to the wall, would push the Confederation to the edge of disaster in the months ahead.[10]

Following Washington's urgent letter Lincoln proposed a hurried visit to camp, a decision that the commander-in-chief warmly seconded. I "strongly urge the Necessity of your presence with me in the Army," he wrote. "Come on immediately; the sooner the better." Lincoln arrived at the Newburgh, New York, encampment on 20 October and spent the next week closeted with Washington and the high command of the army. Their joint effort to "calm the rising billows," as James Madison put it, was at least partially successful. A review of the whole army by Lincoln, in which it received the secretary at war's "fullest approbation," was the only diversion in an otherwise grim week of discussions. While Lincoln did a great deal of listening, as the officers poured out their grievances, it is likely that he used the opportunity to persuade a few, at least, to petition Congress to allow the states to provide for their respective officers.[11]

On his return to Philadelphia Lincoln lost no time reporting the condition of the army. He spent a good part of 30 October with Robert Morris in a "long conference respecting the complaints of the Army." One result of their deliberations in the ensuing month was a comprehensive plan for issuing provisions, which met with general success when implemented in January 1783. Lincoln also wrote Knox to assure him that he had "represented to Congress in very strong terms the distresses which really existed in the army from the want of pay and that the most disagreeable consequences were to be feared if some supply should not be given before the close of the year." The word in Congress, as reported by James Madison, was that Lincoln's visit to camp "has had a very salutary operation, but that some pay must be found for the army." The Virginian put his finger on the problem when he noted: "Where it is to be found God knows."[12]

Any hope that the Confederation's finances would be placed in better train was crushed by the news of Rhode Island's rejection of the 5 percent impost. As Lincoln had foreseen, one state's intransigence had defeated the least objectionable national tax; there was no hope that a land or poll tax would be more successful. It seemed as if the drive to create a more powerful central government, equipped to provide for the army and the country's creditors, had been derailed. For Lincoln the defeat of the impost merely reinforced his belief that the army should turn to the states for help. For Robert Morris and like-minded men in Congress it meant a change of strategy and renewed pressure on the states. In this the army would become an unwitting partner.[13]

Toward the end of November 1782 Knox wrote Lincoln that the army had decided to petition Congress for immediate pay, a settlement of accounts, and a settlement of the half-pay, or commutation. Knox was persuaded that Lincoln would concur in the army's memorial and pressed him to do what he could to further the army's interests. Lincoln told Knox he thought the army committee would have an easy time persuading Congress to agree to all their requests except immediate pay. That, he said, would be impossible, despite all the efforts Robert Morris was making to find funds to pay the army. Congress was already considering a letter that Lincoln had submitted to it after his visit to headquarters, and he believed congressmen would be open to suggestion by the army's representatives. "I am deeply interested in bringing about a speedy settlement with the army and placing the half-pay on a permanent basis," he told Knox. Lincoln assured him that he would "be indulged in giving [his] sentiments freely on the subject" to Congress. Lincoln again stressed his opinion that the army should rely on the states for compensation. Knox sent the letter to Alexander McDougall, noting that Lincoln's ideas conformed with those of the officers' committee, which McDougall was to head, and urged him to consult with the secretary at war on his arrival in Philadelphia. Lincoln, however, planned to spend the winter in Hingham and left the capital in mid-December, stopping to visit Washington at headquarters on his way to Massachusetts. Despite Knox's efforts to hurry the committee, its members arrived in Philadelphia in late December and missed seeing Lincoln by several days. Thus, Lincoln was absent during the critical months when his influence with the committee, and Congress, might have been decisive.[14]

Robert Morris quickly attempted to persuade the officers' committee that the only way the army would receive justice was to link forces with the public creditors to pressure Congress and the states to fund a national debt. Morris still had not given up his principal aim of establishing an independent source of income for the Confederation government. In the high-stakes game that Morris played the army could prove to be the trump card. There were problems, however, in using the army as just another pressure group. As Knox explained: "The influence of the army can exist in one point, that to be sure is a sharp point, which I hope in God will never be directed but against the enemies of the liberties of America." The army was a powerful but unwieldy tool, as Morris would soon find out.[15]

Lincoln vehemently opposed equating the debt owed the army with that of the other public creditors and resented those who would make "an engine of the army to effect a security for their own debts." The army had been paid, when paid at all, with paper securities that depreciated badly. To make matters worse, most officers were obliged to sell what securities they received for a fraction of their value to support themselves or their families. In an argument that anticipated James Madison's position in the first federal Congress, Lincoln insisted that Congress recognize the army's prior claim to justice. The army, he wrote, "should not suffer themselves to be further duped by those who have availed themselves of their distresses, and who have enriched themselves by their misfortunes." To link arms with the public creditors who had speculated in officers' securities, he believed, would make a mockery of the army's sacrifice.[16]

Still, there was enough frustration and bitterness among the officers at West Point to support almost any plan to achieve justice. Despite Robert Morris's agreement to find one month's pay for the army, the officers' disgruntlement only increased as word trickled back from the McDougall mission in Philadelphia that Congress had balked at passing the commutation of the half-pay pension. As Washington put it in a letter to John Armstrong: "The Army, as usual, are without pay; and a great part of the Soldiery without shirts; and tho' the patience of them is equally thread bear, the States seem perfectly indifferent to their cries." The McDougall mission still was hanging fire when Lincoln arrived at army headquarters at West Point on 17 February 1783. Lincoln met with Washington on that day, reviewing a number of technical army matters that the commander-in-chief wanted ironed out in Philadelphia. In the few days that Lincoln stayed at headquarters, however, his discussions with Knox proved to be of weightier stuff. Knox had been in communication with McDougall and was privy to the mission's lack of progress. He also had received letters from Gouverneur Morris urging the army to throw its influence behind the public creditors and the movement to fund a national debt. Knox made it clear to Lincoln that he was caught between the obvious frustrations of the army officers and his reluctance to embroil the army in disloyal activities. After discussing the matter with Lincoln, Knox wrote McDougall a letter that asked him, among other things, "how and in what manner the influence of the army is to be exerted" in order to achieve "permanent continental funds." Whatever path was taken, Knox cautioned, "the reputation of the army must be safeguarded." And he closed by urging McDougall to consult with Lincoln.[17]

When Lincoln returned to Philadelphia in late February there was an atmosphere of tension as Congress tried to grapple with the seemingly intransigent army problems. Discussions between congressmen and the army committee left little doubt that a crisis was brewing at army headquarters. Already the threat of army mutiny had surfaced in congressional debate on the commutation question. To complicate matters, on 12 February news reached Philadelphia of a speech by George III in which the king mentioned the signing of preliminary peace accords between Great Britain and the United States. Paradoxically, the prospect of peace only depressed the spirit of the army further, preoccupied as it was by its postwar situation. And, finally, unknown to Lincoln, Congress also was reeling from the surprise announcement of Robert Morris's conditional resignation as superintendent of finance. On 24 January Morris had issued an ultimatum to Congress: either taxes were passed and funds established by the end of May 1783, or he would resign. Although under an injunction of secrecy, news of his resignation was sure to upset an already unsettled situation at West Point. Without Morris at the helm of the Confederation's finances the army would have little hope of seeing a settlement of its problems other than turning to the states.[18]

In the midst of this turmoil Morris asked Congress for permission to make his resignation public, claiming it was only fair to those with whom he had contractual obligations. When it appeared in the newspapers on 1 March, however, there were howls of disapproval in Congress and dismay elsewhere. By choosing this method of apprising the country of his decision, Morris was evidently trying to shock Congress into passing his financial plan. It is also more than likely that he was trying to ignite the already explosive situation in the army.[19]

For the officers at West Point, anxiously awaiting news of the McDougall mission in Philadelphia, the months of January and February 1783 were long, indeed. Isolated in the frigid north, with little to do and nothing to talk about but their accumulated grievances, the officers' anger and resentment grew. No one in Philadelphia knew the army's situation better than Lincoln. His visit in February had been reinforced afterward by a combination of threat and entreaty contained in a letter of 3 March from Knox. Urging Lincoln to do what he could to see that the army's affairs were settled before peace was proclaimed, Knox added that, should the army be disbanded without a settlement, "they will be so deeply stung by the injustice and ingratitude of their country as to become its tygers and wolves." The rumors of the provisional peace, McDougall's dour letters from Philadelphia, and now the news of Morris's resignation all contributed to an atmosphere of desperation in the army camp at Newburgh.[20]

The quiet was broken on 10 March by a strident call for the officers "to redress their own grievances." An anonymous address proposed a public meeting of the officers to discuss ways of solving their present dilemma through force. Washington headed off the renegade maneuver by asking for a postponement of the meeting and announced one to be held under his auspices. As Knox wrote Lincoln: "What will be the result God only knows. Congress ought not to lose a moment in bringing the affairs of the army to a decision. Push the matter instantly my dear sir with all your might and main."[21]

Before Lincoln had received this letter the crisis at Newburgh was over. Washington's address to the assembled officers some days later was successful in turning their emotions into another channel—one that reiterated their loyalty to Congress and their country and appealed to the nation's sense of justice rather than its fears. Washington's dramatic speech was a masterful performance, scotching the mutinous fever that had momentarily gripped the officer corps. At the last moment they drew back from the "gulph of Civil horror" that their actions would certainly have provoked, hoping that, in Knox's words, "if the people have the most latent spark of gratitude this generous proceeding of the army must call it forth." Like a burst balloon, the pressure behind the army's demand for justice was released in one sharp explosion. Isolated units would prove a threat in the future, but, as a whole, the army would meekly accept whatever settlement it was given.[22]

As Lincoln received the pleasing news from Newburgh, he responded with some of his own. Congress had commuted the half-pay pension into a lump-sum payment worth five years of full pay. Before the officers could rejoice in their good fortune, however, Lincoln reminded Knox that the real question had always been how this sum would be funded and become "of real value to the officers." It had not taken Lincoln very long after his arrival in Philadelphia to detect the aims of the two Morrises and Hamilton. He was adamantly opposed to lumping the debt due the officers with that due the public creditors. Lincoln resented the "mushroom gentry," those who had profited from the discomforts and sacrifices of the army, and he saw no justice in rewarding the former in the same manner as the latter. To clinch his argument Lincoln once again pointed out the near impossibility of passing general taxes to fund the debts of the Confederation. By "jumbling up" the army debt with those of the public creditors, it would make it that much harder to distinguish between them when each would have to apply to the states for payment. And, in the end, Lincoln was convinced that was what would have to be done.[23]

Knox spread Lincoln's sentiments around camp, and it took less than a month for Robert Morris in Philadelphia to learn of them. For the army to apply to the states for funds was diametrically opposed to all Morris's efforts to raise money on behalf of the Confederation. On 23 April Morris confronted Lincoln, complaining that the latter's efforts were undercutting his own (and Congress's) to provide justice for the army. Lincoln stubbornly insisted that "he had a right to give his private Opinion in the Manner he had done," a statement that was more than a trifle disingenuous. Lincoln's public position and his influence with the Massachusetts line made his opposition to a Continental debt more than a "private Opinion." Even though Lincoln had long held these views, which were no secret among his Massachusetts correspondents, his outspokenness at this moment was hardly a coincidence. The Newburgh affair had been a chastening experience, making the prospect of peace and the proper disbanding of the army all the more critical. A settlement with the army was needed immediately, and Lincoln believed the states were more competent to accomplish this than the Confederation.[24]

The testy exchange between Lincoln and Morris was characteristic of the last spring of the war. As Lincoln wrote in a letter home at the end of March: "I am taking every measure in my power to close my affairs and so to arrange the department as to be able to leave it soon. I am tired of war. I wish to sit down in quiet and peace." Even before confirmation of the preliminary peace arrived in Philadelphia on 18 April, Lincoln had begun to settle his accounts with the United States. His lack of confidence in Congress's ability to fund the army debt is illustrated by his instructions to his son to pay strict attention to these affairs: "I have been thus particular that you may have a general knowledge of these matters if I do not obtain a settlement in my lifetime." After discussing his plans with friends in Congress, Lincoln determined to resign upon the receipt of the definitive treaty of peace, expected to arrive by early summer. By the middle of July he wrote his wife, "I expect to be once more in my native town, freed from all public engagements, and master of my own time," returned "to that domestic felicity, from which I have been so long detained, by a cruel war." That, however, was not to be.[25]

As the war wound down, thoughts naturally turned to the future military establishment. With the Continental army soon to be discharged, what provision would be made for national security? As early as April 1783, a congressional committee requested that Washington and Lincoln outline a plan for future Continental military forces. Washington passed along the request to senior officers, whose comments were included in a report submitted to Congress, accompanied by Lincoln's own remarks, in May 1783. Despite American revolutionaries' traditionally fierce opposition to a standing army, all those consulted favored the establishment of a small professional force to patrol the frontiers and provide the core of a larger army in case of a national emergency. Lincoln's major concern, befitting his experience as secretary at war, was how this force was to be fed and supplied. His plan suggested the construction of five magazines to house safely the gunpowder, cannons, ammunition, and other military property of the United States. These magazines would be strategically located throughout the states. In addition, Lincoln advocated the construction of a national armory and foundry so the United States would not be dependent on any foreign power for critical military supplies. Lincoln's proposals and Washington's "Sentiments on a Peace Establishment" were integrated into a committee report written by Alexander Hamilton. But, in the antimilitary atmosphere of Congress during 1783, Hamilton's report was buried, despite several attempts to pass it. Only after Congress had adjourned to Annapolis late in 1783 was a token army (consisting of one regiment) agreed to as an absolute necessity.[26]

Reinforcing Congress's exasperation with military plans was the mutiny of several hundred Pennsylvania troops in June, forcing the legislature to quit Philadelphia and resume deliberations in Princeton, New Jersey. Lincoln's role in the management of this episode is shrouded in mystery; it did, however, almost certainly include a rare instance of dereliction of duty.[27]

Following the announcement of the provisional peace in April, Congress and the high command of the army began to consider how the army could be quickly and peacefully disbanded. Washington knew it would be increasingly difficult to hold those men who had enlisted for the duration of the war once they heard the news of peace. Congress also was concerned that disturbances, such as those at Newburgh, not be repeated. After canvassing the officers, Washington privately communicated his thoughts on how demobilization could best be accomplished to members of Congress. The army officers wished to have a final settlement of all their accounts before disbanding as well as three months' pay in cash. Washington also wished to see Lincoln and Robert Morris, along with a congressional committee with plenary powers, travel to camp in order to bring army affairs to a close. Those wishes were not granted. Given the speed with which the army dissolved, it would receive only a fraction of the requested pay, and that in a highly unsatisfactory way. A settlement of accounts was clearly wishful thinking, given the thousands of individual accounts to be made and the deplorable state of the records. (And, in fact, it would be years before the settlement of accounts was finally completed.) Anxious to be rid of the expense of supporting the army, a charge that every month grew more onerous, Robert Morris agreed to the three months' pay only if the army were disbanded immediately. Congress finally agreed to a compromise and, on 26 May, granted furloughs to all soldiers enlisted for the duration of the war. This, in effect, sent the men home under obligation to report for duty should the provisional peace be broken.[28]

Lincoln carried the furlough resolution to Newburgh in late May. Washington issued the furlough orders on 2 June but, at the request of a delegation of officers, made the acceptance of furloughs voluntary, at least until Congress decided otherwise. Most of those eligible accepted it and left camp, even before the three months' pay arrived. Morris, unable to find cash, had agreed to provide the army with pay in his own notes, but the delay in producing the special paper, printing and signing the notes, and the haste with which many of the troops left camp meant that most soldiers signed over their pay, before they had even received it, for a fraction of its value or for goods from the contractors at West Point, Daniel Parker and Company. Nonetheless, Washington could report to Lafayette on 15 June that those men at Newburgh engaged for the war's duration were furloughed without disorder and with "less discontent than could possibly be expected."[29]

On 11 June Lincoln reported to Congress the result of the furlough resolution at headquarters and received permission to issue the same order to the troops in Pennsylvania, Maryland, Delaware, and Virginia. While Congress was aware that Washington had made the furlough order voluntary, Lincoln's orders to Arthur St. Clair on 13 June for the Pennsylvania troops and those to William Smallwood on 12 June for the Maryland forces said nothing about that alternative.[30]

Before those orders could be issued, however, troops marching home from Newburgh bunked overnight in the Philadelphia barracks with a unit of the Pennsylvania line on 12 June and spread the news of the furlough and pay measure. When the furlough terms were announced to them on 13 June, the Pennsylvania troops refused to accept them. A number of sergeants wrote a remonstrance to Congress, rejecting the furloughs and demanding a settlement of accounts. This remonstrance was passed on to Lincoln, who visited the barracks in an attempt to calm the soldiers. One of the "prudent and soothing measures" Lincoln proposed was to make the furlough voluntary. Unfortunately, the soldiers were in no mood to listen to his overtures, which were drowned in a deafening roar of whistles, hissing, and catcalls. To avoid a recurrence Lincoln ordered most of the troops to Lancaster, Pennsylvania, and arranged for Anthony Wayne's soldiers, scheduled to arrive in Philadelphia, to disembark at Wilmington, Delaware, and march directly to Lancaster to be furloughed. The situation had quieted down enough in the ensuing days for Congressman James Madison to observe on 17 June that the "measures taken by the Secy. at War and G'l Sinclair have I believe obviated the embarrassment." Madison's optimism proved premature.[31]

Inexplicably, Lincoln chose this moment to make a trip to Virginia in order to supervise the placement and construction of a powder magazine. The trip had been planned in advance, but, given the tensions running high within the army units surrounding Philadelphia and the concern with peacefully demobilizing those troops, the errand to Virginia was not of critical importance. Believing that his dispositions had taken care of the army disturbances, Lincoln was absent during the next crucial week, when, on Saturday, 21 June, about three hundred Continental soldiers, commanded by a number of sergeants, surrounded the statehouse, where the Pennsylvania Council was in session on the second floor. A rump session of Congress, with too few members present to make a quorum, occupied the first floor. Though the soldiers' business was with the government of Pennsylvania, the threat of armed force implicit in the demonstration that day and the lack of immediate response by Pennsylvania governor John Dickinson, to provide protection for Congress, convinced a committee of

Congress to order its removal from Philadelphia to Princeton, New Jersey. It sat in session there until the end of November 1783.[32]

Lincoln did not return from Virginia until 17 July. Seemingly unconcerned by what had transpired in his absence, at the first opportunity he wrote a long letter to the members of the American Academy of Arts and Sciences in Boston describing scenes of interest in Virginia and speculating on the future importance of the city of Richmond. After moving on to Princeton, he paused to accept the presidency of the Massachusetts Society of the Cincinnati.[33]

Given the events of the spring and summer of 1783, it was no wonder that many prominent Americans looked askance at the establishment of a military society, the Society of the Cincinnati. As the brainchild of Henry Knox, the society grew, in the words of one officer, "out of the affections of the officers from a desire to perpetuate their friendships." Knox claimed two benevolent goals for his offspring: the society would promote union among the states and serve as a last resort of charity for impoverished officers. As he told Lincoln, "The intention is pure, and uncorrupted by any further design." Others were not so sure. To many, especially in New England, the hereditary nature of the society prefigured the formation of an American aristocracy, the badge of the order reeked of European distinctions. A special class of men dedicated to Unionist sentiments and pressuring the government on its own behalf bespoke European corruption, the decay of a republican order, and the overthrow of republican government. Besides, many argued that thousands of revolutionaries had fought and sacrificed as much as had the officer corps and yet would not benefit from such a distinction. Despite heavy pressure from friends in Congress, Lincoln swung his influence behind the organization. He was elected president of the Massachusetts society, a position he held until his death. As he wrote upon the acceptance of the presidency, "I am flattered by the appointment—I am pleased with the institution . . . to promote the benevolent intentions of it shall claim my early and constant attention."[34]

Lincoln had been back in Philadelphia less than a month before he requested permission of Congress to inspect the army magazines in the northern states. There was little for him to do in the tiny village of Princeton. His primary concerns were the settlement of his accounts—he was being held personally liable for five million dollars drawn on Congress for support of the southern army in 1779 and 1780—and the arrival of the definitive treaty of peace, which would release him from active service in the government. The northern tour lasted until the end of September, with the high point of the trip undoubtedly the social activity at headquarters at West Point. At one point the festivities, no doubt provoked by a few shared bottles of Madeira, included a weighing session, in which Washington (209 lbs.) and Lincoln (224 lbs.) were easily bested by Knox (280 lbs.), Michael Jackson (252 lbs.), and Ebenezer Huntington (232 lbs.) in the battle of the scales.[35]

Back in Philadelphia Lincoln submitted his accounts for settlement to John Pierce on 30 September. (They were finally accepted, with the balance due to him placed on the books of the Treasury on 3 January 1784.) Now it was merely a matter of awaiting the treaty of peace, for Lincoln clearly wished to retire from all public employment. "My friends wish me to remain," he wrote his son Ben, "but I cannot do it." Even with the reduced responsibilities of the proposed peacetime army, Lincoln could not face the yearly journey "from one end of the continent to the other." Nor, after eight years of war and time spent away from home, was the prospect of being called to duty at any moment a welcome one. Most important, however, was Lincoln's sense that "my politicks and those of the times will not agree. I must either be perfectly silent under every measure or must make myself obnoxious to the ill will of those with whom I shall be particularly connected." On the face of it this is a curious statement in light of Lincoln's rough relationship with Robert Morris and those who had sought in the past year to strengthen the Confederation government. From the spring of 1783 on, Morris had been under constant and vicious attack from congressional delegates, who jealously guarded the prerogatives and powers of the states. No matter how much he had disagreed with Morris in the past, Lincoln could not stomach the extreme positions of such congressmen as Arthur Lee, David Howell, or even Stephen Higginson, a delegate from Massachusetts. Lincoln was a moderate at a time when it was difficult to travel in the middle of the road. He wished to do the impossible—respect state power while giving new energy to the federal union. He carefully distinguished his position from Morris's, but he had always remained a strong advocate of the Union. Men such as Samuel Osgood, a friend of Lincoln's, who chipped away at the power and coherence of the Confederation, must have filled him with sadness and contributed to his decision to retire.[36]

And so he did, tendering his resignation to Congress on 29 October. Congress accepted it, on condition that Lincoln remain in office until that body adjourned to Annapolis. Congress tried to ease Lincoln's passage back to civilian life with a glowing tribute, resolving that it entertained "a high sense of his perserverance, fortitude, activity and meritorious services in the field, as well as of his diligence, fidelity and capacity in the execution of the office of Secretary at War, which important trusts he has discharged to their entire approbation." It was a fitting tribute to a man whose quiet and uncomplaining labor, tact, and respect for Congress had helped the army—and Congress— weather heavy seas on the way to the safe harbor of peace.[37]

As he rode away from Princeton in November 1783, eagerly looking forward to a long-awaited reunion with his family, Lincoln might have seen, reflected in Congress's tribute, a hundred scenes from his eight years' service. If he could look back at his experiences as farmer and soldier with a measure of satisfaction, he could only regard what lay ahead with a combination of optimism and anxiety. Notwithstanding the new opportunities open to him as a man of great reputation in his country, he also was a man of fifty, broken in body, exhausted in spirit, and depleted in fortune, with a large family and his position to reestablish in the peacetime world. Like thousands of other Americans, he had greatly sacrificed to create this new country. Now, in the postwar world, he would discover if the sacrifice had been worthwhile.

CHAPTER TEN

Forging a New Life

The objects of the war being so fully & happily accomplished I should
with the highest pleasure again ascend to those private employments to
which I have been so much a stranger for more than seven years but my
hopes are in some measure blasted.

Benjamin Lincoln

However happy Benjamin Lincoln was to be in "the lap of my friends"
and "the arms of my family" in Hingham in the early winter of 1783, his
return to private life required a wholesale reassessment of his past and
present situation. Since the arrival of the preliminary peace in April 1783,
Lincoln had been thinking hard about what the future would bring. It
was obvious that it would be impossible to return to his prewar life. His
age, fifty, and his wounds prevented him from taking up farming again.
Before the war he wrote, "My own industry" was enough for "my little
farm" to prosper, "yielding quite a competency and a surplus which would
have enabled me to have given my children an education suitable to their
expectations and rank in life." But now all that had changed. The resources of the farm, depleted as they were from many years of inattention
and increased expenses, could not meet the demands of the family. Ironically, the war had boosted Lincoln's status, while plundering him of the
means to enjoy it.[1]

It is clear from Lincoln's correspondence that, even if he were capable
of living on the modest scale of his prewar farm, he considered it beneath
his postwar status on two counts. He was on friendly terms with most of
the great men of the infant United States, and maintaining those relations
upon equal terms was of great importance to him. To live otherwise would
be humiliating, all the more so if it were "in consequence of poverty and
want." Second, the education and "appearance in life" of his children,
"who are now considered as the children of Gen. Lincoln," would have to

be "in some proportion to my rank or I shall be charged with having criminally neglected them." Besides the obligation to his children, he was ambitious for them. And, given the proper education, wealth, and connections with the powerful, who could say what future lay in store for them?[2]

Lincoln might have continued in public life, seeking one of the few positions that would have afforded him a living and supported his new aspirations. In Philadelphia, in the spring of 1783, it was an all but foregone conclusion that Lincoln would retire from the war office to become the governor of Massachusetts. But he discouraged his nomination for any public office and seemed eager to be free of all commitments other than private business. His name, however, continued to arise in that regard throughout the 1780s. As an officer of the Confederation, he returned to his native state a man of national consequence. But without an income and the leisure to support a career in public office, he could just as easily sink back into the relative obscurity from which the Revolution had raised him.[3]

Still, the war had left him better off than many of his fellow officers. He was indebted for large sums to only a few people, and his real estate remained unmortgaged. In addition, he had a considerable amount of money tied up in Continental and state securities, which constituted his army pay, rations, and allowances for the past several years. The securities, which Lincoln dryly noted he had been "obliged to loan" to the public, were then selling for a third of their value. Liquidating them was a sacrifice too great for Lincoln to make. At their "present depreciated value," Lincoln wrote, only the "most pressing necessity" could persuade him to sell. To do so would condemn him and his family to "wade through the remainder of life with accumulated distress" because of sacrifices made during the war which ensured the United States "the best of blessings." At least Lincoln had the option of borrowing money from his many "connections" until the securities appreciated in value. That was an avenue closed to many, who also had to make a new beginning after the war.[4]

Although Lincoln protested he was "driven, in this late hour of life, into pursuits which are new," he faced this financial challenge with characteristic energy and a shrewdness that belied his lack of business experience. Borrowing heavily against his real estate, Lincoln built a state-of-the-art flour mill on the Weir River at the eastern edge of Hingham. This became the cornerstone of the commercial firm Lincoln and Sons, which conducted a small-scale triangular trade between Maine, Boston, and the Chesapeake. Lumber from Maine was sold in Alexandria for Virginia wheat to be milled in Hingham. Flour was then sold in Boston or exported from there. Lincoln had several ships built for his firm's operations, which he later leased and then sold as the market took a downturn. Lincoln directed the enterprise with the help of his two sons, Benjamin and Theodore. He also expanded his farm, buying small parcels of land in and around Hingham. And the family continued to run the malt house and brewery that had been in operation before the war.[5]

If Lincoln's reputation and connections now spanned the continent, it was his simplicity and lack of pretension which delighted visitors to his Hingham farmhouse. Charles Van Hogendorp, a young and impressionable Dutch nobleman, who accompanied the Dutch minister Van Berkel to the United States, visited Lincoln in December 1783 and described the general and his family. The young man had met Lincoln earlier in Boston at Lieutenant Governor Cushing's. Despite "the cold manners that characterize the English," Lincoln was quick to invite Hogendorp to his home, where the Dutchman was surprised to see that the general was no more than a farmer. Wonderingly, he wrote that he had heard that Lincoln might be elected governor in the coming year. If that should happen, he wrote, "I have no doubt that at the end of the year he will return to his flocks, his mill and his woods." The idea that men could wield political power for a time and lay it down without a qualm seemed to astonish him. "Imagine the effect on me of his noble simplicity, when, during the evening, sitting in front of the fire, Lincoln spoke to us, smiling all the while, 'I lived here for twenty years after my marriage and never dreamed of war. Here is my place, and here is that of Mrs. Lincoln's, and it's here that we pass our evenings in talking together.'" Hogendorp observed the general up early in the morning, bustling about various household chores and conducting a horseback tour of Hingham and its environs. Only toward the end of his visit did the young Dutchman's sharp eye pick up what he considered a flaw in an otherwise harmonious, if slightly boring, picture of republican domesticity. Referring to an essay on the Romans, Hogendorp wrote that Roman generals often returned from the command of armies to their wives' subordination. "I think Madame Lincoln is a little bit Roman on that point," he snickered. "She is the master within the house." (As well she might be, having managed the Lincoln household and farm single-handedly for eight years.)[6]

Hogendorp made a passing mention of another member of the Lincoln household, a black servant by the name of Juba. It was not until the Dutchman had visited the plantation South that the contrast between the treatment of blacks in the two regions struck him with its full force. In the

North, he wrote, "A negro is a domestic, he works in the fields alongside his master; at home, he takes dinner with him. In the South, the negro is a slave, he is cursed, badly nourished, and mistreated." There is no reason to doubt that Van Hogendorp was referring, in the first instance, to Lincoln's household. The general had held slaves before and during the war. It was only Lincoln's horror at the way slaves were treated in South Carolina and Georgia, which he had seen firsthand while on military campaign, which had led him to renounce "the unjustifiable and wicked practice" of slavery. At the time of Hogendorp's visit the sole slave member of the house was Flora, a woman in her eighties, who died in 1789.[7]

Yet an abhorrence of southern slavery did not translate into an acceptance of black equality or even tolerance of unknown free blacks in the community. Everard Meade of Amelia County, Virginia, one of Lincoln's former aides-de-camp, described the unrest among the slaves provoked by Article 1 of the Virginia Bill of Rights ("all are equally entitled to freedom"), claiming, "Should they [the slaves] emigrate I would most chearfully go to manual labor to emancipate them." Lincoln applauded Meade's sentiments but cautioned him that a wholesale "liberation" of Virginia's slave population would merely "multiply their sorrows." Having been brought up "in the habits of obedience" and to "look to their master for their daily bread," Lincoln believed that emancipation could only be accomplished by "educating the youths in the arts of business & manufactures leading them by degrees to feel their own importance and the necessity of integrity, industry, oeconomy & temperance." This prescription for behavior Lincoln applied to black and white alike. But, when it came to welcoming slave runaways or free blacks into Massachusetts, Lincoln drew the line. Suggesting to Gov. James Bowdoin that the state bar the entrance of free blacks seeking "asylum" in the state, Lincoln wrote that the "ill-consequence of their coming among us" would soon be manifest, since, due to their lack of education, they would "in a short time become a burden on the community." The old Puritan ideal required a community to take care of its own, providing for and disciplining its members. Lincoln's objection to free blacks was merely an atavism of the closed, corporate nature of the early New England town, in which strangers, social misfits, and religious mavericks were warned-out—and kept out of town.[8]

Lincoln's concern with increasing community burdens was reinforced by the slowdown in commerce. The market was glutted with British-made consumer goods and strangled by the lack of cash to buy them. Immediately after the peace American merchants stockpiled bulging inventories of goods by grasping generous offers of credit advanced by British merchants anxious to recover lucrative markets lost during the Revolution. But American shopkeepers were unable to move their goods to consumers, who were strapped for cash. Massive inflation during the war had brought paper money into ill repute, so legislatures (with the exception of Rhode Island) were reluctant to ease the situation by printing money. Merchants found their credit overextended and went bankrupt when called to pay up by British merchants caught in their own credit squeeze. And so the chain of debt became a chain of business failures. In that commercial climate most entrepreneurs, especially those working on limited capital, quickly grew discouraged. Others, even with prominent sponsors, were not slow to get the message. William Jackson, one of Lincoln's former aides-de-camp, had been launched on the mercantile path with Lincoln's blessing and the help of Robert Morris and William Bingham, two of the era's most formidable merchants. But, Jackson wrote in August 1785, even he was quitting business while he was ahead: "The general embarrassment of Commerce affects even merchants of established credit and extensive capital." Lincoln, who had neither, managed to eke out a small profit from his operations, probably because the Chesapeake area was not as hard hit by the downturn as New England. But by January 1786 he was having problems meeting his obligations to one importunate creditor. It was evident that commerce was not the solution to his dilemma.[9]

As he launched his commercial firm in early 1784, Lincoln also explored another potential pathway to wealth. That summer Lincoln traveled to Maine as a Massachusetts state commissioner to, among other things, locate the St. Croix River, named in the 1783 treaty with Great Britain as the boundary between New Brunswick and Maine. In the course of his travels there Lincoln became one of the area's greatest boosters, and on his return he arranged with prominent Bostonians Thomas Russell and John Lowell a joint purchase of some 50,000 acres of wild, or unimproved, land, of which Lincoln took ownership of 20,279 acres. Later, in the 1790s, when William Bingham launched his campaign to sell millions of Maine acres to hungry European speculators, he turned to Lincoln with a list of questions that prompted the latter to write a description of the land and climate of Maine. Land speculation was America's favorite pastime, indulged in by anyone who could rub two coins together. Fortunes were made and lost at a fantastic pace in the postwar period, mostly by buying immense quantities of wilderness, subdividing them, and quickly selling them. Little attention was paid to improving the lands prior to sale. Millions of acres were sold or exchanged in a dizzying pursuit of wealth which often ended in the poorhouse or debtor's prison.[10]

Lincoln's approach to this commerce in land was much different, though how much the difference can be attributed to his shortage of cash and credit is a matter of speculation. Lincoln took seriously the biblical injunction that man should "be fruitful, multiply, and replenish the earth and subdue it." The foundations of America's future prosperity, he believed, depended on opening new lands and making them productive. His Maine property, he found, was "a territory capable of supporting a large number of industrious inhabitants" which would in time, given the right conditions, "add much to the riches, strength, and importance" of the Commonwealth of Massachusetts. To further this project, he sent his son Theodore to begin a settlement on his Passamaquoddy property as the nucleus around which the lands would rise in value, be sold and settled, providing a tidy profit to the proprietors and service to the settlers. From 1786 until failing health prevented it in 1805, Lincoln traveled at least once a year to Maine in order to measure the settlement's progress from a "wild" to a prosperous state.[11]

This idea of gradual development on a modest scale contrasted sharply with the land schemes of one of Lincoln's best friends, Henry Knox. Knox's wife, Lucy Flucker Knox, had inherited vast tracts of Maine land from her mother, Hannah Waldo Flucker. This famous Waldo patent served as the core of the former bookseller and Continental general's domain. Dissatisfied with this huge amount of real estate, Knox mortgaged it to acquire more land. In addition, he built a mansion, called Montpelier, at Thomaston and for two decades lived the life of a nabob, entertaining lavishly and pouring large sums of money into his horse breeding and other farming operations. Knox was chronically short of cash, but, backed by his hundreds of thousands of acres and relying on friendships made during the Revolution, he was able to borrow money for years to sustain his lifestyle. Lincoln was one friend who cosigned many of his friend's notes unquestioningly, a gesture that would have serious consequences when Knox's extravagance caught up with him in the late 1790s.[12]

Of course, the Maine lands, if wild, were certainly not uninhabited when Lincoln acquired them. The grinding march of Lincoln's progress was matched step by step by the retreat and disintegration of the Indian population he found there. Another part of Lincoln's 1784 commission was "to endeavor to form some compromise with the Penobscot Indians respecting the lands which they now occupy." The intent of the last phrase was made explicit by Knox, another member of the commission, when he wrote Lincoln that they should decide on the nature and quantity of the gifts to be presented to the Indians. "We shall appear ridiculous enough in their eyes to ask them for their land," he wrote mockingly, "and not give them any thing to prepare their minds to acquiesce in so modest a request." The treaty, signed in 1786, provided the Penobscots with a small yearly payment, a few wilderness townships, and some land along the Penobscot River. By 1818 both the Penobscot and the Passamaquoddy tribes were relegated to reservations, where they clung defiantly to the older ways of life in the face of white civilization.[13]

Lincoln took on one other obligation from the Massasachusetts government. In December 1785 he was chosen first major general of militia and asked to critique the military structure of the state. After consulting the other newly appointed general officers that winter, Lincoln submitted a report in April 1786, pointing out the lack of supplies, especially gunpowder, and field artillery and asking for a change in the law regarding elections of subordinate officers. While he took the commission seriously, as he did all things military, Lincoln could hardly imagine an occasion that would force him back into the saddle of command. His military maneuvers were reduced to occasional militia review days, when his first division of militia did nothing more dangerous than practice storming the stone walls and pastures of Suffolk County.[14]

While Lincoln's business concerns and government service kept him busy, he still found time to correspond with a wide range of people. Lincoln's interest in the economic development of the United States prompted him to retain a keen interest in political events, which surfaced frequently in his letters. For Lincoln, as for most eighteenth-century leaders, the connection between politics and economics was direct. Governmental power, used wisely and correctly, was a means to promote economic development. "A people must not be left to their own inclinations," Lincoln wrote. Above and beyond the labor needed to sustain their populations, the states were advised to investigate and encourage, by laws, bounties, or other means, those activities that best benefited the state. From a practical standpoint Lincoln observed that all Maine lacked to prosper from its natural advantages were proper legislative regulations. Timber was being taken from public and private lands without the approval of the owner. Dams were built helter-skelter without prior planning. As a result, fish migration was impeded, and fish populations were declining. Laws vesting secure title in the land to those who settled on it were needed. Mill rights should be judiciously allocated by law rather than grabbed indiscriminately. The wholesale slaughter of moose and deer for their hides should be controlled. "Such has been the success of many hunters, that in deep snows when hard crusted, they have killed one hundred moose to a man, in about twenty days." To regulate all this, Lincoln admitted, would be difficult, maybe impossible, but should be tried nonetheless. "The interest of individuals must give way when the general good is consulted."[15]

By defining the general good in this way, Lincoln was undoubtedly one of the nation's first conservationists. It may only have been his aversion to waste and his fondness for economy and order that led him to propose these measures. But he is due credit for looking ahead to the day when the nation's resources would no longer be so bountiful. His argument for the conservation of Maine's tall timber, suited as it was for ships' masts and spars, predicted a time when the United States would be forced to look elsewhere for ship timber to ensure its national security. Of course, Lincoln's plea for government regulation was not wholly disinterested. As a proprietor of Maine lands, his profits depended on orderly settlement, productive farms, and rising land values. As a brewer, Lincoln's advocacy of a bounty on the cultivation of barley and the making of "strong beer," linked as it was to an anti–distilled liquors stance, also stood to put money in his pocket. Lincoln lived in that "best of all possible worlds," in which his own interests were closely aligned with the "general good."[16]

Lincoln's vision of the republican future depended on vigorous government measures to stimulate and regulate the economy. And that, in turn, depended on giving "energy" to government. If Lincoln's immediate concerns were with the Massachusetts state government, he spent a great deal of time in the 1780s mulling over the untenable situation of the Confederation government as well. "That we are drained of our cash, that our trade is embarrassed and our finances deranged are truths which will not be denied," Lincoln wrote Rufus King, a Massachusetts congressman, in February 1786. Samuel Osgood, another congressman from the Bay State and a Lincoln correspondent, was even more discouraged. Though vehemently opposed to an expansion of congressional powers in 1783, Osgood had spent several years as a member of the Board of Treasury and had concluded that nothing but coercive taxation powers and an impost would shore up the weaknesses of the Confederation. Lincoln did not agree. The common answer to the question of how to solve the various ills of the Confederation was "Give Congress more power," he wrote King. Yet only a "coercive" power whose laws would control those of the states would be able to solve the problems caused by a lack of cooperation among the states and the weakness of the Confederation. And that coercive power would annihilate "our republican ideas" and produce a "Union of the

States." Lincoln feared that giving that much power to the federal government would necessarily entail the destruction of the republican experiments—that is, the states—by consolidating them under a government of general powers.[17]

Furthermore, Lincoln went on, "the United States, as they are called, seem to be little more than a name. They are not really embarked in the same bottom." Different economic interests and modes of production, especially in the North and South, dictated that the states take different courses. Massachusetts's support for a Congress with the power to regulate trade was based on its desire to expand its merchant marine and carry the products of the southern states to the rest of the world. For their part the southern states wanted to sell their agricultural products for the best price and thus sought to encourage world buyers to visit southern ports. Southerners feared that a northern monopoly of the carrying trade would result in lower commodity prices. Despite his understanding of each region's economic interests, Lincoln was ready to blame much of the current political stalemate in Congress on the South. The problem was slavery. As long as human bondage continued, he wrote, the southern states would remain "feeble and defenseless." And, rather than uniting firmly with the northern states, as logic would dictate, they only became jealous of them, especially "the enterprising spirit of the Northern hive." Because of these differences, Lincoln did not believe that "these States will, or ever can, be governed, and all enjoy equal advantages, by laws which have a general operation." He concluded on a pessimistic note. "That our interests do & will clash, . . . are the necessary consequences of our great extent, of our difference of climate, Productions, views &c." For those reasons, Lincoln could see no solution other than a breakup of the Confederation into several smaller "divisions," securing peace and safety by a "firm alliance" between them.[18]

As he had during the war, Lincoln continued to believe that republican government must be based on the exertions of a virtuous people within a community of interest. If South and North could not agree because their interests were fundamentally different, Lincoln believed the country should be divided into sections in which people held a common interest. For how could states, composed of a virtuous citizenry, be coerced into supporting a federal government without altering the very nature of republican government? Here Lincoln stumbled over the same hurdle in 1786 as he had in 1783: for him, as for many others, the republican experiment existed in the state governments. And he could not imagine how a federal government could coerce the collected republics without destroying them. By giving Congress a general power of taxation, the states would effectively sign their own death warrants. The power to tax, as America's previous experience with Great Britain had shown, carried with it all the powers of government—police, a standing army and navy, laws and courts, civil servants, and so on. Lincoln could not conceive of a federal government that was effective and yet limited by the powers of the states and the people. He could not imagine a government, such as the one the Constitutional Convention in Philadelphia would devise the next year.[19]

Arguments over the inadequacies of the Confederation were hot topics of conversation and correspondence throughout the continent in the mid-1780s. Calls for a convention to amend the Articles of Confederation were becoming more frequent by 1786. The Massachusetts General Court, as early as the summer of 1785, had instructed its delegates in Congress to move for such a conclave. The delegates had refused, fearing that the proposal would be used as a pretext to overthrow republican state governments. Lincoln had been skeptical of a convention since it was first discussed in the winter of 1782. He had agreed with John Lowell, who said at the time that "governments are rarely made by consultation but grow out of the ground, that is, out of habits, wants and wishes of the People." Lowell continued in a pessimistic vein: "If all the wise men of the East & of the South were to meet in the Center & form a System that other people would admire & lavishly extol, I suspect it would turn out like Shakespeare's 'baseless fabrick of a vision.'" Lincoln, then near exhaustion from trying to keep the war effort afloat, doubtless saw no alternative to Lowell's dreary prediction that the political problems of the Confederation could not be solved. Government in the 1780s would be limited to—"Blunder on, mend where we can, bear what we cannot."[20]

By the fall of 1786 the status quo had become intolerable for many prominent Americans, and the Confederation came under increasing attack. In Massachusetts there seemed to be an added element of desperation in the debate over congressional power (or lack thereof). That was surely the case with Lincoln, whose uneasiness over the agrarian disturbances in western Massachusetts led him to take a closer and more sympathetic look at the Union. Less than a year before Lincoln's disgust for sectional bickering had led him to propose separate confederacies; now he saw safety only in the union of the states. As court closings and the intimidation of state officials rocked Massachusetts that fall, Lincoln saw the republican experiment teeter on the brink of failure. It forced him to rethink his position. In some observations penned while barricaded in his home during a severe snowstorm in December 1786, Lincoln argued for an increase in the powers of the federal government. "The injured state of our commerce; our ruined credit, both at home and abroad, and the contemptible figure we make among the nations of Europe, are the natural consequences and the most conclusive evidences of the want of a federal head." Lincoln had analyzed the report of the grand committee of Congress which recently had proposed a number of amendments to the Articles of Confederation. He found them totally inadequate for the purpose of strengthening the federal government. All of the amendments, to his mind, were fatally flawed, for they made the Confederation subject to the states. It was time, he wrote, that we discard the idea that each state can be a "perfect Republick" and at the same time also adhere to the federal compact. "We should now determine whether we will sacrifice the United States to an attachment, unalterable, to our several constitutions; or whether we will in the first instance, establish an efficient head to the Empire and mould our different constitutions to that. One or the other must be done soon." For his part Lincoln believed that the "wellbeing, if not the very being, of the different States depend on a firm union, and a controuling power at the head of it." Nothing spoke more eloquently to that point than the inability of Massachusetts to come to grips with the western disturbances.[21]

In the three years since the peace Lincoln had laid the foundation for a new life. Struggling to maintain his hard-won reputation and provide the wealth and ease he felt to be his and his family's due, he had launched a number of risky ventures, which in the shaky economic landscape of the mid-1780s were in danger of collapse. Nearly all the reasons for Lincoln's troubles could be traced to the paralysis of the Confederation government. The chaotic trade situation had brought his commercial venture to a near standstill. The lack of public credit and the inability of the Confederation to honor its debt to the officers and soldiers of the army made his officer's pay in the form of Continental securities nearly worthless. Only the steady growth of his Maine settlement bolstered his flagging spirits.

Now, to make a bad situation worse, clouds were amassing on the western horizon. In the summer of 1786 farmers, protesting taxes and debt collection, forced the courts in western Massachusetts to close. For Lincoln the specter of agrarian revolt shook the very foundations of government in the Commonwealth. As Washington asked Lincoln in November 1786: "Are we to have the goodly fabric, that eight years were spent in raising, pulled over our heads?" For the next few months that question would hang in the balance as Lincoln was called to arms once again.[22]

CHAPTER ELEVEN

Shays's Rebellion

Every revolution, and even every war, creates illusions and is conducted
in the name of unrealizable ideals.

Milovan Djilas

As Lincoln paused in December 1786 to give George Washington the
news from Massachusetts, he began on a personal and optimistic note.
After three trips to Maine this year, he wrote, he had successfully settled
his son Theodore there. His younger son, Martin, was ready to accompany him north in the spring. Lincoln was ebullient about Maine's prospects. He had erected "two saw mills on a large scale" and was well on his
way to attracting "the number of families" he was "obliged to settle (viz.
sixty in six years)." Indeed, he wrote, "I am so pleased with the country
that I frequently wish myself there where I might be free from the present
noise and tumults." Unfortunately, because of his position as first major
general of the Massachusetts militia, that was impossible. He was busy
organizing and training the first militia division, "at all times a duty," but
"especially so now, when the State is convulsed and the bands of government, in some parts of it, are cast off."[1]

The agrarian disturbances that began in the summer of 1786 in western Massachusetts were a protest against the onerous tax burden imposed
by the state in the postwar period. Already plagued with slumping farm
prices, farmers were further hit by calls to pay off their private indebted-
ness. The added tax burden levied by the state to pay off its war debt also
squeezed farm budgets. The credit crunch after the war brought property
seizures, forced farm sales, and imprisonment for debt in its wake. County
conventions and towns showered petitions on the General Court seeking
debt relief. The state legislature, in a special 1786 autumn session, granted
an eight-month debt moratorium, but, along with its conciliatory measures, the General Court suspended habeas corpus and passed a new Riot

Act. The insurgents remained unappeased, and the protest quickly grew more radical and menacing. Roving bodies of armed men closed the state courts, harassed government officials, and reportedly planned the take-over of the federal armory in Springfield to march on Boston and topple the existing government.[2]

Massachusetts had a long history of protest and turmoil in the eighteenth century. And the western part of the state had been in an uproar since the agitation against Great Britain began in the 1760s. By the 1780s discontent focused directly on the General Court. Farmers in the western part of the state complained bitterly as the general agricultural prosperity of the war years gave way to the postwar slump. Added to that was a tax burden that weighed more heavily on farming communities than on the commercial towns of the coast. The adoption of the Massachusetts Constitution of 1780, so proudly framed by John Adams and his colleagues as the basis of state government, did little to assuage the disgruntled westerners. The constitution was a conservative document, requiring property qualifications for voting and for office, providing for a strong executive, and tenuring judges for life. It is clear from subsequent events that many in the western counties did not regard the constitution as legitimate.[3]

Western insurgents evoked enough sympathy throughout the Commonwealth to divide the government on how best to resolve the matter. For a time it did nothing but watch and wait. The fall session of the General Court further antagonized the protesters. By December the insurgents, emboldened by the lack of opposition, had sharpened their rhetoric and begun to entertain more ambitious plans than merely closing local courts. Washington, who looked on with growing apprehension and exasperation, wrote Henry Lee that the best way to handle the situation was to "know precisely what the insurgents aim at. If they have *real* grievances, redress them if possible. . . . If they have not, employ the force of government against them at once."[4]

If the Shaysites (named after one of their leaders, Daniel Shays) could claim "*real* grievances," as in hindsight they could, Lincoln did not think them so. The same economic conditions that preoccupied him—reduced trade, the scarcity of money, the lack of public credit—concerned the insurgents. Yet, in analyzing the reasons for the western turmoil, Lincoln drew in broad strokes a picture of moral turpitude. "The want of industry, oeconomy, and common honesty seem to be the causes of the present commotions," he wrote Washington. In Lincoln's estimation, property and credit had been too easily acquired by farmers during the war. Debts were paid off with depreciated paper money, which led to easy living and profligacy. The prewar habits of hard work, frugality, and simple living were forgotten. Now, when "things were fast returning back into their original channels," it was clear "that the industrious were to reap the fruits of their industry, and that the indolent and improvident would soon experience the evils of their idleness and sloth." To put off the day of reckoning the insurgents' petitioned the General Court for paper money. This request was rejected. They then stopped the courts and tried to suspend government operations, ultimately seeking to "sap the foundations of our constitution." For Lincoln the Shaysites showed "evidences of insanity," and it seemed likely that government in Massachusetts would collapse because "there doth not appear to be virtue enough among the people to preserve a perfect republican government."[5]

Part of Lincoln's moral stridency could be traced to the striking parallels that existed between the crowd action of the Shaysites and the extralegal activities of the American revolutionaries. County conventions and petitions by the insurgents recalled the town protests and remonstrances that had inundated provincial governments in the early 1770s. Court closings were another tactic of the revolutionaries, as was the organization of militia units and the stockpiling of arms, powder, and ammunition. Men such as Lincoln had only to remember their own successful use of these tactics to fear their use by the Shaysites. As the British had been overthrown, so could the product of their own revolutionary republicanism, the Massachusetts constitution of 1780. A newspaper writer had the gall to make the connection explicit. An Englishman in Pennsylvania, writing to an American Tory friend in Great Britain, could find no difference between the insurgents of 1776 and 1786: "The unparalleled impudence of these pretended friends to good government," he wrote, nearly apoplectic with the incongruity of the situation. "Good God! That rebels in grain should pretend, by force of arms, to suppress rebellion! What is LINCOLN but a more fortunate SHAYS?"[6]

If the irony escaped Lincoln, it did not fail to strike other observers. Long after the events of 1786–87, in which Lincoln would lead the government forces against the insurgents, the Reverend William Bentley of Salem (a fierce Republican partisan) wrote a lengthy note in his diary summing up the life of the Revolutionary War veteran. Lincoln, he observed, "embarked warmly in the Cause of the Colonies. This heroism gave him influence beyond his own personal merits & after the revolution, like Stark had he maintained the same ground the highest opinions might have been entertained of his integrity. But as situation[s] brought him to public notice, so after the revolution it threw him into the arms of men exactly in manners & character resembling those he had opposed at the commencement of the revolution." Bentley saw Lincoln as a man who had betrayed the cause. In his mind Lincoln had journeyed across the political spectrum from revolutionary to reactionary. Once he had fought vigorously for the promise of equality in the pursuit of life, liberty, and happiness. Now he had become a pillar of an abusive and unresponsive government. He had allied himself with the merchant class and sold out for personal gain. The security of property took precedence over the well-being of individual citizens. Had he actually made that political journey? Or was Bentley extrapolating from Lincoln's support of the Revolution that he also had supported an egalitarian society?[7]

For Lincoln there was no contradiction between his role in the Revolution and the suppression of Shays's Rebellion. There was a crucial difference between the two situations: the adoption in 1780 of the Massachusetts constitution. Lincoln's prewar radicalism had stemmed from a wish for political and economic autonomy, not from a belief that "all men are created equal." It was the British claim to "bind us in all cases whatever" and its "encroaching demands" which led him to take an active role in the conflict. He feared "enslavement," the impoverishment that followed the loss of property. The constitution, framed and adopted by the Commonwealth's citizens, in Lincoln's mind supplied the revolutionary settlement upon which government authority rested. Since the document provided for a representative government, to rebel against it was to rebel against oneself. Lincoln would certainly have agreed with the idea, elicited during a later American agrarian revolt, that "opposition to the laws, in a free government, is a crime which liberty cannot tolerate." As the General Court had announced in its "Address to the People" in the autumn of 1786: "In a republican government the majority must govern: if the minor part governs it becomes aristocracy, if every one opposed at his pleasure, it is no government, it is anarchy and confusion." It was just such chaos that Lincoln experienced during the war and feared would tear his state apart now. It is little wonder that he preferred the status quo.[8]

Moreover, if the constitution were to be changed at all, it should contain more safeguards for property rather than fewer, or so Lincoln's son Benjamin Jr. thought. In a series of ten articles under the title of "The Free Republican," which first appeared in 1784 in the *Boston Magazine* and were later reprinted in the Boston *Independent Chronicle* in 1785 and 1786, the younger Lincoln declared that the real danger to republican government came from the fickleness of popular assemblies. The young lawyer analyzed the constitution of 1780 in the light of its obligation to provide security for the rights of persons and of property. Drawing examples from history, he argued that "no government can be free, where civil power is not proportioned to the rights of individuals, and consequently that men possessed of property are entitled to a greater share in political authority than those who are destitute of it." In his profoundly conservative vision Lincoln's son declared that republican governments could survive only if they struck the right balance between property rights and personal liberties. The science of government consisted in finding that balance. The security of property, however, "must, in the minds of all men, be ranked among the first objects of civil society." Critical to achieving this balance was choosing leaders of "great wisdom and great virtue."[9]

The close and sympathetic exchange of views which Lincoln shared with his son over the years would suggest that the father held similar opinions about society in general and the government of Massachusetts in particular. Lincoln inherited his vision of society from his Puritan forebears. It was an organic and harmonious conception in which society was ordered by wealth, property, and talents, in which men chose those of "great wisdom and great virtue" to govern in the interests of the whole society. Even if men were equal in the sight of God, that did not mean they were equal within society. Differences stood at the heart of an orderly community. If, say in Hingham, a rough equality existed, it was because everyone knew his place. Thus, it is not surprising to find that Lincoln feared the Shaysites far more than he ever had feared the British bayonet. In his mind the insurgents promised to level all distinctions, erase the security of property, and upset the harmony of the personal relations which provided for the sure and smooth functioning of the social system.[10]

To heighten Lincoln's anxiety further the Shaysites threatened to undermine the economic foundations of society. In their pursuit of paper money they sought a depreciated currency, which could be used to pay off debts more cheaply than with hard-to-find specie. Given Lincoln's large personal debt and shaky finances, it would have been in his interest to support such a policy himself. By the end of 1786 Lincoln's trading business had come to a near standstill, and he was being squeezed for repayment of his debt to the Bank of Boston. Although he still held his state securities, they were worth only a small percentage of their face value in the market. Yet he never succumbed to the paper money mania sweeping the United States in the 1780s. The commercial system, he believed, rested on the inviolability of contract and a stable medium of exchange. To borrow hard cash and repay with inflated paper currency was to breach the sacredness of contract and to besmirch one's honor as a gentleman. Added to this was the frightening specter of legal tender laws. The passage of this legislation would force property owners to accept spurious paper notes in payment for real estate and other goods. If enough paper money were issued, it could lead to a wholesale redistribution of property. Despite the fact that, like the insurgents, Lincoln was struggling to hold onto the property he had acquired, he still identified with the wealthy men of property and commerce who dominated the Commonwealth's political and economic life.[11]

Thus, the Shaysites' threat to the constitutional and social order of the state, Lincoln's despair over the embattled state of the Confederation, and his own weak finances fueled a desperate sense of crisis in his mind. When the Massachusetts General Court adjourned in the fall, it had not fully addressed the concerns of the insurgents, nor did it provide sufficient means to put down the insurgency. That indecision mirrored divisions among the "friends of government" about how best to proceed. Given the lengths to which the Shaysites seemed willing to go, Lincoln did not see how "the dignity of government" could be supported without bloodshed. Yet, he wrote to Washington, "when a single drop is drawn, the most prophetic spirit will not, in my opinion, be able to determine when it will cease to flow." In Lincoln's mind the best hope for government was to declare a rebellion and gather a force that would overwhelm the insurgents. Anything else would merely encourage their defiance.[12]

In the fall of 1786 Gov. James Bowdoin came under increasing pressure to do something about the turbulence in the western counties. He tried to arrange with the Confederation to have a federal army raised to put down the insurgency. But lack of money and volunteers hampered the federal efforts, and they came to nought. The state militia, especially in the western counties, was unreliable at best. Finally, in early January 1787 Bowdoin proposed to recruit a volunteer army (mostly composed of militia from the eastern counties) to be commanded by Benjamin Lincoln. The old veteran was the logical choice. As first major general of the Commonwealth, Lincoln was first in the line of seniority. He also was widely known and popular. As early as December 1786, Jeremy Belknap, sensing a new spirit of resolution in the government to quell the rebellion, wrote that, "if the matter must come to a bloody contest, our good old Gen. Lincoln is to take the command; he has resumed his uniform and cockade on this occasion." And Gen. William Shepard wrote to Bowdoin on 17

December: "I should presume the command will be given to Gen. Lincoln, whose high reputation will avail much in this State." The choice also was calculated to reclaim lukewarm Shaysite sympathizers.[13]

Lincoln's reaction to the appointment appears nowhere on record. Yet the prospect of facing an army of Massachusetts citizens could not have been pleasant. Lincoln had seen civil war firsthand in the bitter fighting in South Carolina and Georgia. It had been war at its most brutal, a pointless and continuing vendetta, rather than a conflict waged over tangible objectives. Lincoln quite rightly feared the same thing might happen in Massachusetts. Besides, he wrote worriedly to Washington, "a government which has no other basis than the point of the bayonet" was so very different from the one they had fought to establish that it suggested that the Revolution had failed. Moreover, the Shaysites formed a body of troops that was as much a people's army as the volunteer one that Lincoln was to command. Lincoln had to be aware of the great support the insurgents enjoyed in their own communities, and he knew from experience how difficult a military expedition into that country could be.[14]

Added to these difficulties was the fact that the ranks of the insurgents were filled with army veterans, who no doubt had seen service under Lincoln during the Revolution. A few of the Shaysite leaders, such as Luke Day and Daniel Shays, had been officers in the Massachusetts Continental line. Lincoln had commanded militia units in Boston, at White Plains, and Saratoga. All evidence supports the view that he gained and kept the respect and loyalty of the New England units that he led. Now, barely four years after the signing of peace, he was to face the men he had formerly led from the other end of a gun. It was Washington who afterward openly acknowledged the irony of the situation when he wrote Benjamin Jr. that it must have been "very painful" for Lincoln "to be obliged to march against those men whom he had heretofore looked upon as his fellow citizens and some of whom had perhaps been his companions in the field."[15]

Nor did the expedition into the western counties face an easy task. Lincoln's orders were to protect the courts, assist the civil magistrates in executing the laws, and apprehend anyone attempting the destruction, detriment, or annoyance of the Commonwealth. Because no rebellion had been declared, however, Lincoln remained under the command of civil officers. The "rules of engagement" made any confrontation with the Shaysites problematic. As Lincoln explained, after the Riot Act had been read and before one hour elapsed, the Shaysites could disperse, only to reform somewhere else at another time. "So they may conduct themselves in perfect security from day to day untill a favorable moment shall offer, after the well affected to government are worn out, for them to commence the attack." It was a recipe for disaster, unless the insurgents refused to disperse or were provoked into firing on the government's troops. Then Lincoln would have a free hand to respond.[16]

Under these conditions Lincoln had nothing to gain and everything to lose by taking command of the expedition. If he defeated the insurgents and quashed the rebellion, it would add nothing to his military reputation, while it would permanently alienate the affections of great numbers of citizens. If, on the other hand, he lost, his reputation would be ruined, and any chance of political preferment would be lost along with it. It was especially risky given the divisions within the government. At any time the General Court might repudiate Bowdoin's actions, leaving Lincoln as the scapegoat for the government's repressive policies. Under the same circumstances James Warren or John Hancock would have been stricken with a convenient case of gout and begged off. It was, however, an appointment from which Lincoln, again, did not shrink.[17]

Certainly, Lincoln felt it was his duty to lead the expedition. Throughout his army service he had always sought to be a model republican, who would not refuse the call of his country to undertake even the most arduous assignments. It made little difference whether the service required was in the "field or the cabinet," he wrote his son—"a public servant must obey." He had made a virtue of sacrifice and uncomplaining toil. His reward was the public's acknowledgment that he was a man of integrity and public virtue. How better to show the public that one was worthy of high office than by taking on the most difficult and painful tasks? As his son wrote: "The only honours the citizens can of right pursue are those that result from distinguished virtue and reverence of the laws." Lincoln considered his command of the expedition to be correct on both counts.[18]

A volunteer army of forty-four hundred men was raised with some difficulty in January 1787. Since the General Court had not authorized such an expedition, the money had to come from private sources. Now that he had personal responsibility for the success of the expedition, Lincoln threw all his energies into the venture. He met with the principal men of Boston and personally solicited five thousand pounds from them toward the expenses of the expedition. Lincoln made sure these wealthy men "saw their interest" by suggesting to them "the importance of becoming loaners of a part of their property if they wished to secure the remainder." As further backing, he engaged the sons of the Massachusetts commercial elite as his aides. And he shrewdly asked for and received an address of support from the Massachusetts Society of the Cincinnati, of which he was president. Lincoln wanted as many influential men as possible publicly committed to the expedition before he made war on his fellow citizens.[19]

The campaign to subdue Shays's army was over so quickly that it mocked the terrors imagined by Lincoln, Bowdoin, and the supporters of the expedition. Lincoln left Boston on 20 January 1787 "in high spirits," at the head of a "respectable command." His friend Henry Jackson remarked to Henry Knox that Lincoln "stands high in the estimation of his friends and the people in general." The newspapers were filled with bellicose puffery. One writer in the *Massachusetts Centinel* was certain of victory. "Notwithstanding Mr. Shays's rodomontade, of defeating Gen. Lincoln, burning Boston, etc. gentlemen of judgement and discernment in the county of Hampshire, are of opinion, he will not think it adviseable to try an action with this General." It was surely an auspicious beginning.[20]

Along the road to Worcester, where government troops were sent to ensure the safety of the county court session about to open, Lincoln saw "a fine field for the sporting fancy of the Physiognomist to range in." Among the country people he met on the way, he wrote Bowdoin, many wore "the open smile of approbation & the most perfect good wishes . . . while in others a sullen anxiety marked every line of their faces." The latter appeared to be few, but Lincoln's observation points to the ticklish nature of such a civil contest. As Lincoln advanced, for example, reports arrived at headquarters of armed insurgents moving in every direction. Letters, some anonymous, named Shaysite sympathizers in every town. Intelligence, such as it was, poured in to Lincoln from the surrounding countryside, but its accuracy was questionable.[21]

Lincoln's strategy was simple, if difficult to execute. "The movements of the Insurgents must always regulate yours," he wrote to Gen. William Shepard, who had just taken control of the federal armory in Springfield. "Whenever they move in force towards us or elsewhere, tread on their heels." The insurgents, however, struck the first blow. On the day that Lincoln left Boston about twenty-three hundred farmers encircled Springfield, cutting off communications between Shepard's thousand-man militia force and Lincoln's army as it approached Worcester. When news of this reached Lincoln, he sent to Boston for reinforcements. His own force was three thousand, and he estimated the insurgents had gathered two thousand to face him. Lincoln did not command the overwhelming force he had counted on to humble the Shaysites. A young John Quincy Adams noted in his diary on 26 January that Lincoln "finds more difficulties in the affair he has undertaken, than were expected." And Henry Jackson betrayed his anxiety to Knox over this "business of the insurgents," which had become "very serious." Trying to convince himself that Lincoln would "give a good account of them," Jackson continued, "he has a fine body of men, well-officered, the whole of the monied men to support him." Thus, jittery Boston waited as Lincoln pressed on to Springfield.[22]

By the time he reached the town blood already had been spilled. On 25 January Daniel Shays led fifteen hundred farmers, marching in good order, against the defenses of the federal armory. After a warning from the government forces went unheeded, the insurgents attacked. Two cannon shots fired over the heads of the approaching farmers did not slow them, but rounds of grapeshot fired directly at the oncoming farmers broke their advance and dispersed them, leaving four dead and about twenty lying wounded in the snow. Without the force necessary to continue the fight, Shepard waited for Lincoln's troops to arrive, which they did around noon on 27 January. Lincoln lost no time in pursuing one party of the insurgents, led by Luke Day, to West Springfield, across the Connecticut River from the town, which the rebels occupied. With barely three hours' rest from their march, Lincoln's men crossed the frozen river and, with bayonets drawn and instructions to hold fire, forced the Shaysites to retire "in the utmost confusion and disorder." After pausing to reassess the situation, Lincoln canceled orders for reinforcements from Boston and Pittsfield. He then turned north with his troops and followed closely behind Shays, "treading on his heels," as the army of farmers retreated to Amherst and then passed on to defensive positions in Pelham, "a very strong mountainous Country" made further defensible by deep snow. Lincoln posted his men in Hadley and Hatfield and spent the next few days scouting Shays's position and preparing to take it by assault.[23]

As he advanced, Lincoln received a number of petitions from surrounding towns seeking truces so they could lay their grievances before the General Court, which was about to meet in Boston. Better still, they wanted to declare a truce until May, when the elections of town representatives to the next General Court would take place. By then the towns hoped they could muster enough strength legally to oppose the measures the government had taken to quell the revolt. Lincoln's answer was short: "I have not any power to make any compromise with Shays." Nor would he if he had. To Bowdoin he wrote in earnest that Shays was daily receiving supplies and recruits and that it would be difficult "if not impossible to put an end to such disorders, unless a Rebellion is declared to exist."

The insurgents "must be treated as open enemies," he concluded. "The sooner it is done the better." The declaration of a rebellion, he wrote to Gen. John Patterson, would remove "that delicacy which now in a degree fetter all our movements." To Shays himself Lincoln wrote that he should inform his "deluded followers" to surrender themselves and their arms to a justice of the peace and swear allegiance to the state. If done within three days, they would be recommended for a pardon. If not, Shays "must be answerable for all the ills which may exist in consequence thereof." In answer to another letter from the Shaysite leadership, Lincoln replied that he had no powers to "justify a delay of my operations; hostilities," he added, "I have not commenced."[24]

On Friday, 2 February, Lincoln reconnoitered Shays's defenses at Pelham, planning to attack the next day. But the movement so alarmed the insurgents that they retreated to Petersham, where they expected to receive help and reinforcements from the surrounding sympathetic towns. When Lincoln got word of this the next day, he resolved to end the revolt in one fell swoop by force-marching his men the thirty miles to Petersham that night and taking Shays and his men by surprise. The march began about eight o'clock on Saturday night. As Lincoln described it, "The first part of the night was light & the weather clement but between two and three o'clock in the morning, the wind shifting to the westward, it became very cold and squally." The wind rose as snow fell, covering the roads as the men struggled along in intense cold. The blizzard prevented the men from stopping to rest, so they slogged on in a semi-stupor, many suffering from frostbite. By nine o'clock Sunday morning, 4 February, the vanguard had reached the outskirts of Petersham. Even as cold and exhausted as they were, Lincoln's troops immediately attacked the town, climbing a steep hill in deep snow. The appearance of the government troops so surprised the insurgents that 150 were taken prisoner, while the rest escaped "by the most precipitate flight in different directions." They would never gather in such great strength again.[25]

Lincoln's relatively bloodless success was hailed in Boston, and the general and his men were the subjects of a congratulatory resolution by the General Court. The news was met with considerable relief in New York, where members of the Confederation Congress had been casting anxious eyes toward Massachusetts. Lincoln was feted as a hero, and rumors circulated that he would be elected lieutenant governor or even governor in the spring election. For months scores of bad poets flooded the newspapers with heroic couplets and assorted doggerel, including this epic poem published in the *Massachusetts Centinel*:

The mighty wolf is baneful to the sheep;
Storms in the spring will make the farmer weep;
The lagging frosts to blossoms prove unkind;
And county courts disturb a debtor's mind;
Of Lincoln's sword more ills does fame report,
Than of the wolves, and storms, and frosts, and county court.[26]

Even with Shays fleeing to Canada, however, the rebellion—as it had now been declared by the General Court—was by no means over. Pockets of the disaffected remained in Berkshire County to the west as well as in the counties of Hampshire and Worcester. Lincoln divided his troops and occupied many of the towns in those counties, administering the oath of allegiance to the Commonwealth. But, as he had noted to General Brooks just days before, "There is a frenzy among these people which greatly exceeds what I had any idea to find." How, under these circumstances, could the populace be reconciled with their government? Governing at the point of a bayonet was, as Lincoln had foretold, nearly impossible. Rebellion must be crushed, but it also was necessary, Lincoln wrote, to "reclaim its citizens, to bring them back fully to a sense of their duty, and to establish anew those principles, which lead them to embrace the Government with affection." Without this reconciliation the state would be in constant turmoil, and a government resting on republican principles would be impossible.[27]

Even before Lincoln's army had dispersed the rebels at Petersham the general had been trying to deal with the political consequences of the revolt. As prisoners were taken, Lincoln was forced to conduct a kind of political triage, categorizing the insurgents from least to greatest offenders. His orders to General Patterson provided a rough measure to distinguish among the rebels, directing that "any youths or simple men of years" who had been led astray might be sent home after giving up their weapons and taking the oath of allegiance. Those who knew what their actions entailed but now were "convinced of their errors" might be liberated under a bond to keep the peace and to appear in court at a later date. Some, of course, "being too inimical to be at large," should be jailed. And the "most dangerous characters," he advised, should be apprehended by the troops. These, as he pointed out in a private letter to Knox, the state would do well to execute. "A few prompt examples on the spot," he wrote, "will do more real service than ten times the number at a distance attended with the usual delay." How he expected executions to strengthen people's affection for the government, when their disaffection was "much more deeply rooted, and extensive, than was apprehended," is unclear. It was his unalterable opinion, however, that "if they will not submit to government, allured by the blessings of it, they must bend to its force." This yoke, he went on, would be "too galling for them long to bear" and would either result in their submission or "induce them to leave the State."[28]

The General Court passed a number of measures calculated to support Lincoln's efforts, in addition to declaring the western counties in rebellion and giving Governor Bowdoin extensive powers to subdue the rebels. They authorized more troops for a four-month period and a loan to support them. And they passed a law that disenfranchised all rebels who had not surrendered before 31 January 1787—the great majority of the insurgents. The act also made the rebels unfit for jury duty or to hold any office in the state. James Madison thought the measures harsh and was unsure whether the calm that Lincoln had restored would be "durable." He noted that, these measures notwithstanding, opposition to the state government was open and politically popular.[29]

Lincoln also found the opposition to be elusive and tenacious. From March to June bands of Shaysites preyed upon the "friends of government" in the western counties. Insurgents terrorized government officials, merchants, and lawyers, who made up the region's elite, through kidnapping, intimidation, and the destruction of property. John Warner reported from Worcester that "the bitter rebellious spirit of the insurgents in this county having continued unsubdued and stubborn; their insolence can be exceeded by nothing but their stupidity." The selectmen of the town of Brookfield complained that "some insurgents who have not taken the oath, who still wear the badge of rebellion in their hats, remain here very insolent," adding, "You should send soldiers to apprehend them and bring them to condign punishment." But apprehending them was difficult because rebels were striking targets in Massachusetts and then taking refuge in neighboring states, where Lincoln's troops could not follow. The General Court sought the cooperation of the governors of the surrounding states; Gov. George Clinton of New York, for example, proved amenable to helping capture the rebels. At one point the General Court asked Congress to permit Lincoln to march into any territory within the United States to apprehend the Shaysites. That request was denied. The situation, however, was grave enough that even Lincoln admitted that "ten thousand Men could not so cover the frontiers of this, as to prevent lurking parties from entering it over the Mountains, & plundering the Inhabitants & burning their buildings."[30]

173

While Lincoln maintained that only by dealing harshly with the Shaysite ringleaders could an end be put to this kind of social banditry, he nevertheless thought that disenfranchising a substantial body of the state's citizens was a grievous mistake. First, it severed the people from their government and made it impossible for them to obtain legal redress for their grievances. Second, it made no distinction between the leaders and those who followed them. "While they are in this situation," he wrote Knox, "they never will be reconciled to Government, nor will they submit to the terms of it, from any other Motive than fear excited by a constant military force extended over them." Many productive citizens would leave the state rather than submit; others would carry their resentment with them for the rest of their lives. Moreover, Lincoln went on, "these people have now no influence as a body, and their individual votes are not to be dreaded, for we certainly shall not admit the idea, that the Majority is with them in their political sentiments; if thus, how, upon republican principles, can we justly exclude them from the right of Governing." How, indeed? Those principles of representation were as much a part of the "goodly fabrick" Lincoln had fought for during the revolution as the security of persons and property.[31]

Although Lincoln disagreed privately with Governor Bowdoin over the pacification measures, publicly, he backed him to the hilt. The alternative was, in Lincoln's view, much worse. With elections for governor scheduled for early April there was a chance that the government's policy toward the Shaysites would be repudiated. As Benjamin Jr. expressed it to his brother, Theodore, "I am very apprehensive Mr. Hancock will be chosen for Govr and the General Court composed of men of the same kidney— insurgents all!" The election was understood to be a referendum on the handling of the rebellion by Bowdoin and Lincoln, and "many of the real and zealous friends to the government" were understandably fearful of the "probable evils" that would attend "an alteration of the great chair of office."[32]

Nominated for lieutenant governor, Lincoln came in for his share of press adulation and abuse. The winter's events had stimulated a tremendous interest in the coming election, and there was more than the usual newspaper comment. "You will see by the newspapers that the electioneering mania has taken full possession of all ranks of people," wrote William North to Knox in New York. "It is said that Faneuil Hall will be shook to its centre . . . by the clashing of the Bowdoin and Hancock parties." The supporters of Lincoln praised him to the skies as a man "of the *greatest* knowledge, industry and decision in business, strict oeconomy in public and private life; of the purest religion, and the most unimpeachable character for moral honesty." But "Impartialis," among others, thought that was a "farrago of the most gross and palpable flattery." He and others were unsettled by Lincoln's "military character," and especially by his membership in that "order of military nobility," the Society of the Cincinnati. "Candidas" thought Lincoln was "now acting in a station highly proper and fitted to his genius and profession." Thanks for his services in Shays's Rebellion notwithstanding, no amount of "gratitude" from the public would make Lincoln fit to head a republican government. And "Brutus" summed up their fears nicely by exclaiming that if Bowdoin were elected, "and his Friends succeed in the election G_L_n as Lt. Gov., the consequences to be feared from a union of the Military and Monied interest is truly alarming." His conclusion? "Elect Republicans, like Hancock, to office."[33]

Lincoln shared the eighteenth-century distaste for party politics and pretended to ignore the furious electioneering that went on that spring. Benjamin Jr. probably put it best when he wrote Lincoln during the Revolution of his disdain for the "insidious arts" of politics. His maxim was that a man "must be *sought* or must not be had." So, Lincoln maintained the appearance of disinterest, an attitude that was not difficult, as he spent most of April and May in the western counties as part of a three-man commission appointed to deal with the aftermath of the rebellion.[34]

Hancock, always a popular figure in Boston and already a multiterm governor of the state, took advantage of the rancor against Bowdoin and won the governor's chair by a three-to-one margin. Absent from state politics in the past two years, Hancock could afford to take a moderate and disinterested stance. His offer of clemency for convicted rebels and his pledge to alleviate the most grievous of the farmers' wrongs explain the huge margin of victory. The race for lieutenant governor was altogether different. Lincoln ran against the incumbent Thomas Cushing, for years associated with Hancock; Nathaniel Gorham, the speaker of the House of Representatives; and William Heath, the former revolutionary general. Lincoln was the top vote getter by a slim margin but did not receive a majority. The election was thrown into the House, which dropped Lincoln's name because, it was said, of his military character and sent those of Cushing and Gorham to the Senate. Cushing was unanimously reelected to the post. John Quincy Adams, a young Harvard student at the time, reported to his father that the opposition of Samuel Adams, a power in Massachusetts politics, was enough to deny the office to Lincoln. In fact, given the opposition of Adams and Hancock, who between them occupied the governor's chair for fifteen years, it is remarkable that Lincoln garnered as many votes as he did.[35]

While the new governor and General Court carried out their program of amnesty for the rebels and passed legislation easing the situation of debtors, Lincoln returned to private life. His friend Knox wanted Massachusetts to send him as a delegate to the convention scheduled to meet in Philadelphia that summer to amend the Articles of Confederation. But there was little chance of that. Lincoln had been repudiated by the voters and was out of favor with those in power. He was comforted only by his own conviction that he had done his duty and by the congratulations of his old commander George Washington. "The suppression of those tumults and insurrections with so little bloodshed," he wrote, "is an event as happy as it was unexpected." With the resignation of his command he turned his attention to Maine and his Passamaquody settlements.[36]

Yet the repercussions from Shays's Rebellion were much greater than the mere repudiation of Bowdoin and Lincoln in the spring elections. If the epicenter lay in western Massachusetts, strong tremors were felt as far away as South Carolina and Georgia. The turmoil in Massachusetts prodded advocates of a stronger national government to new urgency in their work to strengthen the Confederation Congress or scrap the Articles entirely and design a new frame of government. Unrest in New England so disturbed the leading political figures in other states that even those who opposed the nationalists agreed that changes would have to be made. Thus, the rebellion created a warm reception for the idea of political change at a time when nationalists and localists appeared to be deadlocked over the future course of the Union.[37]

As for Lincoln, he eagerly anticipated the results of the Philadelphia convention. Shays's Rebellion and its aftermath had jeopardized the republican framework, "the goodly fabrick," that he had fought to create. Whether from the weakness of the Confederation or the instability of the individual states, it seemed Lincoln was about to see those republican walls crumble. He would have agreed with his son's exasperation, when he wrote that it was clear that "the present system must go to the Devil." "Must," Ben Jr. asked, "the establishment of another be left to accident?" The conclave in Philadelphia that summer and the subsequent debate over the Constitution it created would provide the answer to his question.[38]

CHAPTER TWELVE

Securing the Revolution

> We must make haste slowly . . . if we act with judgment, temper and
> moderation, we shall, I have no doubt, in a short time, have a Govern-
> ment established, the influences of which will not only promote and
> preserve the happiness and interest of the United States, but the
> beneficial effects of it will be enjoyed by all the different nations of the
> world.
>
> *Benjamin Lincoln*

In its conception of a mixture of federal and state powers, the constitution that resulted from the summer's deliberations in Philadelphia was
both more and less than Lincoln could ever have imagined. In the early
1780s Lincoln had feared the coercive power of a central government,
preferring to rely on the virtuous cooperation of independent republican
states. But by 1787 he had given up the idea of a loose union of republican states for the stability and security of a strong national government.
The proposed constitution, however, divided power so as to preserve the
states as republican experiments while providing for an effective national
government. It was a constitution Lincoln supported unequivocally, and
he would soon cast his vote for it and stand for office on its behalf.

The proposed constitution arrived in Boston on 25 September 1787.
It was published the next day in an extra edition of the *Massachusetts
Centinel* and subsequently ran in all the state's newspapers. While the
early reaction to it was favorable, opposition soon formed, fueling a debate that reached the farthest corners of the state. "Much has been said
for and against it," Lincoln wrote his son Theodore. "I think however the
arguments in favor of it preponderate." Lincoln's assessment of the
constitution's chances for ratification fluctuated over the next two months,
but, despite the high stakes, he never wavered from his belief that the
document should be discussed with "moderation, candor, and fairness."

He was especially concerned that the constitution's friends realize there was more at stake than the mere passage of a frame of government. How the constitution was adopted or rejected was critically important. To adopt it "by precipitate or violent measures" would only ensure hostility toward the new government and sow the seeds of its destruction. The objections of the opposition had to be answered clearly and persuasively, with moderation and tact, to "soothe and reconcile their minds to the exercise of the government."[1]

In October the General Court called a state convention for 9 January 1788 to consider the proposed constitution. The people of Hingham elected Lincoln and the Reverend Daniel Shute as delegates. Among the 364 delegates at the convention Lincoln was not surprised to see many "insurgents" of the previous year's disturbances, including a number of "Shays's officers." Nor was it surprising that, according to him, they formed the kernel of opposition to the constitution.[2]

That opposition seemed to be in the majority, at least initially, but the friends of the constitution—or Federalists, as they came to be called—undertook the patient process of debating each section of the long document. The Federalists mustered a battalion of the most able speakers in the state to answer the criticisms and fears of the opposition. The objections to the constitution centered on a fear of the concentrated power given to the proposed national government and the possibility that individual liberties would be lost by its adoption. As the debates progressed in front of "a vast many people attending in the galleries" of the convention hall, the Federalists gradually broke down the defenses of the Antifederalists point by point. Still, the issue was in doubt until the last moment, when John Hancock was induced to swing his influence behind the Federalists. Even so, the constitution passed by the slim margin of nineteen votes.[3]

There is no record that Lincoln spoke on the convention floor, yet his frequent reports to George Washington show he followed the debates closely. That he did not participate more fully in the debate can be attributed to several factors. First and foremost, the Federalists had a large group of skilled and experienced speakers on which they might draw. Lincoln's lack of formal education and training in public speaking would have led him to defer to those men. His public life had been spent for the most part in small assemblies: the Massachusetts Council, Washington's meetings of general officers, his own councils of war, cabinet meetings, and congressional committees. Also, Lincoln's speech impediment made him uncomfortable speaking before large groups. Second, Lincoln's concern that the debate take place in an atmosphere of moderation would have prompted him to keep silent so as not to alienate those who eyed his military connections with suspicion. This not only included delegates from western Massachusetts who had been involved in Shays's Rebellion but also those who were offended by Lincoln's membership in the Society of the Cincinnati and others concerned about the proposed federal government's power to declare war and create a standing army.[4]

But there was a third, and more personal, reason that explained Lincoln's reticence to speak at the convention. On 18 January, just a week into the convention proceedings, Lincoln's eldest son, Ben Jr., died of a sudden illness. It was a crushing blow, made all the more so since Ben left a wife and two infant sons and had launched a promising law career. Lincoln was devastated. "Our loss is great," he wrote his friend Washington. "Our wounds are deep." Lincoln had lost more than a "beloved son, an agreeable companion, and a sincere and confidential friend"; he had lost many of his hopes for the future. His pride in his son's achievements, his hopes for the young man on the threshold of a brilliant public career, his comfort in knowing that Ben would care for him "in the evening of life," all had been blasted. And, at a time when his own finances were troubled, Lincoln was saddled with the added burden of his son's family. One of the first casualties of his son's death was the sale of Ben's fine library, painstakingly acquired over the past ten years.[5]

Lincoln's money problems were acute. Seriously in arrears on his loan payments to the Massachusetts Bank, Lincoln was forced to sell a schooner that he owned and plead with his son Theodore to send any cash not directly needed by the settlement in Maine. He even went so far as to investigate how much he could get from the sale of the two thousand pounds in state securities he had held for nearly a decade. When Lincoln learned he would receive only "one penny in the pound" he decided to hold onto the notes. If their value did not rise, he confided to Theodore, there was little chance he could remain in Hingham. He would have to move to Maine and "go to farming in good earnest." "While I have my health," he wrote, "I can get my living any where if the land is good." But, he continued, "it is hard, from want of faith in the public, to be driven to hard labor [at this stage of life]."[6]

Lincoln was able to postpone a return to farming, at least for another year, thanks to the determination of the Massachusetts Federalists to nominate him for lieutenant governor in the place of the recently deceased Thomas Cushing. Lincoln's vote-getting ability, demonstrated in the previous year's election, his strong Federalist stance, and his revolutionary background made him an ideal candidate to share the ticket with John

Hancock, who was running for reelection as governor. A strong Federalist showing was a must if the new federal government was to get the backing it needed to succeed. Lincoln feared that "the antifederalists were in hopes of throwing such an influence into the Government by a change of its officers, as to prevent an organization of the General Government by the State." In Elbridge Gerry, one of Massachusetts's delegates to the Constitutional Convention (and a nonsigner), and James Warren, a prominent state revolutionary politician, the Antifederalists had a formidable ticket. Hancock seemed in no danger of defeat, but the Federalists were unable to unite behind one candidate for the lieutenant governorship. A large Boston contingent promoted Samuel Adams for the post, and neither Lincoln nor Adams would give way to the other. In the face of the challenge of antifederalism "A Friend to Union," writing in the *Massachusetts Centinel,* posed the critical question: "Shall the friends to good order and righteous government, with the rancour of party spirit, quarrel which of *two good men* shall have their suffrages—and beat out each other's brains for the promotion of the *same interest?* It is absurd."[7]

Absurd it might be, but the Federalist camp remained divided to election day. Lincoln's supporters, unable to capitalize on his military service during the Revolution to set him apart from his opponents, who had all played prominent civilian roles in the conflict, emphasized his popularity with the voters. Who, asked "Pythias," will acquire the confidence of the people through "the popularity and condescension of his manners?" Who, asked "Candour," has "the most pleasing manners, the happiest talent at conciliation," and has engaged "the affections and esteem of the people in the country?" And, after pointing out Lincoln's plurality of seven thousand votes in the previous year's election, another wrote: "Is it not possible that Mr. *Lincoln* will have a much greater number of votes than Mr. *Adams?* It certainly is, and a candid man will confess it." Private letters harped on the same themes. "It is my opinion," wrote Martin Gay, who followed the election from London, "[that] Lincoln is the man to succeed to that Honble and lucrative post. The faculty of pleasing all parties, and the great abilities he has Display'd [will ensure his election]."[8]

Though the opposition did all it could to tar Lincoln with a militaristic brush—one newspaper published a serial diatribe against the Society of the Cincinnati which ran all spring—the "Man of the People," as another article called him, won 10,204 of the 21,096 votes cast. Warren, the Antifederalist candidate, with 6,157 votes, came in a distant second. But Adams had polled 3,495 votes, and that was enough to prevent Lincoln from getting a majority of the Federalist supporters. As it had the year before, the election was thrown into the House of Representatives, which constitutionally was required to pick two candidates to send to the Senate. Unlike the year before, however, they chose the winner and runner-up, Lincoln and Warren. The Federalist-dominated Senate then chose Lincoln by a vote of 20 to 8. It was, according to Lincoln, a victory for the new constitution.[9]

It was a year full of honors. Aside from the lieutenant governorship Lincoln was elected captain of Massachusetts's oldest military unit, the Ancient and Honorable Artillery Company, in an elegant ceremony conducted in a flower-bedecked hall. The yearly election was one of Boston's main events, and the recipient of the office had reached the pinnacle of society. In another public ceremony Lincoln presided over the 1788 Harvard Commencement. And, at the annual Fourth of July dinner of the Society of the Cincinnati at the Bunch of Grapes Tavern, Lincoln was reelected president, chairing the dinner and proposing the toasts. How the veteran of those difficult campaigns must have basked in the admiration of his fellow citizens, quietly relishing the acknowledgment of his stature.[10]

The eighth toast that Lincoln gave at the Fourth of July dinner read: "A Speedy and efficacious operation to the new Constitution." Elections for the new Congress were being organized in the states, and electors would soon be selected to choose a president and vice president of the United States. Once again Lincoln took it upon himself to report to Washington on the outcome of political events in Massachusetts. The Federalists could claim victory in the battle to adopt the constitution; by August eleven of the thirteen states had ratified it. But Lincoln feared that "every exertion will be made to introduce into the new government . . . characters unfriendly to those parts of it, which in my opinion are its highest orniments and its most precious jewels." The election of Antifederalists into federal office would clog the operation of the government and turn the people against it. It was critical, therefore to elect Federalists so that the new government would have a chance to succeed. Lincoln was confident that Washington would be chosen president, but he was anxious to put in a good word for John Adams as vice president. Although John Hancock also had been mentioned in this connection, Lincoln was quick to deprecate the governor's chances and even hinted that Hancock was a tool of Antifederalist interests. Lincoln's pleasure was tangible as he reported to Washington during the fall and winter the predominately Federalist results of the Senate and House elections and the choice of presidential electors. The ultimate triumph occurred on 4 February 1789, when Massachusetts cast its ballots unanimously for Washington and Adams.[11]

Still, as the new federal Congress met in New York City in March 1789, Lincoln expressed his fear that influential Antifederalists would succeed in sabotaging the new government. "It doth not require the spirit of prophecy to foresee that various cloggs and embarrassments will be thrown in the way of its progress," he wrote John Adams in April. It would greatly surprise him, he continued, "that the very people who were so lately intoxicated with large draughts of liberty and were thirsting for more . . . should so soon be brought to adopt" the new system. "We cannot yet," he warned Adams, "consider ourselves in the Harbour of Safety." Adams, replying in July 1789, shared his apprehension, noting that, with John Hancock and Samuel Adams at the head of the Massachusetts government, Gov. George Clinton in New York, and former governor Patrick Henry in Virginia, all known to be either lukewarm or vehemently opposed to the constitution, "a convulsion with such men engaged openly, or secretly, in favor of it would be a serious evil." Lincoln's reply was uncharacteristically bitter. Speaking of John Hancock, Lincoln wrote: "The conduct of our great man, is no less painful to us, than alarming to you. By his frequent addresses to the people, and by the trumpeters of his fame, they are taught to believe that he is, almost, the only guardian, in the commonwealth, of their rights." Hancock may "sport with the rights of the people and trample upon our constitution with impunity." But when he is called to account, he has only to whip up the people against the "aristocratical junto," men, Lincoln pointed out, who favored good energetic government. That was enough to preserve Hancock in the good graces of the people, who considered him "the source of liberty and the people's patron." That, Lincoln said, was a "Strange delusion!"[12]

Lincoln's bilious portrait of the governor was not entirely the result of his fears that Hancock might undermine the federal government. A year earlier, in the summer of 1788, Lincoln's quiet enjoyment of the public's plaudits had been broken by Hancock's announcement that the lieutenant governor would not be appointed captain of the Castle (formerly Fort William and now Fort Independence). This fort, which defended Boston's harbor, traditionally had been commanded by the lieutenant governor, who received a considerable sum in lieu of a salary. Hancock's decision was publicly humiliating: previous lieutenant governors, including the far-from-military Thomas Cushing, always had been appointed to the post. But it also created personal difficulties for Lincoln. It meant that Lincoln received no remuneration whatsoever for his largely ceremonial office. The reason for the slight can only be ascribed to the petty jealousy of John Hancock, whose ambition was monumental and whose hunger for public acclaim likewise was ravenous. Hancock suspected Lincoln of seeking to supplant him in the governor's chair, and this probably led him to deny Lincoln the office. But Hancock, who considered himself a military man as well as a politician, was aware that Lincoln's extensive army service eclipsed his own brief tenure as head of the Massachusetts militia. And in Hancock's mind there was room for only one hero in the affections of the people—himself. In a letter of June 1788 Lincoln attempted to persuade Hancock that rumors of his alleged ambitions to become governor were not only groundless but that they also placed Lincoln in "a sad predicament." As Lincoln explained, if he were inattentive to Hancock, it would be interpreted as an omission of duty; if attentive, that it "proceeds from the worst of designs." And Lincoln closed by asking for a personal interview with the governor to straighten out any misunderstanding that might have arisen between them.[13]

Lincoln's explanation fell on deaf ears. Hancock withheld the appointment, which provoked a yearlong newspaper war and a debate in the General Court over the governor's high-handed action. Friends of each man eagerly joined in the battle. Lincoln's friends hoped to unite all the "true" Federalists behind him and break Hancock's stranglehold on power for good. Hancock's backers defended him warmly. They shrewdly chose Samuel Adams, a lukewarm supporter of the new federal government but a man whose revolutionary credentials were impeccable, to join with the governor in an all-out attack on Lincoln's friends in the Federalist faction. The polemics became so bitter and the breach between Hancock and Lincoln so wide that it was clear that one or the other would have to be replaced in the coming election. In the end Lincoln lost not only the election but his political career as well.

The battle was joined in the summer of 1788. In the early exchange of views both sides claimed that some provision should be made for the lieutenant governor—some through the command of the Castle, others through a salary. Various writers who approved Hancock's decision explained that the command was unimportant, merely a sinecure that should be done away with; or that a military man independent of high office should be appointed to command such an important post; or that, constitutionally, the governor was not obliged to appoint the lieutenant governor; and so on. Most of these articles called for the General Court to allow the lieutenant governor a salary. Those who deplored the decision to withhold the appointment pointed out that all the previous lieutenant governors since 1780 had held the post and that Hancock's decision was based more on personal pique than a desire to economize government spending. They also noted that the General Court would find it politically difficult to provide a salary for the "second magistrate," and thus the affront to Lincoln would continue.[14]

If it made Lincoln uncomfortable to see his circumstances bandied about in the newspapers, it must have been downright humiliating for him to read the debates in the General Court on the "Support of the Lieut Governor," which began on 15 January 1789. Lincoln had kept "a most perfect silence both publick and private" on the matter, only intimating to a few friends his distaste for its public discussion. But the debates in the legislature played to a full gallery, and beneath the polite discussion of constitutionality, republican government, and the division of powers between the executive and legislative branches, clothed as it was in "the charms of eloquence," lay the naked conflict between two powerful bodies of men. Lincoln's friends were unable to challenge Hancock's decision on the Castle, but they did manage to pass a resolution—by a mere four votes—creating a salary for the lieutenant governor. Unable to pass the committee's recommendation of a salary of £300 (the average return from the command of the Castle), the House ultimately decided on £160. This was seen as another slap in Lincoln's face by many Federalists; even so, as it turned out, he saw not a penny of this sum.[15]

There the matter might have stood but for the publication of an extraordinarily vituperative series of articles which appeared in the *Massachusetts Centinel* in February and March 1789. These pieces, signed "Laco" and since attributed to Stephen Higginson, a Boston merchant and politician, attacked Hancock with such bitter fury and bile as to provoke a storm of disapproval, even from those who had never found Hancock a particularly attractive politician. The backlash was so intense that it swept Lincoln in its wake; his silence was interpreted as "giving encouragement to the slander." Moreover, it was true, as "Junius" stated in another article, that, in all the controversy over the command of the Castle, no writer had ever "attempted any thing against His Honour's [Lincoln's] private or personal character." Even Hancock's supporters were careful to give Lincoln his full due as a revolutionary patriot and an honest and able man. That made it all the more glaring when Higginson gave way to the "utmost extent of personal abuse" in his attacks on Hancock.[16]

After Laco's appearance in print there seemed to be nothing Lincoln's friends could do to sustain his support and popularity in the Commonwealth. It was clear that either Hancock or Lincoln must be replaced in the April elections, and the governor's popularity had never been higher. As "Sidney" wrote, "A divided house is pregnant with every mischief."

Calls to replace Lincoln with Samuel Adams multiplied as the elections approached. Lincoln's supporters argued in vain that their man had garnered more votes in the last election than any previous lieutenant governor and that his "integrity, publick and private virtues" would ensure him a similar result in 1789. Even the recounting by "No Party Man" of a litany of Lincoln's services to the Commonwealth could not sustain him in his fight against Sam Adams. For Lincoln the year's wrangling came to a humiliating close with the election of Hancock and Adams.[17]

The election did more than turn Lincoln out of office. It was clear to all that, as long as John Hancock retained his grip on Massachusetts politics, Lincoln would have no place there. Their estrangement was permanent and can be illustrated by an incident that happened soon after Lincoln left office. The artillery election was held on 1 June and as captain Lincoln was to resign his post in favor of the newly elected candidate. As Jeremy Belknap told it: "The most extraordinary part of the story is that Gov. H[ancock] had a *convenient* fit of the gout, and could not appear on the Common, the usual place where the old officers resign and the new ones are invested. However, Lincoln proved himself an *older* general, by insisting on a personal interview, and actually entering the bed-chamber, where the ceremonies were performed under the inspection of the physician and nurse." Lincoln had outflanked Hancock, and, as Belknap added, "much risibility was thereby occasioned among those who know the *real* character of the popular idol." Laugh as they might, however, the real victory was Hancock's, for by his studied contempt he had made it clear that Lincoln's career in state politics was over.[18]

Lincoln's mortification was complete. James Warren was right on two counts when he wrote that Lincoln "must wish he had never been in [the lieutenant governorship], unless the predicament he is now placed in may make him more an Object of Attention in the General Government, and secure him a place there." Lincoln had not waited until his defeat was announced in order to solicit a place in the new federal government. In February Lincoln had written to his old friend George Washington, who had just been elected president of the United States. In it he described the predicament in which he found himself: financially embarrassed by the inability of the state to fund its debt; having invested his Continental securities in Maine lands that would "not now sell, or yeild any considerable profit"; and deprived of the emoluments of state office by the jealousy of Hancock and the penuriousness of the General Court. "After forty years close application to business," Lincoln continued, "I am stripped of those means of support, upon which I had leaned with too much confidence, for my own interest and happiness." Lincoln ended the letter by asking for a position in the new government.[19]

Washington declined to promise anything, preferring to keep his options open, being "at liberty to act with a sole reference to justice & the public good." But he held out the hope of an appointment. While he would not be swayed by motives arising from "friendship or blood," Washington told his friend, "My inclinations are very sincere & very strong to serve you," because he had witnessed Lincoln's abilities during the war. That was enough for Lincoln, who began to solicit letters of recommendation from Massachusett's newly elected senators, Caleb Strong and Tristam Dalton, former governor James Bowdoin, speaker of the Massachusetts House of Representatives Nathaniel Gorham, his old friend Henry Knox, who had replaced him as secretary at war of the Confederation government, and the new vice president of the United States, John Adams. These were men he had known for years, men who knew his talents and abilities and had no problem recommending him for a federal post. Still, his failures since those days of promise at the end of the war had left him weary. As he wrote to Strong of his wish to return to public life, "I am like an old Gambler, who having lost his property is disposed to take one game more hoping for better luck so that he may make himself whole in the sum."[20]

Soliciting an office might have been a gamble, but Lincoln left little to chance. When he learned that rumor had it that he would refuse anything less than one of the first offices of the government—a cabinet position, for example—he quickly wrote Washington and his Massachusetts sponsors that this idea was untrue. As he told Washington, "This is so far from being the case that I should feel well satisfied to hold that, in which I might be thought by your Excellency to be most useful." That letter signaled Lincoln's desperation better than any amount of pleading might have done. Despite letters from Congress in New York which sought to reassure him, the summer months passed anxiously. The alternative Lincoln had mentioned to Washington—that without an office in the new government he would be obliged to take up farming again—was reopened that summer. As Lincoln's son Theodore told his brother, Martin: "The appointments from Congress have not yet come on, if my father should not be provided for he intends to come down and live with me [in Maine]."[21]

After Washington's appointments were made known on 3 August it was clear that he had, for the most part, retained officers appointed by the states in the new federal jobs whenever he could, from a belief that those appointments would please the states better than men imposed upon localities by a central government. An exception was Lincoln's appointment to the collectorship of Boston. Three men had worked in revenue positions in that city in the past decade; all three were superseded by Lincoln's appointment. Two of the men, James Lovell and Thomas Melville, became subordinate officers in Lincoln's office. Heavy lobbying by Theodore Sedgwick, a congressman from western Massachusetts, and John Adams was partly responsible for the decision. Sedgwick's insistence that "all men who wished well to the measures of this government and were the means of obtaining it in Massa. most ardently wished" for Lincoln's appointment had its effect on the president, especially when it was reinforced by the body of Massachusetts Federalists. The opposition to Lincoln, Sedgwick had told Washington, "was founded solely on a knowledge and dread of your [Lincoln's] virtues and talents." That the decision was not an easy one, however, is shown by Adams's assertion that "his exertions for Gen. Lincoln had torn open an hornet's nest at Boston."[22]

Massachusetts Federalists were happy about the appointment. Fisher Ames, writing from New York, where Congress was in session, made it a test of political orthodoxy by stating, "Every good man in Massachusetts will be gratified." Some of Lincoln's friends were afraid that he would think the position beneath him; Knox thought the collectorship was inadequate but conceded that it was "the best thing that can be offered at present." They need not have worried. Christopher Gore wrote to a friend that the appointment seemed to have renewed Lincoln's "youth and happiness." The collectorship was a safe and lucrative haven from the uncertainties of commercial life and the vicissitudes of popular government. Lincoln was extremely pleased with the prospect of a steady income and not having to move to New York or live away from home for most of the year. To Theodore he wrote that the position "will give us a handsom living & I think some over." He readily accepted the appointment. One of the first decisions he made, probably with a great deal of satisfaction, was to write Hancock and resign his commission as first major general of militia. Lincoln then lost no time appointing his subordinates and arranging his personal affairs to begin his duties as soon as possible.[23]

What the position lacked in national prestige, it made up for in hard cash. From the beginning the post gave Lincoln more than a "hansom living." As early as 1793, the collector made over four thousand dollars, an immense sum for the time. In 1801, as foreign trade began a decade-long rise to record levels, the port of Boston poured almost one and a half million dollars into the federal Treasury; Lincoln's share that year was over eight thousand dollars. For the first time since leaving Hingham to join the Continental army in 1777, Lincoln had a stable income and one he believed to be commensurate with his position in life.[24]

Despite America's inveterate dislike of taxation in general, and customs duties in particular, the collection of import duties was on the whole cheerfully accepted. Smuggling did take place, as did other ingenious practices, such as an attempt to disguise fish from Nova Scotia as a local product, not only to avoid paying taxes but to collect a bounty as well. But a few well-publicized prosecutions seemed to keep those tricks at a tolerable level. More difficult was enforcing the law fairly without alienating Boston's rich and powerful mercantile community, or, as Lincoln put it, to avoid interpreting the revenue laws so as to "sour many of our best merchants & friends to the government." Enforcing the law was a delicate business, especially at the beginning of the fragile new Republic, when the support of influential men was doubly important. Lincoln's prestige in the Massachusetts Federalist camp and his connections with national leaders surely helped enforce his rulings in the early days of the revenue system.[25]

The most lucrative of Lincoln's duties was the actual collection of federal taxes, and with an office filled with reliable men and efficient lieutenants the work went smoothly. Lincoln's biggest headache, and least remunerative responsibility, was his supervision of "Light-houses, Beacons, Buoys and Public Piers." More time, travel, and effort went into that thankless task than all the rest combined. In 1793 Lincoln supervised seven lighthouses—that is, contracted for a lighthouse keeper, supplied the oil, inspected the premises, handled complaints, and so forth—for fifty-four dollars. The settlement of Maine and the growth of commerce there required the building of several lighthouses along that coast in the 1790s. The Portland light, contracted for by Lincoln in 1789 was, complained one man to his congressman in 1792, already beginning "to tumble down." Lincoln, although "a good man," had been taken advantage of and the place would have to be rebuilt. The collector quickly learned his lesson and farmed out lighthouse contracts to his sons, Theodore and Martin, to build under his direct supervision. They built the Cape Cod Lighthouse in 1797. After past complaints Lincoln was anxious to have "the Light a good one & everything done as it ought to be done."[26]

Lincoln's influence was great, not only from the income and stature the office brought him but also from appointments he had the power to make. The collector's office normally employed more than fifty men in the 1790s—a naval officer, a surveyor, ship captain and crew, clerks, inspectors of customs, gaugers, weighers, and measurers. Add to that the lighthouse contractors, the shipbuilders, the suppliers of lighthouse oil, the day-to-day contacts with the mercantile community, and Lincoln presided over the makings of a political machine. His influence also extended to places not under his immediate control. His son-in-law Hodijah Baylies, a former aide-de-camp of George Washington, was appointed to the collectorship of Dighton, Massachusetts. Not surprisingly, Lincoln's initial appointments were all "friends to government," those who fervently supported the new constitutional order. Applicants seeking federal office in Massachusetts were advised to get Lincoln's recommendation before sending their requests to the president. Lincoln's influence was estimated to be so great that by the end of the decade—years that saw Americans divided into bitterly partisan Federalist and Republican camps—he was accused by the Republicans of having "but one republican under all his appointments as collector." After Thomas Jefferson's election as president in 1800 brought the Republicans to power, calls for Lincoln's removal became louder, because, it was asserted, only his replacement with a Republican would allow that party to "rise with brilliance." If that seemed a trifle exaggerated, there was no doubt that Lincoln was a formidable force in Massachusetts federalism.[27]

CHAPTER THIRTEEN

Frontier Diplomat

> The savage arm is too feeble, in any other way, to counteract the
> progress of their civilized neighbours; they . . . will continue retiring
> before the enlightened husbandman, until they shall meet those regions
> of the north, into which he cannot pursue them.
>
> *Benjamin Lincoln*

Lincoln had barely managed to get the Boston collector's department "arranged agreeably to my liking" in August 1789 when he received a letter from President Washington informing him that Congress was contemplating a diplomatic mission to the southern Indians. Would Lincoln accept an appointment as a commissioner to "establish a permanent and lasting peace" between the Creek Nation and the United States? Lincoln's only experience with Indian negotiations had been a short stint as a state commissioner in talks with the Penobscot tribe in Maine in 1785–86. Nonetheless, in order to give the proper weight and dignity to this diplomatic effort, Washington explained that he needed "persons who have been known in public life," "respectable characters," and preferably men who are "held in high estimation in the Southern States" without being from that region. It was a flattering proposition and one that Lincoln, so recently on the receiving end of federal largesse, could not refuse. He was prepared, therefore, when Washington wrote him on 20 August from New York City to "come on *immediately.*" After packing a good "suit of Regimentals," he set off for New York by stage at 4 A.M. on 26 August with his secretary son-in-law, Abner Lincoln, arriving three days later.[1]

Lincoln spent several days in New York with Secretary of War Henry Knox and President Washington, discussing the administration's expectations and the situation in the South. The new federal government was trying to wrest control of Indian affairs from the states, whose record in dealing with Native Americans had been far from successful. The constant encroachment of white settlers on tribal lands sparked incessant conflict along the borders between Indian and white settlements. Southern and western whites called on the federal government for protection at the same time they sought agressively to expand their land holdings at the expense of the Indians. Washington and Knox were loathe to intervene militarily, primarily because of the financial burden it would create for the fragile new government. An expensive, drawn-out Indian war had to be avoided at all costs. Yet the new government needed the support of the states if it were to govern successfully. And part of the reason states such as Georgia had ratified the Constitution was to engage the power of the federal union in their fight against the Indians. Besides, the administration was as interested as the states in securing Indian lands for white settlement. The 1783 Treaty of Paris between Great Britain and the United States had vested in the latter all the lands east of the Mississippi River and north of the thirty-first parallel. To exercise control over those lands for which it claimed sovereignty, however, the United States had to deal with the various independent Indian nations that occupied them. It sought to make the Indians acknowledge their dependence on the United States, even as it negotiated with them as independent nations. And in contrast to the individual states, which exerted little control over white migration, the federal government sought a more orderly, controlled expansion based on acquiring lands through purchase rather than conquest. It believed that the arts of diplomacy reflected the ideals of the new Republic better than the exterminating sword.[2]

Thus, it was that Lincoln, David Humphreys, a former aide to Washington, and Cyrus Griffin, a former president of Congress, set sail for Georgia on 31 August with two companies of soldiers. They arrived in Savannah after an "unusually rough" passage of nearly a fortnight. After ten days of traveling—including "a fatiguing journey through the deep sands" from Savannah to Augusta, the breakdown of their wagon, and a ride on horseback of some seventy-five miles through "a dreary wilderness"—they reached the treaty site at Rock Landing on 20 September. Their instructions were to negotiate a peace between Georgia and the Creek Nation, while confirming the cessions made by the Indians in previous treaties. To swing this deal the commissioners were authorized to guarantee the integrity of the remaining Creek lands, offer gifts, and arrange a secure port of call for their import trade. It would not be enough.[3]

The two thousand Creeks whom Lincoln found waiting at Rock Landing were led, after a fashion, by the tough and wily Alexander McGillivray, the son of a Scottish trader and French mestizo mother. Over the years McGillivray had become the spokesman for a number of the Creek clans, and the federal government saw him as the key to persuading the Creeks to accept the treaty. As David Humphreys noted, McGillivray's "word is a Law to the Creeks." McGillivray had fashioned strong political and trading ties with Spanish officials in Florida and New Orleans which had enabled the Creeks to maintain their independent and agressive stance against the United States. At times stridently anti-American, McGillivray's diplomacy rested on the willingness of Spain to stand behind the Creeks as well as the reluctance of the United States to engage in open war.[4]

McGillivray was not predisposed to be helpful during negotiations with the United States. He thought the Americans were "intoxicated with High Ideas of National Consequence" after their victorious war with the British. In their dreams of "greatness and Power" the Americans felt they could "Seize with impunity every foot of Territory belonging to the Red Natives," exterminating them, if necessary, to gain their ends. Nor did he have much faith in the negotiating process itself, given the sorry history of Creek-American relations to that point. But he was suitably impressed by the importance of the commissioners coming to treat with the Creeks. "So respectable" an appointment, he wrote hopefully, "was purposely made to give us full and ample satisfaction in regard to our Land grievances." Thus, the negotiations began on a mistaken, if amicable, footing.[5]

While Lincoln and Humphreys waited for Cyrus Griffin and the wagon laden with gifts to arrive in camp, the two commissioners had informal talks with McGillivray and other Creek chiefs. There was "much general talk," Humphreys noted, "expressive of real desire to establish a permanent peace upon equitable terms." The dining, drinking, and flattery continued for several days until the morning of 24 September, when the commissioners were invited to give their treaty proposals to the Creeks in council.[6]

Seated "three or four deep" around the council square, which was enclosed with "boughs and branches," were the notables of the Creek nation. After the ceremony of the black drink, a caffeinated tea used by the Creeks as a purifying beverage and as a gesture of welcome, Lincoln presented the commission's credentials and made a speech that carried as much threat as entreaty for peace. "Our Union," Lincoln said, "which was a child, is grown up to manhood; so that it can speak with a louder voice, and strike with a stronger arm, than ever it has done before." Lincoln tried to convince the Creeks that commercial arrangements with the Americans, including a free port, would be in their interest. After making the case for peace, he read the proposed treaty and then left to give the council a chance to discuss the proposals. That Lincoln might have had an inkling of what the Indian response would be is shown by a story he alledgedly told some years later. At some point in the negotiations Lincoln was invited by a chief to sit down on a log. "It was not long before he was desired to move, and in a few moments to proceed, and the request was repeated, till he found himself at the end of the log." The chief once again asked him to move down, to which Lincoln replied that "he could move no farther. 'Just so it was with us,' the chief answered. 'You have moved us back to the sea, and now ask us to go further.'"[7]

The draft treaty did, indeed, seek to push the Creeks ever farther from the lands they had heretofore enjoyed. They strongly objected to two articles of the draft treaty: the first required them to acknowledge themselves under the authority and protection of the United States and banned them from treaty making with any other power, and the second delineated the proposed boundary line according to Georgian territorial claims. The Creeks proposed to end negotiations and maintain a truce until these articles were changed. According to McGillivray, the "puppy" Humphreys spent the following three days trying to persuade him to accept the disputed articles, until at last the Creek chief told him "By G I would not have such a Treaty cram'd down my throat." At that McGillivray left the treaty grounds, and the negotiations came to an end.[8]

In their report the commissioners insisted that it was McGillivray alone who was the stumbling block on the road to peace. Lincoln, in a private conversation, stated that McGillivray was "a Man of Sagacity and much political & commercial information" but that he was "totally averse to all coalition of the Indians with the United States." That proved to be untrue, for McGillivray traveled to New York in 1790 and signed, for the Creeks, a treaty with the United States. What Lincoln missed entirely was the importance of McGillivray's ties to Spain and the leverage they allowed him in his dealings with the United States. Only Spanish friendship and trade enabled McGillivray to be, as he put it, "stout in my heart and strong in my mouth." Without assurances from the Spanish, he admitted later, "I would have been in an embarrassing and painful situation dealing with Lincollen and Company."[9]

Thus, Lincoln had little success to report when the commissioners finally made their way back to New York in November 1789. For all their efforts Lincoln could only bring back the "White Fan" of peace as a gift to Washington and, with it, the prospect of an uneasy truce. In private conversations Lincoln put as friendly a face on the negotiations as he could, informing one acquaintance that "such arrangements were made, as would, if the Georgians were wise and prudent, prevent a war." But his official report was not so optimistic. Lincoln spent more than a week in New York preparing a long report on the short negotiations, concluding that, if another treaty attempt ended in failure or the Indians "commit further hostilities and depredations . . . that the Creek nation ought to be deemed the enemies of the United States and punished accordingly." That drew acerbic comments from Sen. William Maclay of Pennsylvania that the negotiations were "a spoiled peice of business" and that, to justify their lack of success, Lincoln and his colleagues "seem disposed to precipitate the United States into war." This was, he added, "the not uncommon fruits of employing military men" in peace negotiations.[10]

One advantage to employing military men was in gathering military intelligence. The commission had been instructed to gather accurate information about the Creeks, their numbers, arms, towns, commercial activity, and so on. "The accurate knowledge of this subject is of considerable importance but the enquiries thereto should be circuitously conducted," Knox had ordered. Lincoln wrote a separate report on the measures to be taken by the federal government in case of a war with the Creeks. Part military intelligence—information on roads, distances between principal Creek towns, and strength estimates—and part recommendation, it suggested that five or six posts be built immediately along the frontier to provide magazines, security, and a rallying point, should hostilities begin. Lincoln advised invasion only as a last resort and then only if the attack could be made to coincide with the fall hunt and harvest. Disruption of these events would bring the Creeks to the "most distressing want and misery." And, thus, in Lincoln's euphemistic but entirely logical phrase, the Indians would then "be brought to reason and induced to submit to peace upon the principles of justice."[11]

In the next several years Lincoln thought and wrote a great deal about the place (or absence) of the Indian in the new American Republic. Native Americans were a topic of fascination for Lincoln's generation. With the Indian threat removed from the coastal areas of the country, educated men discussed the origins, practices, and future of the North American Indian. Like the sentiments expressed by Lincoln, the discussion was based on the assumption that Indians were savages and occupied a lower rung on the "Great Chain of Being" than whites. Characteristic of this paternalism was the assertion in the commissioners' report on the Creek negotiations that the disputed treaties between Georgia and the Creeks had been conducted with as much good faith and understanding as most Indian treaties can be, in which "one of the contracting parties is destitute of the benefits of enlightened society."[12]

Yet, within the narrow limits set by the period's conception of Indian life, Lincoln was one of a few men who tried to imagine the future of the North American Indian with sympathy. His experiences in Maine and Georgia, and his later mission to the Ohio country, spurred his curiosity about Indian life. And his deep religious faith prompted him to try to reconcile his understanding of Native Americans as equal members of the human family with his belief in human progress and the march of Western civilization. But the humanitarianism of this small coterie of easterners was speedily overtaken by events, as an army of settlers force-marched across the Appalachian Mountains in the 1780s and 1790s and advanced into the western territories. The vanguard of the settler hordes fought hundreds of skirmishes with the Indians, while behind them farms and towns were built on Indian corn land and hunting grounds. Even so, the attempt to create a rational and humane Indian policy worthy of the new Republic's ideals was in itself an achievement of sorts.[13]

Men such as Lincoln sought to control expansion, making it an orderly and deliberate process, accompanied by religion and the rule of law. The unhampered, landgrabbing free-for-all on the margins of "civilization" frightened them, especially when they recognized how swiftly these rough-and-ready frontier republics would be admitted into the Union. But, above all, uncontrolled expansion threatened to ignite a major Indian war—one the United States could not afford and was not ready to fight.[14]

Such wars were unnecessary, Lincoln believed. "Civilization is the most fatal enemy, by which, barbarism can be surrounded," he wrote to the natural historian Jeremy Belknap. The early settlers of New England had established their first farms on lands cleared by the Indians for agricultural use; they had let their livestock graze in the forests, thus driving the "wild beasts" from the area; and they had monopolized the shellfish on the coastline and the fish in the rivers. "As we have extended our possessions & increased our cultivations, we have rendered those possessions & the country in their vicinity of no importance to the natives," he continued. And so their lands were abandoned, purchased, or taken by whites, and the Indians retreated farther into the woods. "This has been," wrote Lincoln, "an easy & a natural mode of extending our limits." When any other way was tried "war, bloodshed & carnage" had been the consequence. The slow, steady march of civilization would accomplish the same goal without bloodshed.[15]

As he eventually realized, Lincoln was condemning the Indian populations to a slow rather than a rapid death. If he deplored the idea that "there is no faith to be kept with savages" and that "fire and sword" should be spread over "the face of their country," he nonetheless realized that the Indians must "either be civilized or become extinct." "Nature forbids the civilized and the uncivilized possessing the same territory," he explained, and the power of the whites was overwhelming. Lincoln pointed to the near extinction of the New England tribes as an illustration.[16]

At one time Lincoln believed that only the Europeanization of the Indians could save them from extinction. "That they must totally change their pursuits and their modes of living or become extinct as a people I have no doubt," he wrote. "The civilized and enlightened part of the world" was under an obligation to teach the Indians the arts of civilization, science, and agriculture. Only by adopting white methods of cultivation, the Christian religion, and European schooling could the Indian fight the enemies of his society—ignorance and savagery.[17]

Yet Lincoln realized that the problems plaguing Indian culture were not those of ignorance and savagery at all but, rather, ills brought to the Indians by contact with white civilization. The Indians' adoption of European clothing, firearms, and iron weapons and the devastating sweep of European disease had nearly annihilated Indian populations. Having given up "their ancient dress, Furrs and skins," they suffered from wearing poor quality blankets and European clothing in periods of inclement weather. "Ardent spirits" contributed to random violence and the social disintegration of families and tribal ties. Venereal disease, as Lincoln believed, contracted by their "connexion to the Europeans," further ravaged Indian families. Most important, Native American reliance on trade with Europeans had made a travesty of their political economy. Indians neglected to till their fields while wantonly destroying great numbers of game for their valuable furs and skins. And, in a development that shocked Lincoln to the core, hunger forced Indian women to "practice every art to prevent their bearing" children, including "the destruction of those children which are in any degree imperfect or deformed." But Lincoln made no attempt to reconcile those ills with the benefits of civilization. It was as if he were blind to the conclusions drawn from his own observations.[18]

Eventually, Lincoln was forced to concede that civilizing and converting the Indian was impractical. Indians, he wrote, see no benefit in Christianity because the first missionaries among them were those "who were seeking their property." How could they be persuaded of the truth of a religion that permitted "a forcible possession of their lands and an after settlement on them" by white foreigners? Even if white settlers had acted well in the past, Lincoln continued, it would still be an exacting task to civilize the Indians. "All men naturally wish for ease and to avoid the shackles of restraint," even those who have "tasted fully the pleasures of civilization and government." How then could one expect the Indian, who had never experienced those pleasures, "to leave the troden path in which he has long traveled with a degree of safety for one unexplored?"[19]

The point was that he could not. However much Lincoln wished to see "their minds better informed, their Hearts meliorated, the Habit of the Savage lost in the Blessings of Civilization and their Infidelity sacrificed to Christianity," his was a sterile and pessimistic vision. Stripped of their land by "natural law" and the surging white American population, locked into a trade that shattered their dignity and traditional political economy, and battered by the agents of Christian civilization, who only hastened their social disintegration, the Indians would be forced to "retire to those barren regions of the north where the husbandmen cannot pursue them." And even there they would not be left in peace.[20]

In 1793 Lincoln again was asked to negotiate an Indian treaty—this time with the Indian Confederacy in the Old Northwest, the territory that lies north of the Ohio River and east of the Mississippi River. There the United States faced an even more aggravated situation than it had earlier with the Creek Nation. Since 1789 the federal government had vacillated between policies of negotiated settlement and military pacification. Washington's original policy had been one of peace, primarily because the use of federal troops was expensive and impolitic. But the situation in the Northwest had deteriorated. The Indians had repudiated the Treaty of Fort Harmar (1789), which had allowed some settlement north of the Ohio River. White settlers had murdered Indians in senseless outbreaks of violence, and Indians had retaliated, burning isolated farms and killing the inhabitants. The cycle of violence had brought United States policy to the crisis point. Arthur St. Clair's combined army and militia force, destroyed along the Wabash River in 1791, was only one of several unsucessful military expeditions sent to pacify the region. These bloody defeats had led to increasing calls for a professional army to end the Indian threat. At the same time that frontier voices clamored for military protection, public opinion east of the Allegheny Mountains called for a negotiated settlement with the Indians.[21]

To further complicate matters Great Britain still occupied garrisons on U.S. territory in defiance of the Treaty of Paris of 1783. The British governors of Canada meddled in Indian affairs from time to time as their interests dictated, sometimes to cool the passion for war, at other times to stiffen Indian resolve. Once news of the declaration of war between France and Great Britain reached Canada in May 1793, however, the British sought to prolong peace negotiations and avoid a United States–Indian war. But that was a delicate undertaking, as the lieutenant governor of Upper Canada, John Graves Simcoe, acknowledged: "It will be extremely difficult so to manage as not to lose the affections of the Indians and yet not to give that pretext to the Government of the United States for the commencement of hostilities in this country."[22]

The object of greatest American and British anxiety was the Indian Confederacy, an association of tribes whose principal lands lay north of the Ohio River which had managed to resist white encroachment there with some success. The Shawnee Nation, the most aggressive in this regard, dominated the confederacy in the 1790s, replacing representatives of the Six Nations, or Iroquois League, who spoke with a more conciliatory voice. At the Grand Glaize Council of 1792 the Indians delivered an ultimatum to the United States, which was offering continued negotiations. The confederacy would sponsor a peace council at Lower Sandusky in 1793 if the United States would agree beforehand to an Ohio River boundary and the evacuation of its forts in the Old Northwest.[23]

By 1792, however, the Washington administration was committed to a military solution. The government had reorganized its armed forces into a legion commanded by Revolutionary War veteran Anthony Wayne. At the same time, Washington initiated a series of diplomatic overtures designed to undermine the unity of the Indian confederation, arrange a truce to give Wayne time to train his legionnaires, and appease the strong public pressure for a negotiated peace. The diplomatic mission to Ohio in the summer of 1793 was the last chance for peace, but no one in the administration believed it would succeed. Washington took care to appoint emissaries of great stature so that the mission carried "with it the perfect confidence of our citizens that every endeavor will have been used to obtain peace." Nonetheless, Secretary of State Thomas Jefferson would recall, after the treaty negotiations failed, "We expected nothing else, and had gone into negotiations only to prove to all our citizens that peace was unattainable on terms which any one of them would admit." For the very grounds on which the Indian offered to negotiate—an Ohio River boundary—was unacceptable to the Washington administration.[24]

Secretary of War Knox offered the commission to Lincoln in a letter dated 9 March 1793. Lincoln arrived in Philadelphia in early April and spent the next three weeks studying the history of Indian-white relations in the Old Northwest. He was aware of the problems dogging the mission from the start, but he was not made privy to the cabinet's utter pessimism about its outcome. The gist of the long and complex instructions to Lincoln and his fellow commissioners, Timothy Pickering and Beverly Randolph, was to reaffirm the Fort Harmar boundaries for the United States. In exchange for those lands north of the Ohio River, the United States would guarantee the right of soil to the Indians for the land acquired from Great Britain at the Treaty of Paris of 1783. The United States, of course, would remain the only purchaser of Indian land. In addition, the commissioners were authorized to promise the evacuation of trading posts, along with an outright payment of fifty thousand dollars immediately and ten thousand dollars annually for the land already purchased. The commissioners were to avoid recognizing the confederacy by attempting to deal with each nation separately. And they were to bring negotiations to a close by 1 August, informing Wayne of the result immediately. Wayne would hold his troops in readiness for a late summer campaign should the treaty fail. He also was to refrain from any aggressive acts while negotiations took place. Wayne had the difficult task of training his men and preparing a major military expedition while maintaining a facade of peaceful intent.[25]

Lincoln left Philadelphia on 27 April. As the senior commissioner, he took charge of the supplies, including two trunks of silverware, gifts, and cash to be distributed at the council fire. His route took him north through New York to Albany, west along the Mohawk River to Wood Creek, Oneida Lake, and on to Lake Ontario. There a vessel carried his party to Niagara, where Lincoln met Pickering and Randolph, who had traveled there by a direct overland route.[26]

Lincoln kept a journal of his trip to Sandusky, which he later published. In some ways it was a typical account, for the record, written by a public servant. It contained copies of all the important correspondence sent by the commissioners as well as the speeches heard and given at the negotiations. But Lincoln also, as he had done on all his previous travels, indulged his curiosity by making observations of the land, rivers, and natural phenomena that he encountered along the way. These, and the descriptions of towns he passed through and people he met, reveal a man with strong New England roots, a practical bent, a keen interest in agriculture, and a face resolutely set to the future greatness of the American Republic.[27]

Lincoln's long descriptions of the floodwaters, navigation, and landscape of the Hudson and Mohawk rivers reveal a curiosity about the physical world which was characteristic of his age. Travelers' accounts consistently mentioned the natural wonders of the New World as they ventured out beyond its settled bounds.[28]

But there was another aspect to Lincoln's interest in these rivers—their value as commercial highways. Looking out over the broad expanse of the Hudson River, Lincoln imagined rivers of produce pouring into eastern cities from the newly settled backcountry. After visiting Albany, he was convinced that the old Dutch city lacked only the construction of canals from the Hudson River to Lake Champlain and from the Mohawk River to Lake Ontario to make it "the seat of a great Empire." That it was New York City and not Albany which would grow into the great commercial center he envisaged does not dim the strength of his vision: when Lincoln looked at the vast wilderness, he saw only opportunities for those with the energy and vision to grasp them.[29]

As for Albany itself, it was clear that Lincoln measured the world with a New England yardstick. The Dutch, by retaining their language and manners and having "secluded themselves from the world at large . . . their reservedness has the appearance of a want of hospitality." What sounded like tolerance was really the smugness of a traveler abroad observing a culture he considered inferior to his own. "The jealousy which has always existed between the Dutch and the New England people is fast subsiding," Lincoln wrote. "It should never have existed. It is important to the present governing interest to put an end to these things." Besides, he continued, "the time is not far distant when the Sons of New England and New England manners will prevail." Albany's lack of a good water system demonstrated its inferiority. The city's residents took their water from the river, from the same place "in which is washed all the filth of the city." Behind it, however, were bluffs with good water "which might with great ease be drawn by pipes to all parts of the city, even into the upper chambers of their houses." This would also eliminate the hard labor of carrying water from the river. But the citizens were oblivious to the idea of this technical improvement, which only reinforced Lincoln's sense of cultural superiority. As for religious worship in New York state, Lincoln noted the churches he passed but confined himself to a terse comment after attending services in Albany. "At meeting towards evening, I came out with strong prejudices in favour of my own minister."[30]

Lincoln and his party left Schenectady, New York, on 9 May and reached Niagara on 25 May, where they found Pickering and Randolph enjoying the hospitality of John Graves Simcoe, the lieutenant governor of Upper Canada. After several days Lincoln questioned the propriety of staying at Simcoe's residence, Navy Hall, and the commissioners decided to join the Quakers at their camp some six miles away. Simcoe insisted that they remain with him, however, and "his politeness and hospitality, of which he has a large share," prevented them from carrying out their intentions. The visit threatened to become an endless one, as Lincoln remarked, for "we could not see a period to it, as the time of assembling the Indians was uncertain." The council, originally scheduled for 1 June, had been delayed.[31]

In February 1793 the Indians had called for a meeting of the confederated tribes to present a united front during the treaty proceedings. Riven by strong factionalism between the prowar Shawnee and the moderate New York Iroquois, the Indians were hammering out their position at a council fire at the Maumee Rapids. They were encouraged to do so by the British, whose plans for Canada optimistically called for a strong Indian buffer state in the Old Northwest. Thus, Simcoe blocked the movement of the commissioners to the treaty ground until the council proceedings had ended. In fact, the proceedings wore on thoughout June and July, as the Shawnee, by turns insulting and persuasive, tried to convince Joseph Brant's moderate faction and the Cornplanter Seneca to join them in defending the Ohio River border. The eventual triumph of the war party in early August meant that the treaty negotiations would never get off the ground.[32]

For six long weeks Lincoln was confined to the vicinity of Niagara, while the commissioners waited for the result of the Indian conclave. Simcoe found Lincoln "very civil," but on the whole the situation grew unpleasant. Lincoln took every opportunity to make sidetrips of interest. He explored Niagara Falls, finding "their appearance was far short of the idea I had formed of them." During the same trip he visited one of the Seneca towns in the Buffalo Creek settlement, where he was well received. The day passed in speech making and dancing. Here, and later when visiting a Tuscarora village, Lincoln remarked on the log houses with chimneys settled on good land, surrounded by abundant, well-tended cornfields. The Tuscaroras even raised cattle.[33]

Lincoln was also surprised, at a "splendid ball" given by Simcoe in honor of the king's birthday, to meet some ladies "whose mothers sprang from the aborigines of the country": "They appeared as well dressed as the company in general, and intermixed with them in a manner which evinced at once the dignity of their own minds and the good sense of others." He went on to remark that these ladies' great ingenuity and industry in pursuing their educations were due largely to their own efforts, since their fathers were dead and their mothers "retained the dress and manners of the tribe." Here was proof for Lincoln that Indians who made the effort could become civilized.[34]

Finally, toward the end of June the commissioners secured a passport from Simcoe to travel to a point just south of Detroit, which, as a British fort, was off-limits to Americans. The commissioners were given a guard of British soldiers and a letter from Simcoe in which he strongly urged that, in case the treaty failed, "the Commissioners should not be injured or insulted by the Savages." It was rumored that, if peace were not achieved, the Indians intended "to commence hostilities on the spot, by sacrificing the commissioners."[35]

They left Navy Hall on 26 June for the landing some ten miles away, where their boat lay at anchor. Contrary winds kept them in port for a week, by which time a deputation of Indians from the council fire arrived at Niagara. The Indians desired a meeting with the commissioners but only in Simcoe's presence. Thus, on 7 July Lincoln and his colleagues found themselves back at Navy Hall in discussions with the Indian delegation.[36]

The Indians, whose spokesman was Joseph Brant, were anxious to know why Wayne was proceeding with "warlike appearances," stating emphatically, "Your warriors being in our Neighborhood have prevented our meeting at the appointed place." They also warily asked the commissioners to clarify their powers to negotiate by establishing a new boundary line.[37]

The commissioners assured the Indians that all military excursions north of the Ohio River had been expressly forbidden by President Washington until the treaty results were known. Wayne had, however, been provisioning the northern forts for a late summer expedition, and the enormous pack trains with their armed escorts were proof to the Indians of his intentions. Wayne's actions placed Lincoln and his colleagues in a dubious position. Ironically, Pickering spoke more truly than he knew when he labored to convince the Indians of the government's intent: "Is it possible that the same Great Chief [Washington] and his great council could order their warriors to make fresh war, while we are sitting around the same fire with you, in order to make *peace?*" Only the assurance that the commissioners would write to the president, which they did on 10 July, convinced the delegation that the Americans honestly wished for peace.[38]

As for the second point, Pickering assured the Indians that the commissioners had the power to establish a new boundary line, but he stated explicitly that the negotiations would require concessions from both parties. Brant ignored the implications of that statement, which was, in effect, that the United States would never agree to the Ohio River boundary, and on 9 July he expressed his satisfaction with the talks, saying "Now business may be done, so we take you by the hand and conduct you to the meeting."[39]

On 14 July Lincoln and his colleagues left Fort Erie for Detroit, arriving a week later and camping at the home of Matthew Elliott, a British Indian agent. They were received with hospitality. The morning after their arrival Lincoln reported, "We had a full supply of boyled green corn . . . from the best farm I have seen in the country by far." The commissioners wrote to Alexander McKee, another influential Indian agent who was at the Indian council, to inform him of their arrival and ask him to "expedite the councils of the Indians, that we may meet them without more delay."[40]

McKee's answer was hand-carried by Elliott, who arrived in the company of "upward of twenty Indians" on 29 July. John Heckwelder, a Moravian missionary who had accompanied Lincoln to the Ohio country and whose experience with Indians made him skeptical of the prospects for peace, wrote in his journal, "We soon learnt the Errand they were come upon, and which was to undo all which had been done by the first Deputation with the Commissioners at Navy Hall." Despite the hopes of the commissioners, Heckwelder wrote, he "doubted very much, whether we should ever see the Treaty Ground."[41]

The missionary proved prescient. When the Indian deputation gathered on the broad grassy expanse in front of Elliott's house the next day, they delivered an ultimatum. The speaker, a Wyandot chief, first repudiated the understanding reached at Navy Hall in early July and then presented the commissioners with a written statement that demanded to know whether Lincoln and his colleagues were authorized to establish the boundary at the Ohio River. "If you seriously design to make a firm and lasting peace, you will immediately remove all your people from our side of that River." Taken aback by the tone and nature of the communication, the commissioners promised to review it and reply.[42]

When the assembly met the next day Pickering gave a "plain, generous, but determined Answer," in Heckwelder's opinion. He confirmed that the boundary line was a fit topic for discussion and negotiation but complained that this "speaking at a distance, prevents our knowing one another, and keeps alive those jealousies which are a great obstacle to peace."[43]

Pickering then reviewed the history of treaties between the two parties, demonstrating the impossibility of establishing an Ohio River boundary but offering compensation for the lands already transferred to the United States by the Fort Harmar treaty. "Such a large sum in money or goods as was never given at one time for any quantity of Indian land since the white people first set their foot on this Island" would be offered, plus an annual rent. Pickering then produced a major concession to the Indians—the investiture of the "right of soil" of the remaining lands in the Old Northwest in the Indian nations. The speech was a straightforward presentation of the commissioners' instructions, and upon it rested all their hopes of success.[44]

The next day, 1 August, the Wyandot chief spoke again, rejecting the American offers. Previous treaties, he said, were invalid because they were conducted without the consent of the whole people. "You have not bought our lands," he said. "They belong to us. You may return whence you came and tell Washington." Elliott then went to the chief and told him the last part of the speech was wrong, and the chief amended it by saying that he wished the commissioners to remain until the Indians had conferred in council at the Miami Rapids and had sent word of the results. Lincoln agreed to this, only desiring that the answer be returned without delay.[45]

Reports received on 8 August revived hope that the moderate factions had won over the prowar tribes. Single Indians traveling home from the treaty grounds reinforced the idea that peace was at hand. By 12 August the anxious commissioners tried to travel to the treaty site but were prevented by their British guards. Two days later the commissioners wrote McKee, threatening to end negotiations if an answer were not immediately forthcoming. On 16 August two young Wyandots arrived with a written answer that put an end to any hopes of a treaty.[46]

The council's message protested the commissioners' version of past treaties, stating that, in the past, deeds of cession were forced upon individual tribes under the guise of peace negotiations. "Your commissioner was informed," it went on, "long before he held the Treaty of Fort Harmar, that the consent of a general Council was absolutely necessary to convey any part of those lands to the United States." As for the promise of payment and an annual rent, he wrote, "Money to us is of no value, and to most of us is unknown." Nothing could induce them to sell the land, on which, he explained, "we get sustenance for our women and children." And in a clever riposte the council proposed that the money intended for them be divided among the settlers north of the Ohio River as repayment for land and improvements once they had been removed.[47]

Finally, the council commented on the commissioners' concession of the Indian right of soil. "You want to make this act of common justice a great part of your concession, and seem to expect that because you have at last acknowledged our independence, we should for such a favor surrender to you our country." And, as for the right of preemption, "we consider ourselves free to make any bargain or cession of lands whenever and to whomsoever we please." Treaties between the United States and Great Britain had nothing to do with them.[48]

Faced with the Indians' insistence on the Ohio boundary, the commissioners ended negotiations. Citing the "upright and liberal views of the United States," Lincoln and his colleagues could only trust that the "continuance of the war" would not be attributed to them. On 17 August the disappointed commissioners took ship for Niagara, anxious for their personal safety and in a hurry to notify Wayne of the failed negotiations.[49]

From Fort Erie, which they reached on 21 August, the party split up. Pickering and Randolph returned overland along the Mohawk Valley, and Lincoln, Heckwelder, and some others took the water route down the St. Lawrence River and the Lake Champlain Valley. The trip passed uneventfully, except for the "embarrassments" attendent upon reporting to British military garrisons that remained on United States soil and a rough passage on Lake Champlain. By 17 September Lincoln had returned safely to New York City, where he took leave of the company. Heckwelder noted in his journal that he had traveled upward of twenty-two hundred miles with "his good friend Gen. Lincoln," a long, arduous trip that had ended in failure.[50]

Flushed with victories over the armies of the United States, the Western Confederacy proved obdurate in its demands for an Ohio River boundary. Confident of its ability to thwart white settlement on Indian lands and backed, as it thought, by the might of the British Empire, the Indian Confederacy proposed to turn back the clock and so rejected the last and most generous of a number of peace offerings. Spurning a bad bargain, it received worse. Freed of restrictions, Wayne and his legion crushed Indian opposition in the Old Northwest in a series of military encounters the following year, in 1794. The decisive battle at Fallen Timbers on 20 August led to the Treaty of Greenville a year later. The old boundaries of the Harmar Treaty became a thing of the past, as the Indians were driven to retreat farther into the forest.[51]

CHAPTER FOURTEEN

The Old Federalist

General Lincoln—Grown gray in the service of his country, may he long
continue to enjoy its esteem and confidence.

Federalist toast, 1798

Benjamin Lincoln was a fixture in Boston society during the two decades he spent as collector of the port of that city. In all seasons but winter, which he spent in Hingham, his familiar figure could be seen limping
down State Street to the customs office. Habitually dressed in a blue coat,
light smallclothes, and boots, his gray hair tied back in a long queue and
wearing a cocked hat, Lincoln went about the duties of his office in his
usual dignified and courteous way.[1]

Lincoln was also a fixture in the Federalist Party in Massachusetts.
He was a Federalist by inclination and experience. Brought up to value
reason, order, and moderation, Lincoln found the federal government,
with its balance of powers and its precisely delimited charter, analogous
to God's intricate plan of the universe. Federalism's reliance on the "best
men" to chart the course of government also attracted Lincoln, reminding
him of prewar Massachusetts, when deference oiled the workings of society and the government. Finally, Lincoln's war experience, in which "the
idea of different states, and distinct & separate interests, has in too many
instances, distracted our affairs and retarded the public weal," impelled
him to support the idea of a strong central government with vigor.[2]

Yet his was a moderate Federalism. Lincoln was closely tied to the
Washington and Adams administrations through friendships with both
presidents. Even after the Federalists split into two factions in the last
rocky years of Adams's presidency, Lincoln supported his Quincy neighbor wholeheartedly. For taking that stand, Lincoln was denounced, at
least privately, by both Republicans and extreme Federalists. Republicans
saw his domination of federal appointments as an obstacle to their party's

enjoyment of "the loaves and fishes" of political office. The extreme Federalists—Timothy Pickering, Fisher Ames, George Cabot, Stephen Higginson, and others—regarded Lincoln as a traitor to the true cause of New England Federalism. During the Quasi-War, when naval clashes between the United States and France threatened to escalate into all-out war, the extreme Federalists—or Essex Junto, as they came to be called—vociferously supported war against the French. In their minds Lincoln, and other moderate New Englanders such as Henry Knox and Elbridge Gerry, had influenced President Adams to abandon his rigid anti-Gallican stance in favor of temporizing peace negotiations. The consequences of peace with France, according to the Essex Junto, were the abandonment of all they held dear—a standing army, a navy, a host of internal taxes, and, above all, American pride.[3]

Lincoln supported the government and the Federalist Party in a number of public and private ways. As collector, he controlled a host of appointments and contracts that exerted an influence in support of the government throughout the mercantile community. In the early 1790s his lengthy correspondence with Alexander Hamilton, then secretary of the Treasury, kept the latter informed of the political temperature of the Commonwealth as well as offering advice on the revenue system. Publicly, he used dozens of ceremonial occasions over the years to reinforce support for the federal government and, later in the 1790s, for the Federalist Party.[4]

For most of the decade Lincoln was content to manage the customhouse and rebuild his shattered fortune. There were plenty of distractions. He traveled to Georgia and the Ohio country on diplomatic missions. His annual pilgrimages to Philadelphia and to Theodore's home in Maine provided welcome changes from life at the office. He oversaw improvements to the Boston Customs House on State Street, enlarged his ancestral home in Hingham with the addition of a double-wide staircase (no doubt to accommodate his growing bulk), and had homes built for his son-in-law and secretary, Abner Lincoln, and his minister, the Reverend Henry Ware. Lincoln also provided for Ben. Jr.'s widow, Mary Otis Lincoln, and the education and well-being of her two boys, Benjamin and James Otis. Lincoln continued as an active member of the American Academy of Arts and Sciences, reviewing papers from all over the nation on behalf of the agricultural committee. And he supervised the education of as many as a dozen children of friends in the private schools of Hingham. Men like Thomas Willing of Philadelphia, Flynt Boudinot of New Jersey, Charles Ferguson of South Carolina, and R. K. Meade of Virginia sent their sons to be supervised by Lincoln. Hingham housed over a dozen private academies preparing students for entrance to Harvard College. But nearly all the parents would have agreed with Meade's reason for sending his son to Lincoln's care: "The improvement of my childrens minds I conceive a serious object, but the purity of their hearts & the practice of morality is the primary one. Here then I feel rejoiced, when I consider that my son will often see you, that he will know you & will benefit from your example." For Lincoln the custodianship of these adoptive sons was a triumph of sorts. For years he had tried to persuade men from other parts of the country, especially the South, to send their children to New England rather than Europe for their educations. Only by so doing, he believed, could a truly American generation be produced, with regional differences muted and foreign influences destroyed.[5]

Lincoln rarely exerted his political influence overtly. By 1798, however, a combination of events forced Lincoln to intervene in politics, as George Cabot disapprovingly pointed out, "in a manner more decisive than is usual for him of late years." Earlier political battles had driven a wedge between the old Federalists, the supporters of the U.S. Constitution in 1788–89. The assumption of state Revolutionary War debts by the federal government, an act that Lincoln supported wholeheartedly, began to divide the nation into Republican and Federalist camps early in Washington's first administration. By 1795 the uproar over the Jay Treaty with Great Britain nearly completed it. But it was not until George Washington announced his intention to retire, in 1796, that the two fledgling parties began openly to confront each other. That year, in the contest for the presidency, John Adams defeated Thomas Jefferson by a mere three electoral votes, and the scene was set for the bitter wrangling of the next four years.[6]

By 1798 the Federalist administration of John Adams had launched a number of numbingly expensive defensive measures to counter the diplomatic chicanery and hostility of France. The Federalist-dominated Congress blatantly exploited the public's outrage at the XYZ affair in 1798 to authorize a sizable standing army and to pay for it by, among other measures, the first direct tax levied in the United States. Washington came out of his second retirement to lead the troops. Persuading the reluctant old general was not easy; one of the conditions Washington insisted on was the power to select his subordinates. Adams reluctantly agreed to the conditions but gave James McHenry, his secretary of war, a list of acceptable officers from which he hoped Washington would pick. Unfortunately for Adams, Washington chose the energetic and ambitious Alexander Hamilton to be his second-in-command. Charles Cotesworth Pinckney and Henry

Knox, respectively, were to be second and third major generals. Adams, never slow to anger, was furious. Knox was senior to the other two in terms of rank and service and was an old friend of the president and an avid Adams supporter besides, whereas Hamilton was Adams's bête noire. It was Hamilton who had unsuccessfully conspired to have Pinckney's brother Thomas elected as president in place of Adams in the 1796 election, and the New Yorker's influence dominated the members of the president's own cabinet. Washington's choice was an unforgivable affront, one Adams could not excuse. When he made out the commissions, Adams reversed the order of the appointments, giving Knox the first place.[7]

Knox obliged the president by demanding rank over Hamilton. The action unleashed a firestorm of protest within the Federalist Party, especially among the extreme Federalists, who regarded Adams with suspicion and considered Hamilton their champion. Knox and Lincoln were observed visiting the president's farm at Quincy where Adams was summering, and the Essex Junto quivered with righteous indignation. Their speculations were particularly unlovely. George Cabot blamed Lincoln for bolstering Knox's pretensions to the commission, noting that Lincoln had endorsed a great number of Knox's notes, amounting to a large sum of money. "Why is Lincoln intriguing with the President?" asked Timothy Pickering. "What had Knox done for him or Hamilton against him?" The secretary of state went on to answer his own question. Both Lincoln and Knox were "envious of Hamilton's eminently superior abilities." Both were "extremely vain" and "overated."[8]

Lincoln's actions lay less in his vanity or financial worries than in his pride and a sense that Knox's revolutionary service—and, by extension, Lincoln's own—was being denigrated. The conduct of war was being revolutionized in Europe. Even as the Americans argued over rank, the old rules of war they had learned so painfully could no longer meet the new French threat looming across the Atlantic. No matter—all the old revolutionary generals, now past their prime, were sensitive to slights on their war records. A good example of this was Lincoln's reaction to a passage in William Heath's 1798 *Memoirs* describing Lincoln's wounding at Saratoga as possibly the work of American soldiers. Lincoln wrote Heath in a decidedly chilly tone that readers of the general's book could interpret the passage in a multitude of ways, all of them bad. Lincoln could be "impeached for rashness" and "intemperate zeal" by being so far in front of his own troops as to become a target. His wound could be seen as "the infliction of a just punishment for timidity and cowardice" for attempting to desert his post. Or it might be "an act of private revenge" for having performed some act of "unjustifiable cruelty" on the troops. Lincoln's real concern about the book and the way he was described in it was that it would be "read by after Generations, when all those who now know us shall neither know us or be known any more." Anything that reflected on the war years—Heath's *Memoirs*, Knox's appointment—should preserve the truth of that time, as the old veterans saw it.[9]

But the real reason Adams, and Lincoln, preferred Knox for the post was that they trusted him. Despite his great talents, Hamilton was known to be "a proud, spirited, conceited, aspiring Mortal." Abigail Adams considered him a potential "Buonaparty," whose ambition was boundless. Neither Washington nor the extreme Federalists who touted Hamilton for second-in-command realized the extent to which Hamilton's ambition was feared by the rest of the country. Talent was well and good, but in a republican government it must be balanced by reason, order, and a sense of limits. Knox may have been vain and his talents overrated, but he understood the military's subordinate place in a republic. That was more than could be said for Hamilton. Lincoln's opposition, of course, was nowhere near sufficient to block Hamilton's appointment. Even Adams's wishes were quashed by Washington's threat to resign if his choices were not respected. But opposition to men and measures can be carried out in indirect ways, and Lincoln certainly played his part. He advised the Adams administration on military appointments, and the president moved so slowly on them that Hamilton was thwarted at every turn. If the Essex Junto had to speculate about the reason for Lincoln's trip to Philadelphia in 1800, believing him called there "to consult about changes contemplated in the Army," they could be sure of one thing: Lincoln would "join in anything to get rid of Hamilton."[10]

Lincoln's support of Adams was conveyed privately as well as publicly. During a particularly brutal session of Congress, when Adams was excoriated for launching a new diplomatic initiative to heal the rift with France, Abigail Adams, writing from Quincy, informed her husband that "good old Genll Lincoln call'd on saturday evening to inquire if they had not killed you yet. I told him no that you would live to kill half a dozen more politically if they did not stear steady."[11]

National politics were for a time, however, overshadowed by a personal crisis of dramatic proportions. For nearly a year Lincoln had been endorsing—that is, guaranteeing—his friend Henry Knox's personal financial notes. Knox's extravagant lifestyle and land speculation on a grand scale had left him strapped for cash. As his notes came due, he paid them off with money raised by borrowing at ever-higher interest rates. Thus,

Lincoln and Henry Jackson were drawn into Knox's financial embarrassments on the strength of their mutual friendship. The boom was lowered in October 1798, during the controversy over the army command. Unable to pay off notes as they came due, Knox was summoned to Boston by "urgent and anxious creditors," and in consequence Lincoln's property—his home, mills, orchards, and farmlands—was "attached" to pay off Knox's creditors. Rumor in Boston had it that Knox owed over $100,000, and of this Lincoln was responsible for $50,000—"much more," it was said, "than he can pay." By the time the news reached Philadelphia the gossip mill had inflated the sums to astronomical proportions. Jefferson wrote to Madison that Knox owed $400,000, Lincoln $150,000. George Cabot could hardly contain his glee. He wrote to Pickering, suggesting that Lincoln could no longer be trusted with public office. "I have so often seen men made desperate by pecuniary wants that I am always grieved to see men of influence reduced on account of what they may do as well as what they may suffer."[12]

Along with the need to redeem his personal property, Lincoln was in the uncomfortable position of handling large sums of public money, while wild rumors circulated about the extent of his personal debts. His hopes of quickly paying off his portion of Knox's debt rested on keeping his job as collector. For that reason Lincoln raced to scotch the rumor that the Boston banks were not honoring his drafts. He wrote Adams to reassure the president that his personal affairs could never affect the public funds. Knox, he wrote, had given him ample security for his endorsements. Of the public funds, he insisted, "there has not one penny gone to pay any of the notes nor will any ever go from me for that purpose." And, he added, "death would certainly be preferred to an action so base and unjust as it relates to the U.S."[13]

That did not stop others in the administration from initiating discreet inquiries of their own. Oliver Wolcott Jr., the secretary of the Treasury and a close associate of Alexander Hamilton, wrote to Boston merchant Stephen Higginson of his disappointment in the collector. "Though I cannot doubt of his integrity, yet his conduct has certainly diminished my confidence in his discretion and judgement." Is it safe, he concluded, to retain Lincoln as collector? Higginson's answer damned Lincoln with faint praise. "He has been generally esteemed a man of integrity; & his own safety & interest seem to forbid his private affairs having an unfavourable influence upon his official conduct & duties." But, Higginson went on, "it is a hard trial of a man's integrity" when his property is taken from him and he is harassed by creditors from dawn until dusk. "To have the command of public monies & not to resort to them for relief," he wrote, "requires much more than common firmness & prudence." And the financial situation of the three generals was so bad that their credit was "intirely at an end." Wolcott could hardly have been reassured by Higginson's report. Still, nothing came of the Treasury secretary's investigation. Lincoln's stainless reputation for integrity was proof against the insinuations of the Essex Junto, and President Adams refused to consider dismissing his old friend.[14]

Some of Lincoln's friends advised him to shelter his personal property by signing it over to his sons or a trustee in an effort to avoid his obligations. But this Lincoln refused to do. "I could not reconcile the measure to my opinion of justice," he told his son Theodore. "A man may be beggared and after enjoy great happiness in Life but when by an improper action he has lost all confidence in himself, he disturbs the streams if he doth not dry up the source of it." Knox was expected to redeem Lincoln's property. When he could not, Lincoln was given a year's stay of execution in order to buy back his home and farm. The final tally of his proportion of Knox's debt came to more than twenty-five thousand dollars. He paid it all, but the final settlement with Knox was strung out until 1806. Only Lincoln's threat to launch a lawsuit induced Knox to bring the affair to an end. That Lincoln had been taken advantage of was clear; that he remained unembittered was astonishing. The last meeting of the three generals was remembered as amicable, though Knox purportedly shed tears of shame. In the midst of all these distressing troubles Lincoln could still write his son that he "enjoyed many mercies . . . I enjoy great health, am capable of attending to my business," of which there was plenty, "and besides my nerves are yet firm" enough to support "my disappointments."[15]

The defeat of the Federalists in the presidential election of 1800 followed hard on the heels of Lincoln's financial reverses. Lincoln consoled Adams on the loss of the presidency and faced a few anxious moments himself. Some Federalists and many Republicans expected Jefferson to divide the spoils of victory and replace each officeholder with one of his own supporters. Lincoln put on a brave face, writing to a friend in South Carolina that he was ready to be removed if the new administration desired it but thought it unlikely to happen. Lincoln had always kept his political lines open to the opposition, keeping "fair wheather" with both sides, as the ultra-Federalists derisively called it. And his party influence was exerted, it seems, with a light touch. As he himself claimed in a letter to his subordinates in the customhouse: "I have never attempted to controul your political creed, or influence any of your votes in the choice of officers at any of our public meetings." That certainly seemed to be the case. In 1793, for example, Stephen Higginson complained to Hamilton that men in the customhouse were agitating on behalf of French claims to fit out privateers in American ports. Supporters of the government were incensed that these actions ran counter to federal policy. Lincoln hardly seems to have run the customs office with an iron hand. And during the Jefferson administration Lincoln bent over backward not to offend the resurgent Republicans. In 1802 he admonished his employees for public statements contemptuous of the president. "If any of you . . . have in the public walks vilified the chief Magistrate of the Union in terms rude and indecent and should justify yourself herein you only exercise your rights," Lincoln reminded them, "there is an infinite difference between Right and the propriety of exercising that right." For those reasons, and others that pertain more to Jefferson's policy on removals, Lincoln held onto the collectorship.[16]

By 1804 rumors circulated in Boston that Lincoln was about to be replaced. There was enough substance in them that James Sullivan, a highly respected Massachusetts Republican, who served several terms as governor, hastened to write to Secretary of State James Madison to discourage the idea. Sullivan thought that firing Lincoln would hurt the president by inviting the Federalists to make him a cause célèbre. "He is, in general, an inoffensive man," he told Madison, "rather popular than otherwise; the wounds received on the heights of Saratoga would be opened afresh, and wept over, by men, who were, on the day of that battle his enemies, who now dislike him as much as they did then." Sullivan had the Essex Junto in his sights. They openly preached defiance of the federal government. To remove Lincoln at this time, Sullivan thought, would allow the ultra-Federalists to use Lincoln, a symbol of the revolution and the friend of Washington and Adams, to cover the shadowy purposes of those who sought the government's overthrow. Either the rumors were just that or Sullivan's advice was taken, for nothing more was mentioned about Lincoln's removal.[17]

Not that the Republicans were not seeking a legitimate opportunity to replace the collector. The next winter Sullivan again wrote Madison, this time reporting that Lincoln was very ill and unlikely to live through what had been a "remarkably severe winter." Even if he should survive, Sullivan went on, Lincoln would probably be obliged to resign his office. Sullivan wanted to reserve the office for Elbridge Gerry, a revolutionary patriot and elder statesman, who would go on to serve as Republican governor of Massachusetts. Lincoln, however, recovered from his illness that winter, as he had in 1802, and was hale enough to attend to business again until the fall of 1806.[18]

Another measure of Lincoln's popularity was the decision by a group of Boston merchants to subscribe for a portrait of the old general. Painted by Henry Sargent in 1805, the oil portrait shows a red-faced and corpulent Lincoln in his regimental blue coat, one hand resting on a brass cannon, his sword with the ceremonial sword knot, given to him by Washington, at his side. The portrait shows little of the brisk and energetic general whose manner commanded authority. It is more a painting of a sick old man approaching the grave.[19]

Lincoln had survived several severe attacks of the gout since 1801, two of which confined him to Hingham for long periods. For an active man it was hard to give up his annual trip to Maine and his normal bustling about the house. Old age had made him irascible, he conceded to Theodore, but he assured his son that he had not lost his good humor. Celebratory dinners and joyous occasions still marked the years' calendars, but, more and more, pain increasingly filled his days. Nor were all his wounds physical. In the winter of 1807 the Lincoln family suffered a grievous shock when Ben Jr.'s widow, Mary Otis Lincoln, committed suicide. Only a week before she had married Henry Ware, Hingham's former minister, who was the Hollis Professor of Divinity at Harvard College. Abigail Adams wrote tearfully that Mary had been "from her youth all that was amiable, Lovely and good": "I always saw her with pleasure, and parted from her with regret." And she added a note with which Lincoln would have agreed: "The ways of Heaven are dark and intricate."[20]

In October 1806 Lincoln wrote his son Theodore that he was resigning his office at the end of the year. He wished the whole family to gather at Hingham that winter "to make a final arrangement of my property." Lincoln wrote the president in November of his decision, satisfied that Jefferson would be happy to accept his resignation and eager to appoint a Republican in his stead. Instead, Jefferson asked Lincoln to continue in office until a successor was named, promising he would do so before March 1807. Lincoln agreed, once again sacrificing his private wishes for the public good, writing Jefferson, "Your inclination now discovered to me as to the time shall be a law in my mind."[21]

The president, however, did not replace Lincoln. Although little evidence has been found, it seems that an understanding was reached between Lincoln and the administration that Henry Dearborn, the secretary of war, would be nominated for the position in due time. At least Lincoln assumed that was the case. He wrote Albert Gallatin in June 1807 about some arrangements for the Chatham lighthouse and promised to examine the spot "as soon as Mr. Dearborne shall relieve me." It is likely that Jefferson wished to keep the post open for Dearborn, but with the passage of the Embargo Act of December 1807, forbidding the export of American goods to foreign ports, Jefferson preferred to let a Federalist collector enforce a law bitterly opposed by that party. In any case, there was little public comment from Lincoln but a great deal of private grumbling at not being relieved. By the summer of 1808 Lincoln's health was so bad that he could not leave Hingham for his Boston office. When Benjamin Weld, the deputy collector, was asked to explain reports of irregularities in the execution of his duties in November 1808, he replied that enforcing the law was difficult enough without defending himself against "anonimous busybodies." He wanted to resign but said, "Genl Lincoln's situation, and his earnest request that I would continue till he was relieved by another appointment (which he anxiously wishes) is my only inducement [to remain]." When Weld could no longer be "induced" to remain and resigned his post, Lincoln had no choice but to follow. On 16 January 1809 he wrote Jefferson that he was "too feeble to transact any business" and was "compelled" to resign as of that day. To the naval officer of the port, his old friend James Lovell, Lincoln wrote that he was now "so debilitated in my limbs as destroys all hope of being again in Boston." His condition was pathetic: "I am in such a state as to be unable to dress or undress myself or of walking more than a few yards." It was a sad way to end a long and honorable public career.[22]

Even then the collector was not allowed to resign in peace. His decision, though born of desperation, was variously interpreted and used for political gain by Republicans and Federalists alike. In a Boston town meeting on 24 January the Federalists rammed through a resolution praising Lincoln and other "undeviating patriots" for "resigning offices intended to be prostituted to subserve the purposes of oppressing the citizens." The reference was to the Enforcement Act of 9 January 1809, which gave the federal government unprecedented powers to enforce the embargo. On the same day the Washington, D.C., *National Intelligencer* printed a squib that took aim at Lincoln for his "precipitate abandonment" of his post when his "services were most requisite." It should be known, the piece went on, "that the Collector is a *federalist* whom the forbearance of the administration has long retained in office in opposition to the wishes of a respectable class of the community." It finished by connecting Lincoln's resignation directly to the "infamous violations" of the Embargo Act which were frequent in New England. Even so seasoned a political observer as

Levi Lincoln of Massachusetts thought the resignations "unseasonable and regretted" for the political mileage the Federalists were able to wring out of them.[23]

This was too much for U.S. congressman Josiah Quincy Jr., whose honest outrage at the smear on Lincoln's record and zeal to embarrass the president outran his good sense. On the same day that the slap at Lincoln ran in the Washington newspaper Quincy charged President Jefferson with a "high misdemeanor" in keeping Lincoln in the collectorship long after he wished to leave it in order to keep the office open for a member of his administration. He introduced resolutions in Congress to inquire into the affair as a prelude to the impeachment of the president. Quincy's panegyric on Lincoln ("one of the chief glories of our Revolution—a hero, the halting victim of war—his body all seamed and scarred with wounds gotten in the cause of his country, now on the brink of the grave, his laurels never yet tarnished") was matched only by Virginian William Burwell's laconic question: "How could he come forward and impeach the President for keeping in office a man whose merits transcended all description?" In fact, the debate descended nearly to the level of farce before the resolutions were defeated 117 to 1. It was a defense of his record which Lincoln neither anticipated nor deserved.[24]

Once free of public cares Lincoln turned to arranging a final settlement for his children. Martin, who had managed the Hingham property—the farms, mills, and orchards—for his father since he had taken the job of collector, assumed title to them with the responsibility to care for his mother, Mary. Theodore, now firmly settled in Dennysville, Maine, received title to most of his father's lands in the northern country. The daughters, Elizabeth (Betty), Sarah (Sally), and Hannah, had taken their dowries with them at marriage. All were to receive cash on Lincoln's death. His grandsons by Benjamin Jr., James Otis Lincoln and Benjamin Lincoln, were also provided for in the will.[25]

Two primitive portraits, one of Benjamin Lincoln and one of his wife Mary, hang over the fireplace of the Lincoln homestead today, as they did in 1810. Painted by an itinerant artist named J. R. Smith in 1809, the two portraits depict a plain country couple. Lincoln's picture shows an old man sitting in his favorite chair by the window, stolidly facing the viewer. Dressed all in black, with his hands resting on a cane, his expression is empty, his body feeble. There is no hint that this man was anything but a country farmer and perhaps a deacon of his church. The eyes betray no hint of bloody ambushes, sweaty marches, or river crossings. There are no field orders, councils of war, or proud toasts on those silent lips. There is nothing, in fact, that would lead the viewer to know the full and vital part this man had played in founding a nation. It is a portrait of a old man waiting stoically for death. On 9 May 1810, at the age of seventy-seven, Benjamin Lincoln's wait was over.[26]

Two days later Boston church bells tolled for an hour, and flags in the harbor flew at half-mast. In Hingham Lincoln's body was borne to the meetinghouse for the funeral service, in front of a large crowd of neighbors and dignitaries. His honorary pallbearers—"six Skelletons or walking shadows," as John Adams put it—included Adams, Robert Treat Paine, Cotton Tufts, and Thomas Melville. Gov. Christopher Gore attended. Members of the Society of the Cincinnati were there, their left arms swathed in black crepe in tribute to their late president. The funeral sermon, "a cold unanimated and ignorant sketch" (Adams again), was preached by the Reverend Henry Codman. Lincoln's life, Codman said, was "a remarkable instance of a man's rising to great and deserved eminence with few and ordinary advantages." That it certainly was. In a short revolutionary period men and women created a republican world that demanded not extraordinary talents, necessarily, but lives dedicated to public virtue. Many of them, like Lincoln, rose to the challenge. Yet few could claim to have striven harder, for a longer time, and under more trying conditions than Lincoln.[27]

Despite the large turnout at Lincoln's funeral, John Adams was disappointed. Recalling the "mock funerals" of Washington, Hamilton, and Fisher Ames, he wondered why the same outpouring of grief had not accompanied "my ancient my invariable and inestimable Friend Lincoln" to his grave. "How long will fraud prevail over Honesty?" he asked. "Lincolns Education, his Reading his general Knowledge, his Talent at Composition was superiour to Washingtons: his services more arduous dangerous and difficult than Washingtons." And yet Lincoln's services to the nation were then, and would be in the future, eclipsed by the brilliance of Washington's memory.[28]

Oblivion was the one fate the revolutionary generation could not abide. Lincoln had shouldered his duty through long years of war and peace, sacrificing health and family to help found a nation and "earn the perpetual remembrance of posterity." He had gained the respect of his contemporaries and been honored by them on many occasions. But Adams's fear, and Lincoln's fate, was that they would be forgotten.[29]

The day after Lincoln died, the *Boston Gazette* published a testimony to him. "The death of General Lincoln," it began, "is no common misfortune. His great revolutionary services; his irreproachable moral character; his incorruptible personal integrity; and the solidity of his political sentiments, conspire to render his loss, a public calamity." Americans had lost a great patriot. Lincoln was an example of those men—covenanters, in his words—who built the ship of state, sailed it in dark and desperate times through uncharted and dangerous waters, and finally brought it to safe harbor. In the midst of frustration and failure, triumph and happiness, Lincoln stuck to his post until the end. The convenant remained unbroken.[30]

Notes

Introduction

1. Dave Richard Palmer, *The Way of the Fox: American Strategy in the War for America, 1775–1783* (Westport, Conn., 1975), 72. This is only one of many similar characterizations; see also Merrill Jensen, *The New Nation: A History of the United States during the Confederation, 1781–1789* (New York, 1950), 56.

2. David Ramsay, as qtd. in Douglass Adair, *Fame and the Founding Fathers: Essays by Douglass Adair,* ed. Trevor Colbourne (New York, 1974), 5.

3. The literature on republicanism is vast, but a good place to start is the bibliographic essay by Robert E. Shalhope, "Toward a Republican Synthesis: The Emergence of an Understanding of Republicanism in American Historiography," *William and Mary Quarterly (WMQ),* 3d ser., 29 (1972): 49–80; for indications that the concept has run its course, see Daniel T. Rodgers, "Republicanism: The Career of a Concept," *Journal of American History (JAH)* 79 (1992): 11–38.

4. For the sources and traditions of classical republicanism, see Bernard Bailyn, *The Ideological Origins of the American Revolution* (Cambridge, Mass., 1967). For the values inherited from Puritanism, see Edmund S. Morgan, "The Puritan Ethic and the American Revolution," *WMQ,* 3d ser., 24 (1967): 3–43.

5. James Cannon to Benjamin Lincoln (BL), July 1780, in *The Papers of Benjamin Lincoln,* ed. Frederick S. Allis Jr., microfilm ed., 13 reels (Boston, 1967), reel 5; John A. Schutz and Douglass Adair, eds., *The Spur of Fame* (San Marino, Calif., 1966), 147.

Chapter 1: The Wellsprings of Ambition

Epigraph: Adams to Thomas Jefferson, 15 Nov. 1813, in *The Adams-Jefferson Letters,* ed. Lester Cappon, 2 vols. (Chapel Hill, N.C., 1959), 2:402.

1. For the hierarchical nature of colonial American society, see Gordon S. Wood, *The Radicalism of the American Revolution* (New York, 1992), 11–24; BL to an unidentified correspondent, 1782, in Allis, *Lincoln Papers,* reel 6; BL to the Hingham selectmen, 12 Jan. 1790, in ibid., reel 9.

2. Until about 1750 the new year began on 25 March. By such old-style reckoning, Benjamin Lincoln was born in 1732/33. I have rendered all such dates as we do, viz. 1733. On the early days of Hingham, see John J. Waters, "Hingham, Mass., 1631–1661: An East Anglian Oligarchy in the New World," *Journal of Social History* 1 (1968): 351–70; and David Grayson Allen, *In English Ways: The Movement of Societies and the Transferal of English Local Law and Custom* (Chapel Hill, N.C., 1981), 55, 59, 61, 64.

3. For early New England's "errand to the wilderness," see Edmund S. Morgan, *The Puritan Dilemma: The Story of John Winthrop* (Boston, 1958), 69–83.

4. Waters, "Hingham, Mass.," 360–61; Allen, *In English Ways*, 55, 64, 81. The process of Hingham's settlement, especially the division of lands and the establishment of the church, was similar to that of Dedham, Massachusetts, as described in Kenneth A. Lockridge, *A New England Town: The First Hundred Years* (New York, 1970), 1–79.

5. John Coolidge, "Hingham Builds a Meetinghouse," *New England Quarterly* 34 (1961): 441–42; Daniel Scott Smith, "Child-Naming Practices, Kinship Ties, and Change in Family Attitudes in Hingham, Mass., 1641–1880," *Journal of Social History* 18 (1985): 542; Allen, *In English Ways*, 67–69.

6. Allen, *In English Ways*, 56, 59, 61. Through its sea connections with Boston, Hingham "emerged from the purely agricultural frontier stage early in the 18th century." By 1820 only 33 percent of the Hingham work force was engaged in agriculture, as compared to 63 percent, the Massachusetts average; see Daniel Scott Smith, "Population, Family and Society in Hingham, Mass., 1635–1880" (Ph.D. diss., University of California, Berkeley, 1973), 58–59.

7. George Lincoln et al., *History of the Town of Hingham, Massachusetts*, 3 vols. (Cambridge, Mass., 1893), 3:3–4.

8. For the investment in Harvard College, see the *Publications of the Colonial Society of Massachusetts*, 62 vols. to date (Boston, 1892–), 16:412; for the sale of four acres of land to Benjamin Lincoln, maltster, 11 May 1675, see W. Graham Arader III, Autograph Catalog no. 79 (Spring 1988).

9. Lincoln, *History of Hingham*, 3:6.

10. The quotation is from Colonel Lincoln's obituary; see the *Boston Evening Post*, 6 Mar. 1771; Lincoln, *History of Hingham*, 3:8; William H. Whitmore, *The Massachusetts Civil List for the Colonial and Provincial Periods, 1630–1774* (1870; reprint, Baltimore, 1969).

11. Lincoln, *History of Hingham*, 3:8. On the importance of perpetuating the lineage by naming children for their parents, see Smith, "Population, Family and Society," 244–47; for the pervasiveness of the practice, see Smith, "Child-Naming Practices," 546.

12. BL to Benjamin Lincoln Jr., 7 Apr. 1783, in Allis, *Lincoln Papers*, reel 6.

13. John T. Kirkland, "Notices of the Life of Major-General Benjamin Lincoln," *Collections of the Massachusetts Historical Society*, 2d ser. (Boston, 1815), 3:233; Philip Greven, *The Protestant Temperament: Patterns of Child-Rearing, Religious Experience, and the Self in Early America* (New York, 1977), 151–261.

14. Robert J. Wilson, III, *The Benevolent Diety: Ebenezer Gay and the Rise of Rational Religion in New England, 1696–1787* (Philadelphia, 1984); see also Alan Heimert, *Religion and the American Mind from the Great Awakening to the Revolution* (Cambridge, Mass., 1966), 5–6, 415; and Harry S. Stout, *The New England Soul: Preaching and Religious Culture in Colonial New England* (New York, 1986), 224; BL to Theodore Lincoln, 24 June 1781, Lincoln Collection, Boston Public Library (MB). Gay's influence over BL did not extend into the realm of politics. Gay's religious liberalism was profoundly conservative, politically, and the minister became a Tory, though he remained in Hingham throughout the war; see Heimert, *Religion,* viii.

15. See the surviving entries in Colonel Lincoln's diary for 1750 and 1763, in Allis, *Lincoln Papers,* reel 1. For a general picture of life on the New England farm during this period, see Howard S. Russell, *A Long Deep Furrow: Three Centuries of Farming in New England* (Hanover, N.H., 1982), 108–20.

16. For the importance of birth order in determining patrimony, see John J. Waters, "Patrimony, Succession and Social Stability," *Perspectives in American History* 10 (1976): 140–49. Hingham kept a public school from its inception, as the General Court required; see Lincoln, *History of Hingham,* 2:86; William Sullivan, *The Public Men of the Revolution* (Philadelphia, 1847), 129.

17. Sullivan, *Public Men of the Revolution,* 128–29; "Sketch of Major William Jackson," *Pennsylvania Magazine of History and Biography (PMHB)* 2 (1878): 363.

18. John Langdon Sibley and Clifford K. Shipton, *Biographical Sketches of Those Who Attended Harvard College,* 17 vols. (Cambridge and Boston, 1873–1975), 13:455–57; Lyman H. Butterfield, ed., *Diary and Autobiography of John Adams,* 4 vols. (Cambridge, Mass., 1961), 1:87.

19. For Colonel Lincoln's wealth, see the tax lists in Allis, *Lincoln Papers,* reel 1; Benjamin Lincoln Sr. to James Otis, 3 Jan. 1752, Otis Family Papers, New York Public Library (NN); Whitmore, *Massachusetts Civil List,* 59.

20. Lincoln, *History of Hingham,* 3:9; BL's 1754 military commission is in Allis, *Lincoln Papers,* reel 1. On constables, see Edward M. Cook Jr., *The Fathers of the Towns: Leadership and Community Structure in Eighteenth Century New England* (Baltimore, 1976), 26; Michael Zuckerman, *Peaceable Kingdoms: New England Towns in the Eighteenth Century* (New York, 1978), 85–88; and Dirk Hoerder, *Society and Government 1760–1780: The Power Structure in Massachusetts Townships* (Berlin, 1972), 19.

21. Lincoln, *History of Hingham,* 3:9. For evidence that marriage was linked to economic independence, see Daniel Scott Smith, "Parental Power and Marriage Patterns: An Analysis of Historical Trends in Hingham, Mass.," *Journal of Marriage and the Family* 35 (1973): 422. For the names and dates of birth and death of Lincoln's children, see genealogical chart.

22. Charles van Hogendorp to his mother, 7 Dec. 1783, in *Brieven en Gedenkshriften van Gijsbert Karel von Hogendorp uitgegeven door zijn jongsten, thans eenigen zoon,* 2 vols. (The Hague, 1866), 1:266–69. BL to Mary Lincoln,

12 Oct. 1781, and 15 May and 9 July 1793, in Allis, *Lincoln Papers,* reels 6 and 10.

23. Cook, *Fathers of the Towns,* 102.

24. Fred Anderson, *A People's Army: Massachusetts Soldiers and Society in the Seven Years' War* (Chapel Hill, N.C., 1984), 26–27, 39; BL's commission dated 3 June 1763 is in Allis, *Lincoln Papers,* reel 1.

25. Allis, *Lincoln Papers,* reel 1; the legacy of Elijah Cushing is discussed in John C. Cavanaugh, "The Military Career of General Benjamin Lincoln in the War of the American Revolution, 1775–1781" (Ph.D. diss., Duke University, 1969), 19; Lincoln, *History of Hingham,* 3:9.

26. William Pencak, *War, Politics and Revolution in Provincial Massachusetts* (Boston, 1981), 174, 243, 254; Butterfield, *Diary and Autobiography,* 1:279; Benjamin Lincoln Sr. to John Cushing, 4 Feb. 1766, in William Cushing Papers, Massachusetts Historical Society (MHi).

27. Thomas Cushing to John Cushing, 28 Jan. 1766, in William Cushing Papers (MHi); Jackson Turner Main, *The Upper House in Revolutionary America, 1763–1788* (Madison, Wis., 1967), 69–73. The average length of service on the council was ten years. Colonel Lincoln served sixteen years, a circumstance that might be explained by his political neutrality and social status; see Cook, *Fathers of the Towns,* 148–49.

28. Pencak, *War, Politics and Revolution,* 196; Butterfield, *Diary and Autobiography,* 1:312; instructions to Joshua Hearsey, 21 Sept. 1768, in Lincoln, *History of Hingham,* 1:271.

29. Butterfield, *Diary and Autobiography,* 1:279; Wilson, *Benevolent Deity,* 214. For evidence that Ebenezer Gay, among the New England clergy, was bucking an increasingly radical tide, see Stout, *New England Soul,* 259. For a definition of the country party and its definition of a good ruler, see Timothy H. Breen, *The Character of the Good Ruler: Puritan Political Ideas in New England, 1630–1730* (New York, 1970), 240–69.

30. Kirkland, "Notices of General Lincoln," 234; *Massachusetts Gazette and the Boston Weekly News-Letter,* 26 Nov. 1772; James Warren to Samuel Adams, 8 Dec. 1772, in *Collections of the Massachusetts Historical Society,* 73:401; BL to the Boston Committee of Merchants, 19 Mar. 1770, in Lincoln, *History of Hingham,* 1:272.

31. Circular to the brigadier generals of the Massachusetts militia, 18 May 1776, in Allis, *Lincoln Papers,* reel 1.

32. Sibley and Shipton, *Biographical Sketches of Harvard Graduates,* 12:416; *Boston Evening Post,* 6 Mar. 1771.

33. The progress of Bela's illness was, as early as July 1771, "in a dangerous state"; see Edmund Quincy to Catherine Quincy, in Sibley and Shipton, *Biographical Sketches of Harvard Graduates,* 13:457. For BL's occupation with Bela's affairs and their affectionate relationship, see Bela Lincoln to BL, 20 June 1772, in Allis, *Lincoln Papers,* reel 1. The friend's quotation is in Sibley and Shipton, *Biographical Sketches.*

34. For the purchase of land and the settlement of his brother's estate, see the

deed of sale, 4 Feb. 1768, and probate of Bela's estate, Aug. 1773, in Allis, *Lincoln Papers,* reel 1; BL to Martin Gay, 9 Dec. 1767, Special Misc. Collection, Otis-Gay Papers, Columbia University Libraries (NNC).

35. Francis Bowen, *Life of Benjamin Lincoln, Major General in the Army of the Revolution* (Boston, 1847), 221; for BL's militia commission, 15 Jan. 1772, and the deed of sale for Cato, 27 June 1772, see Allis, *Lincoln Papers,* reel 1; for BL's description of slavery in Georgia, see his letter to Benjamin Lincoln Jr., 16 May 1782, ibid., reel 6; for the presence of blacks in the Lincoln household, see Charles van Hogendorp to his mother, 7 Dec. 1783, Hogendorp, *Brieven en Gedenkshriften van Gijsbert Karel von Hogendorp,* 1:266–69; and H. J. Hill to BL, 6 May 1782, in Allis, *Lincoln Papers,* reel 6. For the distinctive pattern of "family slavery" in New England, see William D. Piersen, *Black Yankees: The Development of an Afro-American Subculture in Eighteenth-Century New England* (Amherst, Mass., 1988), 25–36; see also Lorenzo J. Greene, *The Negro in Colonial New England, 1620–1776* (New York, 1942), 104, 218–19, 222.

36. Lincoln, *History of Hingham,* 3:10.

37. Bowen, *Life of Lincoln,* 221–22; Lincoln, *History of Hingham,* 1:273–74.

38. Richard L. Bushman, *King and People in Provincial Massachusetts* (Chapel Hill, N.C., 1985), 214–16; Cavanaugh, "Military Career of Lincoln," 27–31; David R. Millar, "The Militia, the Army, and Independency in Colonial Massachusetts" (Ph.D. diss., Cornell University, 1967), 286–87.

39. Henry S. Nourse, "A Forgotten Patriot," *Proceedings of the American Antiquarian Society,* 96 vols. to date (Worcester, Mass., 1880–), 7:102; Cavanaugh, "Military Career of Lincoln," 33–44; David Hackett Fischer, *Paul Revere's Ride* (New York, 1994), 44–64, 165–73.

40. Bushman, *King and People in Provincial Massachusetts,* 216–18; Bowen, *Life of Lincoln,* 226; BL to the Hingham selectmen, 29 July 1775, in Allis, *Lincoln Papers,* reel 1.

41. BL to Benjamin Lincoln Jr., 25 Nov. 1781, in Allis, *Lincoln Papers,* reel 6.

Chapter 2: From Boardroom to Field Command

Epigraph: Abigail Adams to John Adams, 22 Aug. 1776, in *The Adams Family Correspondence,* ed. Lyman H. Butterfield, 4 vols. to date (Cambridge, Mass., 1963–), 2:105.

1. For general background and the context of the military conflict, I have used Don Higginbotham's excellent survey *The War of American Independence: Military Attitudes, Policies, and Practice, 1763–1789* (Boston, 1983), 82–85; Massachusetts Provincial Congress to the Continental Congress, 16 May 1775, in *American Archives,* ed. Peter Force, ser. 4, 6 vols. (Washington, D.C., 1837–46), 2:621. One of the pillars of Republican ideology was fear of a standing army. Even their own army was seen by revolutionaries as a potential threat to their liberties; see Charles Royster, *A Revolutionary People at War: The Continental Army and American Character, 1775–1783* (Chapel Hill, N.C., 1979), 35–37.

2. Higginbotham, *War of American Independence,* 99; for BL as a member of the Massachusetts Committee of Supply, see Joseph Reed to BL, 7 Sept. 1775, in *The Papers of George Washington,* ed. William W. Abbot et al., Revolutionary War series, 6 vols. to date (Charlottesville, Va., 1983–), 1:401–2 and n. 3; for Washington's request for blankets, see his Circular to the New England Governments, 23 Dec. 1775, in ibid., 2:591–92; Force, *American Archives,* 4:1219–97.

3. James Warren to John Adams, 3 Dec. 1775, in *The Warren-Adams Letters, Massachusetts Historical Society Collections,* vols. 72 and 73 (Boston, 1917–25), 72:190. In Feb. 1776 the council authorized BL as one of a committee to "make some further experiments of the saltpetre that is manufactured in this colony," see Force, *American Archives,* 4th ser., 4:1311.

4. The balloting for general officers was held in the House of Representatives on 30 Jan. 1776. The House's choice of BL to replace Warren took place on 8 Feb. 1776; see Force, *American Archives,* 4th ser., 4:1295, 1426, 1438–39; BL to moderator of Hingham town meeting (Feb. 1776?), in Allis, *Lincoln Papers,* reel 1.

5. Higginbotham, *War of American Independence,* 105; Christopher Ward, *The War of the Revolution,* 2 vols. (New York, 1952), 1:202.

6. Allen French, *The First Year of the American Revolution* (Boston, 1934), 681–83 and nn. For BL as one of a committee to inspect the harbor fortifications, see BL to Artemas Ward, 8 and 15 Apr. 1776, Artemas Ward Papers (MHi); BL to Joseph Andrews, 6 May 1776, in Allis, *Lincoln Papers,* reel 1. The lack of energy can be traced in part to the deficiencies of command, although Ward complained that he had neither the men nor resources to carry out the extensive works planned for Boston; see Washington to Richard Gridley, 28 Apr., and to Ward, 29 Apr. 1776, in Abbot et al., *Papers of Washington,* rev. ser., 4:159, 171.

7. Resolution of the Committee of War, 17 May 1776; and BL's Circular to the Brigadiers, 18 May 1776, in Allis, *Lincoln Papers,* reel 1. BL commanded the brigades from the counties of Suffolk, Essex, Middlesex, and Plymouth.

8. Instructions to Hingham representatives, 23 May 1776, in Lincoln, *History of Hingham,* 1:302; for BL's belief in British "designs," see his Circular to the Brigadiers, 18 May 1776, in Allis, *Lincoln Papers,* reel 1.

9. Richard Frothingham, *History of the Siege of Boston* (Boston, 1851), 314–15; French, *First Year of the Revolution,* 683 and nn.; Gardner W. Allen, *A Naval History of the American Revolution,* 2 vols. (1913; reprint, Williamstown, Mass., 1970), 1:78–83; Samuel Cooper to John Adams, 1 July 1776, cited in *The Divine Politician: Samuel Cooper and the American Revolution in Boston,* ed. Charles W. Akers (Boston, 1982), 229. Two troopships were captured when they sailed unawares into the harbor. For the attempt to capture the whole fleet, see BL to Ward, 23 June, and BL to the commander on Long Island, 23 and 24 June 1776, in Allis, *Lincoln Papers,* reel 1; and Thomas Legate to BL, 17 June 1776, in ibid.

10. Akers, *Divine Politician,* 232; Abigail Adams to John Adams, 13 July 1776, in *The Book of Abigail and John: Selected Letters of the Adams Family, 1762–1784,* ed. Lyman H. Butterfield et al. (Cambridge, Mass., 1975), 144–45;

Thomas Legate to BL, 3 Aug. 1776, in Allis, *Lincoln Papers,* reel 1; Mary Palmer to John Adams, 4 Aug. 1776, in Butterfield, *Adams Family Correspondence,* 2:77. Eventually, Washington would order the entire Continental army to be innoculated for smallpox; see Washington to Gov. Nicholas Cooke, 10 Feb. 1777, in *The Writings of George Washington, from the Original Sources, 1745–1799,* ed. John C. Fitzpatrick, 39 vols. (Washington, D.C., 1931–44), 7:131.

11. Abigail Adams to John Adams, 22 Aug. 1776; and John to Abigail, 20 Aug. 1778, in Butterfield, *Adams Family Correspondence,* 2:105, 115; John Lowell to John Adams, 14 Aug. 1776, in *The Historical Magazine and Notes and Queries concerning the Antiquities, History, and Biography of America,* ser. 1, 10 vols. (Boston, 1857–66), 1:258; Joseph Ward to John Adams, 6 Sept. 1776, in *The Papers of John Adams,* ed. Robert J. Taylor, 6 vols. to date (Cambridge, Mass., 1977–), 5:18; John Rowe Diary, *Proceedings of the Massachusetts Historical Society,* 2d ser. (Boston, 1895–96), 10:102–4; Adams to James Warren, 26 July 1776, *Warren-Adams Letters,* 72:264. Whether Adams's low opinion of BL was merely a reflection of his resentment of Bela Lincoln's marriage to Hannah Quincy, whom Adams had unsucessfully wooed, or whether he had other grounds for deprecating BL's abilities is not known.

12. Samuel Adams to Elbridge Gerry, 23 Sept. 1776, in *The Life and Public Services of Samuel Adams,* ed. William V. Wells, 3 vols. (Boston, 1865), 2:447–48; James Warren to John Adams, 19 Sept. 1776, in *Warren-Adams Letters,* 72:274; Adams to James Warren, 5 Oct. 1776, in Taylor, *Papers of John Adams,* 5:46.

13. BL to Washington, 28 Sept. 1776, in Allis, *Lincoln Papers,* reel 1. Washington to the officer commanding the Massachusetts militia, 19 Sept. 1776; to BL, 30 Sept. 1776; and to George Clinton, 30 Sept. 1776, in Fitzpatrick, *Writings of Washington,* 6:74, 141–42.

14. Expenses for BL and Clinton's stay in New Haven are given in *Public Papers of George Clinton, First Governor of New York,* ed. Hugh Hastings, 10 vols. (Albany, N.Y., 1914), 1:372–73. Jonathan Trumbull Sr. to BL, 2 Oct. 1776, in Trumbull Papers, Connecticut Historical Society (Chi). Washington to BL, 7 Oct. 1776; to the president of Congress, 11 Oct. 1776; to Jonathan Trumbull, 16 Oct. 1776; and General Orders, 15 Oct. 1776, in Fitzpatrick, *Writings of Washington,* 6:176, 196, 207, 210. Jonathan Hobart to BL, 17 Oct. 1776, Emmet Collection, NN.

15. Higginbotham, *War of American Independence,* 160–61; BL to John Browne, 23 Oct. 1776, in Allis, *Lincoln Papers,* reel 1.

16. Ward, *War of the Revolution,* 1:260–8; Minutes of a Council of War, 6 Nov. 1776, in *Papers of the Continental Congress* (PCC), microfilm ed., reel 167, item 152, 217.

17. BL to (?), 21 Oct. 1776, in Allis, *Lincoln Papers,* reel 1; Robert K. Wright Jr., "Nor Is Their Standing Army to Be Despised: The Emergence of the Continental Army as a Military Institution," in *Arms and Independence: The Military Character of the American Revolution,* ed. Ronald Hoffman and Peter J. Albert (Charlottesville, Va., 1984), 54. George Washington to the Massachusetts Legis-

lature, 6 Nov. 1776, and to the president of Congress, 11 Nov. 1776, in Fitzpatrick, *Writings of Washington,* 6:247, 271.

18. Anderson, *A People's Army,* 167–95.

19. Col. Lincoln to (?), 18 Jan. 1760, Lloyd W. Smith Collection, Morristown National Historical Park.

20. The debate over the effectiveness of the militia versus the Continental army began early in the Revolutionary War and has continued to the present day. One of the first to point out the defects of the citizen soldier and to argue for a professional army was Emory Upton (*Military Policy of the United States* [Washington, D.C., 1904]). Recent arguments have concentrated on the political or ideological consequences of a reliance on the militia or standing army; see Lawrence Delbert Cress, *Citizens in Arms: The Army and Militia in American Society to the War of 1812* (Chapel Hill, N.C., 1982), 51–57; Don Higginbotham, "The American Militia: A Traditional Institution with Revolutionary Responsibilities," in *Reconsiderations on the Revolutionary War: Selected Essays,* ed. Don Higginbotham (Westport, Conn., 1978); John Shy, "American Society and Its War for Independence," in ibid; Paul D. Nelson, "Citizen Soldiers or Regulars: The Views of American General Officers on the Military Establishment, 1775–1781," *Military Affairs* 43 (1979): 126–32; Royster, *A Revolutionary People at War,* 114–18.

21. BL to Gov. Richard Caswell (N.C.), 3 Jan. 1780, Charleston Letterbook, BL Papers (MB). One problem with the militia was that they were asked to do a bit of everything, from defending against British raids and quelling Loyalists and Indians to participating in major campaigns; see Higginbotham, "The American Militia," in Higginbotham, *Reconsiderations,* 95–100. For national service and the development of a Continental vision, see Stanley Elkins and Eric McKitrick, "The Founding Fathers: Young Men of the Revolution," *Political Science Quarterly* 76 (1961): 181–216.

22. BL to Gen. Jotham Moulton, 13 Dec. 1776; BL to Mr. Andrews, n.d.; and Ebenezer Gay to BL, 15 Dec. 1776, in Allis, *Lincoln Papers,* reel 1.

23. BL to Warner, 13 Dec. 1776, in ibid., reel 1.

24. Washington to Heath, 18 Dec. 1776, in Fitzpatrick, *Writings of Washington,* 6:392; James Bowdoin to the president of Congress, 30–31 Dec. 1776, in *PCC,* reel 79, item 65, 155.

25. Washington to BL, 18 Dec. 1776, and to Heath of same date, in Fitzpatrick, *Writings of Washington,* 6:392, 394.

26. Washington to the president of Congress, 20 Dec. 1776, in Fitzpatrick, *Writings of Washington,* 6:399–409. The jealousy and bitterness caused by the appointments of general officers by Congress is amply described in Jonathan Gregory Rossie, *The Politics of Command in the American Revolution* (Syracuse, N.Y., 1975), esp. 17–30.

27. The comment on Sullivan's appointment is qtd. in Royster, *A Revolutionary People at War,* 43; Washington to the president of Congress, 4 Apr. 1776, in Fitzpatrick, *Writings of Washington,* 4:472. Warren was not the only one reluc-

tant to act in a Continental capacity. David Wooster, though commissioned as a Continental general, thought his commission as a Connecticut major general had priority; see Rossie, *Politics of Command*, 21.

28. The idea that citizen-soldiers required a special kind of commander is discussed in Royster, *A Revolutionary Army at War*, 43–46; for Charles Lee, see Cress, *Citizens in Arms*, 55; for Montgomery and for Philip Schuyler's problems with the lack of deference of New England officers and men, see Rossie, *Politics of Command*, 38, 43. Washington often complained of lazy officers, see his letter to Joseph Reed, 1 Apr. 1776, in Fitzpatrick, *Writings of Washington*, 4:453.

29. See the notice of BL's appointment to command in Rhode Island in the Boston *Independent Chronicle*, 26 Dec. 1776. For BL's movements in and around Providence, see Marquis de Malmedy to Gen. Charles Lee, 20 Dec. 1776, in *PCC*, reel 99, item 78, 151. BL's report to Washington of British movements in Rhode Island was written from Peekskill, 4 Jan. 1777, in *Correspondence of the American Revolution*, ed. Jared Sparks, 4 vols. (Boston, 1853), 1:320. Heath to Washington, 26 and 28 Dec. 1776 and 4 Jan. 1777, William Heath Papers, in *Collections of the Massachusetts Historical Society*, 64:45, 50, 56. Washington to Heath, 5 Jan. 1777, and to BL, 7 Jan. 1777, in Fitzpatrick, *Writings of Washington*, 6:472, 476.

30. See "Lt. George Matthew's Narrative," in *Historical Magazine*, 1:103; BL to David Wooster and Samuel Parsons, 12 Jan. 1777, *Proceedings of the American Antiquarian Society*, 29:74; BL to Clinton, Jan. 1777, in Hastings, *Public Papers of George Clinton*, 1:536.

31. William Heath, *Memoirs of the American War* (1798; reprint, New York, 1904), 118–25.

32. See Pickering's diary in Octavius Pickering, *The Life of Timothy Pickering*, 4 vols. (Boston, 1867), 1:94; and Pickering to John Pickering, 31 Jan. 1777, Pickering Papers (MHi).

33. Timothy Pickering to John Pickering, 31 Jan. 1777, Pickering Papers (MHi); Washington to Heath, 4 Feb. 1777, in Fitzpatrick, *Writings of Washington*, 7:99.

34. John Adams to Abigail Adams, 21 Feb. 1777, in *Letters of Members of the Continental Congress*, ed. Edmund C. Burnett, 8 vols. (Washington, D.C., 1921–36), 2:269; William Tudor to John Adams, 7 Mar. 1777, in Taylor, *Papers of John Adams*, 5:104; Washington to the president of Congress, 22 Jan. 1777, in Fitzpatrick, *Writings of Washington*, 7:48.

35. The march into New Jersey is found in Pickering, *Life of Timothy Pickering*, 1:114–18; for BL's arrival, see Washington to the president of Congress, 14 Feb. 1777, in Fitzpatrick, *Writings of Washington*, 7:145. BL's commission was enclosed in John Hancock to BL, 22 Feb. 1777; and BL's acceptance is in BL to the president of Congress, 4 Mar. 1777, in *PCC*, reel 23, item 12A, 147, 177. For Adams's inquiry, see Adams to Tudor, 11 Mar. 1777, and Tudor to Adams, 16 Mar. 1777, in *Papers of John Adams*, 5:110, 112.

36. William Tudor to John Adams, 11 Mar. 1777, in Taylor, *Papers of John Adams*, 5:110; the description of Bound Brook and daily life there is given in

Pickering, *Life of Timothy Pickering*, 1:118–25; for the militia, see Washington to Robert Morris, George Clymer, and George Walton, 27 Feb. 1777, in Fitzpatrick, *Writings of Washington*, 7:202.

37. For desertion, see BL to Col. Brodhead, 8 May 1777, and BL to Washington, 22 May 1777, in Allis, *Lincoln Papers*, reel 2; Pickering, *Life of Timothy Pickering*, 1:126; BL to Washington, 12 Apr. 1777, in Allis, *Lincoln Papers*, reel 2.

38. Nathanael Greene to John Adams, 13 Apr. 1777, in *The Papers of Nathanael Greene*, ed. Richard K. Showman et al., 6 vols. to date (Chapel Hill, N.C., 1976–), 2:55; Joseph Ward to John Adams, 19 Apr. 1777, in Taylor, *Papers of John Adams*, 5:156. The Bound Brook raid became a favorite story and is found in a number of garbled versions; see, for example, Marquis de Chastellux, *Travels in North America in the Years 1780, 1781, and 1782*, ed. Howard C. Rice Jr., 2 vols. (Chapel Hill, 1963), 1:119; and John Bernard, *Retrospections of America, 1797–1811* (New York, 1887), 61.

39. Joseph Trumbull to Jonathan Trumbull, 19 Apr. 1777, *Collections of the Massachusetts Historical Society*, 62:42; Washington to the president of Congress, 12 Apr. 1777, in Fitzpatrick, *Writings of Washington*, 7:399; Greene to Adams, 2 May 1777, in Showman, *Papers of Nathanael Greene*, 2:64; Ward to Adams, 19 Apr. 1777, in Taylor, *Papers of John Adams*, 5:156; BL to Washington, 14 May 1777, George Washington Papers, Library of Congress (DLC).

40. See the letters of BL to Washington, 14, 18, 20, and 22 May 1777, in Allis, *Lincoln Papers*, reel 2.

41. Christopher Duffy, *The Military Experience in the Age of Reason* (London, 1987), 97; and Royster, *A Revolutionary People at War*, 61; Benjamin Lincoln Jr. to BL, 26 May 1777, in Allis, *Lincoln Papers*, reel 2.

42. See the letters of Benjamin Lincoln Jr. to BL, 26 and 29 May, 2 and 10 June, and 16 July 1777, in Allis, *Lincoln Papers*, reel 2.

43. Benjamin Lincoln Jr. to BL, 26 May 1777, in Allis, *Lincoln Papers*, reel 2.

44. Nathanael Greene to BL, 9 June 1777, in Showman, *Papers of Nathanael Greene*, 2:105; Ward, *War of the Revolution*, 1:325–28; BL to Samuel Horton, 22 June 1777, in Allis, *Lincoln Papers*, reel 2.

45. Benjamin Lincoln Jr. to BL, 16 July 1777, in Allis, *Lincoln Papers*, reel 2; Ward, *War of the Revolution*, 1:328–29.

46. Ward, *War of the Revolution*, 1:329; Benjamin Lincoln Jr. to BL, 16 July 1777, in Allis, *Lincoln Papers*, reel 2; Washington to BL, 24 July 1777, in Fitzpatrick, *Writings of Washington*, 8:462; for BL's illness, see Benjamin Lincoln Jr. to BL, 11 Aug. 1777, in Allis, *Lincoln Papers*, reel 2.

47. For Abigail Adams, see the epigraph to this chapter. Washington's estimate of BL as a "judicious, brave, active officer" is in Washington to Philip Schuyler, 24 July 1777, in Fitzpatrick, *Writings of Washington*, 8:459; Don Higginbotham, "Military Leadership in the American Revolution," in *Leadership in the American Revolution* (Washington, D.C., 1974), 96; Timothy Pickering to John Pickering, 22 Oct. 1777, Pickering Papers (MHi); Washington to Trumbull, 31 July 1777, in Fitzpatrick, *Writings of Washington*, 8:506.

Chapter 3: Saratoga

Epigraph: Washington to Philip Schuyler, 24 July 1777, in *The Writings of George Washington, From the Original Sources,* ed. John C. Fitzpatrick, 39 vols. (Washington, D.C., 1931–44), 8:459.

1. BL to George Washington, 4 Aug. 1777, in *The Benjamin Lincoln Papers,* ed. Frederick S. Allis Jr., Massachusetts Historical Society microfilm ed., 13 reels (Boston, 1968), reel 2. For Schuyler's delaying activities, see Don Higginbotham, *The War of American Independence: Military Attitudes, Policies and Practice, 1763–1789* (Boston, 1983), 188–90; and Christopher Ward, *The War of the Revolution,* ed. John R. Alden, 2 vols. (New York, 1952), 1:418–19. For the worst construction placed on Schuyler's actions, see Jonathan Gregory Rossie, *The Politics of Command in the American Revolution* (Syracuse, N.Y., 1975), 165–66. For a sympathetic, indeed celebrationist, view of the New York general, see Don R. Gerlach, *Proud Patriot: Philip Schuyler and the War of Independence, 1775–1783* (Syracuse, N.Y., 1987), 251–325; BL to Washington, 12 Aug. 1777, Washington Papers (DLC); and Warren to John Adams, 10 Aug. 1777, in *The Papers of John Adams,* ed. Robert J. Taylor, 6 vols. to date (Cambridge, Mass., 1977–), 5:269.

2. See the letters of Washington to Schuyler, 27 July 1777, to Jonathan Trumbull, 31 July, and to the N.Y. Council of Safety, 4 Aug., in *The Writings of George Washington, from the Original Sources, 1745–1799,* ed. John C. Fitzpatrick, 39 vols. (Washington, D.C., 1931–44), 8:484, 506, and 9:12. For militia morale and desertion, see Ward, *War of the Revolution,* 1:420–21.

3. Washington to Schuyler, 24 July 1777, in Fitzpatrick, *Writings of Washington,* 8:456; Schuyler to BL, 31 July 1777, *Copy of Orders.* Clifford K. Shipton and James E. Mooney. *National Index of American Imprints through 1800: The Short-Title Evans.* American Antiquarian Society, 1969, 16142.

4. BL to Washington, 12 Aug. 1777, Washington Papers (DLC); BL to Schuyler, to Ward, and to Washington, all 4 Aug. 1777, in Allis, *Lincoln Papers,* reel 2.

5. Higginbotham, *War of American Independence,* 188–91; BL to Schuyler, 6 Aug. 1777, in Allis, *Lincoln Papers,* reel 2; Schuyler to BL, 9 Aug. 1777, misc. bound MSS (MHi); Schuyler to BL, 8 Aug., qtd. in Caleb Stark, *Memoir and Official Correspondence of Gen. John Stark . . .* (1860; reprint, Boston, 1972), 125. Schuyler resented the lack of support he had been given by the New England governors and feared the outcome of a general engagement with Burgoyne unless heavily reinforced; see Jonathan Trumbull to Schuyler, 1 Aug. 1777, in *Public Papers of George Clinton, First Governor of New York,* ed. Hugh Hastings, 10 vols. (Albany, N.Y., 1914), 2:148; and Schuyler to Trumbull, 8 Aug. 1777, *Collections of the Massachusetts Historical Society,* 62:106. When Washington got wind of Schuyler's plans to unite all his forces to oppose Burgoyne's advance, he called it "a very ineligible plan" and insisted that rear and flank attacks were absolutely critical for success; see Washington to George Clinton, 16 Aug. 1777, in Fitzpatrick, *Writings of Washington,* 9:75.

6. BL to Schuyler, 8 Aug., and Schuyler to BL, 9 Aug. 1777, misc. bound MSS (MHi). When Enoch Poor was promoted to brigadier general over his head in Feb. 1777, Stark resigned his Continental commission; see Rossie, *Politics of Command,* 140; see also the notes of George Frost to Josiah Bartlett, 19 Aug. 1777, in *Letters of Delegates to Congress, 1774–1789,* ed. Paul H. Smith, 20 vols. to date (Washington, D.C., 1976–), 7:510.

7. BL to Washington, 12 Aug. 1777, Washington Papers (DLC). Lincoln had received intelligence of 4 Aug. from Cambridge "that the enemy will attack that place on Wed. next and move on and fortify themselves at Bennington. I believe the story is thrown out to terrify the inhabitants but I will be on my guard and will make such disposition of the troops as in my opinion will best counteract their designs." Thus, "our plan" probably revolved around a movement to Cambridge from Bennington; see BL to Schuyler, 4 Aug., and to John Stark, 14 Aug., in Allis, *Lincoln Papers,* reel 2. For Stark's account of the battle of Bennington, see his letter to the Council of New Hampshire, 18 Aug., in Stark, *Memoirs,* 126. Lincoln's account was published as a handbill, an act that led to more friction between him and the prickly Stark, who thought that BL had given short shrift to the contributions of the N.H. militia; see BL to the Massachusetts Council, 18 Aug., in ibid., 132. Stark was soon promoted to brigadier general in the Continental line; see Rossie, *Politics of Command,* 167. Indicative of the way Stark's insubordination was viewed is this letter from James Duane to R. R. Livingston, 3 Sept. 1777: "Stark will also be provided for tho' he is something under the clouds for refusing to serve under Gen. Lincoln to whom he refusd the Command of the Troops. . . . Gen. Schuyler prevailed on him to submit to Lincoln: but before that General's Arrival at Bennington he took Care to attack and defeat the Enemy. You'l allow this to be a handsome Apology for intemperate Expressions" (Smith, *Letters of Delegates,* 7:598).

8. Congress replaced Schuyler with Gates on 4 Aug. 1777 by the vote of eleven states; see Paul David Nelson, *General Horatio Gates: A Biography* (Baton Rouge, La., 1976), 103. Nelson's biography has generally superseded the more partisan one by Samuel White Patterson, *Horatio Gates: Defender of American Liberties* (New York, 1941). For a dual biography of Gates and John Burgoyne, see Max M. Mintz, *The Generals of Saratoga* (New Haven, Conn. 1990). For the political battles fought in the Northern Department and in Congress, see Rossie, *Politics of Command,* 118–53; John Adams to Abigail Adams, 4 Aug. 1777, in *The Adams Family Correspondence,* ed. Lyman H. Butterfield, 4 vols. to date (Cambridge, Mass., 1963–), 2:299.

9. Gerlach, *Proud Patriot,* 296–97; Schuyler to BL, 15 Aug. 1777, BL Papers (MHi), reel 2; BL to Gates, 20 Aug. 1777, Horatio Gates Papers (New-York Historical Society [NHi]), reel 5.

10. Gates to BL, 23 Aug. 1777, Gates Papers (NHi), reel 5; and George Clinton to the New York Council of Safety, 22 Aug., in Hastings, *Public Papers of George Clinton,* 2:247. For BL's efforts to expedite the militia, see BL to the Massachusetts council, 23 Aug., and to the New Hampshire council, 27 Aug., in Allis,

Lincoln Papers, reel 2. For his communications with Gates, see (among others) BL to Gates, 29 Aug., and 12 Sept. 1777, in ibid., reel 2. For Arnold and the relief of Fort Schuyler (Stanwix), see Ward, *War of the Revolution,* 2:477–91; and Willard M. Wallace, *Traitorous Hero: The Life and Fortunes of Benedict Arnold* (New York, 1954), 137–44. Burgoyne's army crossed the river on 14 Sept.; for his movements, see Richard J. Hargrove, *General John Burgoyne* (Newark, Del., 1983), 176–80.

11. BL to Gates, 12, 14, and 17 Sept. 1777, Gates Papers (NHi).

12. Gates to BL, 15, 19, and 22 Sept. 1777; and BL to Gates, 20 Sept. (two letters), Gates Papers (NHi). BL was also under pressure to provide reinforcements for his attacking parties; see John Brown to BL, 19 Sept. 1777, Emmet Collection (NN). Lincoln originally intended the Brown and Johnson forces to remain near Ticonderoga, but enemy forces proved too strong for them to capture the fort; see the report of Jacob Bayley to the New Hampshire Committee of Safety, 22 Sept. 1777, in Franklin B. Dexter, *The Literary Diary of Ezra Stiles,* 4 vols. (New York, 1901), 2:212. For a firsthand account of the attack on Ticonderoga and Mt. Independence, see the journal of Ralph Cross, commander of the Essex (Mass.) Regiment in the *Historical Magazine,* 17:8–11.

13. The attack on Lake George landing is described in Ward, *War of the Revolution,* 2:523–24; BL to John Brown, and to Gen. Warner, both 23 Sept. 1777, in Allis, *Lincoln Papers,* reel 2; Gen. Bayley to the New Hampshire Council of Safety, 22 Sept., qtd. in Dexter, *Diary of Ezra Stiles,* 2:212. The effect of the northern fighting on the British army is found in Hargrove, *General John Burgoyne,* 186; and Nelson, *Horatio Gates,* 114; see also "Letters from Cambridge, Mass." (15 Nov. 1777), in *Letters from America, 1776–1779: Being Letters of Brunswick, Hessian and Waldeck Officers with the British Armies during the Revolution,* ed. Ray Pettingill (Boston, 1924), 103.

14. A fair treatment of the Arnold-Gates feud is given in Wallace, *Traitorous Hero,* 149–59; and Nelson, *Horatio Gates,* 122–32; see also Rossie, *Politics of Command,* 169–72.

15. Nelson, *Horatio Gates,* 116–21. The most complete treatment of the entire Saratoga campaign, although marred by a lack of source notes, is still Hoffman Nickerson, *The Turning Point of the Revolution, or Burgoyne in America* (Boston, 1928). A shorter version that integrates the Saratoga campaign with movements around Philadelphia is John S. Pancake, *1777: The Year of the Hangman* (University, Ala., 1977); see also Mintz, *Generals of Saratoga,* 131–227. For a British viewpoint, see Hargrove, *General John Burgoyne,* 135–205.

16. Ward, *War of the Revolution,* 2:525–32. According to the recollections of one eyewitness, BL was active in reconnoitering the British positions prior to the battle and instrumental in persuading Gates to make the attack in force; see Ebenezer Mattoon to Philip Schuyler, 7 Oct. 1835, in William L. Stone, *The Campaign of Lieut. Gen. John Burgoyne . . .* (Albany, N.Y., 1877), 371–75.

17. BL to William Heath, 9 Mar. 1799, in Allis, *Lincoln Papers,* reel 10.

18. BL to William Heath, 9 Mar. 1799, in ibid., reel 10.

19. BL to George Washington, 19 Oct. 1777, in ibid., reel 2; Gates to the president of Congress, 12 Oct. 1777, Emmet Collection (NN); Clinton to BL, 22 Oct. 1777, in Hastings, *Public Papers of George Clinton*, 2:471; Washington to BL, 25 Oct. 1777, in Fitzpatrick, *Writings of Washington*, 9:428; Pickering to John Pickering, 22 Oct. 1777, Pickering Papers (MHi).

20. Ward, *War of the Revolution*, 2:533–40.

21. Resolution of Congress, 4 Nov. 1777, *Journals of the Continental Congress (JCC)*, 9:861; Henry Knox to BL, 18 Jan. 1778, Knox Papers (MHi); Dr. Browne to [?], *New England Historical and Geneological Register* (1864) 18:34. "[Lincoln] was still very lame, and was conveyed from place to place on a moveable bed, with handles, which was fixed on the runners of his sleigh, with a canopy and curtains, and was convenient also to remove into the house"; see Heath, *Memoirs*, 168. BL to Judge Hobart, 1 Dec. 1777; Benjamin Lincoln Jr. to Samuel Norton, 14 Dec. 1777; and BL to Dr. James Browne, 23 Apr. 1778, in Allis, *Lincoln Papers*, reel 2.

22. Benjamin Lincoln Jr. to BL, 17 Sept. and 14 Oct. 1777, in Allis, *Lincoln Papers*, reel 2; John Glover to William Heath, 9 Oct. 1777, *Independent Chronicle and the Universal Advertiser* (Boston), 16 Oct. 1777. An extract from a letter in the same day's paper was even more graphic: "Yesterday Gen. Lincoln received an unfortunate wound in his leg, from a random shot of the enemy, his leg is to be taken off"; see John Glover to BL, 11 Dec. 1777, BL Papers (MB).

23. Resolution of Congress, 29 Nov. 1777, *JCC* 9:981; Washington to BL, 20 Jan. 1778, in Fitzpatrick, *Writings of Washington*, 10:325; James Lovell to BL, 2 Feb. 1778, in Burnett, *Letters*, 3:67.

24. BL to James Lovell, 15 Feb. 1778, in Allis, *Lincoln Papers*, reel 2.

25. BL to (?), 18 Aug. 1779, in ibid., reel 4.

26. On the covenant, see Perry Miller, *The New England Mind: The Seventeenth Century* (1939; reprint, Boston, 1961), 365–462; and Edmund S. Morgan, *The Puritan Family: Religion and Domestic Relations in Seventeenth-Century New England* (1944; reprint, New York, 1966).

27. Washington to BL, 7 May, and BL to Washington, 20 May 1778, in Allis, *Lincoln Papers*, reel 2.

28. BL to Horatio Gates, 17 Mar. and 25 June 1778, Gates Papers (NHi). The crutch is among the mementos kept by Gen. Lincoln's descendants in the Lincoln House in Hingham, Mass. I owe this information to Mrs. Elizabeth Beveridge, who kindly showed me the house during a visit on 29 May 1988.

29. BL to Washington, 1 June 1778, Washington Papers (DLC). Samuel Norton to BL, 2 Sept., and Benjamin Lincoln Jr. to BL, 23 Sept. 1778, in Allis, *Lincoln Papers*, reel 2. The letter from his son reported, "My mother is entirely recovered from the smallpox and her eyes have acquired their usual strength."

30. BL to George Washington, 11 Mar. 1778, in Allis, *Lincoln Papers*, reel 2.

31. Washington to the president of Congress, 7 Aug. 1778, in Fitzpatrick, *Writings of Washington*, 12:291; for the Monmouth and Newport campaigns, see Ward, *War of the Revolution*, 2:570–95.

32. For Lincoln's appointment as president of the court, see General Orders, 23 Aug. 1778, in Fitzpatrick, *Writings of Washington,* 12:352; for the trials, see Gerlach, *Proud Patriot,* 358–62; and *The St. Clair Papers,* ed. William Henry Smith, 2 vols. (Cincinnati, 1882), 1:447n–57n.

33. BL to Washington, 2 Sept. 1778, in Allis, *Lincoln Papers,* reel 2; Ward, *War of the Revolution,* 2:593–95.

Chapter 4: Independent Command

Epigraph: Horatio Gates to Elizabeth Gates, 22 Sept. 1777, qtd. in Don Higginbotham, "Military Leadership in the American Revolution," in *Leadership in the American Revolution,* Library of Congress Symposia on the American Revolution (Washington, D.C., 1974), 103.

1. For congressional assessments of BL as a "brave and able officer" and as an "officer of great military merit," see Richard Henry Lee to Patrick Henry, 21 Oct.; and Cornelius Harnett to Richard Caswell, 24 Oct. 1778, in *Letters of Members of the Continental Congress,* ed. Edmund C. Burnett, 8 vols. (Washington, D.C., 1921–36), 3:459, 461. For Robert Howe's difficulties with the South Carolina and Georgia authorities, see Charles E. Bennett and Donald R. Lennon, *A Quest for Glory: Major General Robert Howe and the American Revolution* (Chapel Hill, N.C., 1991), 52–84; and E. Stanley Gobold Jr. and Robert H. Woody, *Christopher Gadsden and the American Revolution* (Knoxville, 1982), 178–88.

2. For the choice of Washington as commander-in-chief and the "geopolitical debate" it involved, see Jonathan Gregory Rossie, *The Politics of Command in the American Revolution* (Syracuse, N.Y., 1975), 10–12.

3. That Lincoln was chosen at the behest of the South Carolina delegates is asserted by David Ramsay (*The History of the American Revolution,* 2 vols. [London, 1793], 2:112) and John T. Kirkland ("Notices of the Life of Lincoln," *Massachusetts Historical Society Collections, 3:238*).

4. MS Journal of BL's trip to South Carolina, 1778 (DLC). Lincoln described his defense of Charleston as "an important transaction, the most so to me of any one in which I held a part"; see BL to Mercy Warren, 21 Sept. 1790, *Warren-Adams Letters,* 73:321; see the diary entries of Samuel Holten, a Massachusetts delegate to Congress, for 18, 20, 22, 23, and 24 Oct. 1778 in Burnett, *Letters,* 3:455, 461; BL to Washington, 24 Oct. 1778, Washington Papers (DLC).

5. Dr. Browne to BL, 14 Oct. 1778, in *The Papers of Benjamin Lincoln,* ed. Frederick S. Allis Jr., microfilm ed., 13 reels (Boston, 1967), reel 2.

6. For BL's lightness of heart, see the journal entry for 25 Oct., a day when he rode from Chester, Pennsylvania, to head of Elk, Maryland: "The day very pleasant, the girls barefooted & the Blackbirds cheerful." For Williamsburg and the rest of the journey, see MS journal of BL's trip to South Carolina, 1778 (DLC).

7. Rutledge to Washington, 18 Dec. 1778, Washington Papers (DLC). BL to the commander of the Georgia Continentals, 6 Dec., and to the president of Congress, 9 Nov. and 19 Dec. 1778, in Allis, *Lincoln Papers,* reel 3.

8. Robert Howe to BL, 14 Dec. 1778, in Allis, *Lincoln Papers,* reel 2; BL to Washington, 19 Dec., and to Rawlins Lowndes, 22 Dec. 1778, in ibid., reel 3.

9. BL to Georgia governor John Houstoun, 6 Dec.; to John Ashe, 8 Dec.; to Robert Howe, 8 Dec.; and to the president of Congress, 19 Dec. 1778, in ibid., reel 3.

10. The foregoing analysis is taken from John Shy, "British Strategy for Pacifying the Southern Colonies, 1778–1781," in *The Southern Experience in the American Revolution,* ed. Jeffrey J. Crow and Larry E. Tise (Chapel Hill, N.C., 1978), 155–73.

11. Resolution of Congress, 25 Sept. 1778, *JCC* 12:951. BL to Rawlins Lowndes, 20 Dec., and to Robert Howe, 21 Dec. 1778, in Allis, *Lincoln Papers,* reel 3. See BL's answer to a memorandum on the taking of St. Augustine (n.d. but probably end of Dec. 1778), BL Papers (MHi), reel 2. Some were skeptical of the expedition for other reasons. Edward Rutledge thought "it would hardly be attempted this winter": "The season is now far advanced, and but few things in readiness." There were too few Continental troops, and militia forces were useless for a siege. "Congress should have converted measures earlier and better than they have"; see Rutledge to George Washington, 18 Dec. 1778, Washington Papers (DLC).

12. BL to Rawlins Lowndes, 20, 22 (9 A.M.), and 22 (11 A.M.) Dec., and to John Houstoun, 25 Dec. 1778, in Allis, *Lincoln Papers,* reel 3. Rawlins Lowndes to BL, 25 Dec. 1778, in ibid., reel 2.

13. John Houstoun to BL, 19 Dec. 1778, Houstoun Collection (GHi); BL to the president of Congress, 26 Dec. 1778, in Allis, *Lincoln Papers,* reel 3; Houstoun to BL, 24 Dec. 1778, misc. MSS (NN).

14. See Howe's report to BL, 30 Dec. 1778, in *PCC,* reel 177 item 158, 189–92; for a description of the battle, see Kenneth Coleman, *The American Revolution in Georgia, 1763–1789* (Athens, Ga., 1958), 116–21; see also Bennett and Lennon, *Quest for Glory,* 85–99.

15. BL to Henry Laurens, 31 Dec. 1778, in Allis, *Lincoln Papers,* reel 3.

16. Coleman, *American Revolution in Georgia,* 121–23. For the role of the Tory militia in Georgia, see Edward J. Cashin, *The King's Ranger: Thomas Brown and the American Revolution on the Southern Frontier* (Athens, Ga., 1989), 83–101.

17. BL to Henry Laurens, 4 Jan. 1779, in Allis, *Lincoln Papers,* reel 3.

18. BL to Washington, 5 Jan. 1779, in ibid., reel 3. For an example of how frustrating high command could be, see BL to John Houstoun, 25 Dec. 1778, in ibid.: "I have felt myself much interested as a man, for the welfare of your harassed and invaded state, and my feelings have been much heightened by having its safety, in some measure, committed to my care, and those sensations are raised to distress, when applications are made to me for relief while the means thereof are not within my power."

19. Lowndes to BL, 1 Jan. 1779, Emmet Collection (NN). BL to Lowndes, 6 Jan.; to Mr. Valentine, 14 and 20 Jan.; to Col. Marbury, 15 Jan.; to Mr. Ingram,

15 Jan.; to Col. Drayton, 20 Jan.; and to George Galphin, 20 Jan. 1779, in Allis, *Lincoln Papers,* reel 3.

20. BL to Col. Glascock, 21 Jan. 1779, in Allis, *Lincoln Papers,* reel 3; Coleman, *American Revolution in Georgia,* 123. For a more particular description of the Battle of Kettle Creek, see Otis Ashmore and Charles H. Olmstead, "The Battles of Kettle Creek and Brier Creek," *Georgia Historical Quarterly* 10 (1926): 85–125.

21. "An Ordinance to prevent persons from withdrawing from the defence of this state to join the enemies thereof," passed 20 Feb. 1779 (in R. W. Gibbes, *Documentary History of the American Revolution,* 3 vols. [New York, 1857], 2:104). BL to Col. Elbert, 25 Jan. 1779, in Allis, *Lincoln Papers,* reel 3. Cases like the following were not exceptional:

> The man you sent prisoner here charged with mangling the corps of a British soldier, returned with this. Such actions are detestable, to be frowned upon and guarded against. This person informs me that he had a son killed by the enemy and that his body was cut to pieces in a most savage manner, and that although he disapproves his own conduct, yet he thinks it some palliation of his offence that the example was set on their side. . . . My soul abhores such inhuman deeds. I shall guard against their taking place by the troops of this army in future.

Lincoln went on, however: "This offense bears, in guilt, no proportion to that of refusing quarter when it is asked or taking the life of the prisoner who became such an encouragement that he might expect mercy." From Lincoln's tone the latter acts would seem to have been common behavior at the time; see BL to Gen. Williamson, 16 Feb. 1779, in ibid., reel 3. For more on the ethnic, religious, and economic divisions among southerners and their effect on the war, see Jerome J. Nadelhaft, *The Disorders of War: The Revolution in South Carolina* (Orono, Me., 1981), 58–69.

22. BL to Rawlins Lowndes, 26 Jan. 1779, in Allis, *Lincoln Papers,* reel 3; Charles Pinckney Jr. to Mrs. Charles Pinckney, 24 Feb. 1779, in Gibbes, *Documentary History of the American Revolution,* 2:106; Edward McCrady, *The History of South Carolina in the Revolution, 1775–1783,* 2 vols. (New York, 1902), 1:333–36, 341–43.

23. BL to Elbert, 31 Jan. and 4 Feb. 1779; to Ashe, 4 Feb.; to Lowndes, 4 Feb.; and to the president of Congress, 6 Feb. 1779, in Allis, *Lincoln Papers,* reel 3. Charles Pinckney Jr. to Mrs. Charles Pinckney, 24 Feb. 1779, in Gibbes, *Documentary History of the American Revolution,* 2:106. For Moultrie's successful attack on Port Royal Island, see McCrady, *History of South Carolina,* 1:340.

24. John Ashe to BL, 4 Feb. 1779, misc. MSS (NN). Charles Pinckney to Mrs. Charles Pinckney, 24 Feb. 1779, in Gibbes, *Documentary History of the American Revolution,* 2:107. Moultrie to BL, 8 Feb.; Ashe to BL, 14 Feb.; BL to Ashe, 16 Feb.; and Williamson to Ashe, 16 Feb. 1779, in Allis, *Lincoln Papers,* reel 3.

25. BL to Ashe, 18 and 22 Feb. 1779, in Allis, *Lincoln Papers,* reel 3.

26. Council of War, 1 Mar. 1779, Emmet Collection (NN); BL to the president of Congress, 27 Feb. 1779, in Allis, *Lincoln Papers,* reel 3.

27. The Battle of Briar Creek is described in detail in David S. Heidler, "The American Defeat at Briar Creek, 3 March 1779," *Georgia Historical Quarterly* 66 (1982): 317–31; see also Ashmore and Olmstead, "Battles of Kettle Creek and Briar Creek," 101–25. For Ashe's letter to BL of 3 Mar. 1779 announcing his defeat and Moultrie's transcription of Ashe's court-martial proceedings, see William Moultrie, *Memoirs of the American Revolution,* 2 vols. (New York, 1802), 1:323–24, 337–53. BL describes the battle in his letter to the Massachusetts delegates (to Congress), 6 Mar., and BL to John Rutledge, 4 Mar. 1779, in Allis, *Lincoln Papers,* reel 3; see also Henry Lee, *Memoirs of the War in the Southern Department of the United States* (1812; reprint, New York, 1870), 123–24; and McCrady, *History of South Carolina,* 1:343–45.

28. Minutes of a council of war, 4 and 5 Mar. 1779, in Allis, *Lincoln Papers,* reel 3.

29. BL to Gov. Richard Caswell, 7 Apr. 1779, in ibid., reel 3.

30. Everarde Meade to BL, 29 Mar., and BL to James Lovell, 12 Apr. 1779, in ibid., reel 3.

31. Gen. Williamson to BL, 26 Mar.; BL to Williamson, 29 Mar. and 4 Apr.; and George Galphin to BL, 2 Apr. 1779, in ibid., reel 3. For a statement of British Indian policy, see Martha Condray Searcy, "1779: The First Year of the British Occupation of Georgia," *Georgia Historical Quarterly* 67 (1983): 179–80.

32. BL to John Rutledge, 1 Apr. and to Richard Caswell, 3 Apr. 1779, in Allis, *Lincoln Papers,* reel 3.

33. BL to Moultrie, 22 Apr.; to Rutledge, 23 and 27 Apr.; and to the president of Congress, 4 June 1779, in ibid., reel 3.

34. BL to Gen. Williamson, 1 May, and to Gov. Rutledge, 2 May 1779, in ibid., reel 3.

35. Moultrie to BL, 2 and 5 May, and BL to Moultrie, 2 and 6 May 1779, in ibid., reel 3.

36. Moultrie to BL, 5 May 1779, in ibid., reel 3. Lincoln was not the only one who did not believe Prevost's aim was Charleston. Even as late as 5 May, John Rutledge wrote that "the Enemy do not seriously mean a march to Charles-town"; see Rutledge to BL, 5 May 1779, in ibid., reel 3.

37. Council of War, 6 May 1779, in ibid., reel 3. Fortifications were begun in April by Col. Cambrey, a French engineering officer, but had not been completed by the time of the first attack on Charleston; see BL to Lt. Gov. Thomas Bee, 3 Apr., and Bee to BL, 9 Apr. 1779, in ibid., reel 3. For the collapse of American resistance, see Butler to (?), 5 May. For morale in Charleston, see Moultrie to BL, 8 May (2 letters), and McHugo to BL, 8 May 1779, in ibid., reel 3.

38. BL to Rutledge, 10 May 1779, in ibid., reel 3.

39. The most complete treatment of the parley between Prevost and the South Carolina government which carefully sifts the evidence provided in accounts given

by Moultrie and John Laurens is given in McCrady, *History of South Carolina,* 1:351–81; for an account written from the perspective of one who opposed the parley, see Gobold and Woody, *Christopher Gadsden, 193–95.*

40. There are differing accounts over the contents of the messages. I have used the version given in Moultrie, *Memoirs,* 427–35.

41. McCrady, *History of South Carolina,* 1:376–78.

42. BL to Rutledge, 14, 19, 24, and 26 May; to Moultrie, 16 and 17 May; and to Pulaski, 22 May 1779, in Allis, *Lincoln Papers,* reel 3. For a dramatic account of the panic and terror spread by the British throughout the tidewater region south of Charleston, see *Letters of Eliza Wilkinson, during the Invasion and Possession of Charlestown, S.C. by the British in the Revolutionary War,* ed. Caroline Gilman (New York, 1839). There is an interesting eyewitness account of Lincoln's long-looked-for arrival at the Wilkinson plantation. Upon hearing that Lincoln had arrived, Eliza rushed to the door:

> For we had heard such a character of the General, that we wanted to see him much. When he quitted his horse, and I saw him limp along, I can't describe my feelings. The thought that his limping was occasioned by defending his country from the invasion of a cruel and unjust enemy, created in me the utmost veneration and tender concern for him. . . . I think he has something exceeding grave, and even solemn, in his aspect; not forbiddingly so neither, but a something in his countenance that commands respect, and strikes assurance dumb. (77)

43. BL to Rutledge, 26 and 28 May; to Pulaski, 31 May; and to Moultrie, 1 June 1779, in Allis, *Lincoln Papers,* reel 3.

44. Everard Meade to BL, 6 May 1779, in ibid., reel 3; Resolution of Congress, 17 Apr. 1779, *JCC* 13:465. "Sat. 17 April. Long debate about the manner of Genl. Lincolns leaving the S. army, on account of his Ill State of Health" (Donald W. Whisenhunt, ed. *Delegate from New Jersey: The Journal of John Fell* [Port Washington, N.Y., 1973], 73). The news caused some stir and a little consternation, as the public wondered who would replace him. See Edmund Pendleton to William Woodford, 26 April 1779, in *The Letters and Papers of Edmund Pendleton, 1734–1803,* ed. David John Mays, 2 vols. (Charlottesville, Va., 1967), 1:280: "We hear that Genl Lincoln has desired to be recalled, on account of his Leg being bad & his health much declined, if he is indulged, I imagine the appointment to succeed him in that unhealthy climate will not be anxiously sought after." One man at least was anxious for the appointment. Nathanael Greene, quartermaster general of the army, pressed Washington for the assignment; see Greene to Washington, 22 Apr., and Washington to Greene, 26 Apr. 1779, in Showman, *Papers of Nathanael Greene,* 3:423, 429.

45. BL to Rutledge, 9 June, and to Moultrie, 9 and 10 June 1779, in Allis, *Lincoln Papers,* reel 3; Moultrie to BL, 8 June 1779, Emmet Collection (NN).

46. Rutledge to BL, 13 June 1779, in Allis, *Lincoln Papers,* reel 3; BL to Washington, 9 July 1779, in ibid., reel 4. As Lincoln explained to Washington after

Rutledge's request, "I found it difficult after that to leave camp suddenly, and especially as I had not ill health to plead in excuse for it: I am yet in good health; I suffer a little from my leg." What made the decision to stay all the more difficult was the fact that the resolves of Congress had raised the expectations of Lincoln's family and friends that he would be home soon; see Benjamin Lincoln Jr. to BL, 15 July 1779, in ibid., reel 4.

47. BL to Rutledge, 21 June 1779, in ibid., reel 3. Moultrie to BL, 20 June, and BL to Washington, 7 July 1779, in ibid., reel 4.

48. What the British hoped to accomplish by their invasion of Georgia is analyzed in depth in Paul H. Smith, *Loyalists and Redcoats: A Study of British Revolutionary Policy* (New York, 1972), 100–106.

49. BL to Washington, 7 July 1779, in Allis, *Lincoln Papers*, reel 4; Henry Knox to BL, 29 Jan. 1779, Henry Knox Papers (MHi).

Chapter 5: Storm over Savannah

Epigraph: Clay to William Palfrey, 27 Sept. 1779, qtd. in Adolph B. Benson, *Sweden and the American Revolution* (New Haven, Conn., 1926), 145.

1. BL to George Washington, 7 July 1779, in *The Papers of Benjamin Lincoln,* ed. Frederick S. Allis Jr., microfilm ed., 13 reels (Boston, 1967), reel 3.

2. "I have often written them, but have received no answer or a line from Congress since the 10th of December last. I think it exceedingly hard to be kept in such painful suspence for so many months; was this seeming neglect from any other quarter but from Congress, I should venture to suggest that it was wrong" (BL to James Lovell, 12 Apr. 1779, in ibid., reel 3). Despite Lincoln's request for advice, Washington gave none. "I am so utter a stranger to the country in which you are, that I cannot pretend to offer my opinion upon the measures that ought or ought not to be pursued." Yet he was not loathe to comment on Lincoln's situation to the officers in his family; see Washington to Lincoln, 15 Mar., and to Lafayette, 8 Mar., 1779, in *The Writings of George Washington, from the Original Sources, 1745–1799,* ed. John C. Fitzpatrick, 39 vols. (Washington, D.C., 1931–44), 14:219, 240. For the extract of Lincoln's letter of 5 June, see Lovell to James Warren, 13 July 1779, in *Letters of Delegates to Congress, 1774–1789,* ed. Paul H. Smith, 20 vols. to date (Washington, D.C., 1976–), 13:211. "We are in great want of money, we have none but what is borrowed from Private Gentlemen" (BL to Henry Laurens, 27 July 1779, in Allis, *Lincoln Papers,* reel 4).

3. BL to Washington, and to John Jay, 9 July 1779; John Rutledge to BL, 17 July; and BL to Thomas Rutledge, 28 July 1779, in Allis, *Lincoln Papers,* reel 4.

4. BL to Rutledge, 30 July 1779, in ibid., reel 4; BL to Rutledge, 6 Aug. 1779, Benjamin Lincoln Letterbook (hereafter BL Lbk) (MB).

5. BL to Lachlan McIntosh, 10 July 1779, in Allis, *Lincoln Papers,* reel 4; see also Harvey H. Jackson, *Lachlan McIntosh and the Politics of Revolutionary Georgia* (Athens, Ga., 1979), 94–96.

6. Congress decided that newly recruited Virginians earlier destined for the main army would be diverted southward, see John Jay to Charles Scott, 29 July 1779, in Smith, *Letters of Delegates,* 13:308 and n.; see also Harry M. Ward, *Charles Scott and the "Spirit of '76"* (Charlottesville, Va., 1988), 69–72; Maj. Jameson to BL, 12 July 1779, Emmet Collection (NN); BL to Gen. McIntosh, 14 Aug. 1779, Charleston Lbk I (MB); BL to Col. Parker, 20 July, and to Gen. McIntosh, 22 July, and Parker to BL, 28 July and 5 Aug., and Jameson to BL, 30 July 1779, in Allis, *Lincoln Papers,* reel 4.

7. BL to John Rutledge, 9 and 23 Aug. and to Col. Beekman, 23 Aug. 1779, Charleston Lbk I (MB).

8. BL to (Rutledge?), 18 Aug. 1779, in Allis, *Lincoln Papers,* reel 4; "This idea of different states, and distinct & separate interests, has in too many instances, distracted our affairs and retarded the public weal" (BL to Gen. McIntosh, 14 Aug. 1779; see also BL to Col. Wylly, 19 Aug. 1779, in Charleston Lbk I [MB]).

9. BL to Lowndes, 15 Jan. 1779, in Allis, *Lincoln Papers,* reel 3; BL to [Rutledge?], 18 Aug. 1779, in ibid., reel 4. Differences in rations and pay were a constant problem, see BL to the Council of Georgia and to Gen. McIntosh, both 14 Aug. 1779, Charleston Lbk I (MB).

10. Higginbotham, *War of American Independence,* 248–49. The most complete treatment of the siege of Savannah is Alexander A. Lawrence, *Storm over Savannah: The Story of Count d'Estaing and the Siege of the Town in 1779* (Athens, Ga., 1951). Lawrence relies heavily on French sources, especially the journals kept and reports written by d'Estaing. For American requests for French succor, see 21. D'Estaing's reply of 31 Aug. to Rutledge's letter of 20 July 1779 is given in Jacques Michel, *La Vie adventureuse et mouvementee de Charles-Henri Comte d'Estaing* (Verdun, 1976), 226.

11. Lincoln's journal of the siege is in the Library of Congress, see 1–2 (hereafter cited as BL Journal, Savannah [DLC]). See also BL to Gen. McIntosh, 4 Sept., pers. misc. MSS (NN), and 5 Sept. 1779, Charleston Lbk I (MB).

12. BL Journal, Savannah (DLC), 2; see also the Plan of Operations between Count d'Estaing and Gen. Lincoln, n.d., Emmet Collection (NN).

13. BL Journal, Savannah (DLC), 3–6; BL to Gen. McIntosh, 4 Sept. 1779, pers. misc. MSS (NN); BL to Gen. Huger, 6 Sept. 1779, Charleston Lbk I (MB).

14. BL to Washington, 7 Feb. 1779, in Allis, *Lincoln Papers,* reel 3; BL Journal, Savannah (DLC), 6–7; BL to John Rutledge, 12 and 14 Sept. and to Pulaski, 14 Sept. 1779, Charleston Lbk I (MB).

15. Lawrence, *Storm over Savannah,* 31–37; Michel, *Vie de Comte d'Estaing,* 233–34; extract of a letter from Prevost to Lord George Germain, 1 Nov. 1779, *Historical Magazine,* 8:291, 294.

16. Prevost to Germain, 1 Nov. 1779, *Historical Magazine,* 8:294–95.

17. Prevost to Germain, 1 Nov. 1779, *Historical Magazine,* 8:295; BL Journal, Savannah (DLC), 7–9; see Col. Francis Marion's outburst: "Who ever heard

anything like this before!—first allow an enemy to entrench, and then fight him!" as qtd. in Hugh F. Rankin, *Francis Marion: The Swamp Fox* (New York, 1973), 35.

18. Prevost to Germain, 1 Nov. 1779, *Historical Magazine,* 8:291; BL Journal, Savannah (DLC), 9–10; Lawrence, *Storm over Savannah,* 46–53. There is substantial evidence, including the statements of Prevost and other contemporaries, that d'Estaing could have taken Savannah by storm at any time before Maitland's arrival, even without the aid of the American forces (ibid., 58–59).

19. Lawrence, *Storm over Savannah,* 60, 67, 69–75; BL Journal, Savannah (DLC), 10.

20. Lawrence, *Storm over Savannah,* 60–63; the d'Estaing quotation is on 62; BL Journal, Savannah (DLC), 11–12; d'Estaing to BL, 23 Sept. 1779, Emmet Collection (NN); BL to Thomas Rutledge, 20 Sept., and to d'Estaing, 22 Sept. 1779, Charleston Lbk I (MB).

21. For example, BL wrote to Rutledge that "the Count and his officers seem much engaged in the cause," 22 Sept. 1779, Charleston Lbk I (MB); see also BL to the president of Congress, 22 Oct. 1779, in *PCC,* reel 177, item 158; Bretigny's letter is qtd. in Michel, *Vie de Comte d'Estaing,* 219; d'Estaing is qtd. in Lawrence, *Storm over Savannah,* 71.

22. Lee, *Memoirs of the War in the Southern Department,* 139.

23. Lawrence, *Storm over Savannah,* 60–63; BL Journal, Savannah (DLC), 12–15.

24. BL Journal, Savannah (DLC), 15; Lawrence, *Storm over Savannah,* 76–84; see "An English Journal of the Siege of Savannah in 1779," *Historical Magazine,* 8:14; Prevost to d'Estaing, 6 Oct. 1779, in Allis, *Lincoln Papers,* reel 4; BL to Col. Simons, 28 Sept. 1779, Charleston Lbk I (MB); see also the exchange of letters between the allied commanders and Prevost and Prevost to Germain, 1 Nov. 1779, *Historical Magazine,* 8:296.

25. BL Journal, Savannah (DLC), 15; Lawrence, *Storm over Savannah,* 90–94. Lincoln seemed to vacillate from day to day about the best approach to make to the town. On 30 Sept. he wrote to Rutledge in anticipation of the bombardment that he hoped that the allies would need no other attack. The next day, however, he wrote Rutledge again, saying "I am fully of opinion that a more determined mode of attack must be adopted and pursued before Savannah is ours," Charleston Lbk I (MB).

26. Orders for the attack on Savannah, 8 Oct. 1779, Emmet Collection (NN); Lawrence, *Storm over Savannah,* 96–99.

27. Lawrence, *Storm over Savannah,* 100–112; see also McCrady, *History of South Carolina,* 1:412–17; Lee, *Memoirs of the War in the Southern Department,* 139–42; Ward, *War of the Revolution,* 2:692–94. Thomas Pinckney is the only source for the statement that Lincoln commanded the reserve and covered the retreat; all others agree that he joined d'Estaing in leading the attack. Given the ill-feeling between the two commanders and the rivalry between the allies, I doubt that Lincoln would have let slip the opportunity to lead the American attack.

28. Lawrence, *Storm over Savannah,* 127–28; BL Journal, Savannah (DLC), 15; BL to the president of Congress, 22 Oct. 1779, in *PCC,* reel 177, item 158; BL to Rutledge, 10 Oct. 1779, Charleston Lbk I (MB); "Convention entre son excellence le General Lincoln et le Cte d'Estaing pour la retraite de devant Savannah," 13 Oct. 1779, Emmet Collection (NN); allied movements of the last week of the siege as witnessed by the British are found in "An English Journal," *Historical Magazine,* 8:15–16.

29. BL to the president of Congress, 22 Oct. 1779, in *PCC,* reel 177, item 158; BL to Everarde Meade, 1 Nov. 1779, Emmet Collection (NN); BL Journal, Savannah (DLC), 15.

30. Samuel Holten's Diary (10–11 Nov. 1779), James Lovell to Horatio Gates, 11 Nov., Committee of Congress to BL, 12 Nov., Jesse Root to Jonathan Trumbull Sr., 12 Nov., Thomas McKean to William A. Atlee, 13 Nov., 1779, Smith, *Letters of Delegates,* 14:172, 178, 180, 188, 193; "Journal of Samuel Rowland Fisher," *Pennsylvania Magazine of History and Biography,* 41:171; Samuel Shaw to Winthrop Sargeant, 17 Nov. 1779, in ibid., 70:307.

31. Washington to BL, 12 Dec. 1779, in Fitzpatrick, *Writings of Washington,* 17:247.

Chapter 6: The Siege of Charleston

Epigraph: Knox to Lincoln, 29 Jan. 1779, Knox Papers (MHi).

1. For Charleston as a commercial center of importance, see George C. Rogers Jr., *Charleston in the Age of the Pinckneys* (Norman, Okla., 1969), 3–16.

2. Charleston's political centrality is shown by the committee elected to draft a constitution in 1776 by the South Carolina Provincial Congress. Of its eleven members six were from Charleston, four from the surrounding districts. See Jerome J. Nadelhaft, *The Disorders of War: The Revolution in South Carolina* (Orono, Me., 1981), 28; Ramsay to William Henry Drayton, 1 Sept. 1779, in *Documentary History of the American Revolution,* ed. R. W. Gibbs, 3 vols. (New York, 1857), 2:121.

3. The day after the failed assault at Savannah, BL requested Rutledge to see to the completion of the Charleston works and the floating batteries, to have provisions stocked, regiments filled, and an asylum readied for the town's women and children, 10 Oct. 1779, Charleston, Benjamin Lincoln Letterbook (Lbk) I (MB); BL to Washington, 7 Nov. 1779, Washington Papers (DLC).

4. BL to a Committee of Congress, 27 Oct. 1779, included in BL to Washington, 17 July 1780, Emmet Collection (NN); BL to John Wereat, 1 Nov., and to John Laurens, 30 Nov. 1779, Charleston Lbk I (MB); BL to Washington, 7 Nov. 1779, Washington Papers (DLC); BL to Gov. Richard Caswell (N.C.), 3 Jan. 1780, Charleston Lbk I (MB).

5. BL to a Committee of Congress, 27 Oct. 1779, included in BL to Washington, 17 July 1780, Emmet Collection (NN).

6. Henry Laurens to John Laurens, 21 Sept., Lovell to Horatio Gates, 11 Nov., Committee of Congress to BL, 12 Nov., John Matthews to BL, 9 Dec. 1779, and to Thomas Bee, [5?] Jan. 1780, in *Letters of Delegates to Congress, 1774–1789*, ed. Paul H. Smith, 20 vols. to date (Washington, D.C., 1976–), 13:522, 14:178, 180, 257, 320.

7. BL to John Laurens, 9 and 30 Nov., to John Rutledge, 12 Nov., and to Col. Wylly, 26 Nov. 1779, Charleston Lbk I (MB).

8. BL to Rutledge, 12 Jan., to the governor of Georgia, 12 Jan., and to Richard Caswell, 24 Jan. 1780, Charleston Lbk I (MB); Committee of Congress to BL, 27 Dec., and Elbridge Gerry to BL, 27 Dec. 1779, in Smith, *Letters of Delegates,* 14:303–4; BL to a Committee of Congress, 31 Jan. 1780, Emmet Collection (NN).

9. Ira D. Gruber, "Britain's Southern Strategy," in *The Revolutionary War in the South: Power, Conflict and Leadership,* ed. W. Robert Higgins (Durham, N.C., 1979), 217–26.

10. BL to a Committee of Congress, 31 Jan. 1780, Emmet Collection (NN); BL to Richard Caswell, 24 Jan., to Thomas Jefferson, 24 Jan., and to John Rutledge, 30 Jan. 1780, Charleston Lbk II (MB).

11. *JCC* 13:387–88. For the background of the development of a national policy toward the recruitment of blacks in the Continental army, see Pete Maslowski, "National Policy toward the use of Black Troops in the Revolution," *South Carolina Historical Magazine* 73 (1972): 1–17; William Whipple to Josiah Bartlett, 28 Mar. 1779, in *The Papers of Josiah Bartlett,* ed. Frank C. Mevers (Hanover, N.H., 1979), 250. For a view of the war in the South as a "triangular" war among British, Americans, and African-Americans, see Sylvia R. Frey, *Water from the Rock: Black Resistance in a Revolutionary Age* (Princeton, N.J., 1991).

12. BL to Rutledge, 24 July 1779, in *The Papers of Benjamin Lincoln,* ed. Frederick S. Allis Jr., microfilm ed., 13 reels (Boston, 1967), reel 4; BL to Col. Beekman, 23 Aug. 1779 and to Rutledge, 28 and 30 Jan. 1780, Charleston Lbk II (MB).

13. BL to Rutledge, 14 Feb. 1780, Charleston Lbk II (MB).

14. BL to Rutledge, 28 Feb. and 13 Mar. 1780, Charleston Lbk II (MB); Rutledge to BL, 14 Mar. 1780, Trumbull Collection (NHi); Alexander Hamilton to John Laurens (11 Sept. 1779), in *The Papers of Alexander Hamilton,* ed. Harold C. Syrett and Jacob E. Cooke, 27 vols. (New York, 1961–87), 2:166.

15. BL to George Washington, 17 July 1780, Emmet Collection (NN). In Washington's letter to BL informing him of his appointment to the southern command he wrote "Congress have determined on measures for securing Charles Town, in case the enemy should form an expedition against it," Washington to BL, 3 Oct. 1778, BL MSS (MH); *Letters and Papers of Major-General John Sullivan, Continental Army,* ed. Otis G. Hammond, 3 vols. (Concord, N.H., 1930), 3:422.

16. BL to George Washington, 17 July 1780, Emmet Collection (NN). BL was not alone in thinking Charleston was defensible, see Richard K. Murdoch, ed., "A French Account of the Siege of Charleston, 1780," *South Carolina Historical Magazine* 67 (1966): 141; and Johann Ewald, *Diary of the American War: A Hessian Journal* (New Haven, Conn., 1979), 240–41.

17. Alex Macshorter to Elisha Boudinot, 18 Nov. 1780, Emmet Collection (NN).

18. Even though Americans practiced Fabian tactics, they measured the war's progress by ground held and strong points won or lost, ses Royster, *A Revolutionary People at War,* 117. Lincoln probably felt like Washington at the time of the British attack on Philadelphia. As Ira Gruber notes, "Congress, popular feeling and revolutionary ideology all required that he fight for Philadelphia, that he put aside what Samuel Adams called his Fabian tactics and engage the British army." See Gruber, "The Anglo-American Military Tradition and the War of American Independence," in *Against All Enemies: Interpretations of American Military History from Colonial Times to the Present,* ed. Kenneth J. Hagan and William R. Roberts (Westport, Conn., 1986), 36.

19. BL to Commodore Whipple, 30 Jan., 13 and 27 Feb. 1780, in BL to Washington, 17 July 1780, Emmet Collection (NN). Whipple's less than enthusiastic cooperation with Lincoln and the naval side of the siege of Charleston is described in P. C. Coker III, *Charleston's Maritime Heritage, 1670–1865: An Illustrated History* (Charleston, S.C., 1987), 103–14.

20. BL to Washington, 23 Jan. 1780, Washington Papers (DLC).

21. Ibid., 386.

22. George Fenwick Jones, "The 1780 Siege of Charlestown as Experienced by a Hessian Officer," *South Carolina Historical Magazine* 88 (1987): 27–33.

23. Christopher Duffy, *Siege Warfare: The Fortress in the Early Modern World, 1494–1660* (London, 1979), 249–50.

24. Ibid., 249–50.

25. Laumoy to BL, 8 Mar. 1780, Emmet Collection (NN). For evidence of BL's diligence in superintending the construction of the works, see the depositions of James Cannon, 28 June, and Archibald Gamble, 30 June 1780, as copied in BL to George Washington, 17 July 1780, Emmet Collection (NN).

26. Entry of 17 Mar. 1780, in "Diary of Captain Hinrichs," in *The Siege of Charleston. With an Account of the Province of South Carolina: Diaries and Letters of Hessian Officers from the von Jungken Papers in the William L. Clements Library,* ed. and trans. Bernard A. Uhlendorf (Ann Arbor, Mich., 1938), 211; Banastre Tarleton, *A History of the Campaigns of 1780 and 1781, in the Southern Provinces of North America* (London, 1787), 12–13; Ewald, *Diary of the Revolution,* 240–41.

27. BL to Malmedy, 8 Mar., 11, 13 and 18 Apr., and to Isaac Huger, 8 Apr. 1780; Malmedy to BL, 9 and 12 Apr. 1780 and Simons to BL, 9 Apr. 1780, in Allis, *Lincoln Papers,* reel 5; BL to Rutledge, 8 Apr., and to Col. Pinckney, 11 Apr. 1780, Charleston Lbk II (MB).

28. BL to Moultrie, 11 Feb., and to Huger, 7, 13 and 15 Mar. 1780, Charleston Lbk II (MB); Moultrie to BL, 22, 25, 26 and 29 Feb., and Phillip Neyle to BL, 9 Mar. 1780, in Allis, *Lincoln Papers,* reel 5.

29. BL to George Washington, 4 Mar. 1780, Washington Papers (DLC); Hugh F. Rankin, *The North Carolina Continentals* (Chapel Hill, N.C., 1971), 218–19;

BL to Washington, 17 July 1780, Emmet Collection (NN); BL to the president of Congress, 24 Mar. 1780, in *PCC*, reel 177, item 158.

30. BL to Washington, 17 July 1780, Emmet Collection (NN); BL to Abraham Whipple, 20 Mar. 1780, Charleston Lbk II (MB); Washington to John Laurens, 26 Apr. 1780, in *The Writings of George Washington, from the Original Sources, 1745–1799*, ed. John C. Fitzpatrick, 39 vols. (Washington, D.C., 1931–44), 18:299.

31. BL to Washington, 9 Apr. 1780, Washington Papers (DLC); Ewald, *Diary of the American War*, 226.

32. Woodford to Washington, 8 Apr. 1780, Washington Papers (DLC); BL to the president of Congress, 24 Mar. 1780, in *PCC*, reel 177, 158; Ewald, *Diary of the American War*, 226; Ward, *War of the Revolution*, 2:698; James Duane to Washington, Washington Papers (DLC). Duane had heard from a Mr. Cannon who had talked with BL on 9 April. Duane wrote, "We have endeavoured to learn from him the sentiments of General Lincoln on the fate of the town; but it appears that he is as reserved in his conversation as his letters, though his activity and vigor inspire the highest respect and confidence."

33. "Sir Henry Clinton's Journal of the Siege of Charleston, 1780," *South Carolina Historical Magazine* 66 (1965): 149, 155; Ewald, *Diary of the American War*, 223–25.

34. "Clinton's Journal, *SCHM* 66 (1965): 157–58; Lee, *Memoirs of the War in the Southern Department*, 149.

35. George Fenwick Jones, "The 1780 Siege of Charleston as Experienced by a Hessian Officer," *SCHM* 88 (1987): 63–65; Jac Weller, "Revolutionary War Artillery in the South," *GHQ* 46 (1962): 378–79; Duffy, *Military Experience in the Age of Reason*, 217.

36. Lila Mills Hawes, ed., *Lachlan McIntosh Papers in the University of Georgia Libraries* (Athens, Ga., 1968), 100–101; for Rutledge's efforts, see his letter to BL, 25 Apr. 1780, BL Papers (NcD).

37. Minutes of a Council of War, 16 Apr. 1780, in *PCC*, reel 177, item 158, 431; Hawes, *Lachlan McIntosh Papers*, 101.

38. For the attack, see Tarleton, *Campaigns of 1780 and 1781*, 15–16; for British exploitation of the victory, see Lord Cornwallis to Tarleton, 25 Apr., and Sir Henry Clinton to George Germain, 13 May 1780, in ibid., 37, 39; Major von Wilmowsky to Baron von Jungkenn, 13 May 1780, Uhlendorf, *Siege of Charleston*, 409.

39. "Clinton's Journal," *SCHM* 66 (1965): 164; Minutes of a Council of War, 20 and 21 Apr. 1780, in *PCC*, reel 177, item 158, 391; Hawes, *Lachlan McIntosh Papers*, 103–4. McCrady believes that inviting Gadsden was an extraordinary breach of military custom. Lincoln "shirked his responsibility" to Congress and the Continental troops he commanded by bowing to the authority of South Carolina. McCrady ignores the unique circumstances involved in the American Revolution. In a formal European siege, the military governor of a besieged city united civilian and military authority in one head. In contrast, one of

the striking aspects of the revolutionary war and a lasting consequence of it was the subordination of the military to civil authority. Lincoln never conceived himself able to command the elected representatives of South Carolina. Besides, on a practical level, he needed the cooperation of those government officials. He could hardly have carried out an evacuation in the face of both British and South Carolinian resistance, see McCrady, *History of South Carolina,* 473–77.

40. Hawes, *Lachlan McIntosh Papers,* 104. Lincoln's respect for civil authority was such as to bring forth this testimonial from David Ramsay after the surrender: "I think it here justice to your character to state . . . that neither in this [negotiation with the British], nor in any other instance, did you ever appear to me to intend anything either disrespectful to the civil authority, or derogatory to the rights of the people," Ramsay to BL, 27 May 1780, Emmet Collection (NN).

41. Hawes, *Lachlan McIntosh Papers,* 104.

42. Ibid., 105; Minutes of a Council of War, 20 and 21 Apr. 1780, *PCC,* reel 177, item 158, 391–92.

43. "Diary of Captain Hinrichs," 21 Apr. 1780, in Uhlendorf, *Siege of Charleston,* 257, 259; "Articles of Capitulation proposed April 21st 1780," in *PCC,* reel 177, item 158, 395–96; Duffy, *Siege Warfare,* 293; "Clinton's Journal," *SCHM* 66 (1965): 164; Hawes, *Lachlan McIntosh Papers,* 106.

44. Hawes, *Lachlan McIntosh Papers,* 108; John Laurens to Washington, 9 Apr. 1780, Washington Papers (DLC); "Diary of Captain Hinrichs," Uhlendorf, *Siege of Charleston,* 237, 251, 259, 279; Major von Wilmowsky to Baron von Jungkenn, 13 May 1780, in ibid., 407; Ewald, *Diary of the American War,* 234.

45. "Diary of Captain Hinrichs," in Uhlendorf, *Siege of Charleston,* 261–63; Hawes, *Lachlan McIntosh Papers,* 107. The fact that the Americans made only this one sortie puzzled one Hessian officer, see Ewald, *Diary of the American War,* 233.

46. Hawes, *Lachlan McIntosh Papers,* 108; Duportail to Washington, 17 May 1780, in *Correspondence of the American Revolution,* ed. Jared Sparks, 4 vols. (Boston, 1853), 3:450.

47. Minutes of a Council of War, 26 Apr. 1780, *PCC,* reel 177, item 158, 433; Duportail to Washington, 17 May 1780, in Sparks, *Correspondence of the American Revolution,* 3:450.

48. Ewald, *Diary of the American War,* 241; Hawes, *Lachlan McIntosh Papers,* 109–10.

49. "Clinton's Journal," *SCHM* 66 (1965): 168; Hawes, *Lachlan McIntosh Papers,* 109, 121; "Diary of Captain Hinrichs," in Uhlendorf, *Siege of Charleston,* 273–75. BL's attempts to procure enough salted meat to sustain six thousand men for a long siege proved unavailing. As long as communications were kept open to the country, fresh beef was in plentiful supply, see BL to Washington, 17 July 1780, Emmet Collection (NN).

50. Ewald, *Diary of the American War,* 235; Hawes, *Lachlan McIntosh Papers,* 109.

51. "Subaltern's Journal," in Hawes, *Lachlan McIntosh Papers,* 118; "Diary of Captain Hinrich," in Uhlendorf, *Siege of Charleston,* 283–85.

52. Ewald, *Diary of the American War,* 236; Clinton to BL, Articles of Capitulation proposed [by the Americans], and Minutes of a Council of War, all 8 May 1780, BL to Clinton, 9 May 1780, in *PCC,* reel 177, item 158, 399–413.

53. Moultrie, *Memoirs,* 2:96–97.

54. Moultrie, *Memoirs,* 97; Murdoch, "French Account of the Siege of Charleston," *SCHM* 67 (1966): 150; "Subaltern's Journal," Hawes, *Lachlan McIntosh Papers,* 118–20; *Diary of Lieut. Anthony Allaire* (New York, 1968; reprint), 16; "Petitions of the County Militia," received 11 May, Gadsden to BL, BL to Clinton, Clinton to BL, all 11 May 1780, in *PCC,* reel 177, item 158, 419–21, 425–29. Hinrichs wrote that the artillery fire was so violent that the British could not see the first flag of truce and it was only when a large white flag was displayed on the hornwork that a truce could be obtained by the Americans (Uhlendorf, *Siege of Charleston,* 289).

55. Cavanaugh, "American Military Leadership in the Southern Campaign," 128, in Higgins, *The Revolutionary War in the South.* Ewald wrote that "the garrison consisted of handsome young men whose apparel was extremely ragged, and on the whole the people looked greatly starved," *Diary of the American War,* 238; Lee, *Memoirs of the War in the Southern Department,* 159; Uhlendorf, *Siege of Charleston,* 293; Boston *Independent Chronicle and the Universal Advertiser,* 29 June 1780; Moultrie, *Memoirs,* 2:108–11.

56. Ward, *War of the Revolution,* 2:708; "Return of the Continental Troops, Prisoners of War," in *PCC,* reel 177, item 158, 437.

57. Elizabeth S. Kite, *Brigadier-General Louis Lebegue Duportail: Commandant of Engineers in the Continental Army, 1777–1783* (Baltimore, 1933), 174; Fitzpatrick, *Writings of Washington,* 18:264.

Chapter 7: The Long Road to Yorktown

Epigraph: Knox to BL, 24 Apr. 1781, Knox Papers (MHi).

1. BL to the president of Congress, 22 June 1780, in *PCC,* reel 177, item 158, 439; Clinton to BL, 21 May, and John Andre to [?], 3 June 1780, Emmet Collection (NN).

2. Baron von Steuben to Washington, and Nathanael Greene to Washington, both 28 Mar. 1780, Washington Papers (DLC); Greene to Jeremiah Wadsworth, 2 Apr. 1780, Nathanael Greene Papers (DLC); Louis Lebegue Duportail to Marquis de Barbe-Marbois, 7 July 1780, in Kite, *Brigadier-General,* 176; William Churchill Houston to Joseph Ward, 23 May, John Morin Scott to George Clinton, 19 Apr., James Duane to Washington, 9 and 26 May, Oliver Ellsworth to Jonathan Trumbull Sr., 9 May, Samuel Huntington to BL, 17 May, and Philip Schuyler to George Clinton, 20 May 1780, in *Letters of Delegates to Congress, 1774–1789,* ed. Paul H. Smith, 20 vols. to date (Washington, D.C., 1976–), 15:57, 97, 103, 144, 164, 181, 193; Udney Hay to George Clinton, 8 May 1780, in *Public Papers of George*

Clinton, First Governor of New York, ed. Hugh Hastings, 10 vols. (Albany, N.Y., 1914), 5:692.

3. Joseph Jones to James Hunter, 2 June, James Madison to Thomas Jefferson, 2 June, Robert R. Livingston to Philip Schuyler, 9 June, Samuel Holten's diary, 14–15 June, James Lovell to Baron von Steuben, 15 June 1780, in Smith, *Letters of Delegates,* 15:235, 238, 281, 323, 325; Timothy Pickering to John Pickering, 14 June 1780, Timothy Pickering Papers (MHi); Marshall Diary, 15 June 1780, in *Extracts from the Diary of Christopher Marshall, 1774–1781,* ed. William Duane (Albany, N.Y., 1877), 246.

4. Resolution of Congress, 28 Nov. 1777, and extract from the minutes, 23 June 1780, *JCC* 9:976, 17:552; Samuel Holten to George Peabody, 30 June 1780, Emmet Collection (NN); Oliver Ellsworth to Jonathan Trumbull Sr., 23 June 1780, in Smith, *Letters of Delegates,* 15:366; diary entries, 22 and 29 June 1780, in Duane, *Diary of Christopher Marshall,* 248–49; Joseph Pierce to Henry Knox, 22 Nov. 1781, Knox Papers (MHi).

5. John Armstrong to Horatio Gates, 6 June, Thomas McKean to William Atlee, 12 June, and Philip Schuyler to Robert R. Livingston, 12 June 1780, in Smith, *Letters of Delegates,* 15:260, 304, 307.

6. Philip Schuyler to Robert R. Livingston, 12 June, Samuel Holten to George Partridge, 27 June, John Matthews to BL, 4 Aug., and Thomas Bee to BL, 18 Aug. 1780, in Smith, *Letters of Delegates,* 15:307, 378, 543, 597; Matthew Clarkson to BL, 17 July 1780, in *Letters of Members of the Continental Congress,* ed. Edmund C. Burnett, 8 vols. (Washington, D.C., 1921–36), 5:278 n. 2; Gates to BL, 4 June 1780, Horatio Gates Papers (NHi); David Ramsay to BL, 13 Aug. 1781, Emmet Collection (NN).

7. William Clajon to Horatio Gates, 7 June 1780, Gates Papers (NHi); Washington to the president of Congress, 10 July 1780, in *The Writings of George Washington, from the Original Sources, 1745–1799,* ed. John C. Fitzpatrick, 39 vols. (Washington, D.C., 1931–44), 19:147. For James Lovell's apology for the delay in the inquiry, see his letter to BL, 19 July 1780, in Smith, *Letters of Delegates,* 15:472; BL was still interested in pursuing the inquiry as late as Apr. 1781, see Knox to BL, 24 Apr. 1781, Knox Papers (MHi).

8. Houston to William Livingston, 4 and 5 June, Thomas Bee to Henry Laurens, 6 June, James Duane to Philip Schuyler, 16 June, Samuel Holten to Francis Dana, 8 July 1780, in Smith, *Letters of Delegates,* 15:245, 251, 329, 408; Joseph Reed to Washington, 20 June 1780, Washington Papers (DLC); Hamilton to Barbe-Marbois, 31 May 1780, in *The Papers of Alexander Hamilton,* ed. Harold C. Syrett and Jacob E. Cooke, 27 vols. (New York, 1961–87), 2:332; Abigail Adams to John Adams, 5 July 1780, in Butterfield, *Book of Abigail and John,* 263.

9. Benjamin Lincoln Jr. to BL, 18 Apr. 1780, in *The Papers of Benjamin Lincoln,* ed. Frederick S. Allis Jr., microfilm ed., 13 reels (Boston, 1967), reel 5; Benjamin Lincoln Jr. to Elizabeth Lincoln (three letters), Mar. 1779, in ibid., reel

4. One measure of Ben's eagerness to see his father resume his place within the family was his reluctance to see Lincoln exchanged as a prisoner of war, see William Jackson to Benjamin Lincoln Jr., 20 Aug. 1780, in ibid., reel 5.

10. Benjamin Lincoln Jr. to BL, 18 Apr. 1780, in ibid., reel 5.

11. William Jackson to Benjamin Lincoln Jr., 20 Aug. 1780, in ibid., reel 5; see also BL's letter to Major Douglas, 7 Jan. 1781, congratulating him on his exchange and the "freedom and independence which makes life a blessing," in ibid., reel 6; George Washington to the president of Congress, 10 July and 7 Nov., to BL, 26 July, 10 Sept., and 8 Nov. 1780, in Fitzpatrick, *Writings of Washington,* 19:147, 259, 20:27, 322; BL to Sir Henry Clinton, 5 July and 11 Aug., and Clinton to BL, 19 July and 4 Sept. 1780, *Report on American Manuscripts in the Royal Institution of Great Britain,* 4 vols., [Dublin, 1904–9], 2:152, 160, 168, 176; BL to Washington, 11 Aug., and 25 Sept. 1780, Washington Papers (DLC); BL to John Sullivan, 1 Oct. 1780, in Hammond, *Letters of Sullivan,* 3:190.

12. Washington to BL, 8 Nov. 1780, in Fitzpatrick, *Writings of Washington,* 20:322; Shipton, *Sibley's Harvard Graduates,* 12:425–26; Wiiliam Gordon to Horatio Gates, 5 Oct. 1780, *Proceedings of the Massachusetts Historical Society* 63:440; Charles Cushing to BL, 20 Dec. 1780, in Allis, *Lincoln Papers,* reel 5.

13. BL to Washington, 7 Jan. and 1 Mar. 1781, Washington to BL, 11 Dec. 1780, BL to William Shephard, 19 Jan., and Shephard to BL, 5 Mar. 1781, in Allis, *Lincoln Papers,* reel 6; BL to Washington, 25 Dec. 1780 and 15 Feb. 1781, Laurens to Washington, 4 Feb. 1781, in *Correspondence of the American Revolution,* ed. Jared Sparks, 4 vols. (Boston, 1853), 3:181, 221, 231; BL to Caleb Davis, 22 Feb. and to the Massachusetts members of Congress, 27 Feb. 1781, in Allis, *Lincoln Papers,* reel 6.

14. BL to the Count de Rochambeau, and to Washington, both 1 Mar., to John Hancock, 17 Mar. 1781, in Allis, *Lincoln Papers,* reel 6.

15. BL to John Hancock, 15 June 1781, in ibid., reel 6; Ward, *War of the Revolution,* 2:880–81. Washington requested Lincoln's presence at headquarters on 11 May, one month later he wrote Lincoln to come as soon as possible, Washington to Lincoln, 11 May and 13 June, 1781, in Fitzpatrick, *Writings of Washington,* 22:72, 211; for Lincoln's orders, see "Instructions to Major General Benjamin Lincoln," 1 July 1781, in ibid., 21:301; Thomas Rodney to Caesar Rodney, 10 July 1781, in George H. Ryden, *Letters to and from Caesar Rodney, 1756–1784* (Philadelphia, 1933), 419; for a concise and judicious account, see Howard C. Rice Jr. and Anne S. K. Brown, eds. and trans., *The American Campaigns of Rochambeau's Army, 1780, 1781, 1782, 1783,* 2 vols. (Princeton, N.J., and Providence, R.I., 1972), 1:32 and n. 33.

16. Washington to George Clinton, 5 Aug., George Clinton to James Clinton, 7 and 14 Aug. 1781, in Hastings, *Public Papers of George Clinton,* 7:167, 174, 197; BL to the brigadiers of Berkshire and Hampshire Counties, 9 Aug., and to John Hancock, 10 Aug. 1781, in Allis, *Lincoln Papers,* reel 6.

17. For example, Lincoln hosted a dinner for the allied command on 14 July

1781 at Phillipsburg where campaign discussions took place, "Diary of Baron Cromot du Bourg," *PMHB*, 15:166.

18. William Calderhead, "Prelude to Yorktown: A Critical Week in a Major Campaign," *Maryland Historical Magazine* 77 (1982): 123.

19. Washington's decision was made between 19 Aug., when he offered the job to McDougall, and 24 Aug. when he issued marching orders to BL. For Washington's rationale, see also his letter to Robert Howe, 24 Sept. 1781, in Fitzpatrick, *Writings of Washington*, 23:19, 41, 131.

20. The story of the Yorktown campaign has been told many times. Lincoln's part in it was distinctly subordinate: he was Washington's executive officer. Therefore, I have not felt bound to retell the story in great detail. There is no definitive history of the campaign. The best accounts are popular histories, Burke Davis, *The Campaign That Won America: The Story of Yorktown* (New York, 1970); and Thomas J. Fleming, *Beat the Last Drum: The Siege of Yorktown, 1781* (New York, 1963). For a wonderful two volume collection of itineraries, maps, and journals describing the French participation in the campaign, see Rice and Brown, eds., *American Campaigns of Rochambeau's Army;* Davis, *Campaign,* 25–28; Washington kept tight control of all campaign details, even down to the routes of march of both armies, see Washington to BL, 24 Aug. 1781, in Fitzpatrick, *Writings of Washington*, 23:41.

21. James Thatcher, *Military Journal of the American Revolution* (Hartford, Conn., 1862), 274.

22. Ibid., 271.

23. E. James Ferguson et al., eds., *The Papers of Robert Morris, 1781–1784,* 7 vols. to date, (Pittsburgh, 1973–), 2:172–73.

24. Calderhead, "Prelude to Yorktown," *Maryland Historical Magazine* 77 (1982): 128; "Extract of a letter from a continental officer," 12 Sept. 1781, in Hastings, *Public Papers of George Clinton,* 7:326; BL to Washington, and to James Clinton, both 11 Sept. 1781, in Allis, *Lincoln Papers,* reel 6; "Journal of Jonathan Trumbull Jr., 23 Sept. 1781, *Massachusetts Historical Society Proceedings,* 14:334; Washington to BL, 31 Aug., 11 and 15 Sept. 1781, in Fitzpatrick, *Writings of Washington*, 23:69, 113, 119; Douglas Southall Freeman, *George Washington: A Biography,* 7 vols. (New York, 1948–57), 5:345.

25. Franklin and Mary Wickwire, *Cornwallis: The American Adventure* (Boston, 1970), 354–74.

26. For Lafayette's attempt to oust Lincoln from the command of the right wing, see Lafayette to Washington, 30 Sept. 1781, in *Lafayette in the Age of the American Revolution,* ed. Stanley Idzerda, 5 vols. to date, (Ithaca, N.Y., 1977–), 4:411 and nn.; Thatcher, *Military Journal,* 281, 283; BL to Mrs. Lincoln, 12 Oct. 1781, in Allis, *Lincoln Papers,* reel 6.

27. The drama of the British surrender is recreated in Freeman, *Washington,* 5:386–91.

28. Joseph Pierce to Henry Knox, 22 Nov. 1781, Knox Papers (MHi).

Chapter 8: Secretary at War

Epigraph: Livingston to John Jay, 1 Nov. 1781, in *The Revolutionary Diplomatic Correspondence of the United States,* ed. Francis Wharton, 6 vols. (Washington, D.C., 1889), 4:814.

1. Don Higginbotham, *The War of American Independence: Military Attitudes, Policies and Practice, 1763–1789* (Boston, 1983), 292–99; Charles Royster, *A Revolutionary People at War: The Continental Army and American Character, 1775–1783* (Chapel Hill, N.C., 1979), 282–311; E. James Ferguson, *The Power of the Purse: A History of American Finance, 1776–1790* (Chapel Hill, N.C., 1961), 109–19.

2. For Robert Morris's conditions for accepting the appointment and the delay they caused, see Morris to a Committee of Congress, 26 Mar. 1781, in *The Papers of Robert Morris, 1781–1784,* ed. E. James Ferguson et al., 7 vols. to date, (Pittsburgh, 1973–), 1:20–21.

3. Joseph Jones to Washington, 21 Feb. 1781, Washington Papers (DLC); Jared Sparks, *The Life of Gouverneur Morris,* 3 vols. (Boston, 1832), 1:229.

4. Sparks, *Life of Gouverneur Morris,* 1:239; Washington to Schuyler, 20 Feb. 1781, in *The Writings of George Washington, from the Original Sources, 1745–1799,* ed. John C. Fitzpatrick, 39 vols. (Washington, D.C., 1931–44), 21:262; Schuyler to Washington, 3 Apr. 1781, Washington Papers (DLC); Sullivan to Washington, 6 Mar. 1781, in *Letters of Members of the Continental Congress,* ed. Edmund C. Burnett, 8 vols. (Washington, D.C., 1921–36), 6:11.

5. Washington to Schuyler, 20 Feb., and 23 Mar. 1781, Fitzpatrick, *Writings of Washington,* 21:261, 360; Schuyler to Washington, 3 Apr. 1781, Washington Papers (DLC); Sullivan to Washington, 6 Mar. 1781, in Hammond, *Letters of Sullivan,* 3:293; Samuel Adams to Thomas McKean, 29 Aug., and Gouverneur Morris to R. R. Livingston, 14 Mar. 1781, in Burnett, *Letters,* 6:26 n. 2, 139 n. 3.

6. Sullivan to Washington, 17 May 1781, in Hammond, *Letters of Sullivan,* 3:320.

7. John Mitchell Varnum to Washington, 2 Oct. 1781, in Burnett, *Letters,* 6:231; Joseph Reed to Greene, 1 Nov. 1781, in William B. Reed, *Life and Correspondence of Joseph Reed,* 2 vols. (Philadelphia, 1847), 2:375.

8. The president of Congress to BL, 31 Oct., R. R. Livingston to James Duane, 2 Nov. 1781, in Burnett, *Letters,* 6:254 and n. 2; Gouverneur Morris to Greene, 24 Dec. 1781, Sparks, *Life of Gouverneur Morris,* 1:239; William Ellery and Ezekial Cornell to William Greene, 6 Dec. 1781, William R. Staples, *Rhode Island in the Continental Congress* (Providence, R.I., 1870), 360; BL to the president of Congress, 20 Nov., and to Benjamin Lincoln Jr., 25 Nov. 1781, in *The Papers of Benjamin Lincoln,* ed. Frederick S. Allis Jr., microfilm ed., 13 reels (Boston, 1967), reel 6.

9. Very little has been written about Lincoln and the office of secretary at war. Jennings Sanders limits his discussion of BL's administration of the office to seven pages, describing it as "largely clerical in character," and leaving the impres-

sion that the post was relatively unimportant and its occupant even less so (Sanders, *Evolution of Executive Departments of the Continental Congress, 1774–1789* [Chapel Hill, N.C., 1935], 98–104). Harry Ward was more thorough, describing the war department of 1781–83 in three short chapters. He thought that BL's methodical habits and administrative abilities made him an excellent choice for the post and gave BL credit for tackling the unenviable job (Ward, *The Department of War, 1781–1795* [Pittsburgh, 1962], 7–38). BL's appointment seems to have given "universal satisfaction" in New England (*Boston Independent Chronicle and the Universal Advertiser,* 14 Dec. 1781).

10. *Boston Independent Chronicle,* 14 Dec. 1781; Diary, 1 Dec. 1781, in Ferguson, *Papers of Robert Morris,* 3:308; Washington to BL, 4, 5, and 9 Dec. 1781, in Fitzpatrick, *Writings of Washington,* 23:370, 371, 377; William Livingston to BL, 24 Dec. 1781, in *The Papers of William Livingston,* ed. Carl E. Prince and Mary Lou Lustig, 5 vols. (New Brunswick, N.J., 1979–89), 4:354. For BL's insistence on appointing his own subordinates, see his letter to the president of Congress, 14 Jan. 1782, in *PCC,* reel 162, item 149, 101. For Alexander Hamilton's interest in the job of assistant secretary, see Charles Stewart to Hamilton, 27 Mar. 1782 (Stewart Papers [MHi]).

11. Resolution of Congress, 7 Feb. 1781, *JCC* 19:126–27; Elizabeth Cometti, "Civil Servants during the Revolution," *PMHB* 75 (1951): 169.

12. Washington to Lafayette, 4 Jan. 1782, in Fitzpatrick, *Writings of Washington,* 23:430; Resolution of Congress, 10 Apr. 1782, *JCC* 22:177–79; Ward, *Department of War,* 14.

13. BL to Henry Knox, 10 and 12 Aug. 1782, Knox Papers (MHi); Washington to James McHenry, 11 Dec. 1781, and to BL, 20 Jan. 1782, in Fitzpatrick, *Writings of Washington,* 23:381, 452–56.

14. For the Monday evening meetings, see Diary, 3, 10, 17, 24 Dec. 1781; for Robert Morris's statement, see Diary, 22 Jan. 1782, in Ferguson, *Papers of Robert Morris,* 3:317, 356, 399, 435; 4:85; BL to the president of Congress, 10 Jan. 1782, in Allis, *Lincoln Papers,* reel 6.

15. E. Wayne Carp, *To Starve the Army at Pleasure: Continental Army Administration and American Political Culture, 1775–1783* (Chapel Hill, N.C., 1984), 214, 217. The topic of one of the first Monday evening roundtables was how "to promote System and Oeconomy in the Management of Public Business," Diary, 17 Dec. 1781, in Ferguson, *Papers of Robert Morris,* 3:399; Henry Knox to Gouverneur Morris, 21 Feb. 1783, Knox Papers (MHi).

16. BL to Theodore Lincoln, 5 Aug. 1781, BL Papers (MB); on the necessity of economizing, see BL to Samuel Holten, 27 Aug. 1782, in ibid.

17. Diary, 24 Jan., 5 and 24 Apr., 13 July 1782, in Ferguson, *Papers of Robert Morris,* 4:107, 518; 5:45, 578; Washington to BL, 28 May 1782, in Fitzpatrick, *Writings of Washington,* 24:296.

18. For examples of BL's work on the contract supply system, see his memorandum to Comfort Sands, the original contractor for West Point, enclosed in

Robert Morris to Comfort Sands and Co., 19 Jan. 1782, in Ferguson, *Papers of Robert Morris,* 4:76–77; and Washington to BL, 21 Dec. 1781, in Fitzpatrick, *Writings of Washington,* 23:401.

19. Knox to BL, 12 Nov. 1781, Knox Papers (MHi); George Partridge to Elbridge Gerry, 22 Dec. 1781, in Burnett, *Letters,* 6:283: Ward, *Department of War,* 30–31.

20. BL to the president of Congress, 10 Jan. 1782 and Knox to BL, 23 Dec. 1781, in Allis, *Lincoln Papers,* reel 6; Diary, 23 Jan., Morris to the governors of the New England states, 23 Jan., Morris to Comfort Sands, 28 Jan., and Morris to BL, 2, 4, 6 and 9 Feb. 1782, in Ferguson, *Papers of Robert Morris,* 4:97, 104, 130, 153, 160, 175, 198; see the notices in the *Boston Independent Chronicle,* 14 Feb. 1782, and the *Boston Independent Ledger,* 18 Feb. 1782.

21. Morris to Comfort Sands, 28 Jan., and Diary, 8 Apr. 1782, in Ferguson, *Papers of Robert Morris,* 4:130, 538; for BL's help with the supply contracts, see Morris to BL, 2, 4, 6 and 9 Feb., and to Comfort Sands, 11 Mar., and Diary, 28 Mar., 2–6 and 13 Apr., 22 May, and 3, 7, and 11 June 1782, in ibid., 4:153, 160, 175, 198, 389, 467, 503, 512, 518, 522, 570; 5:237, 317, 363, 376.

22. Diary, 24 Apr.; Morris to BL, 7 May 1782, in Ferguson, *Papers of Robert Morris,* 5:45, 120.

23. BL to the president of Congress, *JCC* 22:302 and n.; Madison to Edmund Randolph, and John Lowell to Samuel Adams, 28 May 1782, in Burnett, *Letters,* 6:359, 360.

24. Diary, 12 July 1782, in Ferguson, *Papers of Robert Morris,* 5:567; BL to Knox (private), 7 Aug. 1782, Knox Papers (MHi).

26. For the elegance of Philadelphia society and the quote from Pierre Du Simitiere, see Kenneth Silverman, *A Cultural History of the American Revolution* (New York, 1976), 412; New Year's dinner, *PMHB,* 15:291; BL to Theodore Lincoln, 8 Oct. 1782, BL Papers (MB). For Luzerne's public audience and Van Berkels reception by Congress, see the secretary of Congress to the secretary of foreign affairs, 10 May 1782 and the president of Congress to BL, 25 Oct. 1783, in Burnett, *Letters,* 6:347 and n., 7:356. A wonderful description of La Luzerne's lavish party is given in Benjamin Rush to Elizabeth Graeme Ferguson, 16 July 1782, in *Letters of Benjamin Rush,* ed. Lyman H. Butterfield, 2 vols. (Princeton, 1951), 1:278–283. The portrait of BL by Charles Willson Peale is now in Independence Hall, Philadelphia; for the Du Simitiere portrait, see *PMHB,* 13:370.

26. Jacob Cox Parsons, ed., *Extracts from the Diary of Jacob Hiltzheimer of Philadelphia, 1765–1798* (Philadelphia, 1893), 50, 52, 59; BL to Dr. Barker, 16 Aug. 1782, in Allis, *Lincoln Papers,* reel 6; Charles Burr Todd, *Life and Letters of Joel Barlow, L.L.D.* (New York, 1886), 43.

27. BL to Theodore Lincoln, 24 June, 12 July, 5 Aug. 1781 and 12 Aug. and 8 Oct. 1782, BL Papers (MB); BL to Mr. Howard, 19 Apr., 24 July 1782; to Mr. Jackson, 29 July 1782; to the American Academy, 19 July 1783, and to Benjamin Lincoln Jr., 13 Apr., 16 May, 28 May, 15 July, 25 July, 23 Aug. 1782, in Allis, *Lincoln Papers,* reel 6.

28. Robert Morris to BL, 25 July, Diary, 26 July, BL to Morris, 6 Aug., Samuel Hodgdon to Morris, 7 Aug., "Report on Public Credit" and headnote, 29 July, Morris to Washington, 22 Sept. 1782, in Ferguson, *Papers of Robert Morris,* 6:25, 26–27, 149, 151, 36–84, 415–16.

29. BL to John Lowell, 24 Sept. 1782, in Allis, *Lincoln Papers,* reel 6.

30. BL to John Lowell, 24 Sept. 1782, in ibid., reel 6.

Chapter 9: Peace at Last

Epigraph: E. S. Thomas, *Reminiscences of the Last Sixty-Five Years,* 2 vols. (Hartford, Conn., 1840), 1:125.

1. Diary, 8 Aug. 1782, in *The Papers of Robert Morris, 1781–1784,* ed. E. James Ferguson et al., 7 vols. to date, (Pittsburgh, 1973–), 6:152; BL to Knox, 10 and 12 Aug. 1782, Knox Papers (MHi).

2. Robert Morris to Washington, 29 Aug. 1782, in Ferguson, *Papers of Robert Morris,* 6:282; Knox to BL, 19 Aug. 1782, Knox Papers (MHi).

3. Lawrence Delbert Cress, *Citizens in Arms: The Army and Militia in American Society to the War of 1812* (Chapel Hill, N.C., 1982), 67–68.

4. Ibid., 68–69; Wood, *Creation of the Republic,* 32–36.

5. Jack N. Rakove, *The Beginnings of National Politics: An Interpretive History of the Continental Congress* (New York, 1979), 310.

6. BL to John Lowell, 24 Sept. 1782, and to George Washington, 14 Oct. 1782, in *The Papers of Benjamin Lincoln,* ed. Frederick S. Allis Jr., microfilm ed., 13 reels (Boston, 1967), reel 6.

7. BL to Henry Knox, 23 Jan. 1781, Knox Papers (MHi).

8. BL to John Lowell, 24 Sept. and to Cobb, 24 Sept. 1782, in Allis, *Lincoln Papers,* reel 6. In the fall of 1782 the Massachusetts Continental line sent a committee of officers to the state legislature with a petition requesting that the state settle their accounts, adjust their pay, rations and clothing allowances for depreciation, and assume the responsibility for the officers' half-pay pensions or a commutation payment. The legislature postponed proceedings until Congress decided how it was going to handle the matter (Knox to BL, 19 Aug. and 25 Nov. 1782, and BL to Knox, 26 Aug. 1782, Knox Papers (MHi); Louis C. Hatch, *The Administration of the American Revolutionary Army* [New York, 1904], 143–46).

9. Washington to BL, 2 Oct. 1782, in Fitzpatrick, *Writings of Washington,* 25:226–29; Washington enclosed a copy in a letter to Robert Morris, Washington to Morris, 2 Oct. 1782, in Ferguson, *Papers of Robert Morris,* 6:477; BL sent an extract of the letter to Congress, James Madison to Edmund Randolph, 22 Oct. 1782, in Burnett, *Letters,* 6:514; BL to Washington, 14 Oct. 1782, in Allis, *Lincoln Papers,* reel 6.

10. Heath, *Memoirs,* 368; BL to John Adams, 25 Sept. 1782, *Joseph Rubenfine Autograph Catalogue,* no. 93 (1988); BL wrote a similar letter to Benjamin Franklin in Paris, 25 Sept. 1782, in *The Works of Benjamin Franklin,* ed. Jared Sparks, 10 vols. (Boston, 1856), 9:413–14.

11. Washington to BL, 7 Oct. 1782, in Fitzpatrick, *Writings of Washington,* 25:240; BL to the president of Congress, 14 Oct. 1782, in *PCC,* reel 163, item 149, 50; James Madison to Edmund Randolph, 22 Oct. 1782, in Burnett, *Letters,* 6:514; Heath, *Memoirs,* 373.

12. BL to the president of Congress, 30 Oct. 1782, in *PCC,* reel 163, item 149, 101; Diary, 30 Oct. 1782, and "Plan of Robert Morris and Benjamin Lincoln for Issuing Provision under Contracts, 20 Nov. 1782, in Ferguson, *Papers of Robert Morris,* 6:677, 7:67–78; BL to Knox, 3 Dec. 1782, Knox Papers (MHi); Madison to Edmund Randolph, 29 Oct. 1782, in Burnett, *Letters,* 6:528.

13. E. James Ferguson, *The Power of the Purse: A History of American Public Finance, 1776–1790* (Chapel Hill, N.C., 1961), 152–54; Richard H. Kohn, *Eagle and Sword: The Beginnings of the Military Establishment in America* (New York, 1975), 20; BL to Knox, 3 Dec. 1782, Knox Papers (MHi).

14. Knox to BL, 25 Nov. and BL to Knox, 3 Dec. 1782, Knox Papers (MHi); Washington to Morris, 8 Jan. 1783, in Ferguson, *Papers of Robert Morris,* 7:284; Knox to Alexander McDougall, 17 Dec. 1782, Alexander McDougall Papers (NHi); Ferguson, *Power of the Purse,* 155–56.

15. Ferguson, *Power of the Purse,* 157–59; Knox to Alexander McDougall, 21 Feb. 1783, Knox Papers (MHi).

16. BL to Knox, 22 Mar. 1783, in Allis, *Lincoln Papers,* reel 6.

17. Washington to Armstrong, 10 Jan. 1783, and Washington memorandum of meeting with BL, 17 Feb. 1783, in Fitzpatrick, *Writings of Washington,* 26:26, 140; Knox to Alexander McDougall, 21 Feb. 1783, Knox Papers (MHi).

18. Arthur Lee to Samuel Adams, 29 Jan. 1783, James Duane to Alexander Hamilton, 17 Feb. 1783, in Burnett, *Letters,* 7:28, 45; see the headnote to Robert Morris to the president of Congress, 24 Jan. 1783, in Ferguson, *Papers of Robert Morris,* 7:361–68.

19. This is the interpretation of Morris's motives given in the most persuasive account of the Newburgh Conspiracy, Richard Kohn, "The Inside History of the Newburgh Conspiracy: America and the Coup d'Etat," *WMQ,* 3d ser., 27 (1970): 187–220, which still stands despite challenges from Paul David Nelson, "Horatio Gates at Newburgh, 1783: A Misunderstood Role," in ibid., 29 (1972): 143–58, and C. Edward Skeen, "The Newburgh Conspiracy Reconsidered," in ibid., 31 (1974): 273–290. Kohn's interpretation of Robert Morris's role in the affair has been questioned by the editors of *The Papers of Robert Morris,* see Morris to the president of Congress, 26 Feb. 1783, 7:462–70 and nn.

20. Knox to BL, 3 Mar. 1783, Knox Papers (MHi).

21. Knox to BL, 12 Mar. 1783, in Allis, *Lincoln Papers,* reel 6.

22. Kohn, *Eagle and Sword,* 30–33; Washington to Alexander Hamilton, 12 Mar. 1783, in *The Papers of Alexander Hamilton,* ed. Harold C. Syrett and Jacob E. Cooke, 27 vols. (New York, 1961–87), 3:286; Knox to BL, 16 Mar. 1783, in Allis, *Lincoln Papers,* reel 6.

23. BL to Knox, 22 Mar. 1783, in Allis, *Lincoln Papers,* reel 6.

24. Diary, 23 Apr. 1783 and n. 5, in Ferguson, *Papers of Robert Morris,* 7:734.

25. BL to Benjamin Lincoln Jr., 31 Mar., and to Mrs. Mary Lincoln, 10 May 1783, in Allis, *Lincoln Papers,* reel 6.

26. Kohn, *Eagle and Sword,* 40–53; Cress, *Citizens in Arms,* 78–87.

27. The most complete description of the Philadelphia mutiny of 1783 is Kenneth R. Bowling, "New Light on the Philadelphia Mutiny of 1783: Federal-State Confrontation at the Close of the War of Independence," *PMHB* 101 (1977): 419–50. I am indebted to Mary A. Gallagher and Elizabeth M. Nuxoll of the *Papers of Robert Morris* for sharing their research on the mutiny. Their interpretation of the episode, which differs at critical points from Bowling's, will appear in vol. 8 (forthcoming) of the *The Papers of Robert Morris.*

28. Washington to Theodorick Bland, 4 Apr. 1783, in Fitzpatrick, *Writings of Washington,* 26:285–91; BL to the president of Congress, 14 Apr. 1783, in *PCC,* reel 163, item 149, 439–42; Resolution of Congress, 26 May 1783, *JCC* 24:364; Bowling, "Philadelphia Mutiny," 422–23.

29. Note on army pay, in Gallagher and Nuxoll, *Papers of Robert Morris,* vol. 8 (forthcoming). Washington to the president of Congress, 18 Apr. 1783; to Theodorick Bland, 4 Apr. 1783; and to Lafayette, 15 June 1783, in Fitzpatrick, *Writings of Washington,* 26:285–91, 330–34, 27:14.

30. BL to the president of Congress, 11 June 1783, in *PCC,* reel 163, item 149, 539; BL to Smallwood, 12 June 1783, Emmet Collection (NN).

31. Bowling, "Philadelphia Mutiny," 424–25; Report of Richard Humpton, 24 June 1783, in *PCC,* reel 45, item 38, 4, 5–6; La Luzerne to Vergennes, 18 June 1783, AMAE: Correspondence politique, Etats-Unis, 24:357; Madison's "Notes on Debates," 13 June 1783, in *The Papers of James Madison,* ed. William T. Hutchinson et al., 1st ser., vols. 1–10 (Chicago, 1962–77), vols. 11–17 (Charlottesville, Va., 1977–91), 7:141 and n. 1; James Madison to Edmund Randolph, 17 June 1783, in Burnett, *Letters,* 7:189.

32. BL to the president of Congress, 11 June 1783, in *PCC,* reel 163, item 149, 1–2; Bowling, "Philadelphia Mutiny," 426–38.

33. BL to James Warren, 22 July 1783; to the American Academy, 19 July 1783; and to Capt. Shaw, 23 July 1783, in Allis, *Lincoln Papers,* reel 7.

34. For the organization and early criticism of the society, see Minor Myers Jr., *Liberty without Anarchy: A History of the Society of the Cincinnati* (Charlottesville, Va., 1983), 15–69. For the William Eustis quote, see ibid., 17, 22 n. 47. Samuel Osgood to BL, 24 Nov. 1783, and BL to Capt. Samuel Shaw, 23 July 1783, in Allis, *Lincoln Papers,* reel 7.

35. BL to the president of Congress, 8 Aug. 1783, in Allis, *Lincoln Papers,* reel 7; BL to the president of Congress, 30 Mar. 1783, in *PCC,* reel 163, item 149, 411–14; Joseph B. Berry, ed., "Ward Chipman Diary," 21 Sept. 1783, *Essex Institute Historical Collections* 87 (1951): 217; "Weight of Officers," *PMHB* 36 (1912): 508.

36. BL to Pierce, 30 Sept. 1783, in Allis, *Lincoln Papers,* reel 7. According to Treasury Waste Book E, 114, Records of the U.S. General Accounting Office, RG 217 (DNA), $3,608 was placed on interest for BL; BL to Benjamin Lincoln, Jr., 21 Oct. 1783, and Samuel Osgood to BL, 5 and 24 Nov. 1783, in Allis, *Lincoln Papers,* reel 7.

37. Washington to Knox, 2 Nov. 1783, in Fitzpatrick, *Writings of Washington,* 27:220; *JCC* 25:803–4.

Chapter 10: Forging a New Life

Epigraph: BL to Ebenezer Storer, 18 Oct. 1783, in *The Papers of Benjamin Lincoln,* ed. Frederick S. Allis Jr., microfilm ed., 13 reels (Boston, 1967), reel 7.

1. Ibid., reel 7.

2. Ibid., reel 7.

3. Joseph Reed to Nathanael Greene, 14 Mar. 1783, in William B. Reed, *Life and Correspondence of Joseph Reed,* 2 vols. (Philadelphia, 1847), 2:394; William Gordon to Horatio Gates, 26 Feb. 1783, *Massachusetts Historical Society Proceedings* 63 (1931): 487; Benjamin Walker to Baron von Steuben, 12 Feb. 1783, Steuben Papers (NHi); Ezra Badlam to BL, 28 Apr. 1783, and BL to Benjamin Lincoln Jr., 8 Oct. 1783, in Allis, *Lincoln Papers,* reels 6 and 7.

4. BL to Ebenezer Storer, 18 Oct. 1783, in Allis, *Lincoln Papers,* reel 7. For BL's debt, see, for example, the thousand dollars borrowed from John Hancock in July 1778, Hancock to BL, 2 Mar. 1785, in ibid.

5. BL to Ebenezer Storer, 18 Oct. 1783, in ibid., reel 7. For loans sought by BL, see his letter to Benjamin Lincoln Jr., 17 Oct. 1783, in ibid., reel 7. For BL's plans to build a flour mill on the latest design, see the exchange of letters between him and Samuel Hodgdon, former army commissioner of stores and BL's Philadelphia agent, beginning 14 Dec. 1783 and continuing throughout 1784, in ibid., reel 7. A description of the mill, fully automated except for "spreading the meal to cool," is found in "Questions and Answers about the Flour Mill lately erected at Hingham," misc. MSS (MHi); see also Lincoln, *History of Hingham,* 3:160–61. For BL's acquisition of property, see the deeds of sale, 6 and 15 Sept. and 13 Dec. 1783; 20 Mar. and 1 and 19 Apr. 1784, in Allis, *Lincoln Papers,* reel 7; Johann David Shoepf, *Travels in the Confederation, 1783–1784,* ed. Alfred J. Morrison, 2 vols. (1788; reprint, New York, 1968), 1:43.

6. F. Van Hogendorp to G. K. Aan Zijne Moeder, 30 Nov. and 7 Dec. 1783, in Frederick van Hogendorp, *Brieven en Gedenkshriften van Gijsbert Karel von Hogendorp uitgegeven door zijn jongsten, thans eenigen zoon,* 2 vols. (The Hague, 1866), 1:257–69. The letters were published in both Dutch and French; my free translations are taken from the latter.

7. Van Hogendorp to his mother, 7 Dec. 1783 and 26 Mar. 1784, in ibid., 1:266–69, 338. H. J. Hill to BL, 6 May 1782; and BL to Benjamin Lincoln Jr., 16

May 1782, in Allis, *Lincoln Papers,* reel 7. "List of Births and Deaths in the Lincoln Household," in ibid., reel 12. As for Lincoln's treatment of slaves and servants within his household, it would be entirely characteristic for him to follow the old Puritan ideal of family government; see Edmund S. Morgan, *The Puritan Family: Religion and Domestic Relations in Seventeenth-Century New England* (New York, 1966), 109–32. For "family slavery" in New England, see Piersen, *Black Yankees,* 25–36.

8. Everard Meade to BL, 25 July 1785, and BL to Meade (ca. August 1785), in Allis, *Lincoln Papers,* reel 7; BL to James Bowdoin, 16 Sept. 1785, Lloyd W. Smith Collection (NjMoHP). Hingham's social development was similar to the closed, corporate, utopian character of Dedham, as described by Kenneth Lockridge (*A New England Town: The First Hundred Years* [New York, 1970]).

9. Richard B. Morris, *The Forging of the Union, 1781–1789* (New York, 1987), 130–34. William Jackson to BL, 16 July 1784, and 30 Aug. 1785, in Allis, *Lincoln Papers,* reel 7. For BL's business affairs generally and for their tenuous nature after December 1785, see BL's orders to Mark Clark, captain of the sloop *Polly,* and his correspondence with Thomas Porter of Porter and Ingraham, Alexandria; William Lyles of Lyles and Company, Alexandria; and Thomas Peters of Peters and Company, Baltimore, in ibid., reel 7. For the debt, see BL to Hobby, 25 Jan. and 21 Feb. 1786, in ibid., reel 7.

10. Rebecca W. Hobart, *Dennysville, 1786–1986 . . . and Edmunds, Too!* (Ellsworth, Maine, 1986), p. 7; BL to James Bowdoin, 16 Sept. 1785, Lloyd W. Smith Collection (NjMoHP); Benjamin Lincoln, *A Description of the Situation, Climate, Soil, and Productions of Certain Tracts of Land in the District of Maine, and Commonwealth of Massachusetts* ([Philadelphia?], 1793; Evans 25720). A summary of BL's pamphlet in the context of Bingham's land schemes is in Robert C. Alberts, *The Golden Voyage: The Life and Times of William Bingham, 1752–1804* (Boston, 1969), 232; Robert H. Wiebe, *The Opening of American Society: From the Adoption of the Constitution to the Eve of Disunion* (New York, 1984), 138–39. I am using Wiebe's point that land speculation in the 1780s and 1790s was distinguished by a kind of mindless rapacity, "an essentially spaceless, placeless quest for wealth," which was not informed by much real knowledge or interest in the land itself.

11. The injunction formed one leg of BL's criticism of American Indian society; see BL to John Heckwelder, Oct. 1793, in Allis, *Lincoln Papers,* reel 10; and chap. 13 of the present study. BL to James Bowdoin, 16 Sept. 1785, Lloyd W. Smith Collection (NjMoHP). For the timing of the purchase and mention of the partnership, see BL to Samuel Holden Parsons, 12 May 1786, and Charles Storer to BL, 25 Jan. 1787, in Allis, *Lincoln Papers,* reel 7. To follow the expansion of the settlement at Dennys River (later Dennysville), see the correspondence between BL and Theodore Lincoln, in ibid., reels 7–12; and in the Lincoln collection (MB). Lincoln is depicted as a wealthy land speculator in James S. Leamon, *Revolution Downeast: The War for American Independence in Maine* (Amherst, Mass., 1993), 192.

12. North Callahan, *Henry Knox: General Washington's General* (New York, 1958), 338–64; Carolyn S. Parsons, "'Bordering on Magnificence': Urban Domestic Planning in the Maine Woods," in *Maine in the Early Republic,* ed. Charles E. Clark, James S. Leamon, and Karen Bowden (Hanover, N.H., 1988), 62–82. The endorsement of Knox's notes began in 1797 when Knox, unbeknownst to BL, was trying to get out of financial difficulties; see the BL-Knox correspondence from 1797 to the end of Knox's life, in Allis, *Lincoln Papers,* reels 10–11; and chapter 14 of the present study. For an unflattering portrait of Lincoln as a "great proprietor," see Alan Taylor, *Liberty Men and Great Proprietors: The Revolutionary Settlement on the Maine Frontier, 1760–1820* (Chapel Hill, N.C., 1990), 31–59, 61, 85, 148.

13. Knox to BL (ca. August), and 16 Aug. 1784, Knox Papers (MHi); BL's report to Gov. Bowdoin, 30 Aug. 1786, and "Letter of a Committee to the Governor," 30 Aug. 1786, in *Documentary History of the State of Maine,* ed. James Phinney Baxter, 24 vols. (Portland, Me., 1869–1916), 21:239–49, 247–49; Richard M. Candee, "Maine Towns, Maine People: Architecture and the Community, 1783–1820," in Clark et al., *Maine in the Early Republic,* 34–35.

14. John Avery to BL, 20 Dec. 1785, and BL to Gov. James Bowdoin, 26 Dec. 1785 and 23 Apr. 1786, in Allis, *Lincoln Papers,* reel 7; BL to Bowdoin, 24 Mar. 1786, BL Papers (MB); in 1789 the militia held a review on John Adams's farm in Braintree. Adams's comment was that he wished "that Gov. Hancock and Gen. Lincoln would not erect their military reputations upon the ruins of my stone walls"; qtd. in Page Smith, *John Adams,* 2 vols. (New York, 1962), 2:739.

15. Draft in BL's hand, 1783, in Allis, *Lincoln Papers,* reel 7; BL to James Bowdoin, 16 Sept. 1785, Lloyd W. Smith Collection (NjMoHP).

16. The essay, "Remarks on the Cultivation of the Oak," was found in BL's papers after his death and published in the *Massachusetts Historical Society Collections,* 2d ser., 1 (1814): 187–94; see also Charles Van Ravenswaay, "America's Age of Wood," *American Antiquarian Society Proceedings* 80 (1970): 49–66; BL to James Bowdoin, 16 Sept. 1786, Lloyd W. Smith Collection (NjMoHP). The letter included an early condemnation of "the excessive use of distilled spirits." Lincoln suggested that beer replace liquor because the latter not only "serves to impoverish the people, and ruin their morals, but . . . it enervates and enfeebles their bodies, the effect of which must be, that the next generation will be in a degree effeminate and puny."

17. BL to Rufus King, 11 Feb. 1786, in *The Life and Correspondence of Rufus King,* ed. Charles R. King, 6 vols. (New York, 1894–1900), 1:156–60; Samuel Osgood to BL, 11 May 1786, in Allis, *Lincoln Papers,* reel 7. For Osgood's change of heart, see Rakove, *The Beginnings of National Politics,* 340–41; for a concise statement of the problems faced by the Confederation government in the 1780s, see ibid., 333–59.

18. BL to Rufus King, 11 Feb. 1786, in King, *Life and Correspondence of Rufus King,* 1:156–60. Much of Lincoln's thought mirrored debate in Congress at

this time; see Rakove, *Beginnings of National Politics,* 346–50. For themes of union and disunion in the early Republic, see Paul C. Nagle, *One Nation Indivisible: The Union in American Thought* (New York, 1964), 23–31.

19. John Lowell to BL, 28 (Dec.?) 1782, misc. MSS (MHi); BL to Rufus King, 11 Feb. 1786, in King, *Life and Correspondence of Rufus King,* 1:156–60.

20. Rakove, *Beginnings of National Politics,* 348, 370–71; John Lowell to BL, 28 [December?] 1782, misc. MSS (MHi).

21. Benjamin Lincoln, "Observations," 9 Dec. 1786, in Allis, *Lincoln Papers,* reel 7. The amendments of the Grand Committee are discussed in greater detail in Rakove, *Beginnings of National Politics,* 370–72. For the western disturbances—or Shays's Rebellion, as it came to be called—see chap. 11 of the present study.

22. George Washington to BL, 7 November 1786, in Fitzpatrick, *Writings of Washington,* 29:59.

Chapter 11: Shay's Rebellion

Epigraph: Milovan Djilas, *The New Class* (New York, 1957), 22.

1. BL to George Washington, 4 Dec. 1786–4 Mar. 1787, Washington Papers (DLC).

2. David Szatmary, *Shays' Rebellion: The Making of an Agrarian Insurrection* (Amherst, Mass., 1980), 31–39; Robert A. East, "The Massachusetts Conservatives in the Critical Period," in *The Era of the American Revolution,* ed. Richard B. Morris (New York, 1939), 349–57; Jonathan Smith, "The Depression of 1785 and Daniel Shays' Rebellion," *WMQ,* 3d ser., 5 (1948): 80–86.

3. Pauline Maier, *From Resistance to Revolution: Colonial Radicals and the Development of American Opposition to Britain, 1765–1776* (New York, 1972), 3–26; see also Benjamin Lincoln Jr.'s comment on previous disturbances in the western counties in his letter to BL, 10 July 1782, in *The Papers of Benjamin Lincoln,* ed. Frederick S. Allis Jr., microfilm ed., 13 reels (Boston, 1967), reel 6. The concept of a revolutionary settlement that rested on "a broad consensus concerning the authority of institutions" is explored in John L. Brooke, "To the Quiet of the People: Revolutionary Settlements and Civil Unrest in Western Massachusetts, 1774–1789," *WMQ,* 3d ser., 46 (1989): 425–62. Brooke finds the "roots of Shays' Rebellion lay in great part in a failure of a revolutionary settlement of civil institutions unique to Hampshire County" (426).

4. The hesitant response of the Massachusetts government in contrast to those of the surrounding states is described in Szatmary, *Shays' Rebellion,* 76–84; Washington to Henry Lee, 31 Oct. 1786, in *The Writings of George Washington, from the Original Sources, 1745–1799,* ed. John C. Fitzpatrick, 39 vols. (Washington, D.C., 1931–44), 29:34.

5. BL to Washington, 4 Dec. 1786–4 Mar. 1787, Washington Papers (DLC). Merchants, professionals, and those whose livelihood depended on a commercial

nexus shared many of BL's beliefs about the rebellion; see Szatmary, *Shays' Rebellion,* 70–76. Szatmary had described the Shaysites as operating within a moral economy—that is, an economy in which social relationships had priority over market relationships—and that the basis of the rebellion was found in the reaction against the intrusion of the free market. But I find that the Shaysites—in their support of paper money, for example—were attempting to manipulate the new market economy in their favor. They failed initially because they could not muster enough political weight. If any one was operating in a moral economy, it was Lincoln; see ibid., 1–18. For arguments supporting the point that Massachusetts elites were public-minded men acting from public virtue, see Richard Buel Jr., "The Public Creditor Interest in Massachusetts Politics, 1780–86"; and William Pencak, "'The Fine Theoretical Government of Massachusetts Is Prostrated to the Earth': The Response to Shays's Rebellion Reconsidered," in *In Debt to Shays: The Bicentennial of an Agrarian Rebellion,* ed. Robert A. Gross (Charlottesville, Va., 1993), 47–56, 121–44. For the insecurity of eastern merchants, see Stephen E. Patterson, "The Federalist Reaction to Shays's Rebellion," in ibid., 101–20.

    6. Richard D. Brown, "Shays' Rebellion and Its Aftermath: A View from Springfield, Massachusetts, 1787," *WMQ,* 3d ser., 40 (1983): 598; "Political Miscellany," Boston *Massachusetts Centinel,* 28 Apr. 1787.

    7. *The Diary of William Bentley, D.D.,* 4 vols. (Salem, Mass., 1905), 3:514–15. According to Szatmary, the irony was all on the surface; see *Shays' Rebellion,* 76–77.

    8. BL to Dr. Barker, 15 Apr. 1783, and to Mrs. Mary Lincoln, 10 May 1783, in Allis, *Lincoln Papers,* reel 6. The motivation of Massachusetts farmers, of which BL was one, is persuasively laid out in Richard Bushman, "Massachusetts Farmers and the Revolution," in *Society, Freedom and Conscience,* ed. Richard M. Jellison (New York, 1976), 77–124. The clergy's reaction to the Whiskey Rebellion is qtd. in Nathan O. Hatch, *The Sacred Cause of Liberty: Republican Thought and the Millenium in Revolutionary New England* (New Haven, Conn., 1977), 124; *Address from the General Court to the People of Massachusetts* (Boston, 1786; Evans 19781), 33.

    9. Boston *Independent Chronicle,* 24 Nov. 1785–9 Feb. 1786. For a response to Benjamin Lincoln Jr.'s essays, see William Manning, *The Key to Liberty: The Life and Democratic Writings of William Manning, "A Laborer," 1747–1814* (Cambridge, Mass., 1993).

    10. BL's influence on his son can be seen at several points in the "Free Republican" essays, but see especially the remarks on reason and education in no. 10 of the Boston *Independent Chronicle,* 9 Feb. 1786; see also the correspondence of BL and his son in Allis, *Lincoln Papers,* reels 6 and 7; Morgan, *The Puritan Family,* 17–21. An example of deference in Hingham is found in Hogendorp, *Brieven en Gedenkshriften van Gijsbert Karel von Hogendorp,* 1:344: "I heard this from General Lincoln: You would not imagine how difficult it is to get my old soldiers to sit with me at my table even though all distinctions ceased with the peace" (my

trans.). For BL's fear of the agrarian law, see BL to Washington, 4 Dec. 1786–4 Mar. 1787, Washington Papers (DLC).

11. BL to (?), 25 Jan. 1786, in Allis, *Lincoln Papers,* reel 7. BL's belief in the sacredness of contract proved dangerously expensive for him when Henry Knox defaulted in 1799 on notes BL endorsed. BL nearly lost his own property by refusing to shelter it by signing it over to his sons, see BL to (?), 8 Oct. 1800, in ibid., reel 11; and chap. 13 of the present study. Szatmary, *Shays' Rebellion,* 44–48; Janet Riesman, "Money, Credit, and Federalist Political Economy," in *Beyond Confederation: Origins of the Constitution and American National Identity,* ed. Richard Beeman et al. (Chapel Hill, N.C., 1987), 150–51.

12. BL to George Washington, 4 Dec. 1786–4 Mar. 1787, Washington Papers (DLC). For a similar belief expressed by his son in an earlier disturbance in the western counties, see Benjamin Lincoln Jr. to BL, 10 July 1782, in Allis, *Lincoln Papers,* reel 6.

13. See, for example, Artemas Ward to James Bowdoin, 16 Dec. 1786, and William Shepard to Bowdoin, 30 Dec. 1786, in "Temple-Bowdoin Papers, *Massachusetts Historical Society Collections* 7 (1907): 118, 127; Szatmary, *Shays' Rebellion,* 82–85; James Bowdoin to BL, 19 Jan. 1787, qtd. in George Richards Minot, *The History of the Insurrections, in Massachusetts, in the Year 1786 and the Rebellion Consequent Thereon* (Worchester, Mass., 1788), 99–101; Jeremy Belknap to Ebenezer Hazard, 2 Dec. 1786, *Massachusetts Historical Society Collections,* 5th ser., 2:447; Shepard to Bowdoin, 17 Dec. 1786, in "Temple-Bowdoin Papers," 120.

14. BL to Washington, 4 Dec. 1786–4 Mar. 1787, Washington Papers (DLC).

15. Szatmary, *Shays' Rebellion,* 64–65; Washington to Benjamin Lincoln Jr., 24 Feb. 1787, in Fitzpatrick, *Writings of Washington,* 29:168.

16. Bowdoin to BL, 19 Jan. 1787, in Minot, *History of the Insurrections,* 99–101; BL to Washington, 4 Dec. 1786–4 Mar. 1787, Washington Papers (DLC).

17. Knox to Lafayette, 13 Feb. 1787, and Knox to BL, 14 Feb. 1787, Knox Papers (MHi). For divisions within the government, see diary entry, 3 Dec. 1786, in Fitch Edward Oliver, *The Diary of William Pynchon of Salem* (Boston, 1890), 257.

18. BL to Benjamin Lincoln Jr., 25 Nov. 1781, in Allis, *Lincoln Papers,* reel 6; "Free Republican," no. 2, Boston *Independent Chronicle,* 1 Dec. 1785.

19. Benjamin Lincoln Jr. to Hodijah Baylies, 4 Jan. 1787, in Allis, *Lincoln Papers,* reel 7; BL to Washington, 4 Dec. 1786—4 Mar. 1787, Washington Papers (DLC); Jeremy Belknap to Elizabeth Belknap, 14 Jan. 1787, in *Massachusetts Historical Society Collections,* 5th ser., 4:325; Szatmary, *Shays' Rebellion,* 87; Wallace E. Davies, "The Society of the Cincinnati in New England, 1783–1800," *WMQ,* 3d ser., 5 (1948): 21–22.

20. Henry Jackson to Knox, 21 Jan. 1787, Knox Papers (MHi); *Massachusetts Centinel,* 20 Jan. 1787.

21. BL to James Bowdoin, 21 and 24 Jan. 1787, and (?) to BL, 20 Jan. 1787, in Allis, *Lincoln Papers,* reel 8.

22. BL to William Shepard, 23 Jan. 1787, and Shepard to BL, 19 and 23 Jan. 1787, in ibid., reels 8 and 7; diary entry, 26 Jan. 1787, in *The Diary of John Quincy Adams,* ed. Marc Friedlaender and Robert J. Taylor, 2 vols. to date (Cambridge, Mass., 1981–), 2:152; Jackson to Henry Knox, 28 Jan. 1787, Knox Papers (MHi).

23. BL to James Bowdoin, to John Brooks, and to John Patterson, all 28 Jan. 1787, and to Bowdoin, 30 Jan. 1787, in Allis, *Lincoln Papers,* reel 8. BL to Knox, 28 Jan. 1787, Knox Papers (MHi).

24. Petitions from the towns of Williamstown, Hardwick, Oakham, Granby, New Braintree, etc., ca. 28 Jan. 1787; BL to the selectmen of Williamstown, 30 Jan. 1787; BL to James Bowdoin, 30 Jan. 1787; BL to John Patterson, 1 Feb. 1787; BL to "Capt. Shays & the officers commanding the men in arms against the Government of this Commonwealth," 30 Jan. 1787; "to Francis Stone, Capt. Daniel Shays, & Adam Wheeler," 31 Jan. 1787, in Allis, *Lincoln Papers,* reel 8.

25. BL to James Bowdoin, 4 Feb. 1787, in ibid., reel 8; see also Herbert T. Wade, "The Essex Regiment in Shays' Rebellion, 1787," *Essex Institute Historical Collections* 90 (1954): 337–38.

26. Henry Jackson to Knox, 18 Feb. 1787, Knox Papers (MHi); "Resolution of the General Court," 6 Feb. 1787, in Allis, *Lincoln Papers,* reel 8; Stephen Mix Mitchell to Jeremiah Wadsworth, 24 Jan. 1787, and Rufus King to BL, 21 Jan. 1787, in *Letters of Members of the Continental Congress,* ed. Edmund C. Burnett, 8 vols. (Washington, D.C., 1921–36), 8:531–32; Rufus King to John Adams, 10 Feb. 1787, and to Elbridge Gerry, 11 Feb. 1787, in *The Life and Correspondence of Rufus King,* ed. Charles R. King, 6 vols. (New York, 1894–1900), 1:201, 213; "Shays: A Rebel Eclogue," *Massachusetts Centinel,* 19 May 1787.

27. BL to James Bowdoin, 5 and 6 Feb. 1787, and BL to John Brooks, 2 Feb. 1787, in Allis, *Lincoln Papers,* reel 8; BL to Knox, 14 Mar. 1787, Knox Papers (MHi).

28. BL to John Patterson, 31 Jan. 1787, in Allis, *Lincoln Papers,* reel 8; BL to Knox, 17 Feb. 1787, Knox Papers (MHi); James Sullivan to Rufus King, 25 Feb. 1787, in King, *Life and Correspondence of Rufus King,* 1:214; Stephen Higginson to Knox, 13 Feb. 1787, "Letters of Stephen Higginson," *Annual Report of the American Historical Association for the Year 1896,* 2 vols. (Washington, D.C., 1897), 1:751; BL to James Bowdoin, 14 Feb. 1787, in Allis, *Lincoln Papers,* reel 8.

29. Szatmary, *Shays' Rebellion,* 106; James Madison to Thomas Jefferson, 19 Mar. 1787, in *The Papers of James Madison,* ed. William T. Hutchinson et al., 1st ser., vols. 1–10 (Chicago, 1962–77), vols. 11–17 (Charlottesville, Va., 1977–91), 9:321.

30. Szatmary, *Shays' Rebellion,* 107–14. For an example of this kind of social banditry, see BL to James Bowdoin, 27 Feb. 1787; John Warner to BL, 18 Feb. 1787; Woodbridge Little to BL, 26 Mar. 1787; the selectmen of Brookfield, 2 Apr.

1787; BL to Chittendon, and to Clinton, both 21 Feb. 1787; and BL to James Bowdoin, 9 Mar. 1787, in Allis, *Lincoln Papers,* reel 8. James Bowdoin to Rufus King and Nathan Dane, 11 Mar. 1787, in "Temple-Bowdoin Papers," *Massachusetts Historical Society Collections* 7:170. BL to James Bowdoin, 27 Feb. 1787, in Allis, *Lincoln Papers,* reel 8.

31. BL to Knox, 14 Mar. 1787, Knox Papers (MHi).

32. Benjamin Lincoln Jr. to Theodore Lincoln, 27 Mar. 1787, BL Papers (MB); Peter Van Schaak to BL, 8 Apr. 1787, in Allis, *Lincoln Papers,* reel 8.

33. North to Knox, 31 Mar. 1787, Knox Papers (MHi). In an era of low-turnout elections, this one brought out a substantial 28 percent of the electorate; see Ronald Formisano, *The Transformation of Political Culture: Massachusetts Parties, 1790s–1840s* (New York, 1983), 30–31; "Impartialis," *Boston Gazette,* 2 Apr. 1787; "Candidas," Boston *Independent Chronicle,* 29 Mar. 1787; "Brutus," *Boston Gazette,* 2 Apr. 1787.

34. Richard Hofstadter, *The Idea of a Party System: The Rise of Legitimate Opposition in the United States, 1780–1840* (Berkeley, Ca., 1969), 1–39; Benjamin Lincoln Jr. to BL, 14 Sept. 1780, in Allis, *Lincoln Papers,* reel 6; *Massachusetts Centinel,* 14 Mar. 1787.

35. For John Hancock, see Formisano, *Transformation of Political Culture,* 31–32; Herbert S. Allan, *John Hancock: Patriot in Purple* (New York, 1953), 323; William H. Fowler Jr., *The Baron of Beacon Hill: A Biography of John Hancock* (Boston, 1980), 263, 265–66; John Quincy Adams to John Adams, 30 June 1787, in *Writings of John Quincy Adams,* ed. Worthington Chauncy Ford, 7 vols. (New York, 1913–17), 1:32–33.

36. Morris, *Forging of the Union,* 264; BL to John Hancock, 6 June 1787, in Allis, *Lincoln Papers,* reel 8; Henry Knox to BL, 14 Feb. 1787, Knox Papers (MHi); George Washington to BL, 23 Mar. 1787, Washington Papers (DLC).

37. Szatmary, *Shays' Rebellion,* 120–27; Richard D. Brown, "Shays's Rebellion and the Ratification of the Federal Constitution in Massachusetts," in Beeman et al. *Beyond Confederation,* 113–14.

38. J. R. Pole, "Shays's Rebellion: A Political Interpretation," in *The Reinterpretation of the American Revolution, 1763–1789,* ed. Jack Greene (New York, 1968), 416–17; Benjamin Lincoln Jr. to George Thatcher, 9 May 1787, BL Papers (MB).

Chapter 12: Securing the Revolution

Epigraph: BL to George Washington, 3 June 1788, Washington Papers (DLC).

1. Samuel Bannister Harding, *The Contest over the Ratification of the Federal Constitution in the State of Massachusetts* (Cambridge, Mass., 1896), 15–19; BL to Theodore Lincoln, 14 Dec. 1787, BL Papers (MB); George Washington to BL, 31 Jan. 1788, George Washington Papers (DLC).

2. Harding, *Contest over the Ratification,* 45–47, 59–60; BL to Theodore Lincoln, 14 Dec. 1787, BL Papers (MB); BL to George Washington, 3 Feb. 1788, Washington Papers (DLC).

3. Harding, *Contest over the Ratification,* 60–62, 85–89; BL to George Washington, 27 Jan. and 6 Feb. 1788, Washington Papers (DLC).

4. See BL to Washington, 27 Jan. and 3 and 6 Feb. 1788; and Washington to BL, 31 Jan. and 11 and 28 Feb. 1788, Washington Papers (DLC).

5. BL to Washington, 21 Jan. 1788, in *The Papers of Benjamin Lincoln,* ed. Frederick S. Allis Jr., microfilm ed., 13 reels (Boston, 1967), reel 9; *Catalogue of the Library of Benjamin Lincoln, Jr.* (from a notice of the sale) (Boston, 1788; Evans 21204).

6. BL to Mason and Gore, 1 Jan. 1788, and Maj. Haskell to BL, 4 Mar. 1788, in Allis, *Lincoln Papers,* reel 9; BL to Theodore Lincoln, 16 Feb. and 21 July 1788, BL Papers (MB).

7. Nominations for office took place at the town level among interested parties but rarely had the sanction of a town meeting. See the *Massachusetts Centinel,* 8 Mar. 1788, for the nomination of BL by a "large and respectable assembly" in the town of Roxbury and, in the same paper a week later (15 Mar.), a letter disputing the claim; BL to George Washington, 3 June 1788, Washington Papers (DLC); "A Friend to Union," *Massachusetts Centinel,* 15 Mar. 1788.

8. "Pythias," 15 Mar. 1788; "Candour," 2 Apr. 1788; "The Dreg No. II," 5 Apr. 1788, all in *Massachusetts Centinel;* Martin Gay to Mr. James, 7 July 1788, in *Publications of the Colonial Society of Massachusetts,* 62 vols. to date (Boston, 1892–), 3:383.

9. "Considerations on the Noble Order of Cincinnatus," *Boston Gazette,* 24 and 31 Mar. and 7, 14, 21, and 28 Apr. 1788; "Union," *Massachusetts Centinel,* 29 Mar. 1788; "Election Results," ibid., 31 May 1788; BL to George Washington, 3 June 1788, in *Correspondence of the American Revolution,* ed. Jared Sparks, 4 vols. (Boston, 1853), 4:223.

10. "Ancient Artillery Election," *Massachusetts Centinel,* 4 June 1788; "Harvard Commencement," *Independent Chronicle,* 17 July 1788; "Cincinnati," *Boston Gazette,* 7 July 1788.

11. "Society of the Cincinnati Dinner," *Boston Gazette,* 7 July 1788; Theodore Sedgwick to BL, 1 Aug. 1788, in Allis, *Lincoln Papers,* reel 9; BL to George Washington, 24 Sept., 25 Oct., 20 Dec. 1788, and 4 Jan. 1789, in *Papers of George Washington, Presidential Series,* ed. W. W. Abbot et al., 4 vols. to date (Charlottesville, Va., 1987–), 1:5–9, 66, 194, 233–35; Merrill Jensen and Robert A. Becker, eds., *The Documentary History of the First Federal Elections, 1788–1790,* 3 vols. to date (Madison, Wis., 1976–), 1:441; BL received one electoral vote for vice president from Georgia; see ibid., 3:441.

12. BL to John Adams, 22 Apr. and 8 July 1789, in Allis, *Lincoln Papers,* reel 9; Adams to BL, 19 June 1789, in *Historical Magazine,* 5:243.

13. Wells, *Life of Samuel Adams,* 3:285–86; Fowler, *Baron of Beacon Hill,* 273–74; BL to John Hancock, 26 June 1788, in Allis, *Lincoln Papers,* reel 9.

14. "Fair Play," 7 Aug. 1788, editorial note under a Boston 7 Aug. 1788 dateline; and "Propriety," 14 Aug. 1788, in the Boston *Independent Chronicle.* "Saratoga," Boston *Massachusetts Chronicle,* 13 Aug. 1788.

15. "Justice," Boston *Massachusetts Centinel,* 1 Nov. 1788. An earlier debate over the powers and intent of a committee inquiry into the matter by the General Court took place in November 1788, in ibid., 15 Nov. 1788; "Debates," in ibid., 17 and 21 Jan. 1789. For one reaction to the salary amount, see John Fenno to Joseph Ward, 7 Feb. 1789, in *Proceedings of the American Antiquarian Society,* 96 vols. to date (Worcester, Mass., 1880–), 89:318.

16. [Stephen Higginson], *Writings of Laco* (Boston, 1789; Evans 21886); "Junius," Boston *Independent Chronicle,* 5 Mar. 1789. BL's defeat in the April 1789 elections was attributed to "the virulence with which the Gov. had been attacked by a writer, Laco, in the Centinel, Boston"; see the entry for 6 Apr. 1789, *Diary of William Bentley,* 1:121.

17. "Junius," 5 Mar. 1789; "Sidney," 26 Mar. 1789; "An Independent Elector," 12 Mar. 1789, in the Boston *Independent Chronicle.* "Amicron," 28 Jan. 1789; "A Countryman," 7 Feb. 1789; "No Party Man," 18 Feb. 1789, in the Boston *Massachusetts Centinel.* The election results were announced on 27 May but appeared in the *Independent Chronicle,* 4 June 1789.

18. Jeremy Belknap to Ebenezer Hazard, 2 June 1789, *Massachusetts Historical Society Collections,* 43:134; *Independent Chronicle,* 4 June 1789.

19. James Warren to Elbridge Gerry, 19 Apr. 1789, in *A Study in Dissent: The Warren-Gerry Correspondence, 1776–1792,* ed. C. Harvey Gardiner (Carbondale, Ill., 1968), 222; BL to George Washington, 20 Feb. 1789, in Abbot et al., *Papers of George Washington, Presidential Series,* 1:330–32.

20. Washington to BL, 11 Mar. 1789, to James Bowdoin, 9 May 1789, and to Nathaniel Gorham, 9 May 1789, in Abbot et al., *Papers of George Washington, Presidential Series,* 1:383, 2:235–37. BL to Caleb Strong, 15 Apr., to Tristam Dalton, 15 Apr., to Nathaniel Gorham, 9 May, all 1789, and James Bowdoin to Washington, 24 Apr. 1789, in Allis, *Lincoln Papers,* reel 9. BL to Knox, 31 May 1789, Knox Papers (MHi).

21. BL to Nathaniel Gorham, 9 May, to Caleb Strong, 13 May, both 1789, and Jonathan Jackson to BL, 1 Aug. 1789, Theodore Sedgwick to BL, 1 Aug. 1789, and Theodore Lincoln to Martin Lincoln, 21 July 1789, in Allis, *Lincoln Papers,* reel 9. BL to George Washington, 16 July 1789, in Abbot et al., *Papers of George Washington, Presidential Series,* 3:213–14.

22. John Fenno to Joseph Ward, 5 Aug. 1789, *Proceedings of the American Antiquarian Society,* 89:335; Sedgwick to BL, 1 Aug. 1789, in Allis, *Lincoln Papers,* reel 9; Adams to John Lowell, 14 Sept. 1789, as qtd. in Smith, *John Adams,* 2:763.

23. Fisher Ames to Theophilus Parsons, 3 Aug. 1789, in Theophilus Parsons (fils), *Memoir of Theophilus Parsons, Chief Justice of the Supreme Court of Massachusetts* (Boston, 1859), 466. Jonathan Jackson to BL, 3 Aug.; Henry Knox to BL, 4 Aug.; BL to George Washington, 9 Aug.; BL to Theodore Lincoln, 20 Aug.;

and BL to John Hancock, 13 Aug. 1789, in Allis, *Lincoln Papers,* reel 9. Christopher Gore to Rufus King, 11 Aug. 1789, in King, *Life and Correspondence of Rufus King,* 1:366. BL's appointments were announced in an extraordinary edition of the *Massachusetts Centinel,* 12 Aug. 1789. They were: John Rice, deputy collector; William Shattuck and Patrick Phelon, weighers and gaugers; and J. C. Minot, inspector.

24. *ASP, Misc.,* 1:60; "Amount paid into the Treasury from the Collector of Boston for the Year 1801," Feb. 1802, Albert Gallatin Papers (NNU), reel 6.

25. BL to Alexander Hamilton, Nov.–Dec. 1789, 10 Nov. 1791, in Allis, *Lincoln Papers,* reel 9. For smuggling and the case of the Nova Scotia fish, see BL to Hamilton, 29 Apr., 17 May, and 13 and 29 July 1791, in ibid. Collectors of less stature and at smaller ports seemed to have more difficulty in adhering to a strict interpretation of the laws; see Leonard D. White, *The Federalists: A Study in Administrative History* (New York, 1956), 304–8.

26. Commission as Superintendent of Light-Houses, 10 Mar. 1790, in Allis, *Lincoln Papers,* reel 9; 1793 payment as superintendent, *ASP, Misc.,* 1:67; Thomas Wait to George Thaxter, 5 Dec. 1792, BL Papers (MB); Benjamin Goodhue to Oliver Wolcott Jr., 13 Apr. 1799, Wolcott Papers (CHi), 11:69. Representative correspondence about lighthouse construction, personnel, supply, etc., BL to Mr. Fosdick, 30 Nov. 1791; to Alexander Hamilton, 1 Dec. 1791; to Capt. Josiah Saywood, 12 June 1792; to Tench Coxe, 27 Sept., 30 Nov. 1792, 5 and 14 June 1794, and 22 July 1795, Allis, *Lincoln Papers,* reel 9. For Theodore and Martin Lincoln, see BL to Theodore Lincoln, 7 Sept. and 22 Oct. 1797, BL Papers (MB); and John Adams, Journal of executive actions, 25 Mar. 1797, Adams Papers (MHi), reel 195.

27. Carl E. Prince, *The Federalists and the Origins of the U.S. Civil Service* (New York, 1977), 14–16, 26. See the newspaper notice for the building of a "stout schooner" to be built for the U.S. under BL's direction, in the Fredericksburg *Virginia Herald,* 11 Apr. 1798. For the importance of BL's recommendation, see Fisher Ames to Paul Revere, 24 Jan. 1791, Paul Revere Papers (MHi); and Henry Knox to Mercy Warren, 9 July 1789, Warren-Adams Letters, *Massachusetts Historical Society Collections,* 55:316; "Petition to James Madison" (date torn), filed under BL, Letters of Application and Recommendation, Jefferson Administration, 1801–1809 (DNA). For the pressure on Jefferson for a complete removal of Federalists from office, see Noble E. Cunningham, *The Jeffersonian-Republicans in Power: Party Operations, 1801–1809* (Chapel Hill, N.C., 1963), 165–87. For BL's role in party politics during the 1790s, see chap. 14 of the present study.

Chapter 13: Frontier Diplomat

Epigraph: Benjamin Lincoln, "Observations on the Indians of North-America . . . ," *Massachusetts Historical Society Collections,* 1st ser., 5 (1798): 11–12.

1. Washington to BL, 11 and 20 Aug. 1789, and BL to Washington, 16 and

28 Aug. 1789, in *Papers of George Washington, Presidential Series,* ed. W. W. Abbot et al., 4 vols. to date (Charlottesville, Va., 1987–), 3:419–20, 477, 502–3, 551; *Massachusetts Centinel,* 26 Aug. and 5 Sept. 1789.

2. *Massachusetts Centinel,* 5 Sept. 1789. The argument that American expansion was "undergirded" by the "twin props of idealism and greed" is forcefully presented in J. Leitch Wright Jr., *Creeks and Seminoles: The Destruction and Regeneration of the Muscogulge People* (Lincoln, Neb., 1986), 129–37. For Georgia's expectations of the new federal government, see Lucia Burk Kinnaird, "The Rock Landing Conference of 1789," *North Carolina Historical Review* 9 (1932): 349–65. For the costliness of an Indian war, see Richard H. Kohn, *Eagle and Sword: The Beginnings of the Military Establishment in America* (New York, 1975), 96.

3. *Massachusetts Centinel,* 5 Sept. 1789; David Humphreys to George Washington, 21 Sept. 1789, in Frank Landon Humphreys, *Life and Times of David Humphreys,* 2 vols. (New York, 1917), 2:4–5. The commissioners were instructed to judge impartially the validity of the disputed treaties, but it was also noted that "should therefore the result of your investigation be unfavorable to the claims of Georgia it would be highly embarrassing to that State to relinquish the said lands to the Creeks." In other words, the fix was in. See "Instructions for the Commissioners to the Southern Indians," 29 Aug. 1789, in *The Papers of George Washington, Presidential series,* ed. William W. Abbot et al., 4 vols. to date (Charlottesville, Va., 1983–), 3:551–64. "Report of the Commissioners," 17 Nov. 1789, *American State Papers, Indian Affairs* (Washington, D.C., 1832), 1:68–79.

4. Wright, *Creeks and Seminoles,* 103; Charles R. Ritcheson, *Aftermath of Revolution: British Policy toward the U.S., 1783–1795* (Dallas, 1969), 175; Humphreys to George Washington, 21 Sept. 1789, in Humphreys, *Life of David Humphreys,* 2:5.

5. For a detailed look at U.S. relations with the Creeks, see Randolph C. Downes, "Creek-American Relations, 1782–1790," *Georgia Historical Quarterly* 21 (1937): 142–84; Alexander McGillivray to Estavan Miro, 10 Aug. 1789, and McGillivray to William Panton, 8 Oct. 1789, in John Walton Caughey, *McGillivray of the Creeks* (Norman, Okla., 1938), 244, 252.

6. Humphreys to Washington, 26 Sept. 1789, in Humphreys, *Life of David Humphreys,* 6–7; Report of the Commissioners, 17 Nov. 1789, *ASP, Indian Affairs,* 1:68–79.

7. Entry for 24 Nov. 1789, in *The Literary Diary of Ezra Stiles,* ed. Franklin B. Dexter, 4 vols. (New York, 1901), 3:371–72. On the black drink ceremony, see Charles H. Fairbanks, "The Function of Black Drink among the Creeks," in *Black Drink: A Native American Tea,* ed. Charles M. Hudson (Athens, Ga., 1979), 122–23; "Anecdote," Philadelphia *Pennsylvania Gazette,* 27 July 1796; Report of the Commissioners, 17 Nov. 1789, *ASP, Indian Affairs,* 1:73–74.

8. McGillivray to William Panton, 8 Oct. 1789 and 8 May 1790, in Caughey, *McGillivray of the Creeks,* 252–53, 260. American attempts to persuade the Creek chief, in whom, as he wrote, all "the arts of flattery, ambition and intimidation

were exhausted in vain," are detailed in Humphreys to Washington, 26 and 27 Sept. 1789, in Humphreys, *Life of David Humphreys*, 7–12; Report of the Commissioners, 19 Nov. 1789, *ASP, Indian Affairs*, 1:74–76.

9. Report of the Commissioners, 17 Nov. 1789, *ASP, Indian Affairs*, 1:77; entry of 24 Nov. 1780, in Dexter, *Literary Diary of Exra Stiles*, 3:371; Wright, *Creeks and Seminoles*, 137–39; McGillivray to John Leslie, 12 Oct. 1789, in Caughey, *McGillivray of the Creeks*, 255.

10. Entry for 24 Nov. 1789, in Dexter, *Literary Diary of Ezra Stiles*, 3:373; *Massachusetts Centinel*, 21 and 25 Nov. 1789; John Fenno to Joseph Ward, 20, 21, and 28 Nov. 1789, *Proceedings of the American Antiquarian Society*, 89:346–48; entry for 11 Jan. 1790, in *The Diary of William Maclay and Other Notes on Senate Debates*, ed. Kenneth R. Bowling and Helen E. Veit (Baltimore, 1988), 180.

11. "Instructions to Commissioners," 29 Aug. 1789, in Abbot, *Papers of George Washington, Presidential Series*, 3:559–60; Commissioners to the Secretary of War, 20 Nov. 1789, *ASP, Indian Affairs*, 1:78–79; BL's draft report, Nov. 1789, 1792, in *The Papers of Benjamin Lincoln*, ed. Frederick S. Allis Jr., microfilm ed., 13 reels (Boston, 1967), reel 9.

12. Report of the Commissioners, 17 Nov. 1789, *ASP, Indian Affairs*, 1:78.

13. The dynamic behind this fascination with the Indians and the attempt to create an enlightened policy toward them is laid out by Bernard W. Sheehan in *Seeds of Extinction: Jeffersonian Philanthropy and the American Indian* (Chapel Hill, N.C., 1973), esp. 119–47; see also Michael Allen, "Justice for the Indians: The Federalist Quest, 1783–1796," *Essex Institute Historical Collections* 122 (1986): 124–41.

14. Allen, "Justice for the Indians," 124–41; Andrew R. L. Cayton, *The Frontier Republic: Ideology and Politics in the Ohio Country, 1780–1825* (Kent, Ohio, 1986), 13–21.

15. BL to Rev. Jeremy Belknap, 21 Jan. 1792, in Allis, *Lincoln Papers*, reel 9.

16. BL to Rev. Jeremy Belknap, 21 Jan. 1792, in ibid., reel 9; "General Lincoln's Observations on the Indians of North-America, in Answer to some Remarks of Dr. Ramsay's," *Massachusetts Historical Society Collections* 5 (1798): 11.

17. BL to John Heckwelder, 30 Sept. 1795, in Allis, *Lincoln Papers*, reel 10.

18. BL to John Heckwelder, October 1793, in ibid.

19. "General Lincoln's Observations" (draft), October 1795, in ibid.

20. Ibid.

21. The most thorough treatment of U.S. policy toward the Indians of the Old Northwest is Wiley Sword, *President Washington's Indian War: The Struggle for the Old Northwest, 1790–1795* (Norman, Okla., 1985); see also Kohn, *Eagle and Sword*, 91–127, 141–57; Reginald Horsman, *Expansion and American Indian Policy* (E. Lansing, Mich., 1967), 84–103; and Francis Paul Prucha, *The Sword of the Republic: The United States Army on the Frontier, 1783–1846* (New York, 1969), 17–38.

22. The many strands of British interest can be followed in J. Leitch Wright Jr., *Britain and the American Frontier, 1783–1815* (Athens, Ga., 1975), 66–85; Simcoe to Henry Dundas, 17 June 1793, in *The Correspondence of Lt. Gov. John Graves Simcoe,* ed. E. A. Cruikshank, 5 vols. (Toronto, 1923), 1:357.

23. Sword, *Washington's War,* 223–231.

24. Ibid., 203–14. BL had been briefly considered to head the legion but was regarded as too old for such an active command. Washington noted BL's qualifications on his list of candidates: "sober, honest, brave and sensible, but infirm, past the vigor of life" (9 Mar. 1792, in Fitzpatrick, *Writings of Washington,* 31:509; Washington to Charles Carroll of Carrollton, 23 Jan. 1793, in ibid., 32:312–13; Jefferson to Thomas Pinckney, 27 Nov. 1793, in *The Writings of Thomas Jefferson,* ed. Andrew A. Lipscomb and A. E. Bergh, 20 vols. [Washington, D.C., 1903–4], 9:258).

25. Knox to BL, 9 Mar. 1793, in Allis, *Lincoln Papers,* reel 10; Instructions to the Commissioners, 26 Apr. 1793, *ASP, Indian Affairs,* 1:340–42; Kohn, *Eagle and Sword,* 100.

26. List of items for the Negotiations at Sandusky, Pickering Papers (MHi), reel 59; BL's Journal, in Allis, *Lincoln Papers,* reel 10.

27. Benjamin Lincoln, "Journal of a Treaty held in 1793 with the Indian Tribes Northwest of the Ohio, by Commissioners of the United States," *Massachusetts Historical Society Collections,* 3d ser., 5 (1836): 109–76.

28. BL Journal, in Allis, *Lincoln Papers,* reel 10.

29. Ibid.

30. Ibid.

31. For Simcoe's hospitality, see ibid.; Edward Hake Phillips, "Timothy Pickering at his Best: Indian Commissioner, 1790–1794," *Essex Institute Historical Collection* 102 (1966): 186; and Mary Quayle Innis, ed., *Mrs. Simcoe's Diary* (Toronto, 1965), 95, 96.

32. Wright, *British and Frontier,* 75; Sword, *Washington's War,* 239–43, 245–48.

33. Simcoe to Alured Clark, 26 July 1793, Cruikshank, *Correspondence of Simcoe,* 1:400; BL Journal, in Allis, *Lincoln Papers,* reel 10.

34. BL Journal, in Allis, *Lincoln Papers,* reel 10.

35. Ibid.; John Askin to William Robertson, 24 June 1793, in Cruikshank, *Correspondence of Simcoe,* 1:369; Paul A. W. Wallace, ed., *Thirty Thousand Miles with John Heckwelder* (Pittsburgh, Pa., 1958), 312–13.

36. BL Journal, in Allis, *Lincoln Papers,* reel 10.

37. Ibid.

38. Proclamation by Anthony Wayne, 22 Apr. 1793, Knox to Arthur St. Clair, and to the governor of Virginia, both 24 Apr. 1793, in *The Territorial Papers of the United States,* ed. Clarence E. Carter, 28 vols. (Washington, D.C., 1934–75), 2:452–53. For Wayne's activities, see Kohn, *Eagle and Sword,* 151–55; and Sword, *Washington's War,* 235–37. In addition, on 20 June the government had adver-

tised in a Philadelphia newspaper a contract for supplying rations for the coming year to U.S. army posts in the Miami country, including the spot where the Indians were currently convening (Joseph Chew to Alexander McKee, 13 Sept. 1793, in Cruikshank, *Correspondence of Simcoe,* 2:37). Lincoln was not satisfied with the commissioners' public letters to the president and the secretary of war. On 10 July Lincoln wrote Knox a private letter warning of trouble Wayne could cause to the commissioners' mission and personal safety. Knox ordered Wayne to keep his army at Fort Washington on the Ohio River until further orders; see BL Journal, in Allis, *Lincoln Papers,* reel 10; and Kohn, *Eagle and Sword,* 151–53.

39. BL Journal, in Allis, *Lincoln Papers,* reel 10.

40. Ibid.; U.S. Commissioners to Alexander McKee, 21 July 1793, in Cruikshank, *Correspondence of Simcoe,* 1:395. Elliott's role at the Indian council is given in Reginald Horsman, *Matthew Elliott, British Indian Agent* (Detroit, 1964), 73–91.

41. BL Journal, in Allis, *Lincoln Papers,* reel 10; Wallace, *John Heckwelder,* 313–16. Heckwelder had expressed his skepticism weeks earlier after hearing reports that "the [Indian] Nations were assembling for War, there being already 1,100 Men on the Spot, and scarcely a Woman to be seen among them, whereas otherwise, when Indians got to Treaties, they are careful in bringing their Women and Children on, in order to obtain more Presents."

42. BL Journal, in Allis, *Lincoln Papers,* reel 10; Wallace, *John Heckwelder,* 316; Phillips, "Timothy Pickering," 189.

43. Wallace, *John Heckwelder,* 317–18; BL Journal, in Allis, *Lincoln Papers,* reel 10.

44. BL Journal, in Allis, *Lincoln Papers,* reel 10.

45. Ibid.

46. Ibid.; Wallace, *John Heckwelder,* 319–20.

47. BL Journal, in Allis, *Lincoln Papers,* reel 10.

48. Ibid.

49. Ibid.; Phillips, "Timothy Pickering," 193; Kohn, *Eagle and Sword,* 154. Arrangements had been made in the spring to inform Wayne of the results of the treaty; see Knox to the commissioners, 29 Apr. 1793, in Carter, *U.S. Territorial Papers,* 2:454.

50. BL Journal, in Allis, *Lincoln Papers,* reel 10. The voyage from Ohio to New York is related in great detail in Wallace, *John Heckwelder,* 321–31.

51. Sword, *Washington's War,* 272–331; BL to John Heckwelder, Oct. 1795, in Allis, *Lincoln Papers,* reel 10.

Chapter 14: The Old Federalist

Epigraph: Washington birthday dinner, 24 Feb. 1798, Boston *Columbian Centinel.*

1. William Sullivan, *The Public Men of the Revolution* (Philadelphia, 1847), 128–29.

2. BL to Lachlan McIntosh, 14 Aug. 1779, Charleston, Benjamin Lincoln Letterbook (Lbk) I (MB). For the ideological origins of Massachusetts federalism, see James M. Banner Jr., *To the Hartford Convention: The Federalists and the Origins of Party Politics in Massachusetts, 1789–1815* (New York, 1970), 3–52. For a portrait of "Federalists of the Old School," see David Hackett Fischer, *The Revolution of American Conservatism: The Federalist Party in the Era of Jeffersonian Democracy* (New York, 1965), 1–28.

3. See, for example, the letters exchanged between BL and Alexander Hamilton, in vols. 6–15 of *The Papers of Alexander Hamilton,* ed. Harold C. Syrett and Jacob E. Cooke, 27 vols. (New York, 1961–87). Public dinners almost always took on a partisan tone in the late 1790s and thereafter. In New England, especially, the occasion of George Washington's birthday, the Feast of Shells in honor of the Pilgrim landing, or dinners to honor prominent politicians such as John Adams and Alexander Hamilton were synonymous with Federalist rallies. Lincoln attended all the important dinners and presided over many. See, for example, the Feast of Shells in 1798, 1800, and 1802, in *Publications of the Colonial Society of Massachusetts,* 17:313, 324, 335; and, for a dinner honoring Hamilton, see *Columbian Centinel,* 21 June 1800. For a detailed and judicious treatment of the politics of the 1790s, see Stanley Elkins and Eric McKitrick, *The Age of Federalism* (New York, 1993).

4. On the influence of customhouse collectors, see Charles Pinckney to James Madison, 26 May 1801, in *The Papers of James Madison, Secretary of State Series,* ed. Robert J. Brugger et al., 3 vols. to date (Charlottesville, Va., 1986–), 1:230. For BL's support of Adams, see his role as chairman of a committee that organized a public dinner in the president's support (Philadelphia *Gazette of the U.S.,* 12, 22, and 25 Aug. 1797). Stephen Higginson thought that Knox, Gerry, and Lincoln's "obsequious toadying" to Adams was pushing him in the direction of peace (Higginson to Oliver Wolcott Jr., 29 Mar. 1799, Wolcott Papers [CHi]). One indication of BL's moderation is his comment on *Porcupine's Gazette,* an ultra-Federalist newspaper to which he subscribed for a time. For him Peter Porcupine was a "severe writer, too much so I think" (BL to Theodore Lincoln, 7 Sept. 1797, BL Papers [MB]).

5. On BL's visits to Philadelphia, see the report of the marriage of William Jackson to Eliza Willing, 11 Nov. 1795, in *PMHB* 21:27; and Jackson to BL, 26 Sept. 1796, in *The Papers of Benjamin Lincoln,* ed. Frederick S. Allis Jr., microfilm ed., 13 reels (Boston, 1967), reel 10. For the improvement of the customhouse, see the notice, 31 Mar. 1798, as qtd. in Ann Smith Lainhart, ed., "John Haven Dexter and the 1789 Boston City Directory," *New England Historical and Genealogical Register* 140 (1986): 52. For additions to BL's house, see author's conversation with Elizabeth Beveridge, 1987. On houses for Abner Lincoln and Henry Ware, see Lincoln, *History of the Town of Hingham,* 1:198; and Ware to BL, 10 Feb. 1795, in Allis, *Lincoln Papers,* reel 10. BL was a founding member of the American Academy of Arts and Sciences, see *Life, Journals and Correspondence of Rev. Manasseh Cutler, LL.D.,* ed. William Parker Cutler and Julia Perkins

Cutler, 2 vols. (Cincinnati, 1888), 1:93, 2:215–19, 354–55; and letters to BL published in the Boston *Independent Chronicle,* 27 Mar. 1788 and 12 Feb. 1789. For BL's custodianship of children, see his letter to William Jackson, 26 Mar. 1800, in Allis, *Lincoln Papers,* reel 13; and R. K. Meade to BL, 12 June 1798, in ibid., reel 10. That Hingham was "famous for a number of small schools" was recorded by the Duke de la Rochefoucault Liancourt in his book *Travels through the United States of North America . . . ,* 2 vols. (London, 1799), 2:250–53.

6. George Cabot to John Adams, 29 Sept. 1798, qtd. in Henry Cabot Lodge, *Life and Letters of George Cabot* (Boston, 1878), 166; for BL's support of debt assumption, see his letter to Fisher Ames, 20 May 1790, in Allis, *Lincoln Papers,* reel 9.

7. The story of the fight over the army command is told at length in Manning J. Dauer, *The Adams Federalists* (Baltimore, 1953); and Stephen G. Kurtz, *The Presidency of John Adams: The Collapse of Federalism* (Philadelphia, 1957). Adams recalled later that his instinct was to call back into service all the old revolutionary officers and "nominate every Survivor according to the Rank he held at the conclusion of the War." No one, however, "would have heard the proposition with patience" (Adams to Richard Rush, 11 Aug. 1813, *PMHB* 60:445). Pickering told a different version: according to him, Adams refused his advice to name Alexander Hamilton the first major general, saying he would "sooner have Gates or Lincoln or Morgan." Pickering replied that Morgan was an excellent soldier but had a "broken constitution," Gates was "now an old woman," and Lincoln was "always asleep" (Pickering to George Washington, 13 Sept. 1798, Pickering Papers [MHi]).

8. George Cabot to Timothy Pickering, 27 Sept. 1798, in Lodge, *Life of George Cabot,* 164–65; Benjamin Goodhue to Timothy Pickering, 17 Sept., and Pickering to Goodhue, 24 Sept. 1798, Pickering Papers (MHi).

9. BL to William Heath, 19 Mar., and Heath to BL, 25 Mar. 1799, in Allis, *Lincoln Papers,* reel 10.

10. John Adams to Abigail Adams, 9 Jan. 1797, Adams Papers (MHi); Abigail Adams to William Smith, 7 July 1798, Smith-Carter Collection (MHi); Richard H. Kohn, *Eagle and Sword: The Beginnings of the Military Establishment in America* (New York, 1975), 230–34. Oliver Wolcott requested BL's opinion whether current captains "possess the prudence, bravery, diligence and talents for command" in the U.S. navy; see Wolcott to BL, 7 June 1798, in Allis, *Lincoln Papers,* reel 10; Stephen Higginson to Timothy Pickering, 12 Jan. 1800, in "Letters of Stephen Higginson," *Annual Report of the American Historical Association for the Year 1896,* 2 vols. (Washington, D.C., 1897), 1:835.

11. Abigail Adams to John Adams, 2 June 1800, Adams Papers (MHi).

12. Henry Knox to BL, 20 Oct. 1797; 4 Jan.; 29 Mar.; 5 May; 12, 20, 22, 28, and 30 June; 1, 5, and 11 July; and 14 Aug. 1798; and BL to Knox, 28 Dec. 1797, in Allis, *Lincoln Papers,* reel 10. Benjamin Goodhue to Timothy Pickering, 3 Oct. 1798, Pickering Papers (MHi). George Cabot to Pickering, 26 and 31 Oct. 1798, in Lodge, *Life and Letters of George Cabot,* 174, 176. Jefferson to Madison, 3

Jan. 1799, in *The Papers of James Madison,* ed. William T. Hutchinson et al., 1st ser., vols. 1–10 (Chicago, 1962–77), vols. 11–17 (Charlottesville, Va., 1977–91), 17:194.

13. BL to John Adams, 7 Nov. 1798, Adams Papers (MHi).

14. Oliver Wolcott Jr. to Stephen Higginson, 21 Nov. 1798, and Higginson to Wolcott, 13 Dec. 1798, Oliver Wolcott Jr. Papers (CHi).

15. BL to Theodore Lincoln, 8 Nov. 1798, 16 Sept. 1799, and 8 Oct. 1806, BL Papers (MB); BL accounts with Knox, 16 Apr. 1802, BL to Knox, 4 June 1802, in Allis, *Lincoln Papers,* reel 11. BL bought back his home, etc., from Caleb Stimson for $8,003.13 on 2 Oct. 1800. As the story goes, Lincoln said that "these people were given to understand that if Harry Knox did not pay them Ben Lincoln would, and Ben Lincoln will" (unidentified newspaper account, 1886, in ibid., reel 11). Knox to BL, 3 July and 21 Oct. 1804, and BL to Knox, 20 and 26 Sept. 1804, Knox Papers (MHi). The final settlement is described in William Sullivan, *The Public Men of the Revolution* (Philadelphia, 1847), 134n. That BL was exasperated is evident from his letter to Henry Jackson, 27 Nov. 1799, BL Papers (NcD).

16. BL to John Adams, 30 Mar. 1801, Adams Papers (MHi); BL to Thomas Pinckney, 24 Nov. 1801, in Allis, *Lincoln Papers,* reel 11; Benjamin Goodhue to Timothy Pickering, 17 Sept. and 3 Oct. 1798, Pickering Papers (MHi); BL's letter to his subordinates, qtd. in Sibley and Shipton, *Biographical Sketches of Those Who Attended Harvard College,* 12:437. I found no evidence for Carl Prince's assertion that some kind of deal was struck between the administration and Lincoln to allow him to keep the collectorship; see Carl E. Prince, *The Federalists and the Origins of the U.S. Civil Service* (New York, 1977), 26.

17. James Sullivan to James Madison, 8 July 1804, James Madison Papers (DLC); Gallatin wanted Lincoln removed for "indecent and outrageous conduct" that stemmed from Lincoln's hosting a dinner in honor of Christopher Gore on 24 Apr. 1804; see Gallatin to Jefferson, 30 May 1804, qtd. in Henry Adams, *The Life of Albert Gallatin* (1879; reprint, New York, 1943), 193. For the reports of the dinner and toasts, and criticism of them, see *Boston Gazette,* 24 and 26 Apr., *Boston Independent Chronicle,* 30 Apr., and the *Columbian Centinel,* 5 May 1804.

18. James Sullivan to James Madison, 17 Feb. 1805, Letters of Application and Recommendation, Jefferson Administration (DNA) (filed under Elbridge Gerry).

19. Mary Otis Lincoln to BL, 21 Mar. 1805, in Allis, *Lincoln Papers,* reel 11. The portrait was presented to Lincoln and passed on to his descendants. It now hangs in the Massachusetts Historical Society in Boston.

20. James Lovell to Mary Lovell Pickard, 10 Jan. 1802, qtd. in Edward B. Hall, *Memoir of Mary L. Ware* (Boston, 1853), 10–11; BL to Theodore Lincoln, 13 Oct. 1801, BL Papers (MB); Theophilus Parsons (fils), *Memoir of Theophilus Parsons, Chief Justice of the Supreme Court of Massachusetts* (Boston, 1859), 316–18; Abigail Adams to Mercy Otis Warren, 9 Mar. 1807, in *Warren-Adams Letters,* 2:354.

21. BL to Theodore Lincoln, 8 Oct. 1806, BL Papers (MB); Theodore Lincoln to BL, 31 Oct. 1806, in Allis, *Lincoln Papers,* reel 11; Thomas Jefferson to BL, 27 Nov. 1806, and BL to Jefferson, 5 Dec. 1806, Thomas Jefferson Papers (DLC).

22. Marshall Smelser, *The Democratic Republic, 1801–1815* (New York, 1968), 163–69. BL to Albert Gallatin, 4 Mar. and 24 June 1807; Gallatin to Jefferson, 18 Mar. 1807; Benjamin Weld to Gallatin, 22 Nov. 1808, Albert Gallatin Papers (NNU). BL to Jefferson, 16 Jan. 1809, and BL to James Lovell, 20 Jan. 1809, in Allis, *Lincoln Papers,* reel 11.

23. "Resolutions of the Boston Town Meeting," 24 Jan. 1809, *Columbian Centinel* (Boston), 25 Jan. 1809; Smelser, *Democratic Republic,* 168–69; *National Intelligencer* (Washington, D.C.), 25 Jan. 1809; Levi Lincoln to Albert Gallatin, 30 Jan. 1809, Albert Gallatin Papers (NNU).

24. *Annals of Congress,* 10th Cong., 2d sess., 1173–83.

25. For BL's settlement with Martin Lincoln, see deeds made in 1796, in Allis, *Lincoln Papers,* reel 10; and, for Theodore Lincoln, see the series of deeds from 1793 to 1810, BL Papers (MB). For Lincoln's will, see Allis, *Lincoln Papers,* reel 12.

26. Interview with Elizabeth Beveridge at the Lincoln House, Hingham, 1986.

27. Obituary notice, Boston *Columbian Centinel,* 12 May 1810; John Adams to Benjamin Rush, 14 May 1810, in *Old Family Letters,* ed. Alexander Biddle, 2 vols. (Philadelphia, 1892), 1:255–56. Funeral sermon, in Allis, *Lincoln Papers,* reel 11.

28. John Adams to Benjamin Rush, 14 May 1810, in Biddle, *Old Family Letters,* 1:255–56.

29. Douglass Adair, "Fame and the Founding Fathers," in *Fame and the Founding Fathers: Essays by Douglass Adair,* ed. Trevor Colbourne (New York, 1974), 8, 13.

30. *Boston Gazette,* 10 May 1810.

Bibliography

Primary Sources

Manuscript Collections

Boston Public Library, Boston
        Benjamin Lincoln Papers
        Benjamin Lincoln Letterbook, Charleston
Charleston Library Society, Charleston
        John Rutledge Papers
Columbia University Library, New York City
        Otis Family Papers
        Otis-Gay Papers
        Special Miscellaneous Collection
Connecticut Historical Society, Hartford
        Jonathan Trumbull Sr. Papers
        Oliver Wolcott Jr. Papers
        Jeremiah Wadsworth Papers
Duke University Library, Durham, North Carolina
        Benjamin Lincoln Papers
Georgia Historical Society, Savannah
        Houstoun Collection
University of Georgia Library, Athens
        Telamon Cuyler Collection
        Benjamin Lincoln Letterbook
Harvard University, Houghton Library, Cambridge
        Benjamin Lincoln Manuscripts
Library of Congress, Washington, D.C.
        Benjamin Lincoln Journal, Savannah
        Nathanael Greene Papers
        Charles Hogendorp Papers
        Thomas Jefferson Papers
        James Madison Papers
        George Washington Papers

Massachusetts Historical Society, Boston
        Cushing Family Papers
        William Cushing Papers
        C. E. French Papers
        William Heath Papers
        Henry Knox Papers
        Benjamin Lincoln Papers
        Joseph Palmer Papers
        Timothy Pickering Papers
        Quincy Family Papers
        Smith-Carter Collection
        Artemas Ward Papers
Morristown National Historical Park, Morristown, New Jersey
        Lloyd W. Smith Collection
National Archives, Washington, D.C.
        Papers of the Continental Congress
        Records of the U.S. General Accounting Office
        Letters of Application and Recommendation, Jefferson Administration
New-York Historical Society, New York City
        Horatio Gates Papers
        Alexander McDougall Papers
        Steuben Papers
New York Public Library, New York City
        Thomas Addis Emmet Collection
        Miscellaneous Manuscripts
University of North Carolina, Chapel Hill
        Richard Caswell Papers
        Preston Davie Collection
        Revolutionary Papers, Southern Historical Collection
        Jethro Sumner Papers
South Carolina Historical Society
        John Laurens Papers

Newspapers

Boston Evening Post
Boston Gazette
Gazette of the United States (Philadelphia)
Independent Chronicle (Boston)
Massachusetts Centinel (later *Columbian Centinel*, Boston).
Massachusetts Chronicle (Boston)
National Intelligencer (Washington, D.C.)
Pennsylvania Gazette (Philadelphia)
Porcupine's Gazette (Philadelphia)
Virginia Herald (Fredericksburg)

Published Sources

Abbot, William W., et al., eds. *The Papers of George Washington, Revolutionary War series.* 6 vols. to date. Charlottesville, Va., 1983–.

——. *The Papers of George Washington, Presidential Series.* 4 vols. to date. Charlottesville, Va., 1987–.

The Adams Papers. Massachusetts Historical Society microfilm edition. 608 reels. Boston, 1954–59.

Adams, Henry, ed. *The Writings of Albert Gallatin.* 3 vols. Philadelphia, 1879.

Allaire, Anthony. *Diary of Lieutenant Anthony Allaire.* New York, 1968.

Allis, Frederick S., Jr., ed. *The Benjamin Lincoln Papers.* Massachusetts Historical Society microfilm edition. 13 reels. Boston, 1968.

——. *The Timothy Pickering Papers.* Massachusetts Historical Society microfilm edition. 69 reels. Boston, 1966.

American State Papers. Documents, Legislative and Executive . . . . 38 vols. Washington, D.C., 1832–61.

Balch, E. W., trans. "Narrative of the Prince of Broglie." *The Magazine of American History* 1 (1877): 231–35.

Baxter, James Phinney, ed. *Documentary History of the State of Maine.* 19 vols. Portland, Maine, 1889–1916.

Bentley, William. *The Diary of William Bentley, D.D.* 4 vols. Salem, Mass., 1905–14.

Berry, Joseph B., ed. "Ward Chipman Diary." *Essex Institute Historical Collections* 87 (1951): 211–41.

Bowling, Kenneth R., and Helen E. Veit, eds. *The Diary of William Maclay and Other Notes on Senate Debates.* Baltimore, 1988.

"Boyle's Journal of Occurrences in Boston." *New England Historical and Genealogical Register* 85 (1931): 117–33.

Brown, Richard D., ed. "Shays's Rebellion and Its Aftermath: A View from Springfield, Massachusetts, 1787." *William and Mary Quarterly,* 3rd ser., 40 (1983): 598–615.

Brugger, Robert J., et al., eds. *The Papers of James Madison, Secretary of State Series.* 3 vols. to date. Charlottesville, Va., 1986– .

Burnett, Edmund C., ed. *Letters of Members of the Continental Congress.* 8 vols. Washington, D.C., 1921–36.

Butterfield, Lyman H., et al., eds. *Adams Family Correspondence.* 4 vols. to date. Cambridge, Mass., 1963.

——. *The Book of Abigail and John: Selected Letters of the Adams Family, 1762–1784.* Cambridge, Mass., 1975.

——. *Diary and Autobiography of John Adams.* 4 vols. Cambridge, Mass., 1961.

——. *Letters of Benjamin Rush.* 2 vols. Princeton, N.J., 1951.

Campbell, Maria. *Revolutionary Services and Civil Life of Gen. William Hull.* Philadelphia, 1848.

277

Carter, Clarence E., ed. *The Territorial Papers of the United States.* 28 vols. Washington, D.C., 1934–75.

Chastellux, Marquis de. *Travels in North America in the Years 1780, 1781, and 1782.* Translated and edited by Howard C. Rice, Jr. Chapel Hill, N.C., 1963.

"Letters of Joseph Clay, Merchant of Savannah, 1776–1793." *Georgia Historical Society Collections* 8 (1913).

Cruikshank, E. A., ed. *The Correspondence of Lieut. Gov. John Graves Simcoe.* 5 vols. Toronto, 1923.

Cutler, William Parker, and Julia Perkins Cutler, eds. *Life, Journals and Correspondence of Rev. Manasseh Cutler, LL.D.* 2 vols. Cincinnati, 1888.

"Sir Henry Clinton's Journal of the Charlestown Siege." *South Carolina Historical Magazine* 66 (1965): 147–82.

Dexter, Franklin B., ed. *Literary Diary of Ezra Stiles.* 3 vols. New York, 1901.

Duane, William, ed. *Extracts from the Diary of Christopher Marshall, 1774–1781.* Albany, 1877.

Egleston, Thomas. *The Life of John Paterson, Major-General in the Revolutionary Army.* New York, 1894.

Ewald, Johann. *Diary of the American War: A Hessian Journal.* Translated and edited by Joseph P. Tustin. New Haven, Conn., 1979.

Ferguson, E. James, et al., eds. *The Papers of Robert Morris, 1781–1784.* 7 vols. to date. Pittsburgh, 1973–.

Fitzpatrick, John C., ed. *The Writings of George Washington, From the Original Sources.* 39 vols. Washington, D.C., 1931–44.

Force, Peter, ed. *American Archives.* 9 vols. Washington, D.C., 1839–53.

Ford, Worthington, C., et al., eds. *Journals of the Continental Congress, 1774–1789.* 34 vols. Washington, D.C., 1904–37.

Friedlaender, Marc, and Robert J. Taylor, eds. *The Diary of John Quincy Adams.* 2 vols. to date. Cambridge, Mass., 1981–.

Gardiner, C. Harvey, ed. *A Study in Dissent: The Warren-Gerry Correspondence, 1776–1792.* Carbondale, Ill., 1968.

Gibbes, R. W., ed. *Documentary History of the American Revolution.* 3 vols. New York, 1857.

Gilman, Caroline, ed. *Letters of Eliza Wilkinson.* New York, 1839.

William Gordon Letters. *Massachusetts Historical Society Proceedings.* Vol. 63. Boston, Mass., 1929–30.

Hammond, Otis G., ed. *Letters and Papers of General John Sullivan, Continental Army.* 3 vols. Concord, N.H., 1930–39.

Hastings, Hugh, ed. *Public Papers of George Clinton, First Governor of New York.* 10 vols. Albany, N.Y., 1899–1914.

Heath, William. *Memoirs of the American War.* Boston, 1798.

Higginson, Thomas Wentworth. *Life and Times of Stephen Higginson.* Boston, 1907.

Letters of Stephen Higginson. *Annual Report of the American Historical Association for the Year 1896.* 2 vols. Washington, D.C., 1897.

Historical Magazine and Notes and Queries Concerning the Antiquities, History, and Biography of America. 10 vols. Boston, 1857–66.

Hough, Franklin B. *Siege of Savannah.* Albany, 1866.

Humphreys, Frank Landon. *Life and Times of David Humphreys.* 2 vols. New York, 1917.

Hutchinson, William T., et al., eds. *The Papers of James Madison.* 1st ser., 10 vols. Chicago, 1962–77; 7 vols. Charlottesville, Va., 1977–90.

Innis, Mary Quayle, ed. *Mrs. Simcoe's Diary.* Toronto, 1965.

Izerda, Stanley, ed. *Lafayette in the Age of the American Revolution.* 5 vols. to date. Ithaca, N.Y., 1977–.

Papers of Thomas Jefferson. Presidential Microfilm edition.

Jackson, Donald, and Dorothy Twohig, eds. *The Diaries of George Washington.* 6 vols. Charlottesville, Va., 1976–79.

Jones, Charles C., Jr., ed. *The Siege of Savannah in 1779, as Described in Two Contemperaneous Journals of French Officers.* Albany, 1874.

Jones, George Fenwick, ed. "The 1780 Siege of Charlestown as Experienced by a Hessian Officer." *South Carolina Historical Magazine* 88 (1987): 23–33, 63–75.

King, Charles R., ed. *Life and Correspondence of Rufus King.* 6 vols. New York, 1894–1900.

Kirkland, John T. "Notices of the Life of Major-General Benjamin Lincoln." *Massachusetts Historical Society Collections,* 2d ser., 3 (1815): 233–55.

Knight, Russell W., ed. "General John Glover's Letterbook." *Essex Institute Historical Collection* 112 (1976): 1–53.

Lainhart, Ann Smith, ed. "John Haven Dexter and the 1789 Boston City Directory." *New England Historical and Genealogical Register* 140 (1986): 23–62.

Lamb, Roger. "An Original and Authentic Journal of Occurrences during the Late American War, from Its Commencement to the Year 1783." In *South Carolina: The Grand Tour, 1780–1865.* Edited by Thomas D. Clark. Columbia, S.C., 1973.

Lee, Henry. *Memoirs of the War in the Southern Department of the United States.* New York, 1812.

Lincoln, Benjamin. "Journal of a Treaty Held in 1793 with the Indian Tribes Northwest of the Ohio, by Commissioners of the United States." *Massachusetts Historical Society Collections,* 3d ser., 5 (1836): 109–76.

Lipscomb, Andrew A., and Albert E. Bergh, eds. *The Writings of Thomas Jefferson.* 20 vols. Washington, D.C., 1903–4.

MacKenzie, Roderick. *Strictures on Lt. Col. Tarleton's History . . . .* London, 1787.

McRee, Griffith J. *Life and Correspondence of James Iredell.* 2 vols. New York, 1857.

Mays, David John, ed. *The Letters and Papers of Edmund Pendleton, 1734–1803.* 2 vols. Charlottesville, Va., 1967.

Mevers, Frank C., ed. *The Papers of Josiah Bartlett.* Hanover, N.H., 1979.

Minot, George Richards. *The History of the Insurrections, in Massachusetts, in the Year 1786 and the Rebellion Consequent Thereon.* Worcester, Mass., 1788.

Moncrieff, C. K. Scott, trans. *Memoirs of the Duc de Lauzun.* London, 1928.

Moultrie, William. *Memoirs of the American Revolution.* 2 vols. New York, 1802.

Murdoch, Richard K., ed. "A French Account of the Siege of Charleston, 1780." *South Carolina Historical Magazine* 67 (1966): 138–54.

Oliver, Fitch Edward, ed. *The Diary of William Pynchon of Salem.* Boston, 1890.

Pace, Antonio, ed. and trans. *Luigi Castiglioni's Viaggio: Travels in the United States of North America, 1785–87.* Syracuse, N.Y., 1983.

Parsons, Jacob Cox, ed. *Extracts from the Diary of Jacob Hiltzheimer of Philadelphia, 1765–1798.* Philadelphia, 1893.

Parsons, Theophilus (fils). *Memoir of Theophilus Parsons, Chief Justice of the Supreme Court of Massachusetts.* Boston, 1859.

Pettengill, Ray, ed. *Letters from America, 1776–1779: Being Letters of Brunswick, Hessian and Waldeck Officers with the British Armies during the Revolution.* Boston, 1924.

Pickering, Octavius. *The Life of Timothy Pickering.* 4 vols. Boston, 1867–73.

Prince, Carl E., and Helen H. Fineman, eds. *The Papers of Albert Gallatin.* Microfilm edition. 46 reels. Philadelphia, 1969.

Prince, Carl E., and Mary Lou Lustig, eds. *The Papers of William Livingston.* 5 vols. New Brunswick, N.J., 1979–89.

Ramsay, David. *The History of the Revolution of South Carolina.* 2 vols. Trenton, N.J., 1785.

Reed, William B. *Life and Correspondence of Joseph Reed.* 2 vols. Philadelphia, 1847.

Rice, Howard C., Jr., and Anne S. K. Brown, eds. and trans. *The American Campaigns of Rochambeau's Army, 1780, 1781, 1782, 1783.* 2 vols. Princeton, N.J., and Providence, R.I., 1972.

Ryden, George Herbert. *Letters To and From Caesar Rodney, 1756–1784.* Philadelphia, 1933.

Schoepf, Johann David. *Travels in the Confederation, 1783–1784.* Edited by Alfred J. Morrison. 2 vols. Philadelphia, 1911.

Shipton, Clifford K., and James E. Mooney. *National Index of American Imprints through 1800: The Short-Title Evans.* 2 vols. American Antiquarian Society, 1969.

Showman, Richard K., et al., eds. *The Papers of General Nathanael Greene.* 7 vols. to date. Chapel Hill, N.C., 1976–.

Smith, Paul H., ed. *Letters of Delegates to Congress, 1774–1789.* 20 vols. to date. Washington, D.C., 1976–.

Smith, William Henry, ed. *The St. Clair Papers.* 2 vols. Cincinnati, 1882.

Sparks, Jared, ed. *Correspondence of the American Revolution; being the Letters of Eminent Men to George Washington.* 4 vols. Boston, 1853.

———. *The Life of Gouverneur Morris.* 3 vols. Boston, 1832.

———. *The Works of Benjamin Franklin.* 10 vols. Boston, 1856.

Staples, William R., ed. *Rhode Island in the Continental Congress.* Providence, R.I., 1870.

Stark, Caleb. *Memoir and Official Correspondence of General John Stark.* Boston, 1972.

Syrett, Harold C., and Jacob E. Cooke, eds. *The Papers of Alexander Hamilton.* 27 vols. New York, 1961–87.

Tarleton, Banastre. *A History of the Campaigns of 1780 and 1781, in the Southern Provinces of North America.* London, 1787.

Taylor, Robert J., ed. *The Papers of John Adams.* 6 vols. to date. Cambridge, Mass., 1977– .

Temple-Bowdoin Papers. *Massachusetts Historical Society Collections.* Ser. 7, vol. 7. Boston, 1907.

Thatcher, James. *Military Journal of the American Revolution.* Hartford, Conn., 1862.

Thomas, E. S. *Reminiscences of the Last Sixty-five Years.* 2 vols. Hartford, Conn., 1840.

Todd, Charles Burr. *Life and Letters of Joel Barlow, LL.D.* New York, 1886.

Uhlendorf, Bernard A., ed. and trans. *The Siege of Charleston. With an Account of the Province of South Carolina: Diaries and Letters of Hessian Officers from the von Jungkenn Papers in the William L. Clements Library.* Ann Arbor, Mich., 1938.

Wallace, Paul A. W. *Thirty Thousand Miles with John Heckwelder.* Pittsburgh, 1958.

Warren-Adams Letters. *Massachusetts Historical Society Collections.* Vols. 72–73. Boston, 1917–25.

Wells, William V. *The Life and Public Services of Samuel Adams.* 3 vols. Boston, 1865.

Calendar of the General Otho Holland Williams Papers in the Maryland Historical Society. Baltimore, 1940.

Whisenhunt, Donald W., ed. *Delegate from New Jersey: The Journal of John Fell.* Port Washington, N.Y., 1973.

Secondary Sources

Books

Adair, Douglass. *Fame and the Founding Fathers: Essays by Douglass Adair.* Edited by Trevor Colbourne. New York, 1974.

Adams, Henry. *The Life of Albert Gallatin.* 1879. Reprint, New York, 1943.

Akers, Charles W. *The Divine Politician: Samuel Cooper and the American Revolution in Boston.* Boston, 1982.

Alberts, Robert C. *The Golden Voyage: The Life and Times of William Bingham, 1752–1804.* Boston, 1969.

Alden, John R. *General Charles Lee: Traitor or Patriot.* Baton Rouge, La., 1951.

Alexander, Edward P. *A Revolutionary Conservative: James Duane of New York.* New York, 1938.

Allan, Herbert S. *John Hancock: Patriot in Purple.* New York, 1953.

Allen, David Grayson. *In English Ways: The Movement of Societies and the Transferral of English Local Law and Custom.* Chapel Hill, N.C., 1981.

Allen, Gardner W. *A Naval History of the American Revolution.* 2 vols. 1913. Reprint. Williamstown, Mass., 1970.

Anderson, Fred. *A People's Army: Massachusetts Soldiers and Society in the Seven Years' War.* Chapel Hill, N.C., 1984.

Banner, James M., Jr. *To the Hartford Convention: The Federalists and the Origins of Party Politics in Massachusetts, 1789–1815.* New York, 1970.

Beeman, Richard, et al., eds. *Beyond Confederation: Origins of the Constitution and American National Identity.* Chapel Hill, N.C., 1987.

Bennett, Charles E., and Donald R. Lennon. *A Quest For Glory: Major General Robert Howe and the American Revolution.* Chapel Hill, N.C., 1991.

Benson, Adolph B. *Sweden and the American Revolution.* New Haven, Conn., 1926.

Bernard, John. *Retrospections of America, 1797–1811.* New York, 1887.

Bigelow, E. Victor. *A Narrative History of the Town of Cohasset, Massachusetts.* Cohasset, 1898.

Billias, George Athan, ed. *George Washington's Generals.* New York, 1964.

———. *George Washington's Opponents.* New York, 1969.

Bowen, Francis. *Life of Benjamin Lincoln, Major General in the Army of the Revolution.* Boston, 1847.

Breen, T. H. *The Character of the Good Ruler: Puritan Political Ideas in New England, 1630–1730.* New York, 1970.

Brighton, Ray. *The Checkered Career of Tobias Lear.* Portsmouth, N.H., 1985.

Brooke, John L. *The Heart of the Commonwealth: Society and Political Culture in Worchester County, Massachusetts, 1713–1861.* Cambridge, Eng., 1989.

Bushman, Richard L. *King and People in Provincial Massachusetts.* Chapel Hill, N.C., 1985.

Callahan, North. *Henry Knox: General Washington's General.* New York, 1958.

Carp, E. Wayne. *To Starve the Army at Pleasure: Continental Army Administration and American Political Culture, 1775–1783.* Chapel Hill, N.C., 1984.

Cashin, Edward J. *The King's Ranger: Thomas Brown and the American Revolution on the Southern Frontier.* Athens, Ga., 1989.

Caughey, John Walton. *McGillivray of the Creeks.* Norman, Okla., 1938.

Cayton, Andrew R. L. *The Frontier Republic: Ideology and Politics in the Ohio Country, 1780–1825.* Kent, Ohio, 1986.

Clark, Charles E., et al. *Maine in the Early Republic.* Hanover, N.H., 1988.

Coker, P. C., III. *Charleston's Maritime Heritage, 1670–1865: An Illustrated History.* Charleston, S.C., 1987.

Coleman, Kenneth. *The American Revolution in Georgia, 1763–1789.* Athens, Ga., 1958.

Cook, Edward M., Jr. *The Fathers of the Towns: Leadership and Community Structure in Eighteenth Century New England.* Baltimore, 1976.

Cress, Lawrence Delbert. *Citizens in Arms: The Army and Militia in American Society to the War of 1812.* Chapel Hill, N.C., 1982.

Crow, Jeffrey J., and Larry E. Tise, eds. *The Southern Experience in the American Revolution.* Chapel Hill, N.C., 1978.

Cunliffe, Marcus. *Soldiers and Civilians: The Martial Spirit in America, 1775–1865.* Boston, 1968.

Cunningham, Noble E. *The Jeffersonian-Republicans in Power: Party Operations, 1801–1809.* Chapel Hill, N.C., 1963.

Dauer, Manning J. *The Adams Federalists.* Baltimore, 1953.

Davis, Burke. *The Campaign That Won America: The Story of Yorktown.* New York, 1970.

Djilas, Milovan. *The New Class.* New York, 1957.

Duffy, Christopher. *The Military Experience in the Age of Reason.* London, 1987.

———. *Siege Warfare: The Fortress in the Early Modern World, 1494–1660.* London, 1979.

Elkins, Stanley, and Eric McKitrick. *The Age of Federalism.* New York, 1993.

Ferguson, E. James. *The Power of the Purse: A History of American Public Finance, 1776–1790.* Chapel Hill, N.C., 1961.

Fischer, David Hackett. *The Revolution of American Conservatism: The Federalist Party in the Era of Jeffersonian Democracy.* New York, 1965.

———. *Paul Revere's Ride.* New York, 1994.

Fleming, Thomas J. *Beat the Last Drum: The Siege of Yorktown, 1781.* New York, 1963.

Formisano, Ronald P. *The Transformation of Political Culture: Massachusetts Parties, 1790s–1840s.* New York, 1983.

Fowler, William H., Jr. *The Baron of Beacon Hill: A Biography of John Hancock.* Boston, 1980.

Freeman, Douglas Southall. *George Washington: A Biography.* 7 vols. New York, 1948–57.

French, Allen. *The First Year of the American Revolution.* Boston, 1934.

Frey, Sylvia R. *Water from the Rock: Black Resistance in a Revolutionary Age.* Princeton, N.J., 1991.

Frothingham, Richard, Jr. *History of the Siege of Boston.* Boston, 1851.

Gerlach, Don R. *Proud Patriot: Philip Schuyler and the War of Independence, 1775–1783.* Syracuse, N.Y., 1987.

Gobold, E. Stanly, Jr., and Robert H. Woody. *Christopher Gadsden and the American Revolution.* Knoxville, Tenn., 1982.

Greene, Lorenzo J. *The Negro in Colonial New England, 1620–1776.* New York, 1942.

Greven, Philip. *The Protestant Temperament: Patterns of Child-Rearing, Religious Experience, and the Self in Early America.* New York, 1977.

Gross, Robert A., ed. *In Debt to Shays: The Bicentennial of an Agrarian Rebellion.* Charlottesville, Va., 1993.

Hall, Edward B. *Memoir of Mary L. Ware.* Boston, 1853.

Hall, Van Beck. *Politics without Parties: Massachusetts, 1780–1791.* Pittsburgh, 1972.

Harding, Samuel Bannister. *The Contest over the Ratification of the Federal Constitution in the State of Massachusetts.* Cambridge, Mass., 1896.

Hargrove, Richard J., Jr. *General John Burgoyne.* Newark, Del., 1983.

Hatch, Louis C. *The Administration of the American Revolutionary Army.* New York, 1904.

Hatch, Nathan O. *The Sacred Cause of Liberty: Republican Thought and the Millenium in Revolutionary New England.* New Haven, 1977.

Heimert, Alan. *Religion and the American Mind from the Great Awakening to the Revolution.* Cambridge, Mass., 1966.

Higginbotham, Don. *The War of American Independence: Military Attitudes, Policies and Practice, 1763–1789.* Boston, 1983.

———. *George Washington and the American Military Tradition.* Athens, Ga., 1985.

Higgins, W. Robert, ed. *The Revolutionary War in the South: Power, Conflict and Leadership.* Durham, N.C., 1979.

Hobart, Rebecca W. *Dennysville, 1786–1986 . . . and Edmunds, Too!* Ellsworth, Me., 1986.

Hoffman, Ronald, and Peter J. Albert, eds. *Arms and Independence: The Military Character of the American Revolution.* Charlottesville, Va., 1984.

Hofstadter, Richard. *The Idea of a Party System: The Rise of Legitimate Opposition in the United States, 1780–1840.* Berkeley, Calif., 1969.

Hogendorp, Frederick van. *Brieven en Gedenkshriften van Gijsbert Karel van Hogendorp, uitgegeven door zijn jongsten, thans eenigen zoon.* 2 vols. The Hague, 1866.

Hoerder, Dirk. *Society and Government 1760–1780: The Power Structure in Massachusetts Townships.* Berlin, 1972.

Horsman, Reginald. *Expansion and American Indian Policy.* East Lansing, Mich., 1967.

———. *Matthew Elliott, British Indian Agent.* Detroit, 1964.

Jackson, Harvey H. *Lachlan McIntosh and the Politics of Revolutionary Georgia.* Athens, Ga., 1979.

Jensen, Merrill. *The New Nation.* New York, 1950.

Johnston, Henry P. *Yale and Her Honor-Roll in the American Revolution, 1775–1783.* New York, 1888.

Keegan, John. *The Mask of Command.* New York, 1987.

Kite, Elizabeth S. *Brigadier-General Louis Lebegue Duportail: Commandant of Engineers in the Continental Army, 1777–1783.* Baltimore, 1933.

Kohn, Richard H. *Eagle and Sword: The Beginnings of the Military Establishment in America.* New York, 1975.

Kurtz, Stephen G. *The Presidency of John Adams: The Collapse of Federalism.* Philadelphia, 1957.

Kurtz, Stephen G., and James H. Hutson, eds. *Essays on the American Revolution.* New York, 1973.

Lambert, Robert Stansbury. *South Carolina Loyalists in the American Revolution.* Columbia, S.C., 1987.

Lawrence, Alexander A. *Storm over Savannah: The Story of Count d'Estaing and the Siege of the Town in 1779.* Athens, Ga., 1951.

Leamon, James S. *Revolution Downeast: The War for American Independence in Maine.* Amherst, Mass., 1993.

Lincoln, George, et al. *History of the Town of Hingham, Massachusetts.* 3 vols. Cambridge, Mass., 1893.

Lockridge, Kenneth A. *A New England Town: The First Hundred Years.* New York, 1970.

Lumpkin, Henry. *From Savannah to Yorktown: The American Revolution in the South.* Columbia, S.C., 1981.

McCrady, Edward. *The History of South Carolina in the Revolution, 1775–1783.* 2 vols. New York, 1902.

Maier, Pauline. *From Resistance to Revolution: Colonial Radicals and the Development of American Opposition to Britain, 1765–1776.* New York, 1972.

Main, Jackson Turner. *The Upper House in Revolutionary America, 1763–1788.* Madison, Wis., 1967.

Manning, William. *The Key of Liberty: The Life and Democratic Writings of William Manning, "A Laborer," 1747–1814.* Cambridge, Mass., 1993.

Martin, James Kirby. *Men in Rebellion: Higher Governmental Leaders and the Coming of the American Revolution.* New York, 1976.

Michel, Jacques. *La Vie adventureuse et mouvementee de Charles-Henri Comte d'Estaing.* Verdun, 1976.

Miller, Perry. *The New England Mind: The Seventeenth Century.* Boston, 1939.

Mintz, Max M. *The Generals of Saratoga.* New Haven, 1990.

Morgan, Edmund S. *The Puritan Family: Religion and Domestic Relations in Seventeenth Century New England.* Boston, 1944.

———. *The Puritan Dilemma: The Story of John Winthrop.* Boston, 1958.

Morris, Richard B. *The Forging of the Union, 1781–1789.* New York, 1987.

Myers, Minor, Jr. *Liberty without Anarchy: A History of the Society of the Cincinnati.* Charlottesville, Va., 1983.

Nadelhaft, Jerome J. *The Disorders of War: The Revolution in South Carolina.* Orono, Maine, 1981.

Nagel, Paul C. *One Nation Indivisible: The Union in American Thought, 1776–1861.* New York, 1964.

Nelson, Paul David. *General Horatio Gates: A Biography.* Baton Rouge, La., 1976.

Nickerson, Hoffman. *The Turning Point of the Revolution; or, Burgoyne in America.* Boston, 1928.

O'Donnell, William E. *The Chevalier de La Luzerne: French Minister to the United States, 1779–1784*. Bruges, 1938.

Palmer, Dave Richard. *The Way of the Fox: American Strategy in the War for America, 1775–1783*. Westport, Conn., 1975.

Pancake, John S. *1777: The Year of the Hangman*. University, Ala., 1977.

Patterson, Samuel W. *Horatio Gates*. New York, 1941.

Patterson, Stephen E. *Political Parties in Revolutionary Massachusetts*. Madison, Wis., 1973.

Pencak, William. *War, Politics and Revolution in Provincial Massachusetts*. Boston, 1981.

Piersen, William D. *Black Yankees: The Development of an Afro-American Subculture in Eighteenth Century New England*. Amherst, Mass., 1988.

Prince, Carl E. *The Federalists and the Origins of the U.S. Civil Service*. New York, 1977.

Prucha, Francis Paul. *The Sword of the Republic: The United States Army on the Frontier, 1783–1846*. New York, 1969.

Quincy, Edmund. *Life of Josiah Quincy of Massachusetts*. Boston, 1869.

Rakove, Jack N. *The Beginnings of National Politics: An Interpretive History of the Continental Congress*. New York, 1979.

Rankin, Hugh F. *Francis Marion: The Swamp Fox*. New York, 1973.

———. *The North Carolina Continentals*. Chapel Hill, N.C., 1971.

Ritcheson, Charles R. *Aftermath of Revolution: British Policy toward the United States, 1783–1795*. Dallas, 1969.

Rogers, George C., Jr. *Charleston in the Age of the Pinckneys*. Norman, Okla., 1969.

Rossie, Jonathan Gregory. *The Politics of Command in the American Revolution*. Syracuse, N.Y., 1975.

Royster, Charles. *A Revolutionary People at War: The Continental Army and American Character, 1775–1783*. Chapel Hill, N.C., 1979.

Sanders, Jennings. *Evolution of Executive Departments of the Continental Congress, 1774–1789*. Chapel Hill, N.C., 1935.

Seaburg, Carl, and Stanley Paterson. *Merchant Prince of Boston: Colonel T. H. Perkins, 1764–1854*. Cambridge, Mass., 1971.

Severo, Richard, and Lewis Milford. *The Wages of War: When America's Soldiers Came Home—From Valley Forge to Vietnam*. New York, 1989.

Sheehan, Bernard W. *Seeds of Extinction: Jeffersonian Philanthropy and the American Indian*. Chapel Hill, N.C., 1973.

Shy, John. *A People Numerous and Armed: Reflections on the Military Struggle for American Independence*. New York, 1976.

Sibley, John Langdon, and Clifford K. Shipton. *Biographical Sketches of Those Who Attended Harvard College*. 17 vols. Cambridge and Boston, 1873–1975.

Silverman, Kenneth. *A Cultural History of the American Revolution*. New York, 1976.

Smelser, Marshall. *The Democratic Republic, 1801–1815.* New York, 1968.

Smith, Page. *John Adams.* 2 vols. New York, 1962.

Smith, Paul H. *Loyalists and Redcoats: A Study of British Revolutionary Policy.* New York, 1972.

Stewart, Catesby Willis. *The Life of Brigadier General William Woodford of the American Revolution.* Richmond, Va., 1973.

Stout, Harry S. *The New England Soul: Preaching and Religious Culture in Colonial New England.* New York, 1986.

Sullivan, William. *The Public Men of the Revolution.* Philadelphia, 1847.

Sword, Wiley. *President Washington's Indian War: The Struggle for the Old Northwest, 1790–1795.* Norman, Okla., 1985.

Syrett, David. *The Royal Navy in American Waters, 1775–1783.* Brookfield, Vt., 1989.

Szatmary, David P. *Shays' Rebellion: The Making of an Agrarian Insurrection.* Amherst, Mass., 1980.

Taylor, Alan. *Liberty Men and Great Proprietors: The Revolutionary Settlement on the Maine Frontiers, 1760–1820.* Chapel Hill, N.C., 1990.

Taylor, Robert J. *Western Massachusetts in the Revolution.* Providence, R.I., 1954.

Vipperman, Carl J. *The Rise of Rawlins Lowndes.* Columbia, S.C., 1978.

Wallace, Willard M. *Traitorous Hero: The Life and Fortunes of Benedict Arnold.* New York, 1954.

Ward, Christopher. *The War of the Revolution.* Edited by John R. Alden. 2 vols. New York, 1952.

Ward, Harry M. *The Department of War, 1781–1789.* Pittsburgh, 1962.

———. *Charles Scott and the "Spirit of '76."* Charlottesville, Va., 1988.

White, Leonard D. *The Federalists: A Study in Administrative History.* New York, 1956.

———. *The Jeffersonians: A Study in Administrative History, 1801–1829.* New York, 1956.

Whitmore, William H. *The Massachusetts Civil List for the Colonial and Provincial Periods, 1630–1774.* Albany, N.Y., 1870.

Whittemore, Bradford Adams. *Memorials of the Massachusetts Society of the Cincinnati.* Boston, 1964.

Wickwire, Franklin, and Mary Wickwire. *Cornwallis: The American Adventure.* Boston, 1970.

Wiebe, Robert H. *The Opening of American Society: From the Adoption of the Constitution to the Eve of Disunion.* New York, 1984.

Wilson, Robert J., III. *The Benevolent Deity: Ebenezer Gay and the Rise of Rational Religion in New England, 1696–1787.* Philadelphia, 1984.

Wood, Gordon S. *The Creation of the American Republic, 1776–1787.* Chapel Hill, N.C., 1969.

———. *The Radicalism of the American Revolution.* New York, 1991.

Wright, J. Leitch, Jr. *Britain and the American Frontier, 1783–1815.* Athens, Ga., 1975.

————. *Creeks and Seminoles: The Destruction and Regeneration of the Muscogulge People.* Lincoln, Neb., 1986.

Zahniser, Marvin R. *Charles Cotesworth Pinckney, Founding Father.* Chapel Hill, N.C., 1967.

Zuckerman, Michael. *Peaceable Kingdoms: New England Towns in the Eighteenth Century.* New York, 1970.

Articles

Allen, Michael. "Justice for the Indians: The Federalist Quest, 1783–1796." *Essex Institute Historical Collections* 122 (1986): 124–41.

Ashmore, Otis, and Charles H. Olmstead. "The Battles of Kettle Creek and Brier Creek." *Georgia Historical Quarterly* 10 (1926): 85–125.

Bailyn, Bernard. "The Central Themes of the American Revolution." In *Essays on The American Revolution,* edited by Stephen G. Kurtz and James H. Hutson. Chapel Hill, N.C., 1973.

Banning, Lance. "Republican Ideology and the Triumph of the Constitution." *William and Mary Quarterly,* 3d ser., 31 (1974): 167–88.

Bowling, Kenneth R. "New Light on the Philadelphia Mutiny of 1783: Federal-State Confrontation at the Close of the War of Independence." *Pennsylvania Magazine of History and Biography* 101 (1977): 419–50.

Brooke, John L. "To the Quiet of the People: Revolutionary Settlements and Civil Unrest in Western Massachusetts, 1774–1789." *William and Mary Quarterly,* 3d ser., 46 (1989): 425–62.

Brown, Richard D. "Shays's Rebellion and the Ratification of the Federal Constitution in Massachusetts." In *Beyond Confederation: Origins of the Constitution and American National Identity,* edited by Richard Beeman, Stephen Botein, and Edward C. Carter II. Chapel Hill, N.C., 1987.

Bushman, Richard L. "Massachusetts Farmers and the Revolution." In *Society, Freedom and Conscience: The American Revolution in Virginia, Massachusetts, and New York,* edited by Richard M. Jellison. New York, 1976.

Buel, Richard, Jr. "The Public Creditor Interest in Massachusetts Politics, 1780–86." In *In Debt to Shays,* edited by Robert A. Gross. Charlottesville, Va., 1993.

Calderhead, William. "Prelude to Yorktown: A Critical Week in a Major Campaign." *Maryland Historical Magazine* 77 (1982): 123–35.

Candee, Richard M. "Maine Towns, Maine People: Architecture and the Community, 1783–1820." In *Maine in the Early Republic,* edited by Charles E. Clark, James S. Leamon, and Karen Bowden. Hanover, N.H., 1988.

Cavanagh, John C. "American Military Leadership in the Southern Campaign: Benjamin Lincoln." In *The Revolutionary War in the South: Power, Conflict and Leadership,* edited by W. Robert Higgins. Durham, N.C., 1979.

Clodfelter, Mark A. "Between Virtue and Necessity: Nathanael Greene and the Conduct of Civil Military Relations in the South, 1780–1782." *Military Affairs* 52 (1988): 169–75.

Cometti, Elizabeth. "Civil Servants during the Revolution." *Pennsylvania Magazine of History and Biography* 75 (1951): 159–69.

Coolidge, John. "Hingham Builds a Meetinghouse." *New England Quarterly* 34 (1961): 435–61.

Davies, Wallace Evan. "The Society of the Cincinnati in New England, 1783–1800." *William and Mary Quarterly,* 3d ser., 5 (1948): 3–25.

Downes, Randolph C. "Creek-American Relations, 1782–1790." *Georgia Historical Quarterly* 21 (1937): 142–84.

East, Robert A. "The Massachusetts Conservatives in the Critical Period." In *The Era of the American Revolution,* edited by Richard B. Morris. New York, 1939.

Fairbanks, Charles H. "The Function of Black Drink among the Creeks." In *Black Drink: A Native American Tea,* edited by Charles M. Hudson. Athens, Ga., 1979.

Ferguson, Clyde R. "Carolina and Georgia Patriot and Loyalist Militia in Action, 1778–1783." In *The Southern Experience in the American Revolution,* edited by Jeffrey J. Crow and Larry E. Tise. Chapel Hill, N.C., 1978.

Gruber, Ira D. "The Anglo-American Military Tradition and the War for American Independence." In *Against All Enemies: Interpretations of American Military History from Colonial Times to the Present,* edited by Kenneth J. Hagan and William R. Roberts. Westport, Conn., 1986.

Heidler, David S. "The American Defeat at Briar Creek, 3 March 1779." *Georgia Historical Quarterly* 66 (1982): 317–31.

Higginbotham, Don. "The American Militia: A Traditional Institution with Revolutionary Responsibilities." In *Reconsiderations on the Revolutionary War: Selected Essays,* edited by Don Higginbotham. New York, 1978.

———. "The Early American Way of War: Reconnaissance and Appraisal." *William and Mary Quarterly,* 3d ser., 44 (1987): 230–73.

———. "Military Leadership in the American Revolution." In *Leadership in the American Revolution.* Library of Congress Symposia on the American Revolution. Washington, D.C., 1974.

Kaplan, Sidney. "Pay, Pension, and Power: Economic Grievances of the Massachusetts Officers of the Revolution." *Boston Public Library Quarterly* 3 (1951): 15–34, 127–42.

———. "Rank and Status among Massachusetts Continental Officers." *American Historical Review* 56 (1951): 318–26.

———. "Veteran Officers and Politics in Massachusetts, 1783–1787." *William and Mary Quarterly,* 3d ser., 9 (1952): 29–57.

Kinnaird, Lucia Burk. "The Rock Landing Conference of 1789." *North Carolina Historical Review* 9 (1932): 349–65.

Kohn, Richard. "American Generals of the Revolution: Subordination and Restraint." In *Reconsiderations on the Revolutionary War: Selected Essays,* edited by Don Higginbotham. Westport, Conn., 1978.

———. "The Inside History of the Newburgh Conspiracy: America and the Coup d'Etat." *William and Mary Quarterly,* 3d ser., 27 (1970): 187–220.

Maslowski, Pete. "National Policy toward the Use of Black Troops in the Revolution." *South Carolina Historical Magazine* 73 (1972): 1–17.

Nelson, Paul D. "Citizen Soldiers or Regulars: The Views of American General Officers on the Military Establishment, 1775–1781." *Military Affairs* 43 (1979): 126–32.

———. "Horatio Gates at Newburgh, 1783: A Misunderstood Role." *William and Mary Quarterly,* 3d ser., 29 (1972): 143–58.

Parsons, Carolyn S. "'Bordering on Magnificence': Urban Domestic Planning in the Maine Woods." In *Maine in the Early Republic,* edited by Charles E. Clark, James S. Leamon, and Karen Bowden. Hanover, N.H., 1988.

Patterson, Stephen E. "The Federalist Reaction to Shays's Rebellion." In *In Debt to Shays,* edited by Robert A. Gross. Charlottesville, Va., 1993.

Pencak, William. "'The Fine Theoretic Government of Massachusetts Is Prostrated to the Earth': The Response to Shays's Rebellion Reconsidered." In *In Debt to Shays,* edited by Robert A. Gross. Charlottesville, Va., 1993.

Phillips, Edward Hake. "Timothy Pickering at His Best: Indian Commissioner, 1790–1794." *Essex Institute Historical Collection* 102 (1966): 163–202.

Pole, J. R. "Shays's Rebellion: A Political Interpretation." In *The Reinterpretation of the American Revolution, 1763–1789,* edited by Jack P. Greene. New York, 1968.

Ravenswaay, Charles Van. "America's Age of Wood." *American Antiquarian Society Proceedings* 80 (1970): 49–66.

Riesman, Janet A. "Money, Credit, and Federalist Political Economy." In *Beyond Confederation: Origins of the Constitution and American National Identity,* edited by Richard Beeman, Stephen Botein, and Edward C. Carter II. Chapel Hill, N.C., 1987.

Rodgers, Daniel T. "Republicanism: The Career of a Concept." *Journal of American History* 79 (1992): 11–38.

Royster, Charles. "Founding a Nation in Blood: Military Conflict and American Nationality." In *Arms and Independence: The Military Character of the American Revolution,* edited by Ronald Hoffman and Peter J. Albert. Charlottesville, Va., 1984.

Schaffel, Kenneth. "The American Board of War, 1776–1781." *Military Affairs* 50 (1986): 185–89.

Searcy, Martha Condray. "1779: The First Year of the British Occupation of Georgia." *Georgia Historical Quarterly* 67 (1983): 168–88.

Shalhope, Robert E. "Toward a Republican Synthesis: The Emergence of and Understanding of Republicanism in American Historiography." *William and Mary Quarterly,* 3d ser., 29 (1972): 49–80.

Shy, John. "American Society and Its War for Independence." In *Reconsiderations on the Revolutionary War: Selected Essays,* edited by Don Higginbotham. Westport, Conn., 1978.

———. "British Strategy for Pacifying the Southern Colonies, 1778–1781." In *The Southern Experience in the American Revolution,* edited by Jeffrey J. Crow and Larry E. Tise. Chapel Hill, N.C., 1978.

Skeen, C. Edward. "The Newburgh Conspiracy Reconsidered." *William and Mary Quarterly,* 3d ser., 31 (1974): 273–90.

Smith, Daniel Scott. "Parental Power and Marriage Patterns: An Analysis of Historical Trends in Hingham, Massachusetts." *Journal of Marriage and the Family* 35 (1973): 419–28.

———. "Child-Naming Practices, Kinship Ties, and Change in Family Attitudes in Hingham, Massachusetts, 1641–1880." *Journal of Social History* 18 (1985): 541–65.

Smith, Jonathan. "The Depression of 1785 and Daniel Shays' Rebellion." *William and Mary Quarterly,* 3d ser., 5 (1948): 77–94.

Wade, Herbert T. "The Essex Regiment in Shays' Rebellion, 1787." *Essex Institute Historical Collection* 90 (1954): 317–49.

Wallet, Francis G. "The Massachusetts Council, 1776–1774." *William and Mary Quarterly,* 3d ser., 6 (1949): 605–27.

Waters, John J. "Hingham, Massachusetts, 1631–1661: An East Anglian Oligarchy in the New World." *Journal of Social History* 1 (1968): 351–70.

———. "Naming and Kinship in New England." *New England Historical and Genealogical Register* 138 (1984): 161–81.

———. "Patrimony, Succession and Social Stability." *Perspectives in American History* 10 (1976): 131–60.

Weir, Robert M. "Who Shall Rule at Home: The American Revolution as a Crisis of Legitimacy for the Colonial Elite." *Journal of Interdisciplinary History* 6 (1976): 679–700.

Weller, Jac. "Revolutionary War Artillery in the South." *Georgia Historical Quarterly* 46 (1962): 250–73, 378–87.

Wright, Robert K., Jr. "Nor Is Their Standing Army to Be Despised: The Emergence of the Continental Army as a Military Institution." In *Arms and Independence: The Military Character of the American Revolution,* edited by Ronald Hoffman and Peter J. Albert. Charlottesville, Va., 1984.

Dissertations

Bradsher, James G. "Preserving the Revolution: Civil-Military Relations during the American War for Independence, 1775–1783." Ph.D. diss., University of Massachusetts, 1984.

Bulger, William T. "The British Expedition to Charleston, 1779–1780." Ph.D. diss., University of Michigan, 1957.

Cavanagh, John C. "The Military Career of Major-General Benjamin Lincoln in the War of the American Revolution, 1775–1781." Ph.D. diss., Duke University, 1969.

Millar, David R. "The Militia, the Army, and Independency in Colonial Massachusetts." Ph.D. diss., Cornell University, 1967.

Smith, Daniel Scott. "Population, Family and Society in Hingham, Massachusetts, 1635–1880." Ph.D. diss., University of California, Berkeley, 1973.

Index

Page numbers listed below in italics (e.g. *24* and *illus.*) refer to illustrations in the text.

293

requests Continental reinforcements, 89; and defense of Charleston, 90–107; requests recruitment
of black soldiers, 92; and terms of
surrender at Charleston, 106, 107;
as prisoner of war, 110, 112, 114;
returns home from Charleston,
110; criticized on loss of Charleston, 112; plans for Ben, Jr.'s future,
114; and recruitment of Continental troops, 114–15, 116; receives
honorary degree, 115; reinforces
garrison at Newport, R.I., 115–16;
and Yorktown campaign, 116–20;
chosen secretary at war, 123, 124;
duties as secretary at war, 124–25;
on frugality, 127; relations with
Morris, 127, 129, 130, 132–33,
143; and social life in Philadelphia,
130–31; portraits, 131, 214, 216–
17, *illus.*; travels through Pa., 131;
writings of, 131–32; and states'
rights, 133; opposes half-pay
pension plan, 136–37, 138, 143;
expresses pride in army's efficiency,
138; makes recommendations on
military matters, 144, 156; and
remonstrance from Pa. troops,
146; president of Mass. Society of
the Cincinnati, 147; settles wartime
accounts, 147, 148; makes
northern inspection tour, 147–48;
weight of, 148; resigns War Dept.
position, 148–49; on children's
education, 150–51; personal
finances, 151, 154, 165, 179, 187–
88; rejects public office, 151; and
interest in Me., 154, 155, 156,
161, 176; as Mass. state commissioner (1784), 154, 155–56; on
political economy, 156–57, 164; on
Confederation, 157–59, 160; on
Shaysites, 162–63; views on

individual and society, 165;
commands expedition in western
Mass., 165–74; nominated for
lieutenant governor, 174, 175;
delegate to Mass., 178–79; elected
lieutenant governor, 179–81;
relations with Hancock, 182–85;
seeks position from Washington,
185–86; and collectorship of
Boston, 187–89, 206, 211, 212–
13; and diplomatic mission to
southern Indians, 190–94; on
Indian-white relations, 195–97,
and diplomatic mission to Northwest Indians, 197–205; as a
Federalist, 206–7; opposes
Hamilton's appointment, 209–10;
Revolutionary War record, 209–
10; supports Adams administration, 210; resigns collectorship of
Boston, 214, 215; death, 217
Lincoln, Benjamin, Jr. (son), 9, *10–11*,
14–15, 124, 167; education, 19; at
siege of Fort Independence, 35;
reports on family's welfare, 38, 39;
accompanies father home, 50–51;
studies law, 53; on his father's
absences at war, 113, 114;
corresponds with father, 132, 148;
helps father with family business,
152; writes "The Free Republican," 164–65; on Mass. election,
174; on politics, 175; death, 179
Lincoln, Benjamin (grandson), 207,
216
Lincoln, Benjamin, House (Hingham,
Mass.), 8, 12, 207, 216, *illus.*
Lincoln, Deborah "Debby" (daughter), *10–11*, 51
Lincoln, Edmund (son), *10–11*
Lincoln, Elizabeth (sister), *10–11*
Lincoln, Elizabeth (daughter), *10–11*,
216

Lincoln, Elizabeth Thaxter (mother), 9, *10–11*

Lincoln, Hannah (sister), *10–11*

Lincoln, Hannah (daughter), *10–11*, 216

Lincoln, James Otis (grandson), 207, 216

Lincoln, Levi, 114, 215–26

Lincoln, Martin (son) (b/d 1766), *10–11*

Lincoln, Martin (son), *10–11*, 19, 113; visits Me., 161; corresponds with family, 186; builds light-houses, 188; inherits Hingham property, 216

Lincoln, Mary (sister), *10–11*

Lincoln, Mary (daughter), *10–11*

Lincoln, Mary Cushing (Mrs. Benjamin), *10–11*, 39, 113, 216; marries Lincoln, 14–15; inherit-ance of, 15; provides for family, 38; learns of husband's wounding, 51; contracts smallpox, 53; corresponds with husband, 144; description of, 152; portrait, 216, *illus.*

Lincoln, Mary Lewis (grandmother), *10–11*

Lincoln, Mary Otis (daughter-in-law), 207, 214

Lincoln, Olive (sister), *10–11*

Lincoln, Sarah (sister), *10–11*

Lincoln, Sarah (daughter), *10–11*, 216

Lincoln, Sarah Fearing (great-grandmother), *10–11*

Lincoln, Theodore (brother), *10–11*

Lincoln, Theodore (son), *10–11*, 12, 19, 113; corresponds with father, 127, 130–31, 131–32, 177, 187, 212, 214; and family finances, 152, 179; settles in Me., 155, 161, 186; mentioned, 174; builds lighthouses, 188; father visits, in Me., 207;

inherits father's northern land, 216; house in Me., *illus.*

Lincoln, Thomas (great-great-grandfather), 7, 8, 9, *10–ll*

Lincoln and Sons, 151–52

Livingston, Robert R.: observations on Lincoln's War Dept. appoint-ment, 121, 123; as secretary of foreign affairs, 121, 126

Long Island, 25, 27

Loring, Mary (Col. Lincoln's first wife), 9, *10–11*

Lovell, James, 51–52, 68–69, 77, 90, 111, 215; works in office of Boston collector, 187

Lowell, John, 26, 132, 133, 137, 154, 159

Lowndes, Rawlins, 59, 65, 79; refuses request for supplies, 60–61, 62

Loyalists, 38, 75; in the South, 59, 62, 64–65, 74, 91

Luzerne, Chevalier de la, 131

McDougall, Alexander, 117, 121; and officer's committee, 139, 140–41, 141, 142

McGillivray, Alexander, 191–92, 193

McHenry, James, 208

McIntosh, Lachlan, 85; and command of forces in Ga., 78, 80, 82; favors evacuation of Charleston garrison, 100–101, 101, 102

McKee, Alexander, 203, 204

Maclay, William, 194

Macshorter, Alex, 93–94

Madison, James, 129, 138, 139, 140; and republicanism, 3; on troop furlough, 146; on Shays's Rebel-lion, 173; as secretary of state, 213

Maine, 190; defenses of, 115; trade, 151–52; land speculation in, 154–55, 156; Indians in, 155–56; lighthouses in, 188

Benjamin Lincoln and the Ame
rican Revolution